A Passion for Equality

"Democratic institutions awaken and flatter
the passion for equality without ever being
able to satisfy it entirely."

—ALEXIS DE TOQUEVILLE

A PASSION FOR EQUALITY

◆————————————————

George A. Wiley
and the Movement

NICK KOTZ
& MARY LYNN KOTZ

W · W · Norton & Company · Inc. · New York

Copyright © 1977 by The George Wiley Memorial Fund
Published simultaneously in Canada by George J. McLeod Limited,
Toronto. Printed in the United States of America.

All Rights Reserved

First Edition

Library of Congress Cataloging in Publication Data

Kotz, Nick.
A passion for equality.

Bibliography: p.
Includes index.
1. Wiley, George Alvin, 1931–1973.   2. Social
reformers—United States—Biography.   3. Civil rights—
United States.   4. Welfare rights movement—United
States.   5. Afro-Americans—Biography.   I. Kotz, Mary
Lynn, joint author.   II. Title.
HV28.W47K67   1977   361'.0092'4 [B]   77–8015
ISBN 0–393–07517–6

1 2 3 4 5 6 7 8 9 0

CONTENTS

ILLUSTRATIONS

PREFACE

"You make a winning plan and you make it happen."

—GEORGE WILEY

We have tried to tell the story of the life of George Alvin Wiley (1931–1973), a remarkable man who was one of the most effective, yet least understood leaders of the social movements of the 1960s. Beyond that, we attempt to provide perspective to a significant period of American history, which deserves greater attention and scrutiny. In particular, little has been written about the civil rights movement's frustrating efforts to deal with discrimination in the North, and with economic discrimination in general. Wiley was at the heart of that effort, both at the local level and as a national leader of the Congress of Racial Equality (CORE). When the civil rights movement faltered—in part because it could not solve these northern problems—Wiley charted a new course as founder of the National Welfare Rights Organization, through which he pioneered in efforts to organize the poor and to address the problems of welfare and of powerlessness. That was his unique contribution.

George Wiley was a complex man. He struggled throughout his life with the difficulties facing a talented black in a competitive white world; he devoted one compartment of his life to a highly educated white woman and, at the same time, another portion to the very poorest and most downtrodden of black women. He grappled, in addition, with still another division of soul: Half of him was always the intellectual, the scholar; the other half always the activist. At his core was always a commitment to fight for equality.

As a reporter covering the welfare reform fights of the late 1960s and early 1970s, Nick Kotz had a professional acquaintance with George

Wiley. We saw him only once in a personal setting, with his children shortly before he died. We were struck by the difference between the public image and the private man.

The problems to which Wiley devoted himself remain today, and he provided a viewpoint which is highly relevant to the continuing national dilemma. We hope that this book will contribute to the search for solutions and for achieving a more just American society.

Part of Wiley's legacy was the massive amount of material he left behind which made this book possible: Not only did he never give up, he never threw anything away!

From early diaries to invitations to sorority teas, to carbons of letters, piles of news clippings, datebooks, copies of his speeches, and documents he kept in neat files, can be gleaned a picture of the developing George Wiley as well as an invaluable record of the civil rights and welfare rights movements. Especially important were two taped interviews with Wiley in which he told his own story—one by Edward Daner in June, 1964, the other by Wilbur Colom in August, 1973. All the Wiley papers, tapes, and transcripts are in repository in the Social Action collection, Wisconsin State Historical Society, Madison.

However, this story of Wiley, and the story of the movement, is seen primarily through the eyes of those who knew him well: family, friends, aides, supporters, and opponents. From the 175 persons we interviewed and the others who wrote to us, we see a man who, throughout his life, profoundly affected all those who knew him and were involved in his movement.

This story, therefore, is told by his parents, Olive and William Wiley; his brothers and sisters, Lucille Wiley Davis, Shirley Wiley Green, Alton W. Wiley, Edwin K. Wiley, Beverly Wiley LaCorbiniere; his wife, Wretha Wiley Hanson; his children, Daniel K. and Maya D. Wiley; his relatives, Mr. and Mrs. Bill Thomas, Eliza Gladden, Henry Davis, and Jeane Wiley.

And from his early life: Robert Birrell, Wilbert Connery, Roosevelt Greer, Jr., Barrie Hackett, Jr., Russell Hackett, Graham Mann, Ralph Pellicano, Mrs. Joseph Rohloff, and George Yanyar.

College years: Dr. Paul Abell, Stephen Aldrich, David Armor, Dr. Malcolm Bell, Nancy Bell, Clyde Bennett, Dr. Chester A. Berry, Dr. W. D. Cooke, Dr. Norris Culf, Belva Davis, Dr. Robert C. Fahey, Ruth Ann Fahey, Martha Goldsmith Schwartz, Dr. Ralph Helverson, Dr. Hyman Minsky, Dr. Scott McKenzie, Evelyn B. Morris, Dr. Glenn Olds, Dr. John F. Quinn, Dr. Jerrold Meinwald, Carol Condie Stout, Bertha Cooke Waring, Dr. Eugene Winslow, Dr. Henry Wirth.

Petersburg: Dr. Wyatt Tee Walker.

Chemistry: Dr. Jon B. Applequist, Dr. David Braddon, Dr. Donald

Botteron, Dr. James Cason, Dr. Donald Dittmer, Dr. J. D. McCullough, Dr. Kenneth Pitzer, Dr. William Pryor, Dr. Andrew Streitwieser.

Syracuse CORE: Dr. Norman Balbanian, Dr. Robert Blanchard, Philip Booth, Clint Byers, Ronald Corwin, Dr. Edward Daner, Edwin Day, Albert Ettinger, Fern Freel, Charles Goldsmith, Inez Heard, David Jaquith, Rudy Lombard, Susan Rice, Timothy Rice, Barbara Rumsey, Faith Seidenberg, Landers Smith, Bruce Thomas, Dr. and Mrs. William Wasserstrom, Anna Mae Williams, Wretha Wiley.

National CORE: Val Coleman, Dr. Robert Curvin, Edwin Day, David Dennis, James Farmer, Alan Gartner, Richard Haley, Gregg Harris, Rudy Lombard, James T. McCain, Floyd McKissick, Dr. S. M. Miller, The Rt. Rev. Paul Moore, Ruth Turner Perot, Elaine Slater, James Slater, Wretha Wiley.

NWRO: Nancy Amedei, Nancy Barnes, Barbara Bode, Simeon Booker, Richard Boone, Hobart Burch, Joyce Burson, Dr. Kenneth Clark, Dr. Richard Cloward, Audrey Colom, Wilbur Colom, Rep. John Conyers, Shirley Dalton, Edwin Day, Bert DeLeeuw, Rep. Ronald V. Dellums, Gary Delgado, Barbralee Diamonstein, Leslie Dunbar, Ruby Duncan, Marian Wright Edelman, Peter Edelman, Faith Evans, James Evans, Seymour Facher, John Ferren, Harold Fleming, Victor French, Dr. Mitchell Ginsberg, Fred Gipson, Thomas Glynn, Leonard Goodwin, Don Green, Jane Hart, Dr. Joel Handler, Jill Hatch, Robert Hatch, Catherine Jermany, Helen Hess, William Hess, Carl Holman, Etta M. Horn, David Hunter, David Ifshin, Hulbert James, Tom Joe, Roxanne Jones, Frankie Jeter, Vernon Jordan, Jonathan Kaufman, Sen. Edward Kennedy, Michael Kerr, Andrea Kydd, John R. Kramer, Trude Lash, Rhoda Linton, Dr. George T. Martin, Jr., John Marqusee, Robert Maynard, Sen. Eugene McCarthy, Maya Miller, Sen. Daniel P. Moynihan, Andrew Norman, Ben Okner, Sam Orr, Susan Orr, Robert W. Ostrow, Rep. Richard Ottinger, Mary Lou Oates Palmer, William Pastreich, Anne Peretz, Phil Perkins, Geoffrey Peterson, Jennifer Cafritz Phillips, Dr. Frances Fox Piven, Ronald Pollack, Rafe Pomerance, Wade Rathke, Joseph L. Rauh, Jr., Laura Rockefeller, Phyllis Ryan, Dr. William Ryan, Tim Sampson, Beulah Sanders, Austin Scott, Pete Seeger, Paul Sherry, Steve Simonds, Edward Sparer, Mark Splain, Gloria Steinem, Dr. Gilbert Steiner, Terry Szpak, Dr. Robert Theobald, Bruce Thomas, Johnnie Tillmon, Michael Trister, Melvin E. Turner, Betty Vorenberg, Thomas Wahman, The Rev. Lucius Walker, the Rt. Rev. John Walker, Jennette Washington, Stephen Wechsler, Barbara Williams, Joanne Williams, Peggy Winkler, Catherine Wolhowe, Irving Workoff, Rep. Andrew Young, Wretha Wiley.

We owe special gratitude to Wretha Wiley Hanson, Wiley's former wife, who first encouraged us to write this book, and provided endless help and insights. The idealism of George Brockway, the chairman of

W. W. Norton & Company, Inc., made the book a reality. Others who helped greatly with hard work and competence include Candace Mac-Queen, our researcher; Emily Garlin, copy editor; Sheila Harvill, typist; and Barbara Wolfson, editing. We are indebted to Leslie Dunbar and the Field Foundation, who generously gave us a grant to meet in part the expenses of travel and transcriptions of taped interviews.

Finally, we owe special thanks to the welfare mothers we interviewed, who, despite cruel rebuffs, still somehow have faith in America and its promise. It is to those brave women of the welfare rights movement that we dedicate this book.

Chevy Chase, Maryland   Nick Kotz
Broad Run, Virginia   Mary Lynn Kotz
December, 1976

A Passion for Equality

"Democratic institutions awaken and flatter the passion for equality without ever being able to satisfy it entirely."

—ALEXIS DE TOQUEVILLE

1

Master of
the Barely Possible

A big man in a bright African daishiki barreled out of the arriving jet, down the ramp, and into Chicago's O'Hare Airport, apologizing politely as he jostled the other passengers. He tore through the terminal corridors like a broken-field runner, a strange dark figure in the crush of warmly-dressed people.

He raced up to an island of pay telephones just outside the gate for his connecting flight. Quickly, he snatched three receivers from the hooks; he dropped his briefcase on the floor in front of one, stuffed his crumpled raincoat beside another, dug into his pocket for a fistful of change and a list of numbers. He slipped a dime into each coin slot and began dialing.

Passersby watched in astonishment as this tall black man draped in telephone cords kept three lines busy, warded people away from his commandeered position, and craned his neck periodically to make sure he didn't miss his flight. It seemed almost a game, a contest to see how many contacts he could make in an hour.

But for George Alvin Wiley, the telephones were the lifeline to his mission. With a whirlwind balancing act, he ran a social movement the way he captured a bank of telephones: It looked like sheer confusion, but it worked. He had mobilized some of the poorest of America's poor into a cohesive political organization. He had organized 100,000 welfare recipients, many of whom had started out thinking even less of themselves than the general public did. Wiley had imbued them with hope and dignity, taught them their rights under the law, and welded them, through hundreds of small community groups, into the National Welfare Rights Organization, whose red-white-and-blue insignia, NWRO, emblazoned the battered briefcase on the airport floor.

Most political theory held that it was impossible to organize the pariahs at the bottom of society. Wiley had proved that it was possible—but just barely—with a web of connections kept mainly in his head and in his dog-eared list of telephone numbers. Now, on a cold March morning in 1971, he was struggling to keep the fragile links from being jarred loose by a hostile American public.

Wiley knew that welfare recipients were maligned and misunderstood, that they wanted to work at a living wage and to raise their children to lead decent lives; he knew that welfare was a last resort. There was shame in the welfare system, Wiley told them, but the shame was not theirs: "It belongs to a country which chooses to punish its poor instead of opening opportunities to them." Unless they gained a meaningful chance to make it in America, he believed, the American dream would be only a delusion and the movement would forever be blowing in the wind.

Sooner than most civil rights leaders, he had acted on the knowledge that the hard-won right to sit at a lunch counter was worth little if you couldn't afford to buy the hamburger. At the heart of his crusade was the idea that these women, who with their children existed at the sufferance of a government program blandly titled "Aid to Families with Dependent Children," should not spend their lives pleading for crumbs from the table of an affluent society. He sought immediate economic benefits for them, a voice in the system, and the long-range goal of a guaranteed annual income.

There had been remarkable successes. Starting five years before, with neighborhood groups from the ghettoes of Bedford-Stuyvesant to the cane-brakes of Louisiana, he had organized the women. Then he merged hundreds of those neighborhood organizations into citywide groups, and into the national federation which they proudly christened the NWRO.

The mothers had descended upon neighborhood welfare centers, where they demanded that the welfare system obey the law. They had lobbied in their own behalf, from county courthouses to Washington itself. The message Wiley provided was simple but revolutionary: "You cannot do with us what you will, whatever your protestations of benevolence. It is our lives that you are regulating and legislating, and we demand a voice in determining our own lives." For many in the councils of power, the notion that uneducated, dependent people should know what was good for themselves was a delusion, but the women of NWRO had taken the concept to heart.

They had won victories in the streets and in the courts. The welfare rights movement helped force open the welfare system. Five million persons who had been legally entitled before were now receiving benefits for the first time. The welfare system was still a monstrosity, yet Wiley looked upon the explosion as a great accomplishment. Numerous inequities in the society remained. But in his view, the poor were at least getting something—and that something helped them in a society which still could not produce enough family-supporting jobs, or begin to solve the problems of racism and poverty.

His movement had defied the theories of political scientists, the separatist ideology of black nationalists, the prim support of white liberals, and the Calvinist ethos which labeled Wiley's followers as the "undeserving poor" who were expected to accept without question the leftovers from America's abundance.

Most Americans, however, regarded the welfare explosion as a national disgrace. Inflamed by the rhetoric of politicians, led by President Richard Nixon and Vice President Spiro Agnew, people expressed their resentment to the protests of the 1960s by scapegoating the "worthless welfare cheaters." Show them a bushy-haired George Wiley demanding in the streets and they thought they saw an agitator shouting, "Burn, Baby, Burn."

Even when the civil rights movement floundered, Wiley had not despaired or quit. Instead, he had charted this new course, one that set him apart from all of the other national black leaders. While others turned to elective politics or black nationalism or to reruns of conventional strategies, he turned to economics—and to basic grass-roots organizing.

Though many spoke eloquently of organizing the poor, few really bothered with that constituency, and some secretly despised the taint of those noisy welfare mothers. Wiley served as a conscience to the civil rights movement, refusing to let other leaders forget about the least of their number.

He brought to the very poor the tools of organization by which other groups effectively pursue their own self-interest. He caused a transformation in the lives of countless women who learned to stand up and fight back, to depend upon themselves. Their organization affected American social policy, reaching from the smallest county welfare office all the way to the White House, and helped to generate a serious debate over a guaranteed annual income.

In 1971, Wiley was playing a unique role in that continuing national debate called "welfare reform"—a term with several very different meanings. For many, reform simply means ending the so-called welfare mess, getting millions of people off the dole. For some politicians and theorists the stated objectives are gargantuan: Reducing the rolls, getting people to work, finding more jobs, cutting costs, maintaining the work incentive, treating working people fairly, solving American poverty. Wiley understood all these currents, but he was very clear in his own analysis of what would constitute reform: "Any welfare reform proposal must leave poor people better off, not worse off, than they were before. That is the essence of reform."

His flight to Las Vegas was now boarding. Grabbing his briefcase and raincoat, Wiley sprinted to the waiting jet, as always, the last to board. Cutting it close was as much of a habit as capturing a bank of telephones.

He was flying to Nevada to stop a purge. The frantic juggling of telephones in the airport was part of his effort to bar Nevada officials from carrying out a reduction or termination of welfare benefits for more than 50 percent of those women and children who had been receiving them. Without any notice or opportunity for legal appeal, the checks—which averaged $103 per month—had just been stopped. Nevada Welfare Director George Miller had sent proud notice of his action to each of the other forty-nine states. Here's one way to reduce the welfare budget: Just cut 'em off!

The Nevada welfare cutoff was dramatic, but not without precedent. Throughout the thirty-six-year history of the federal-state welfare program, there had been periodic purges of the rolls. Wiley believed that those purges represented a systematic effort to regulate the lives of the poor. In times of great social unrest, society would loosen its grip and permit them the dole. But once the unrest appeared to subside, then society always retightened the traditional control. This was beginning to happen again in 1971, starting with Nevada.

Nevada's social climate combined the most conservative features of the old South and the new West. The glittering façade of Las Vegas and Reno obscured Nevada's real poverty, built upon a low wage scale and a callously meager public expenditure for welfare services. Social welfare acted as a tool for enforcing the system of cheap labor. Welfare case workers even directed women toward employment in prostitution (which is legal in parts of Nevada) as an alternative to welfare.

As Wiley eased back into his airliner seat, he began to plan the next steps of the Nevada campaign. He had made a thousand frantic trips like this one; he was bone tired and could not concentrate. His mind drifted. He was forty years old, and he wondered whether he was not another burnt-out case from the movement. He thought about quitting, about trying to make up for the long neglect of his own family, which had become a casualty of the movement. His life had started out so differently from the course he now pursued. He reflected on the changes in it.

George Wiley had not always battled for the underdog. For his first thirty years he had pursued the American dream for success, grasped it firmly, and believed that it was available to all. He had triumphed in a white world, as a "first": most popular in his high school class, first black in his college fraternity, first black to head the student government, first black research chemist at duPont, first black Ph.D. in chemistry from a prestigious Ivy League university, first black on a faculty crowded with Nobel laureates, first black in a chemistry department which he led in research. He had married a beautiful, intelligent white woman, and they had started raising a family, secure in a cloistered white academic world in which Wiley starred— the tweedy, light-hearted professor, the fellow who zipped around campus in a red sports car and regularly beat the university president at tennis.

He had it made, or so it seemed. But events raced ahead in America, at a pace that disrupted the country and caused Wiley to re-examine the dream. The journey he traveled from the 1930s into the 1970s traces a significant part of our history during those four decades. The changes that evolved in his ideas and actions were part of a national awakening, of a black transformation, and of a new challenge.

Wiley thought of that challenge as the jet sped westward, and he wondered when, if ever, it would be answered satisfactorily. But his reflections were interrupted; he was jarred back into present reality as the big plane touched down on the runway at the Las Vegas airport.

From the moment he walked off of the airplane, his spirits began to lift. The welcoming committee was there, standing like a black mountain in the desert, four welfare mothers hiding their own fear behind a haughty bearing; Johnnie Tillmon of California, Beulah Sanders of New York, Frankie Jeter of Pittsburgh, and Ruby Duncan of Nevada, members of NWRO's executive board, moved toward Wiley and surrounded him. They wore red-white-and-blue buttons that said "Welfare Rights Now."

"We are here to insist that the poor people of Nevada are given back their rights and that state officials obey the law," Wiley told reporters. "We have used the courts, negotiations, hearings, political pressures, and protests. And if all other methods fail, we will stay in the streets for as long as it takes to win this fight."

"Operation Nevada" was a casebook example of Wiley's movement at work. It was a juggling act that brought together all the scarce resources that poor people do not have at their command. Wiley had quickly pulled together those resources from his Washington headquarters, from his nationwide field operations, and from a network of outside supporters. For the Nevada campaign he had summoned organizers from his own NWRO payroll, and also recruited a dozen others from various social action groups and college volunteers. For money he turned to the churches, the foundations and a few wealthy individuals. Then he drew in celebrities to generate publicity.

The effort had taken two months of groundwork, with Wiley orchestrating every move. The lawyers filed suit in federal court, charging that Nevada officials had violated the rights of the state's welfare recipients, depriving them of due process. The organizers carried out the painstaking work of locating the seventy-five hundred persons whose checks had been cut off or cut down, and then, with the lawyers, interviewing them to determine the details of their individual cases, and at the same time trying to convince them that they should join the demonstrations and become members of NWRO. This was the most difficult part. Many welfare recipients sought anonymity rather than notoriety, and feared (with justification) that any protests on their part would make it even more difficult for them to regain their income. "We're going to help you and you are going to help yourselves," exhorted Johnnie Tillmon, NWRO's national chairman. The women responded and a small, weak NWRO chapter in Las Vegas had become a large, strong one.

For weeks they had marched in the streets, sustaining threats, going to jail, building pressure in a well-planned action. With Wiley's arrival, the campaign was building to a climax.

As thousands of weekend revelers moved along the Las Vegas Strip, they suddenly found their way blocked by George Wiley and five thousand singing, chanting demonstrators. Wiley marched out in front with the women and a host of civil rights volunteers, while two aides, his volunteer Secret Service, walked backwards, peering into the crowd for the glint of a gun. Word was out that there was a mob "contract" on Wiley's life.

They came to Caesar's Palace, the ornate hotel that symbolized the whole make-believe world. They blocked the doors and set up for a rally. But then, in that spontaneous surge of bodies which often overtook Wiley's most carefully laid plans, the shouting welfare mothers pushed their way past the guards and into the lobby. For once, the endlessly spinning wheels of chance stood still. Ralph David Abernathy commanded silence as he prayed for "Caesar to render unto the people that which is theirs." Once their point was made, Wiley regained control of the group and marched the women back out into the streets.

The following day leaders of the Nevada gambling industry met secretly and passed their strong judgments to state officials: The demonstrations must stop. Publicity about the disruptions had hurt business. Let the poor have their dole!

Two days later, an alternative Wiley strategy prevailed. Federal District Judge John Foley decreed that the Nevada government had acted illegally. All of the welfare recipients who had been purged from the rolls were to be reinstated immediately and paid the benefits denied them.

That night the demonstrations stopped. Instead, there was a mass victory rally in the streets. George Wiley, who had been so weary before, was jubilant. He danced until he dropped from exhaustion, then he danced some more, clumping his patched-up shoes in rhythm with the music for the first time in anyone's memory. It was a victory for the Wiley method, organizing people at the neighborhood level with the incentive of an immediate, tangible gain, applying pressure by well-orchestrated and publicized demonstrations, using the system against itself by requiring government to follow the rule of law. For the time being, it was a "win."

As the NWRO members danced in their victory celebration, the curious public stood on the sidewalks of Las Vegas and watched, either in puzzlement or in anger. "Why don't you just go to work?" somebody shouted out. At other times the women might shout back an answer, but they ignored the taunt. It would take a long time to explain, anyway.

I

THE EDUCATION OF
GEORGE ALVIN WILEY

2

"Remember, You Are a Wiley."

Almost everyone who had known Wiley as a child or as a young man was shocked to discover this militant champion of the poor. He was not a product of the slums of which he spoke so vividly, those rat- and roach-infested tenements where his constituents were forced to live; he had never been a street fighter, battling for his manhood on dirty pavements.

But he would become a leader; everyone agreed on that point. The Wileys of Rhode Island produced leaders: the valedictorians, the class presidents, the magna cum laudes—the lawyer, the journalist, the pharmacologist, the teacher, the sociologist. . . . And George was the academic star of the family—the Ph.D. whose work broke new ground in organic chemistry, whose colleagues praised him for his easy, outgoing personality as well, and envied his verve as he sped along the highway in a red Austin-Healy or leaped up on a table to recite "Casey at the Bat"; the young button-down professor who lived a confident, secure life in a white world—always "the first black," always "the only black," and proud of it.

And then, later, they saw him on television, noisy and abrasive, in his Afro and daishiki, raising a clenched-fist salute, threatening to tear apart the system unless it shared its affluence with the poor. They saw him barge into the 1972 Democratic Convention with his army of welfare mothers shouting out their demands. He wrestled with the convention manager and yelled out into millions of American homes, "If you don't hand over that microphone, I'm going to punch you in the teeth!"

Will Connery, who had grown up with George Wiley in Warwick, Rhode Island, during the 1940s, in a close-knit gang of innocent young Americans who called themselves "Squeaky," "Beefy," "Pooky," "Turkey," and so on, was watching:

"I couldn't believe my eyes or ears. That's what we used to say when we were all joking around, playing basketball. 'I'm gonna punch you in the teeth,' Bonny would yell, and then he'd smile that big smile of his. They were the same words, but he wasn't smiling. Not this time."

"Bonny" was George Alvin Wiley, so nicknamed by his pals for an old song, "Barney Google with the Goo-Goo-Googley Eyes." "Bah-ney," it was pronounced in New England, and it was soon shortened to "Bonny." The "goo-goo eyes" accompanied a sparkling, dazzling smile he carried with him all his life, an unconscious weapon that disarmed and charmed, winning friends, foundation grants, elections, good will, and a large following of admirers—a smile so uniquely his that it would linger in the memories of all who knew him.

Connery and other friends were puzzled by Wiley the welfare fighter. What kind of metamorphosis had taken place? What had happened to the happy, smiling youth; the bright, obedient student; the popular, fun-loving member of the old neighborhood gang; the son of their good, loyal neighbors, who just happened to be black?

But for a black man who grew up in New England as a "White Negro" (as Wiley described himself), who had met successfully all the expectations and demands of the white world in which he lived, who was called "a credit to his race" because he tried to be raceless, could Wiley's transformation be metamorphosis—an overnight change? Or was it an evolution of the soul? And did it carry another message, a message about what white Americans had never understood about black Americans, and about what was happening in the country in the 1960s?

By 1931, the year George Wiley was born, there were only two thousand black families in all of Rhode Island, but the Wileys lived nowhere near them. Warwick was a sleepy, semi-rural town of twenty-three thousand not yet a suburb of Providence, with woods and clean streams, open fields and ponds, neat green lawns and houses painted the colors of a New England autumn, in quiet neighborhoods like Lakewood and Norwood.

The Wileys lived in Norwood, between the railroad tracks and the Pawtuxet River, on land they had inherited from grandfather Daniel Thomas, who had quarried for stone there. Theirs was "a really nice home," as George's sister Lucille describes it, a modest green shingled cottage down the hill from their grandparents' big Victorian house, and around the corner from Uncle Bill Thomas. Along with their relatives, the Greers, they were the only blacks in Warwick.

George's neighbors were white, his playmates were white, his class-mates were white, and they like to remember him as being "no different."

"I'll tell you, the Wiley family were the leaders in this community," says Ralph Pellicano, a close childhood friend. "They used to set an example and we used to look up to it. Mr. Wiley was a low-key individual who taught discipline through reasoning. He was like a father to all of us. He would explain the rights and wrongs, and lead you into the direction you should have been walking."

George's father, William Daniel Wiley, a devout Christian layman and newspaper editor for Providence's black community, sent six children through college on the salary of a postal clerk; his mother, Olive Thomas Wiley, a tall, indefatigable woman who divided her time between home and community service, later was named Rhode Island's Mother of the Year. The Wileys were a family which white Rhode Islanders often held up as a symbol, both to demonstrate their own tolerance and as a model of what a black family should be.

Will and Olive Wiley and their forebears were not particularly unique among those thousands of black families who had slowly and painfully inched their way up to precarious status in the middle class.* Those families always produced high achievers.

"Our family was very much of a real family," says George's older sister Lucille. "We didn't go visiting much, we didn't have much company, and we spent all day Sunday together at church." But theirs was not the traditional black church experience that proved to be the binding force for much of the black middle class of America. The Wileys' church was a small, fundamentalist, evangelistic sect, the Metropolitan Church Association, which met in members' homes or in humble storefronts—and it was white.

As George's sister Shirley explained: "Wileys were a special breed. We don't fit the black skin/white masks mold. We don't fit the black middle class socialite mode of the *Ebony* magazine variety. We had no ties with family in the Deep South. We didn't belong to one of the established black churches. Even one of these institutions would have given us knowledge of the black life style—from soul food to black colleges. We didn't yearn for, strive to be in the American mainstream. *We were always in it.*"

---

* Commenting on such families, black sociologist Andrew Billingsley has written: ". . . it need not be a great deal of money or education to set the family apart and provide a head start for its young members and those of succeeding generations. Negro families have shown an amazing ability to survive in the face of impossible conditions. They have also shown remarkable ability to take the barest shreds of opportunity and turn them into the social capital of stability and achievement." The Wileys had two other slight advantages which sometimes helped blacks. Their skins were light, an inheritance from slavery; and their forebears generally worked in white homes, rather than fields, gaining better opportunities for at least a limited education.

George Wiley grew up in a strong, secure family that believed in the American dream that anything is possible if you have faith in God and yourself—and work twice as hard as white people.

For generations they had worked hard: Emily Isabelle Pinder, an orphan born in 1867, worked the farm fields along the Chesapeake Bay from the time she was seven years old, and cried because she wasn't allowed to go to school. Her adopted family sent her to Baltimore when she was thirteen to "go into service"—creating the niceties of life in white people's homes, at two dollars a month. "She was proud of what she learned there," her daughter Olive Wiley recalls, "beautiful manners, the proper way to speak, everything about gracious living."

When she was eighteen, she moved to Providence to join an older sister, worked as a maid until she married and had a baby, then took in laundry at home. Widowed at twenty-eight, her husband and baby dead of meningitis, she married Daniel Thomas, who had migrated from Washington, D.C., to become a waiter in Providence's Narragansett Hotel in 1896.

Dan Thomas aspired to more. At the hotel, he served a group of wealthy white men who had founded the exclusive Massasoit Golf Club in Warwick and took him along as caretaker, with living quarters on the country club grounds. Their three children, William, Alton, and Olive, were born there. The Thomases lived frugally, saving enough money to buy a large, rocky plot of land in which Dan saw interesting possibilities. On that land, Thomas not only built a home but quarried ledgestone, which he transported by horse and wagon to lay as foundations for some of the biggest buildings in Providence.

The Thomases lived comfortably in a big house on a hill near the quarry, a beautiful spot with maples, pines, spruces, and a view clear to the Pawtuxet River. "We were never in want," recalls Olive.

During those years, when blacks in America suffered through the cruelest years of deprivation and brutality since the end of slavery,* Providence, with its early tradition of anti-slavery and anti-discrimination laws, offered a better climate—within certain boundaries. The young Thomas family suffered from the same discrepancy between theoretical legal rights and the realities of northern bigotry that had puzzled blacks ever since Frederick Douglass many years earlier was alternately honored by the state's noble abolitionists and pulled off Rhode Island trains because he was black. The

---

* Between 1894 and 1900 more than twenty-five hundred lynchings occurred, the majority in four southern states. But the brutality of racism was in the North, too. From the U.S. Commission on Civil Disorders: "That northern whites would resort to violence was made clear in anti-Negro riots in New York, 1900; Springfield, Ohio, 1904; Greensburg, Indiana, 1906, Springfield, Illinois, 1908." Rampaging whites attacked blacks at random, looting and destroying homes and lynching, by methods ranging from hanging, to mutilation, to burning alive, more than a thousand blacks during the first ten years of the twentieth century.

Thomases found the subtleties of northern discrimination often just as unpredictable. They never knew whether they would encounter benevolence or hostility. Opportunities were limited; certain restaurants and hotels barred their doors. Schools, however, were open, and the Thomas children endured racial taunts—until Dan Thomas threatened to administer a sound beating to each white child who harassed them.

When Olive, an honor graduate from high school, tried to find office work, she was turned away repeatedly with the statement, "Our girls won't work in the same office with colored." Even parents of her white friends shunned her as she applied for a job. Finally she was employed at the Imperial Printing and Finishing Company "by a Jewish man who said the other girls could just leave if they didn't want to work beside me."

George Washington Wiley, whose father was a cook in Charleston, South Carolina, made it out of the South in 1905 with his second wife, the servant of wealthy northern white people who wintered in South Carolina. He worked in Providence as a laborer, then a builder, drove a horse and wagon, and later coal trucks. He had brought his seven-year-old son William (who had been in Camden, South Carolina, shuttling between relatives after his mother died) to live in Providence with him and his new bride, a laundress.

Young Will delivered laundry, and one of his customers was a professor at Brown University who decided to train the boy as a butler: "I would march into the sitting room, bow, and announce to the family, 'Dinner is served.' Then I'd precede them into the dining room, to pull the chairs back for the professor and his wife. They paid me fifteen cents, and I liked to go because I ate well there, a good, fancy meal once a week. But I never got very far with butlering."

Will Wiley was an exceptional student, editor of his high school paper, ambitious to become a journalist, but he could not afford to go to college.* For the next three years, he delivered flowers for a Providence florist; then, in 1918, caught up in patriotism for the war effort, he joined the Navy. Starting as a mess attendant (blacks in the Navy during World War I could serve as either ship's cook or servant in the officers' mess), Wiley made the rank of steward by 1919. Finding a job when he got out was more difficult.

It was not a good year for black people in America, including bright,

* His aunt, who worked for Providence's aristocratic Chafee family (whose son, as governor of Rhode Island, later would honor Will Wiley by appointing him to the State Task Force on Civil Rights), helped pave the way for a scholarship to Brown University. His high school, however, had offered him only a commercial curriculum, and despite his high grades he had not taken enough of the courses required for admission to Brown. He could not afford another year of high school, nor could he afford to go to Howard University in Washington, D.C., where he had been accepted immediately. Had he succeeded, William Wiley would have raised to 397 the number of blacks graduating from college in America in 1920.

ambitious young men like Will Wiley. During the "red summer," long-fermenting racial tensions exploded in twenty-six anti-black race riots, brutal physical combat in which scores of blacks were killed. Tensions in the North ran high. Wiley finally found a job working in the color room of the Imperial Printing and Finishing Company. There, he met Olive Thomas and began a four-year courtship, during which they spent much of their spare time as volunteers in the scouting movement.

In 1923 he took a civil service exam, and in 1924 he went to work in the post office, at sixty-five cents an hour. When the Wileys were married in 1925, Will was twenty-seven and Olive twenty-two, and he could boast of a "good, steady job at seventeen hundred dollars a year." A daughter, Lucille, was born in 1926; another, Shirley, in 1927.

For blacks in the 1920s, the postal service opened an important door by providing a few secure, non-menial jobs, ensuring middle-class (or even higher) social and economic status within the black community. Those jobs were prized by whites as well, and competition for them was intense.

It was, therefore, a brave and surprising step when, in 1928, Will Wiley gave up that secure position and income in the post office and an exciting new position with a black newspaper, rented out the house he had built, packed his wife and two little girls into a 1925 Chevrolet coupe, and headed for Waukesha, Wisconsin. His incentive, he felt, was divine. He and Olive were going to become missionaries.

For the next three years, they lived, worked and studied as the only black family at Fountain House, an old hotel on a lake shore that was converted into a Bible school. Will Wiley helped publish *Burning Bush*, the Metropolitan Church Association's evangelistic magazine.

They had entered the church through Emily Isabelle Thomas, who came home one day and told her daughter, Olive, "I want you to meet some white people I have met who know no color lines. They must be real Christians!" (As Will Wiley stated: "We blacks have often equated true Christianity with the attitudes that some so-called Christians took toward blacks.")

When Olive and William Wiley dedicated their lives to its service, the sect included only forty churches with 1,113 members, all in the North.* Within their charter was the charge to deliver the gospel to the poor, the helpless, and the outcast. Their doctrine stated salvation of the soul through faith in Christ, adherence to the strictest forms of abstinence and simple living, and a literal belief in the Bible.

William Wiley graduated from the Bible school as a certified missionary, but Olive's career was interrupted. Their first son, Alton, was born at Fountain House in 1929. When she became pregnant again the next summer, "it

---

* Begun in Chicago as a mission of the Methodist Episcopal Church in 1894, the Metropolitan Church Association soon became an independent movement and in 1918 set up headquarters and a Bible school in Wisconsin.

was decided that it would be better if we came back to Providence. It looked as though we were going to have a large family, and we had to make a living."

Their dream of going as missionaries to the Virgin Islands permanently shelved, Will Wiley, at thirty-three, scrambled to support his children by selling Bibles, religious calendars and church publications. However, in the midst of the Great Depression, there were few customers for the soft-spoken black man. Unemployment, which would mean hard times for the next ten years, had already hit Providence. Thousands were out of work, and many of them lined up to receive help from the Family Relief Society.

The young family lived in a crowded slum on Gillman Street in South Providence, and the meager rental income from their home out in Warwick kept them from going hungry. But when Olive's time came, in February 1931, there was no money for a doctor, or even a midwife. Late in her eighth month, in below-freezing weather, she took a ferry to New Jersey, where a midwife member of their church had offered to deliver the baby free of charge and care for mother and child.

George Alvin Wiley was born on February 26, 1931, in Bayonne, New Jersey, where he lived for the next three weeks. He was a frail baby who almost died in the chilly Providence apartment during his first year—a crisis his brother Alton remembers with great clarity: the doctor warming his hands at the pot-bellied wood stove, the aunts and uncles on their knees praying. His parents believe that George's survival was a miracle.

For the Wileys, a run of good luck followed George's recovery. Will found a job keeping books for an undertaker. It paid eleven dollars a week; for five dollars Olive could buy a week's worth of groceries.

"Some of our neighbors were on welfare, but the only thing we accepted was flour," she said. "They were giving out big bags of flour to the needy, but after the first time, we felt that we shouldn't accept it, because we should really depend on ourselves and not depend on anyone else for help. We should trust the Lord for what we needed."

George's father again began publishing the Providence edition of the *Boston Chronicle*, New England's black newspaper. He had collected advertising from the Democrats during the 1932 campaign, and after the election of Franklin D. Roosevelt as president and Theodore Francis Green as U. S. senator, Will Wiley used his new political contacts to get a job again at the post office, at thirty-five dollars a week.

At the same time, the Wileys were able to move from South Providence back into their own house in Warwick, where they settled into the home of George Wiley's childhood.

Alton Wiley: "George was the smallest of the four of us. We were always concerned about his health. But he was stubborn. I mean he would *never* give in!"

William Wiley, the father: "George was persistent. He would try a hundred ways to bring you around to his way of thinking. He'd plead his case, and that of his brothers and sisters, too."

Lucille was shy and studious; Shirley, mischievous and exuberant; Al, nonchalant and athletic; George, anxious to please, hiding his feelings behind the radiant smile. Each Wiley child felt responsible for the others, and for sharing in the family life. Edwin and Beverly were born a few years later, and caring for the new babies became part of the older four's responsibility.

Olive Wiley: "The children were taught to work. I said, 'we all live here and we all should help.' "

Alton and George delivered newspapers, harvested vegetables at nearby farms, and spent one grim summer as chimney sweeps.

In the Wiley home there was warmth and laughter and conversation, but Mom and Dad held unquestioned authority. No fighting was allowed at home—Shirley and Lucille clawed each other's arms in total silence, more afraid of their mother's reprimands than of sisterly fingernails; Al and George took their arguments to the baseball diamond.

Alton Wiley: "My father kept a razor strop down in the cellar, and when he resorted to that type of punishment you knew you had done something fairly significant. Mother also was a very strict disciplinarian. She said we were not to talk back, and there were certain things we were not to do—and we didn't do them. I guess we had respect." Alton also remembers what a rare treat it was when Will Wiley could spend the entire evening at home with his family: "He worked all hours as a clerk at the post office—working nights and sleeping days. He published the newspaper, kept books at the funeral home, raised a big garden, and raised chickens, too. He would take chickens and eggs to the post office and sell them. I don't know *when* he did all these things." Another thing Will did was to overcome discrimination in the post office. It took years before he became the first black clerk permitted to serve customers at the window.

Olive Wiley canned the vegetables, made all their clothes, and steered the children into wholesome, competitive activities—Four-H Club, scouting—and, during the school year, followed them around to football games and track meets. In the summertime, the family would drive out to Wisconsin to the Bible school, where the four oldest children sang as a quartet, or to a simple mountain resort in New Hamphire where they knew blacks would be accepted.

"Whatever school they were in, I was involved in PTA," says Olive, "because I felt that when parents were interested in what the children were doing, the teachers seemed more interested in the children. One year I was in four PTAs. Also, it was always hard to get den mothers in cub scouts, but I accepted year after year because my boys were in it." *

* Olive Wiley was Rhode Island Mother of the Year in 1965.

The Wiley home was, above all, deeply religious.

Shirley Wiley Green: "When we grew up in Norwood in the 1930s we were no poorer than anybody else, and we were probably a little better off, because my father is one of the finest human beings who ever existed, and he *lived* by the First Pslam: " 'Blessed is the man who walketh not in the counsel of the ungodly nor standeth in the way of sinners, but his light is the law of the Lord, and in the Lord doth he meditate day and night. And he shall be like a tree planted by the river of waters.' "

The Wiley family discussed the Bible, they studied it, they lived as close to its precepts as they could. Every Sunday, "sick or well, alive or dead," they spent all day in church, and in the evenings during the week there were prayer meetings. By the time he was twelve, George Wiley had memorized a formidable number of Bible verses and was often called upon to "testify." Each of the Wiley children, because of the religion imparted in their everyday living, felt set apart from other children.

Shirley Wiley Green: "I can just see my mother coming out on the porch as we were leaving, and saying in her soft voice, 'Remember, please, you are a Wiley.' And nobody ever said what that meant and I never consciously thought about about it, but my mother said, 'Remember, you are a Wiley.' And we always remembered we were Wileys. We didn't break rules. We didn't go out. We didn't dare come home with anything but honors."

That phrase was full of meaning for each of the six children. There was pride in family and commitment to honor. But underneath lay a reality of the Wiley existence, taught every day to their children by Olive and Will: "To be accepted, you will have to study twice as hard, act twice as nice, be twice as good. You are black, in a white world."

3

The White Negro

On the surface, Wiley's childhood years seemed idyllic, with endless games of kick-the-can and hide-and-seek, adventures in the cave-like mushroom beds, and in the field next door, whatever sport happened to be in season. "It was like Paradise, growing up there," neighbor George Yanyar recalls.

All of the old friends remember the Wileys as "just wonderful kids" and George as the happiest boy in the group. He showed to his family and friends a sunny, almost angelic, disposition. He gathered friends easily and won a popular place in the gang. "Laugh—his laughter was contagious," says George Yanyar.

His other characteristic was dogged persistence. He was small for his age, and never as strong as Alton, but he tried valiantly to compete in athletics. Graham Mann recalls: "Every day George would go out and take a beating in football and come right back the next day. He just wasn't as big as the rest of the guys, but he took it." Ralph Pellicano: "They really put him on the ground. I used to wonder whether he was going to be together when he got up!"

George, too, was working twice as hard. His boyhood world revolved around his white pals. He wrestled with them, played pranks on them, made better grades than most of them, and valued their friendship highly.

Barrie Hackett: "We never considered him black, but then George Wiley just seemed to consider himself as white."

When the stings of racism first pierced his sheltered world, he was bewildered and unprepared. George Wiley remembered clearly the first such instance: "I was very small. Al and I walked to a barbershop in the neighborhood. One day, after we had gone there for a while, the barber asked my parents to come and talk with him. 'Some of the people in the neighborhood have complained about your boys coming here,' he told them, 'and I would appreciate it if you wouldn't send them anymore.' After that, we had to go seven miles downtown to the Negro community and go to Negro barbers."

As Olive Wiley explained their action: "We could have said all white people are like that—they're no good. But we would never do anything like that because of our theology and training. I heard a motto years ago that I made my own and tried to teach my children: I will let no man belittle my soul by hating him. It hurts you more to hate than the other person. A soft answer turns away wrath."

In the 1930s and 1940s, the elder Wileys had to choose carefully which battles could be fought and won in behalf of their children. One incident that made an impact on all of them involved Shirley when she was eleven.

The entire family made a festive holiday trip to take Shirley to girl scout camp at nearby Kingston, only to have the director say, "I am sorry, Mr. and Mrs. Wiley, we don't allow colored girls at this camp." At the time Shirley felt inside that she was being rejected because she was inferior, not because the camp discriminated. She recalled: "My father is a very quiet man, and when he is angry he whispers. I can still hear my father say to the woman, between his teeth: 'It so happens that I run a newspaper and I will fight this thing if it is the last thing I do.'

"So we got back in the car and I am crying and George and Al are crying and Mom was going, 'Tsk, tsk, tsk.' My father wouldn't speak to anybody. When we got home he got out his typewriter and typed like mad an editorial, 'Consistency Is Indeed a Joy,' for that week's paper, about the girl scout law that a scout is a friend to all and a sister to every other girl scout. The banner headline was 'Scout Troop Rejects Negro Girl.' After the paper came out, they were embarrassed and asked me to come back to camp, but Dad wrote another editorial saying they would have to change their policy for all Negro girls. It took him until February to get it changed."

Despite his father's efforts against discrimination* and frank talks with his children about racial issues, after that incident George chose "to avoid the problem whenever possible."

George Wiley: "I was the kind of Negro growing up who was attempting

---

* William Wiley was a founder in 1939 of the Providence Urban League, and fought through this organization and the *Chronicle* to improve conditions for blacks. In 1943, Wiley successfully challenged discrimination by Boilermakers Local 308 at the Walsh Kaiser Shipyards of Providence. He reported on and worked with the Urban League to open the telephone company to black employees in 1945 and pressed the Rhode Island Hospital Nursing School to accept black trainees.

essentially to be white. I did not think of myself as a Negro, but simply as a person who was essentially equal with the other people in the neighborhood who would do anything everybody else did. And it was particularly traumatic for me and particularly embarrassing, and a situation I found very difficult to understand or to grapple with, when I was singled out as a Negro, or when I was set apart from a group. I was attempting to identify as a person, and to do what I could do, but if there was any problem, I avoided it and withdrew."

In *The Souls of Black Folk*, W. E. B. DuBois talks about the black American's search for his identity: "One ever feels his twoness, an American, a Negro; two souls, two thoughts, two unreconciled strivings; two warring ideals in one dark body. The history of the American Negro is the story of this strife—this longing to attain a self-conscious manhood, to merge his double self into a better and truer self. . . . He simply wishes to make it possible for a man to be both a Negro and an American, without having the doors of opportunity roughly closed in his face."

George withdrew from the war with his twoness, choosing the white world and hoping that racial confrontations were something that occurred mostly elsewhere. After all, there was the good old white gang, full of boyish pranks: throwing tomatoes and mudballs at street lights, hiding behind a barn and lobbing apples or snowballs at the cars—just anything for a chase.

George Wiley: "We didn't get into any real trouble, but we were involved in building bonfires in the middle of the streets, and running through people's yards, and minor vandalism. . . . We liked to be chased by the police because that was sport. Finally, we were reaching an age where we could be prosecuted, and so that was the end of that."

Olive and Will Wiley put an end to those boyhood escapades. Not only did they violate the spirit of "loving thy neighbor," but George's parents feared the damage an arrest could do to their hopes for their sons—more so than to "Beefy," "Pooky," "Squeaky," and "Ham." One false step for the Wileys and they could end up as victims rather than noble examples. His parents were all too well aware that while George was happily playing with his white friends in the open fields of Warwick, race riots ripped through other northern and western cities, and lynch mobs continued to shed Negro blood throughout the southern United States. They tried to protect their children from the precariousness of black existence.

William Wiley: "The kids didn't know there was a struggle. We lived there in Warwick in a white community, just the three families, Wileys, Thomases, and Greers. George went to school and grew up without any inhibitions."

But George hid his feelings about race, even from his father: "I remember once I went to a swimming pool with a white friend who had accepted me completely, couldn't understand why we were not being admitted to the pool, and held the proprietor in a big argument, never realizing that it was racial discrimination. But I knew right away what was up, and I was really trying to get out of there! Even after we left I would not tell my friend why we were being turned away, because it embarrassed me. He was my friend and I was happy with the relationship with him where I was a person, not a Negro."

As they grew older, Al and George were at times the targets of racial taunts. They endured them. Their friend, George Yanyar, remembers incidents in which he defended the Wiley brothers against racial epithets: "Al and George would just remain quiet and accept it as it was. They never got into a fight about it, and never came back with abusive language—and they seemed to be the winners by their dignity."

For the Wiley children, the idyll came to an abrupt end with adolescence—experiencing their sexual awakenings in a world where interracial dating was so forbidden it was unspeakable, and where were no other blacks. It was especially lonely for the girls.

Lucille Wiley Davis: "We were already set apart by our religion: no lipstick, no straightened or curled hair, no short-sleeved dresses. Of course, we could say to ourselves that we didn't go to the proms or the parties because our religion forbade movies and dancing, but the reality was that we were excluded."

Lucille, the slender, lovely top student in the Nelson W. Aldrich High School Class of 1943, who thought she was miserably homely because she wasn't white, made her first brave step toward a social life: she joined the choir of the Pond Street Baptist Church* in Providence, a gathering-place for young black people in the community. Shirley followed—fearful that her soul would be endangered by "backsliding" to the Baptists—as did Alton. At Pond Street, the three older Wiley children found comfort and companionship, a first, tentative connection with a black world.

But George refused to go; his white life meant too much to him. Yet he was miserable within the strictures of the Metropolitan church, sitting alone on its hard benches Sunday after Sunday, now the only black teenager in the group, dressed neatly in coat and tie all day while his friends played ball or drove off to the beaches with their dates. The loneliness was almost unbearable.

George's own sense of isolation was painfully complicated because he had developed a hopeless teenage crush on the "queen of the class," a dimpled white cheerleader to whom he wrote secret—and unsent—confessions of his love. He had difficulty reconciling his gregarious need for friends with the reality of the color barrier.

* The historic church, founded in the early nineteenth century, had been the leadership center in the black community for generations and was a stop on the underground railway for runaway slaves. The African Unity Society met there in pioneer battles for black rights.

George Wiley: "The process of growing up was learning what kinds of adjustments were realistic and meaningful and valid. For me, the initial adjustment was one of withdrawal from those situations which I could not deal with as a person.

"When there was some kind of social occasion, for example, when a group of teenagers would get together, or a dance, I always had a problem as to how I would handle it. My own response was to put on a façade of not being particularly interested in girls, and to go in heavily for sports and other activities that didn't involve social relations.

"I never had a date the whole time I was in high school. In fact, I developed the attitude that I was going to be a bachelor and never get married. I never even admitted this to my closest friends, but I routinely came in contact with more white girls who seemed attractive to me than did the Negro girls.

"Now my rebellion was that I was NOT going to be restricted in choice by some reason such as color. And my reaction to not having this choice for a normal social relationship was that I simply withdrew, and threw myself into other pursuits."

It took an uncommon amount of self-control to conceal his misery, but he concealed it well. He was always the good sport who played his heart out, who was funny as a son-of-a-gun, who'd spirit the team off to Boston to catch the afternoon striptease at the old Howard Burlesque and be back in time for basketball practice.

Graham Mann: "You would go into chemistry class to work on your experiment—something you had worked on for two or three weeks—and it would be gone! You would be wild. And George would just sit there, innocent as you please, just couldn't understand what you were so upset about. He would finally pop up and say, 'I put it in the closet, in a nice, safe place for you so nobody else would get it . . .'—and you'd have to laugh."

George's other high school pursuits were an almost total immersion in sports—basketball, football, baseball, and track and Gym Club, and into student activities—Hi-Y, debating, a role in *Julius Caesar*, yearbook staff, and science club. "He was a very good orator," recalled classmate Barrie Hackett. "He won a speaking contest in our senior year—he recited 'Casey at the Bat' probably the best I ever heard it."

In the *Reminder*, 1949 yearbook of Nelson W. Aldrich High School, "Bonny" Wiley was described as "a favorite with everyone in the class, and a fellow with an undying sense of humor. He will someday become an outstanding chemist." He worked summers and after school as a janitor in the Cabana Club in Norwood, then ran errands for the Joseph Maxwell Company in Providence, worked the fountain at a dairy bar, and, in the evenings, ground stones for a costume jewelry manufacturer—finally earning enough money to buy an old Model-A jalopy.

Uncle Bill Thomas: "He used to come over here to work on that car, and I would tell him, 'You've got a lot of nerve even going across the street in that thing.' But he drove it off, and how he made it I don't know. But George was determined. *Really* determined. He would do what he wanted one way or another, whether he had help or whether he had to do it by himself."

Aside from his inner worries, which also included his size (at age 18 he was only five feet six inches tall and weighed 125 pounds), George had won acceptance in the white male world of sports and camaraderie. Outwardly, he brimmed with self-confidence. Whether making a talk at church or a speech to the PTA convention, reciting Lincoln's Gettysburg Address at a Memorial Day service or driving home a point in debate at school, he had learned to hold—and enjoy—an audience.

A huge boost to George's self-esteem was his emergence as a scholar, not only following the Wiley tradition into the Rhode Island Honor Society but showing, to the family's surprise, exceptional aptitude. All the Wiley children tested exceptionally high on IQ tests as "very gifted," but George scored the highest of all: 150. "We were all in awe," remembers Shirley. "Here was old happy-go-lucky, easygoing George, the smartest of all of us."

He had his success models in front of him in school, and had watched them walk through their own fire: Lucille's ambition was to be a nurse, but no nursing school in Rhode Island would take a black student. Instead, she won a scholarship to the Rhode Island College of Pharmacy and eventually became chief biologist at the state hospital. Shirley, encouraged by her grandmother Thomas to become another Sojourner Truth,* turned to study black history. Determined to become a journalist, she was admitted to Pembroke College, earning her way working nights in a hot, dangerous foundry, "because the white girls got the safe jobs upstairs at typewriters." When she lost two fingers in a foundry accident, which temporarily interrupted her income and college career, she joined her father on the newspaper, championing black rights. Al was at Rhode Island State, supported by an athletic scholarship. He was gaining a reputation as a record-breaking runner.

George had always been interested in science and had been encouraged by Lucille. The main inspiration and push, however, came from Joseph Rohloff, a white high school science teacher who spent hours with George, both at school and in the Rohloff home, teaching, counseling, and encouraging him toward a career in chemistry. In George's senior year, Rohloff urged him to enter the statewide science fair. He produced a large and elaborate experiment for making rayon out of milk by-products, a patched-together Rube Goldberg contraption that took up an entire room. Nobody thought it would ever work.

"He kept working on this huge chemistry device right up to the last

---

* Sojourner Truth, an eloquent black woman, spoke out for the abolition of slavery.

minute," Shirley recalls, "and Mother was so afraid that it wasn't going to be finished in time. She was very good about trying to prepare us for things like that. But George told her, 'I am a genius and know I am going to win.'

"My mother answered very softly, quoting Scripture, 'Let another man praise thee and not from thine own lips. . . .'

"And George said, 'But, Mama, I am a genius, and if you are a genius it's foolish to be modest. Those people who go around being modest don't use themselves, don't use themselves completely."

The project did win first prize, a scholarship to Rhode Island State College.* So, in the fall of 1949, after a summer spent working for college money at two jobs, George drove his Model-A jalopy the thirty miles to Kingston to search for a wider world. It was another white world, for which he had been preparing in Warwick.

As Roosevelt Greer said: "We had no awe or fear of white people; they couldn't be any smarter or dumber than we. We'd gone to school together, we'd talked together, we'd intellectualized, and the same thing was true with George. There was nothing special about white people."

George, Shirley remembers, went off to college in a buoyant mood. "He really believed the myth that if you work hard enough you can have the All-American dream."

* Which became the University of Rhode Island in 1952.

4

Joe College, BMOC

George Wiley fairly exploded in college—his dream then seemed as though it could never be deferred. He worked twice as hard, collected all the rewards, grew six inches his freshman year, and believed that his possibilities were limitless. Where he had been "very popular" in high school, he was *most* popular in college, a campus superstar. And his own slow awakening during the so-called silent fifties raises into question whether that decade could so easily be labeled as complacent, smug, and bland. For some, it was a time of unparalleled growth, a gestation period for black leaders.

In the calm, unthreatening college atmosphere that he found so congenial, George Wiley honed the skills needed to become a leader. His workshop was the small world of white campus politics and student organizations, but he learned, nevertheless, how to administer programs, organize students, and persuade his white peers to follow his leadership. He would put all those lessons to good use later, for his college activities gave him an extraordinary education in the very skills that were needed in the civil rights and welfare rights movements of the sixties.

George first set foot on the Rhode Island campus in September 1949, determined to enjoy college life as much as anybody else. In Kingston, a small town with one main street and the university, there was little else to enjoy. Out of twenty-eight hundred students there were six blacks—his brother and himself, one football player, and three African students—but their paths rarely crossed. George was the only black student in chemistry.

He joined Al in the quonset hut dormitory, which provided housing for the entering freshmen and less affluent students who did not belong to fraternities, and he supplemented his science scholarship by working as a dorm janitor.

He kept a diary that freshman year, a meticulous daily record of what he did and, less often, of what he really thought. He writes innocently of his delight in the company of his friends and joy in his new-found freedom to indulge in all-night "bull sessions," card games, and trips to the movies, dairy bar, and pool hall. There was a frustrating, unsuccessful effort to follow in Al's footsteps as a track star. He details his exams, term papers, trips to the lab and to the library. It is the sketch of a diligent student very worried about maintaining the B average he needed to keep his scholarship. The diary gives only a few brief glimpses of the deeper thoughts of a black youth who really wishes he were white, who worries that his color will bar him from enjoying the good life he sees around him.

One of the most poignant episodes concerns his feelings for a white girl named Pat, a vivacious blonde whom he met in chemistry lab and courted by helping with her homework. George had no idea what a black man could expect or demand from a white woman. The college rituals of dating made him tentative and insecure. From March to September of 1950, his diary is filled with wishes that Pat would care for him. He drives past her house late at night but doesn't dare to knock on the door. He makes frequent study dates and telephone calls, but confides his true feeling only to his diary: "She doesn't show much affection to me except at times. Even at these times, it probably doesn't mean anything. The trouble with me is that I believe only what I want to believe until the cold facts are forced upon me. I guess what I'm getting is all a guy like me can expect anyway."

George's pursuit was timid, and despite their growing friendship, Pat remained oblivious to George's feelings and even described her active social life to her anguished secret suitor. Yet he persisted, although he knew the relationship was hopelessly one-sided: "Why is it there are certain things which in my rationalizing mind I don't even admit to myself? For instance, you'll notice that I never face the facts about race."

George also longed for acceptance in the carefree world of fraternities and sororities which dominated social life on the campus. The fraternities selected their initiates, who would become pledges, through "rush feeds" in the springtime. In 1950, no black student had ever been pledged to a fraternity or sorority at Rhode Island. Nevertheless, George dreamed of joining. "One thing brightened my day," he wrote in his diary. "Steve Aldrich asked me over to Phi Mu Delta for dinner sometime. It has added to my inferiority complex seeing the other guys going to 'rush feeds' and being on the outside because of my race."

A week later, he noted: "I had supper early and went to Phi Mu Delta for the rush feed. I had a swell time. There were jokes, acts, refreshments, and a social hour. I met a lot of swell guys. I'd sure like to get in there." It was touch and go. One of the members assured George that "if I didn't get in, it wouldn't be because of me, but because of someone's feeling that a step across the racial precipice was too big for the frat to make at this time." But he did get in: "They let out a big cheer when I came in because I was the last one. We took the oath and Lee gave me my pledge pin. We had refreshments and later went to the union. Pat and the girls from East Hall called to congratulate me."

George did not know that his bid at Phi Mu Delta had aroused controversy all the way up to the fraternity's national office. The cheer that went up when George came in was not because he was the last one in but because he was the first: first black to be accepted by this fraternity anywhere; first black to be admitted to a white fraternity at Rhode Island.*

It was a triumph that black students of the sixties would have scorned, but in the early fifties it was a hopeful breakthrough.

As George's campus life blossomed, he began a painful break from home. He worried about his parents' feelings about the fraternity. "I didn't get much reaction when I told the folks about the frat," he wrote. "It's going to be 'outside' the church—the dances, etc. I know they're not going to like that."

And the strictures of the Metropolitan Church began to seem burdensome: "In church today I was asked to get up in front and, I guess, give my 'testimony.' I always dread this because I don't want to commit myself and don't want to get 'saved.' I want to make any such decisions myself. . . . Dad brought us down to the campus tonight. He's the swellest father a person could ever want. Oh, that I were a better son."

In fact, George misjudged his parents. Despite their total dedication to their religion, they were tolerant of their children's independence. And the Wileys were delighted that their son had broken the fraternity racial barrier. In Will Wiley's view, it was a moment of pride and of opening doors for other blacks.

The Wiley family pursued the same version of the American dream that intrigued and inspired the children and grandchildren of white immigrants. The drive was to be "American" in all respects, to shuck off ethnic loyalties, customs and languages, to be like everyone else. This fervent process of acculturation would later be reconsidered by white ethnics as well as by blacks, but in the 1950s the drive for conformity was never stronger.

Thus, George Wiley thrived in college. A paper he wrote in freshman English, "Communism Is a Threat to the U.S.," was right on the mark. He kept track of the Korean War, worrying in his diary that "I might be called up if it develops into something bigger." He replaced his janitor job with a better one, selling sandwiches in the dorms, sometimes earning as much as two dollars an evening. He studied hard enough to make good grades in

* Wiley was named to the national fraternity's Hall of Fame in 1976.

chemistry, his major, but not too hard to be considered a "grind." Like other students in this period, he was intent on being "well rounded." He played intramural basketball intensely and made the varsity tennis team. And, with the fraternity as a springboard, he became a campus leader.

His fraternity elected him vice president (a position from which he directed its social events), and in his sophomore year, nearly twenty years of age, he made a great social leap—he had his first date, stiffly escorting to an ROTC ball a young black woman from another college. He won the race for president of the junior class, defeating five other candidates, and soon afterwards was elected president of the Student Union, the organization which ran most social events on the campus. At the Student Union, he organized car pools to provide transportation for students from around the state, jam sessions every Saturday morning, bingo games every Saturday night. He became an expert at planning the details of social functions—picnics, publicity, invitations, transportation, food, decorations, movies, tournaments—and stirring up student participation in all these activities.

The honors rolled in. He was elected to Scabbard and Blade, the ROTC honorary society, and to Phi Kappa Phi, the highest scholastic honorary society on campus. And then he received the ultimate: he was selected to Sachems, the senior leadership organization, and elected its moderator. As Sachems moderator, George dressed in regulation blue blazer with white piping, Indian chieftain insignia on his pocket and feather in his lapel, a uniform he wore to lunch with Eleanor Roosevelt, whose National Brotherhood Week address he introduced in February, 1953.

Another important college success was the rapport which he established with college administrators and teachers. At a time when many students and faculty were totally isolated from one another, he made friendships and attracted mentors. He developed a considerable reputation as a negotiator with university officials.

Years later, Wiley would reflect that his preparation for leadership in civil rights came from all that busy work activity on campus. As he recalled in a speech at his alma mater: "The Student Union played a very significant role in my own educational process as a student here in Rhode Island, provided an opportunity for my development, an opportunity for participation. Participation, I might mention, that had grown to proportions where it was very actively discouraged by a number of members of the chemistry faculty on the grounds that it was interfering with my academic pursuits."

George's teachers learned that he could pursue a wide range of activities without apparently short-changing any of them. For while he was running most major campus activities in his junior year, he made A's in Organic Chemistry, Logic, and Ethics, and B's in Calculus, Analytical Geometry, Physical Chemistry, and Public Speaking.

Professor E. C. "Doc" Winslow, the chairman of the chemistry department, recalls that George was an unusual student, even in freshman chemistry: "George's self-confidence led to a certain degree of flippancy that most professors would possibly have regarded as a sign of disrespect, but it didn't bother me. It soon became obvious to me that George was very bright, articulate, and trustworthy." At the end of the year, Professor Winslow chose George as his assistant, a position that previously he had always awarded to a senior.

Another chemistry professor, Paul Abell, also became a Wiley mentor and friend: "We had an excellent relationship—one of the best I have had with any student at any time. He was more mature in outlook than most students. He had an interest in everything that went on around him—an aura of life."

With encouragement from Professors Winslow and Abell, George decided on a career in organic chemistry. As he would later recall, "I had never thought about going to graduate school before, but organic chemistry clicked with me and it was natural for people with pretty good grades to go on. The faculty told me about their graduate schools—Cornell and Illinois—so I applied to both and was offered assistantships at both. Cornell sounded pretty good, and it was a little closer to home, so I chose Cornell."

Throughout Wiley's undergraduate years, his seriousness as a student, his driving bid for leadership, his compelling desire to be accepted in the white world were masked by his casual manner. He didn't drink or smoke, but he was always the life of the party. At a time when many college students dressed immaculately to impress others, George was indifferently casual, to a point that exasperated his mother. As Olive Wiley recalled: "We sometimes would drive down to the campus to bring him some extra food or something—and we'd find George in dungarees and sneakers or warm-up pants and an old sweatshirt. He'd bring home his laundry, and they'd be in tatters. 'Why are you bringing me those rags?' I'd ask. And he'd be shocked. 'Why, Mom, those are my good ones.' "

Despite all of Wiley's successes, he was only beginning to come to grips with the realities of being black in America.

In the summer of 1952, George journeyed into the South for the first time. In the company of two white friends, Norris Culf and Jim McCauley, he went to ROTC summer camp in Virginia. At first it was a lark. They headed for Washington, D.C., in George's old Model-A and planned to take their time getting to camp. Then, as they neared Washington, as Norris Culf recalls, "We could not find a place to spend the night. No black people could stay in the hotels in Washington, D.C. Jim and I were seemingly more upset about it than George was. George drove us to our camp at Fort Meade, Maryland, and then went on alone, late at night, all the way to his camp at Fort Lee in Petersburg, Virginia. That was a low point, but he just accepted it as one of those things, and he went on his way."

When he returned to college in the fall of 1952, however, there was an important change in George Wiley: "I had begun to slowly mature, to the point where I could begin to understand what my situation was, with respect to society. I was beginning, for example, to be willing to discuss the race problem for the first time with a white person, without embarrassment to me. For a long time, it would have been embarrassing for me to enter such discussions. I believe at that time it was very embarrassing to most Negroes to be in such discussions."

His initial, tentative discussions about race were with white people he trusted, his closest classmate friends, and his two key faculty advisors at the Student Union, Bertha Cook Waring and Chester Berry.

"When he came back from that summer camp," recalled his friend Will Connery, "he was sort of bewildered. I asked him about the camp, and he said, 'Will, I just had a shock. We would all go out to the movies and they wouldn't let me in. I couldn't drink at certain water fountains.' I said, 'You're kidding, George.' And he said, 'No, it's true.' "

Bertha Cook Waring: "He was troubled. The commanding officer of the Rhode Island group at Fort Lee decided to take the boys to Virginia Beach for the Fourth of July. But he told George that he would not be able to come because the hotel at Virginia Beach would not admit blacks. All through his senior year it bothered him, to the extent that he began to see himself for the first time as someone who might do something for his race."

"As we talked that senior year," recalled Norris Culf, "George began to speak against racial discrimination. We'd talk for hours about it. But it was always a 'soft sell' on his part. Most people never realized how he felt, because he was so outgoing and friendly and mixed so well with everybody that I don't think people thought it was very much of an issue to him. He was not the type of guy who would get up there and be pushy about it. He never showed a lot of strong emotional hatred or disappointment, but rather, he would look at the problem very rationally, analyzing it from all points of view. I think it was always in the back of his mind to someday try to do something about that."

In 1952, he began serious reading for the first time about problems of racial discrimination. He clipped a series of articles by James Rhea, a black reporter for the *Providence Journal,* describing the mass migration of millions of blacks out of the rural South into the urban North, which doubled the nonwhite population in thirty metropolitan areas. This migration, which began with the opening up of defense jobs in World War II, was really just beginning, and it would later alter the course of George's life as surely as the migration of his grandparents at the turn of the century had determined the course of theirs.

He also filed away stories of racial incidents: about the 1952 murder of NAACP leader Harry T. Moore in Florida; the opening up, as a result of a Supreme Court decision, of graduate schools in Tennessee to a few black students; the stoning of a black family that had dared move into a white neighborhood in suburban Chicago; the total banning of black residents from the first Levittown housing development, built to house workers from the booming Pennsylvania steel industry.

But if George was now reading about race and daring to discuss the issues with his most trusted friends, he was by no means ready to take any action. He reflected years later: "If there had been a CORE [Congress of Racial Equality] chapter at Rhode Island, I would not have joined it, and if there had been an NAACP chapter, I would have been embarrassed by it."

He was still mainly interested in racial problems as they affected him personally. He still wanted to be treated as a person, not as a black, and his relations with women were an important index of his success.

"During the latter part of my senior year," he reflected much later, "I took out a couple of white gals on the campus for the first time, but I really hadn't adventured much—and it tells something about me. A number of girls had resigned from a sorority out of principle because the national of the sorority had refused to admit this alleged Indian girl. These girls were kind of far-outers, independent-minded and probably the more principled people, and after they resigned from the sorority, they formed their own clique. And I dated one of these girls in my senior year. That was safe.

"I took out a girl I knew would have principles, and would be inclined to be unconcerned about what anybody said. I liked these girls—in fact I'd had a secret crush on one of them in high school—but there might have been some other girls I would have liked as well, that I didn't ask out because of some fear they would have turned me down. I was still not very courageous about it."

He carefully picked and chose his spots for asserting his freedom of choice. For big public affairs, he would find a black date. In the friendly surroundings of his own fraternity, he would date one of those few white girls who had asserted their own independence.

The problem of interracial dating also involved the attitudes of his own parents, as he realized with his first serious involvement with a woman, a Finnish student named Irja whom he met at a Student Union conference at another college: "I brought her home once. And it was miserable. My folks were very cool—practically wouldn't speak to her. I really laid into them about that. 'Here you are selling race relations, and when it's turned around, you can't take it.' Philosophically and morally, I thought they had no valid position."

The summer after he graduated from college, he continued to see Irja. As his sister Shirley recalled: "He was very much taken with Irja. I'd say, 'Why don't you take out black girls?' He'd reply that black girls just didn't have what white girls had for him. He didn't mean sexually. He meant intellectually—and he'd say, 'All the things they can talk about and do—Negro girls just don't measure up.' He really believed this. And I used to argue, 'Yeah, if we had the same breaks, maybe we could do some things a little differently.' "

Despite his preference for white companions, in 1953 George for the first time entered the social milieu of black America. The catalyst was tennis. As a youngster, George had become proficient at the game, learning from his uncle Bill Thomas, who built his own rough court in his backyard in Warwick and organized other blacks into the Little Rhody Tennis Club.

In tennis, as in golf, blacks were rigidly segregated. Denied the use of country clubs and banned from the United States Lawn Tennis Association, blacks had years earlier formed their own American Tennis Association, which served as a social network for black doctors, lawyers, teachers, ministers, and their college-age children. George won a place on his uncle's Rhode Island team.

"It was really great," George recalled. "Each weekend a different city along the eastern seaboard would host a tournament. I drove to Washington, Philadelphia, Boston, New York, Hartford. This gave me a lot of very pleasant social contact with the Negro communities along the eastern seaboard— the middle class, the tennis playing set. But, mind you, this was 1953, and I was all the way through college, and this is the first contact I am having with Negro communities."

In June he graduated with high honors from the University of Rhode Island and immediately broke another barrier. He had entered the field of chemistry without knowing that Negroes were rarely hired as chemists in industry: "That was my unrealism. I thought I was white, and I just went out and did these things anyway. I was the first Negro to be on the technical staff at duPont* in their organic chemical department. It was really a big deal because all these people had to come and have a look at me. The plant manager even invited me in to have a talk with him, and everybody was worried about how it was going to work out. I was the least worried of anybody. I knew it was going to work out, because all my life I have been put in this situation of being the first, and there never has been any problem."

As usual, George made friends with the whites in the lab, but the most important relationship that summer was with a black man. The late Al Wilson, who became his first black mentor outside his own family, was a unique and lonely pioneer in the early fifties. He was one of the first black executives hired by a major American industry, and he took on the role of breaking the race barrier for blacks to become executives and high-ranking professionals. The Wilsons found housing for George near their own home, and Al taught him the realities of black life and black hopes.

George was learning slowly, yet he still thought that all blacks could be

---

* In the company's Penn's Grove, N.J., chamber works plant.

as upwardly mobile as he, if they only worked hard enough. For the first time, he envisioned himself as a model for other blacks. It was a role suited to the gradualism of the fifties, and one heartily endorsed by well-meaning whites. As his sister Shirley described his thoughts: "He felt that his contribution as a Negro was to be a 'first,' first black in the fraternity, first black president of his class, first black chemist in that duPont lab, thus opening doors for others, because he was confident of his abilities in science and in persuading people. He was determined to be not only the first black chemist wherever he was going, but the best chemist in the country, setting an example no one could question."

With this dream of glory, George enrolled at Cornell in the fall of 1953, determined to win his Ph.D. in chemistry and to become a great scientist.

5

Deeper Waters

When he began his graduate study in 1953, George Wiley once again stood out in a rarified world within a world. At Cornell, a great Ivy League university of seven thousand students in Ithaca, New York, he was one of 171 Ph.D. candidates in chemistry. In his Baker Hall laboratory he worked happily with his all-white peers and professors for four years. "I am seeking to gain more specialized knowledge in my major field of organic chemistry in preparation for a life of research and teaching," he wrote. "My most earnest desire is to make some substantial contribution to humanity."

He was soon challenged by an intriguing variety of pursuits. He was drawn toward graduate student circles where intellectual accomplishments were more admired than the kind of Joe College activities that had seemed so captivating in Kingston. There were fierce discussions about politics and civil rights, about events in Africa and China, and debates about Senator Joseph McCarthy and academic freedom. It was all new and sometimes baffling to Wiley, who wrote to his old philosophy professor: "The Campus in general professes Ultra-Liberalism which, as far as I can discern, is an extremely nebulous monster." But he did not shrink from the "monster." Instead, he threw himself into the swiftest currents of campus life; he was going to be a leader at Ithaca, too.

He thought there should be more activity for graduate students at Willard Straight Hall, Cornell's Student Union building, and applied for a position on the Union board. He was turned down. No matter, he would keep trying. (After being rejected for three years, he did at last become a member of the board of directors.)

He applied for Telluride, a discussion/living society comprised of "the best minds" at Cornell. He stressed that his ambition was to inspire students to develop a respect for seeking the truth, and to think clearly and objectively. He wanted to relate academia to the challenge of participation in public affairs. His application concluded: "I believe in the dignity of man. . . . It is the degree to which he rises above his environment to assert his dignity which is the measure of how nearly he fulfills his potentiality for perfection. . . ."

Telluride rejected him—a painful blow for the former student leader. But never mind. He was serious about broadening his intellectual base, and he sought other avenues. George once again found mentors with whom he shared ideas, dreams for the future, and the pleasure of good company. These men were Ralph Helverson, minister of the Ithaca Unitarian Church, and Dr. Glenn Olds, the university chaplain, who directed Cornell United Religious Work. Wiley visited frequently in their homes, attended services and ushered at Helverson's church, and became a pivotal member of the graduate seminars which Olds initiated and inspired.

In discussions with Helverson and Olds, George expressed his impatience with both the students of "Silent Generation" and the academics who took refuge in the world of pure thought. "He wanted to teach," recalled Glenn Olds, "but he felt that he could do with chemistry what I had been doing with philosophy: use it as a pretext for opening minds and assailing institutions, trying to enlist and develop a new kind of personal ethic and sympathy and competence and ambition to help us make a new kind of world. He saw himself doing that through chemistry. The university had become for him a focal point for bringing about change in society."

As George wrote to a friend: "The university community is not an 'unreal world,' that many university people think it is, and to participate only in 'sham exercises' is precisely the crux of the important failings of the university. That we can conceive of our ivy-covered halls as an 'ivory tower' in which we can sit back and view the world as spectators is idealistic foolishness."

Glenn Olds: "In one of our first projects, the Graduate Club, which we converted to the One World Club, George became involved and quickly became its leader. There was a dynamic executive committee of the club, a very intellectually sophisticated group, composed of the most thoughtful of the graduate students at Cornell. George was a member of this group and they spent practically every Friday night at our house. We took the world apart and tried to put it back together again. The issue was not simply racial, ethnic, geographic or economic. In that era, we saw the issues in their more cosmic simplicity. We were wrestling with the problems as multi-causal, global, and really rooted in the classical values systems, the relationships of nature, man and God. We analyzed the nature of man, and the objectivity of values, and George just devoured it. We argued that God is love, and that love has a persistent reality that cannot be ignored except at our own peril. George took to this like filings to a magnet."

In a first gesture of activism, George successfully initiated in the chemistry department a seminar titled, "Non-Chemical Chemistry: The Search for Meaningful Values for the Physical Scientist." "This seminar," he said, "should permit us to discuss together some of the value presuppositions upon which our pursuit of chemistry is based. The purpose of the seminar should be to develop an understanding of the proper relation to chemistry and the university in assisting man toward attainment of his highest purpose."

Although he had shed the more puritanical strictures imposed by the Metropolitan Church, he still deeply believed in God and a reverent, purposeful life. George's quest for religious values that he could accept, as both a rational scientist and a secretly troubled black man, emerged from a series of interchanges between himself and Ralph Helverson. In Unitarianism, Helverson preached a nondoctrinaire, encompassing religion in which George found sound principles, though he questioned its "too-easy rejection of ultimate truths and moral authority."

When Helverson preached that "man does not become good by believing in God but comes to believe in God by being good," that man doesn't come to proper religious development by believing in dogmas, but rather comes gradually to accept certain religious doctrines, George noted his enthusiastic agreement. And when Helverson preached tolerance of religious and racial differences, he found an enthusiastic listener.

Those who met Wiley only at a party, or on the tennis court, saw merely the charm and good humor, the joyous mien which he presented to the world. He kept hidden his painful groping towards an understanding of the balance between science and religion, and between his personal goals and his broader human responsibilities.

George's friends at Cornell were amazed not only at the gentleness of this energetic black man who "never smoked, drank, nor cussed," but at his tolerance for the foibles of others. His roommate Malcolm Bell remembers him as accepting whatever people did, without ever questioning or criticizing, no matter how badly someone he knew behaved: "Even if someone had done something really terrible, he'd say, 'Oh, that rascal, that rascal.' "

According to his Cornell datebooks, George rarely had a free moment. Attending chemistry labs and seminars and working on his dissertation research; a regular fan at varsity basketball games (he even played on the Cornell rugby team), graduate student square dances, Student Union coffee hours, the Unitarian Church; taking trips around the country to conferences, tennis tournaments, ROTC camp in New Jersey—he managed to cram an exhausting number of activities into his life.

He had to scrape for money, earning a little from Army Reserve, working at the Providence post office over the Christmas holidays, living on his teaching assistantship—barely enough to buy gasoline for his car. He taught freshman chemistry, had a part-time job at the Student Union running a cigarette stand and serving as a campus guide. It helped, he said, when he "won a big, fat fellowship from the John Hay Whitney Foundation in New York in 1956—so next year I can devote full time to research without having to spend a big slug of time teaching and working at part-time jobs."

Malcolm Bell wondered how he managed. "People like me and most of our friends spent most of our time laboring away in the laboratory, and in scientific journals and books, always studying," yet George made more than a reasonable record for himself as a student in organic chemistry, a demanding field, while plunging into all his extracurricular activities."

At least part of the answer was that George had an extraordinarily quick mind, and with it an unusual ability to compartmentalize his concerns and his time. He had enormous reserves of physical and mental energy, which he used with abandon, stopping rarely to rest. And he did not waste time; he was very well organized, making endless notes to remind himself of all the things he wanted to do. He lived fiercely by the motto that he had decided upon while still in high school—that he should use himself fully. There was a price to be paid for his over-extended schedule and the submersion of his private worries: a stomach ulcer, about which he told no one. That was his private problem, and he thought he should bear it stoically, not use it as excuse for inaction.

Despite his increasingly stimulating excursions into philosophy, the focus of George's work at Cornell was organic chemistry—the chemistry of life. He found a mentor who would guide his development. For his doctoral work, he selected as his advisor Dr. Jerrold Meinwald: "George was academically a good student and he was more than enthusiastic about organic chemistry. He was a confident fellow at all stages.

"Like any good organic chemist, George could keep thousands of details in mind at one time. He had to know hundreds of names, and all the reactions of each name, alone and with each other, which add up to a whole pattern of things he had to work with. To any problem he had to bring to bear a tremendous background of facts and reactions—and he also had to think in three dimensions.

"George Wiley had a taste for problems—he knew how to select ones that were neither too ambitious nor too trivial. The talent of selection is not common at all. George picked nice problems, and he loved organic chemistry!

"George was lucky—he had both the enthusiasm for the subject and a little bit of competitive feeling. If you are not enthusiastic you cannot work hard enough to be successful. By and large, research is a demoralizing experience. About 90 percent of all new chemistry experiments fail. And so you need the character to go back again and say, 'What went wrong with that one? What should I do?' And you go back and try again. After you fight with something long enough, finally it works. To the chemist, a failed experiment is not a failure at all, but a challenge, only a step toward final success. George was well disciplined in that respect."

George's doctoral thesis, in which he set to work for four years on solving an "investigative mystery," was "The Structure of Flavothebaone," an analysis of a molecule found in thebaine, a poisonous substance within the opium poppy.* "His thesis worked out just beautifully," says his professor. "He could, in fact, prove the structure of this product, prove that it had a rational mechanism . . . and that its unusual properties also were interesting in that they taught something about ultraviolet absorption by organic molecules. It was much more interesting than the average thesis."

"We were all so proud of him," recalls his sister Shirley. "He'd be so wrapped up in his thesis, and I'd say, 'How's old Flavo-T?' and he'd get all incensed and try to explain how serious and what an important project it was."

"Frankly the gals around here have kept me busier than a toad on a hot griddle," George wrote to a black tennis circuit companion in Washington, D.C. His earlier constraints about women melted away in Cornell's liberal, more cosmopolitan atmosphere. His most intense relationship at Cornell was with a white woman, Carol Condie, an anthropology student from the West.

Carol was struck by how exceptionally friendly, outgoing, open, and down-to-earth he was—"not ever phony, and naïve in a lot of ways. I, as an anthropologist, had a prejudice against hard scientists, found them narrow and limited. He was interested in the humanities, in the same kind of real-world issues as I was. He was deeply concerned about civil rights. . . . We'd talk for hours, discussing problems in the South.

"He used to amaze me. We would go to parties where neither of us knew anyone. I would feel nervous in the situation and he would walk in with that big smile and say, 'Aren't you glad to see me?'—and it wasn't arrogant. Everyone always looked up, and liked him immediately.

"I asked him if he ever looked in a mirror. He asked what I meant and I said, 'You are black.' 'I know it,' he said. I said, 'How do you *do* this, walking into a room full of people and saying that?'

"He answered, 'Well, I decided a long time ago that I would be interested to see a situation that I couldn't handle.' "

* Part II, "The Synthesis of Some Benzo (1; 2; 5, 6)-Norbornenes," Cornell University, 1957.

At first, he thought he could not possibly marry a white woman, but then, George later reflected: "I thought through the question of whether we could get married or not—and I went back to my original stand: that I ought to be able to marry who my conscience dictated. I threw out the premise that I need restrict myself because of race.* As a result, I made the first realistic adjustment to my situation. I realized that I was a Negro, and that I could have social relationships with Negroes and whites—if I was big enough to do it. In my adolescent years, I would have been inclined to discriminate against Negroes because I thought I was white."

Yet his life still basically was white. His connections with black people were tenuous, and his efforts to show his white friends that he did not "mind" being a Negro at times struck a discordant note. Malcolm Bell recalls one episode: "The graduate students and faculty had put on a party in the chemistry museum—which consisted of a series of skits, a lot of beer, and square dancing. And George was asked to help put on a skit—this was in the spring of 1956—and what he did really shocked me and embarrassed me for him. He did an a cappella recitation of Phil Harris' 'Darktown Poker Club,' with great exaggeration—playing the darky role in front of the whites. I felt very ill at ease when he did this." It was less disquieting and more natural when George recited to the group his "Casey at the Bat," which he joyfully performed over the years. He spoke in the cool voice of white New England.

Still, at Cornell George studied the civil rights issues and was gradually drawn into a commitment, albeit a tentative one. The Wiley who later reflected that he would have been embarrassed by an NAACP chapter at Rhode Island now joined one in Ithaca. He later criticized it as a "do-nothing" organization, yet it fairly matched his own pace at that time. He declined to join the Quaker-sponsored Fellowship of Reconciliation, which campaigned against the proliferation of atomic weapons and had given birth to the Congress of Racial Equality (CORE). In a letter rejecting membership he wrote: "It is too extreme, and extremes often represent themselves as panaceas. In my opinion, the cure for war comes in the day-to-day articulation of love and self-transcendence."

But George was being buffeted, if ever so gently, by the winds of change. As he traveled the black tennis circuit, his friends were discussing the 1954 Supreme Court decision outlawing segregated schools and the 1955 implementation order that desegregation must proceed "with all deliberate speed."

There were shocking tragedies; for instance, the 1955 murder in the Mississippi delta of fourteen-year-old Emmett Till, who had dared to look at a white woman. Other murders were more directly related to the incipient

---

* George and Carol's discussion of marriage never got beyond the theoretical phase, and the relationship eased into a solid friendship that lasted throughout his life.

black movement for civil rights. While Wiley was in ROTC summer camp in New Jersey, voter registration worker Lamar Smith and NAACP leader Reverend Charles Lee were gunned down in the South. They were early martyrs of the new black movement. George Wiley's "personal" file at Cornell was filled with newspaper clippings, as well as editorials by his father, about those events that affected blacks in 1955–1957.

The outrage, as well as the hope and excitement, spilled over into Olive and Will Wiley's dining room in Warwick, where the Wiley family carried on continuing seminars when George drove down from Ithaca on weekends throughout the next year.

Will Wiley, who had always led the discussions, now listened as his sons and daughters* debated the role of blacks in America, and their obligations as the educated "Talented Tenth."** There were so many things to talk about, such as the bravery of the black Alabamans, inspired by Rosa Parks, boycotting the segregated buses in Montgomery under the leadership of a young minister, Martin Luther King, Jr. Blacks were seeking not only to integrate southern schools and public accommodations but to vote. And in the North men like William Wiley, who was now president of the Rhode Island Urban League, were attacking discrimination in employment.

Shirley Wiley Green: "We would start out sitting around the table having breakfast and we would never get up from the table. We'd talk about the atrocities, and what we each could do. I was deep into the richness of the black cultural experience, and felt that there is strength in soul and that we should work within the black communities. I said that it wasn't until every black person was free that I would be free. Dad believed that pressure should be brought to bear on the establishment, through organizations like the Urban League. George believed in integration. He believed that people can be convinced on the basis of reason.

"As we talked about what we each could do about the situation, George thought his contribution was going to be as a black man who just happens to be black who has made it, and that people would see this example and say, 'Wow, blacks can do it.' He no longer wanted to be just a chemistry professor but was interested in becoming president of a university. He wanted to prove that a chemistry professor didn't have to be so ivory-tower that he couldn't deal with people. It was only incidental, but the fact that he was black was also going to be something."

The Wiley family discussions were part of an electric current spreading around the dinner tables and living rooms of millions of black Americans. As

---

* Alton, his two-year stint in the Army completed and now a law student at Boston University, joined the marathon family discussions, as did Shirley, who was now working in a black church in New York. Sometimes the discussions took place at Lucille's house, where her husband, Henry Davis, a businessman, told of the economic difficulties of the blacks in Rhode Island.

** W. E. B. DuBois' term for the educated black class from which leadership was to emerge.

Lerone Bennett wrote: "The myth [of Negro progress] was tangible, the myth was palpable. You could see it, you could touch it—the brass ring was gold."

During this postwar period, blacks were making economic gains in relation to whites. The NAACP was winning battles, and as yet there were no concentrated efforts by whites to stop the trend. They had not yet gotten so close to America's racial nerve.

In 1957, George Wiley received his Ph.D. from Cornell. He was eager for success and fulfillment in the academic world; he would make his black commitment along the way. But first he had a commitment to the U.S. Army for his long-delayed six months of active service. The place was Petersburg, Virginia, where his experience five years earlier as a trainee still burned in his memory. Now the times were different, and George Wiley had changed; he was a first lieutenant in the Army, and he had things on his mind to find out and prove.

6

Confronting
the System

"By the time I finished Cornell," said George Wiley, "I was fully matured and ready for battle on the racial problem. I had a pretty good concept of who I was, what I was. I had never participated in any demonstrations but I think I had adjusted, and was sort of ready. I was cocked and loaded."

When he arrived at Fort Lee he was full of optimism. Inspired by Martin Luther King's victory in the Montgomery bus boycott, buoyed by reading about the progress in Congress of federal civil rights legislation,* and impressed by the turnout in May of fifty thousand people at the Lincoln Memorial in Washington to protest the slow pace of desegregation in the schools, he set out to take on the nearby town of Petersburg.

For the first three weeks, he lived on the Army post. Two-thirds of the class in the Quartermaster School were white second lieutenants from the South. George, as a first lieutenant, had command authority over them, and was quickly elected class president. He was once again the only Negro.

Only twenty-one miles north of the site of Nat Turner's rebellion, Petersburg in 1957 still commemorated its martyrdom in Civil War days. A city of thirty-five thousand then, in tobacco country, it had been described as diehard and intransigent.

---

* The new law established a civil rights commission, a special civil rights division in the Justice Department, and legal penalties for interference in voting in federal elections.

George Wiley: "When the three weeks of basic training were over, I moved into the Negro community, right in the heart of the ghetto. I had a life on the post, but I had a chance, for the first time ever, to live in a Negro community, to see what life was like out there. I joined a Negro church,* mainly because the minister was quite militant, and I thought he was exciting. It was a Baptist church, but he was preaching a Unitarian doctrine: social protest and all this. He was Wyatt Tee Walker, who later became Martin Luther King's chief lieutenant."

Wyatt Tee Walker: I remember this tall, skinny guy showing up at church one morning. He looked very young, and he was very talkative. His accent was different, northeastern. What struck me about George is that here was a young Ph.D. from Cornell who was anxious to join in, who didn't care what Army protocol was. By the yardsticks of society, what did he need this headache for? All he'd have had to do was put in his time in service and then go up the ladder. But here was George, right out there 'working the point,' as they say in the military. He was willing to take risks, and he caught some flak."

Civil rights was in the national headlines. On August 29, 1957, after South Carolina Senator Strom Thurmond set a new Senate filibuster record of twenty-two and a half hours, the Senate passed a law to protect the voting rights of black Americans—the first federal civil rights legislation since 1875. Blacks and their white allies were encouraged by the legislative victory. And in the sleepy southern town of Petersburg, the young minister and the brash young Army officer sought to turn legislative theory into practice.

George Wiley: "Voter registration was hot nationally at the time. And it was hot in Petersburg for a practical kind of reason: if you could register a lot of Negroes in Petersburg, you could actually overturn the power structure. The population ratio was about 60 percent white and 40 percent Negro. The registration among whites was low, although they outnumbered Negroes at the polls by ten to one. Therefore, if *all* the eligible Negroes registered, they would have outnumbered the registered whites by two to one. So the point, as I saw it, was if Negroes could have gotten in with a good registration campaign, they could have completely upset the applecart in Petersburg. This was what I was going to work on."

"Upsetting the applecart" had its price. Wyatt Tee Walker's home in Petersburg had been fire-bombed in retaliation for his activities encouraging blacks to swim at a state park lake. School teachers had been threatened. Blacks who had lived there all their lives were insecure and intimidated.

White Citizens Councils had begun to spread through the South, threatening the new black activists with economic reprisals, social pressures, and

---

* The Gilfield Baptist Church, founded in 1788, was one of the oldest Baptist churches in America.

violence. It was Virginia's Senator Harry F. Byrd who called for "massive resistance." As desegregation petitions were filed against school boards, southern politicians responded with a multiplicity of laws designed to prevent school integration. Virginia proclaimed a doctrine of "interposition"—a declaration of its sovereignty over the federal government—and passed seven anti-NAACP laws, "to investigate, embarrass, curb, or cripple the NAACP in this state." The legislation hit hardest at black voter registration.

Walker: "Virginia in general had a polite kind of tyranny, but in Petersburg it was like the Black Belt. They had signs—'White' and 'Colored'—in every public building. In downtown Petersburg there was nowhere a Negro could go to get a sandwich. The hotel was segregated. Separate schools. All-white police force and fire companies. No blacks in city government. No blacks working in any kind of job other than custodial. There were two USOs, one black and one white."

Wiley was either oblivious of or indifferent to the powerful forces he chose to challenge. He was naïve, idealistic, steeped in academic theory about race relations, and very determined.

George Wiley: "I had asked a Negro on the Army post about joining the local NAACP. He said, 'You can't do it. If you are in the Army you can't join the NAACP.' This, of course, offended me."

For ten days Wiley persistently made his way through the Army chain of command to verify his right to become an NAACP member. At each step he was told that he shouldn't meddle in community affairs, that he would do more harm than good. He was sent to see a black athletic coach who told him to stick to Army business. He was sent to another officer who warned him that any speeches involving Army affairs had to be cleared in advance. Sensing that Wiley was a non-conformist who would cause trouble, each officer he saw bucked him to a higher command. Finally he confronted a colonel, the chief personnel officer of the base. At this point, it dawned on Wiley that his superior officers could cite no regulation to bar him from civil rights work; they were merely trying to exert their higher rank and persuade him to conform. Recognizing the situation, he announced that he would indeed join the NAACP, and the colonel surprised him by saying that he too opposed segregation.

"This was a very significant incident to me because it indicated one level of the way the problem existed, the way it operated," Wiley reflected. "It emphasized the importance of confrontation. We began working on registration, and we set up a very elaborate organization for doing this. We set up an NAACP office, got equipment in, a typewriter, and a secretary. I joined the Voter Registration Committee and said, 'Okay, Wyatt, who do I report to?' And the committee was so defunct that I was the only member, so I became chairman very speedily."

He was further motivated into action by the bravery that September of nine black students in Little Rock who, after a three-week siege, entered

Central High School, but only after President Eisenhower federalized the 9,936-man Arkansas National Guard and called out 1,000 Army troops to enforce a court order and protect the students.

Wiley was burning to change the southern system, and though he had never been a racial activist or experienced the dangers of black southern life, he was impatient with anyone whose fires burned less brightly than his.

Wyatt Tee Walker: "The first confrontation we had was at a meeting at the Jackson Funeral Home. George got up and gave a long diatribe against the churches and the ministers, saying they weren't doing anything. I took him aside and said: 'Now, look, buddy, you won't get to first base in this town or any other town if you start lambasting churches and ministers. That's all we've got! No wonder you're turning people off!' I sat down and showed him that everything that had gone on in that town on civil rights had been either church-sponsored or church-oriented, and the personnel had come from the churches.

"If I had any criticism of him at the time it would be of his youthfulness and brashness, not understanding the realities that in a community organization you have to work with a cross-section of people. It was a town that had been completely cowed by the climate of fear in Virginia."

But Wiley did not understand what Walker was saying. Not only had he not experienced life in the South, but he did not appreciate the survival instincts of southern blacks. He was self-righteous and intolerant.

George Wiley: "One thing that really struck me was the level of apathy in this Negro community. It really used to frustrate me. We had a guy who was sort of a dirt-digging contractor and somewhat of a politician, who someone said would be a good guy for a ward leader. But he never had any time. He was always digging dirt and you never could get together with him.

"I worked on voter registration every night and seldom did anything socially. One day I went to see a friend of my family's and he dragged me out to his social club to play cards and billiards. I went to this man's club and there was this dirt-digger that I never could get to do any work. He had a whole evening to while away and play cards—but no time for the civil rights activity! As bad as the problems were, as immediate as the kinds of things that could be done about them, we could not move that community. But we did get a block organization set up, and we had some rallies and things—successful rallies of fifty people when there were ten thousand Negroes in Petersburg!"*

Not only was there fear of reprisal, but a poll tax and a whole series of stratagies by white officials which made registration a painstakingly slow, frustrating struggle.

Wyatt Tee Walker: "There was a long voter registration form consisting

* "Obviously, if all these people would vote," he wrote to Carol Condie, "they would not have to cry about segregation. They could just change the laws."

of ten to twelve questions. If the people would agree to register, and were literate, and could write, then you had to conduct classes to show them how to answer these questions. After that, we would take people down, one at a time, to register them. And the registrar, down at city hall, would lollygag around, find something wrong, anything, and turn them down. It was that laborious."

In his civilian clothes, driving a sputtering 1948 Oldsmobile sedan he called "The Kangaroo" because it leaped when it started up, squiring about a pretty black Virginia State student whom he'd pressed into voter registration work, Wiley put to work all his organizational training from his college days: recruit volunteer workers, make accurate lists with addresses of potential voters, make written assignments, follow up—old skills put to work in new, dangerous ground.

George had some success, not enough to please his outsized ambitions, but he did register some voters.* By way of contrast, in many towns similar to Petersburg not a single black person succeeded in registering or actually voting that year.

Wyatt Tee Walker: "He never got arrested, and that is surprising because he did have a flint-like personality. He was just steaming all the time at the injustice."

George Wiley: "I remember getting my Ph.D. in social education in a little coffee shop in downtown Petersburg. I had been told that I was among the Talented Tenth, that I was a lieutenant in the Army, and that I was to be treated differently from other people. I remember how indignant the white waitress was when she blurted out, 'Wh-wh-what are you doing here?'

" 'I'm trying to get breakfast,' I said.

" 'Are you colored?' she said.

" 'I am from Rhode Island,' I answered. I remember this woman, who must not have had more than an eighth-grade education. I remember how she split her infinitives, how her fingernails were dirty—that she did not have the social amenities that I'd been told you have to have in order to be accepted.

"I remember how indignant she was as she told me I was not wanted in that restaurant. And as I stubbornly refused to leave, as I stubbornly refused to admit that I was different and was to be treated differently, I remember her crowning phrase: " 'You are not one of them dumb kind. You are an educated nigra. Go back over on the other side of town where you belong.' "

* In the gubernatorial race, Democratic Attorney General J. Lindsay Almond, Jr., had asserted that he was committed to "oppose with every facility at our command, and every ounce of our energy, the attempt to mix white and Negro children in our classrooms." (A year later, Almond would close the schools in Warren County rather than comply with a court order to desegregate.) In Petersburg, in the primarily black Sixth Ward, a majority of the 518 voters voted for Almond's Republican opponent.

The incident in that Petersburg restaurant was a pivotal event in George Wiley's life: "I was told throughout my growing up in Providence, Rhode Island, that I was a colored person who was different from the mass of colored people who lived in that city, because most of these colored people were dirty. Most of the colored people in Providence were uneducated. Most of the colored people in Providence had social behavior that was unacceptable to most of the white community. I was told that I was clean and educated and I would have the opportunities to be accepted in the society on a different basis from the rest of the blacks who inhabited the areas in which I lived.

"And I am sad to say, but I will confess, that I bought the myth that I was one of the Talented Tenth and that I could be treated differently and that I would have a different experience than others in America. And I remember there was only a very slow process by which I began to understand that my freedom was abridged and my opportunities and my dignity were abridged by the fact that there were others who did not have that opportunity and there were others who were not being accorded the same kind of dignity and respect."

Another incident at Fort Lee also left its mark. It seemed trivial, involving "officer rating." Each student was to list the "five most competent" and "five most incompetent" officers in his class. Some students in Wiley's class refused to list any officer as "incompetent." Wiley took the side of the dissidents. The dispute escalated until a colonel threatened court-martials.

Wiley negotiated with the colonel, and his outspoken advocacy made him a hero in the eyes of the southerners, who were convinced he had saved them from court-martials. George took advantage of their gratitude to press home a point. On November 15 he and his black girlfriend were honored by the class at a party—the first integrated social occasion many of the young white officers had ever attended. The next day, Lieutenant Wiley left for Alabama for an interview with the chemistry department of Tuskegee Institute. He had already interviewed for jobs at Southern University in Baton Rouge, and at Fisk and Tennessee State in Nashville. And he used his forays into the deeper South to challenge the racism of his Fort Lee classmates:

"I'd come back from these guys' home cities and then say, 'What are you guys going to do when you go home? *You've* got the segregation problems. If I go to work in Alabama or Louisiana, I am going to be segregated. You guys are doing that to *me!*' And they would get very embarrassed and hang their heads. One said, after his companions had gotten out of earshot, 'Wiley, you know you're right. This situation is intolerable. It is unjust and something ought to be done about it. But I don't know what to do. I will be completely ostracized if I do anything at all, if I get out of line.'

"I was fairly serious about taking a teaching job at Tuskegee. It was the best job I had offered to me at the time [November, 1957], and I knew it was going to be rough. So I used to say to these guys from Alabama and Georgia, whom I played tennis with, and who thought I'd saved their necks, 'You know, here at the post we are good friends. When I come down to Alabama, I'll come visit you. I'll come to your house and ring your doorbell and throw my arms around you.'

"This was very embarrassing to those guys because they knew I'd do it. They knew I wasn't kidding. Some of them were scared. But when I left, to a man they did say, 'Wiley, if you do come South, come see us. You will still be our friend. We will try to make whatever adjustments we can make to continue the friendship.' And I know they were sincere because they knew me too well to make an empty gesture of that sort. But one of those guys also said to me, 'Wiley, if you're coming down South to live you better change your attitude. Because you're coming down South to die.' "

The brief, intense activist fling in Petersburg had touched his conscience, causing an agonizing reconsideration of his ambitions for the future. He was drawn to the black institutions of the South not only because of his new commitment to civil rights, but because for a while they seemed the only source of employment for a black chemist. When another opportunity came through he wrestled now with the direction of his career in teaching: should his contribution as a scholar be to share his knowledge of chemistry at a black college he considered "second-rate," or should he compete with the best at a top-flight university? A grant had come through for post-doctoral study at the University of California at Los Angeles. He would be working with Dr. Saul Winstein, considered a giant in the field of organic chemistry. Wiley consulted his mentors.

Chester Berry, his Student Union advisor from Rhode Island: "The decision involved a consideration of social responsibility. I asked George what kind of chemist he was. He replied that he wasn't concerned about his ability to compete with the very finest."

Jerrold Meinwald, his Cornell professor: "He was superbly qualified. And he was very definitely headed in the direction of any normal graduate student going on to become a major scientist. We talked about his teaching in the black colleges in the South. But in the long run he didn't feel that would be his most important contribution. Going to UCLA for a post-doctorate was exactly the same thing any nonblack student would do."

Chester Berry: " 'I'm not a very good nigger,' George told me."

And in December, 1957, leaving Fort Lee and its problems behind, George Wiley headed West.

7

A Man
for All Seasons

The "Kangaroo" was his mode of transportation, and his "best girl," Olive Wiley, his traveling companion, as George Wiley set out for California on the day after Christmas, 1957.

He prepared methodically for his trip. There were people he wanted to meet—he made a list of male and female John Hay Whitney fellowship recipients on the West Coast whom he might consider as intellectual equals, and another list of friends, and old college acquaintances, and, on a separate list, "women." The Wileys hoped that their twenty-seven-year-old Ph.D. would find a suitable young black woman in Los Angeles and they added all their social contacts to his list of names.

George Wiley and his mother carefully compiled another list as well. Because the "Kangaroo" had a problem with overheating, they would have to make frequent rest stops. And because they were black people traveling across America in the fifties, they had to arrange to stop where they could be reasonably sure of finding a motel room or a meal.

George tucked into the glove compartment a copy of the civil rights laws for every state through which they would drive. In Pennsylvania and Illinois, he and his mother found most motel rooms barred to them; in East St. Louis, they were twice turned down for lunch.

In some instances his list of laws brought service, albeit hostile; in others, their treatment was the same as in East St. Louis. (To their surprise, their warmest reception was in Oklahoma. The coldest was in Nevada.) As soon as they arrived in California, George wrote letters to appropriate officials in every state where they had met discrimination, detailing each incident and citing violations of state laws.

From that New Year's Day in 1958, George Wiley was enchanted by California. He found Saul Winstein exciting, his chemistry stimulating. Winstein had used one of George's Cornell experiments in his own work in solvolysis, and made a place for Wiley in his research group. There was an immediate personal dynamic between the two men that contributed greatly to the young chemist's professional development. In March, George delivered an impressive seminar, "The Chemistry of Some Benzonorbornenes," at the University of California in Berkeley, and by April he was assured a job teaching there for the following two years.

Until September, he worked with the late Dr. Winstein at UCLA, supported by a sixteen-hundred-dollar stipend from the U.S. Public Health Service, on the grounds that his experiments in benzobicyclooctadienone might contribute to cancer research. Professor J. D. McCullough remembers Dr. Wiley as taking part in many seminars, leading others, and as an unusually well-liked person, by faculty and students alike: "It was an unusual case. He was colored, which for that time was unusual, although in appearance he would seem to be at least 50 percent Caucasian. There was absolutely nothing in his manner to indicate an interest in social activism."

On Sunday afternoon, February 23, George attended the First Baptist Church to hear Martin Luther King, Jr. The audience was less than impressed with King's speech,* and although Los Angeles was one of the most segregated cities in the United States in 1958, Wiley found little there to invite social activism.

George Wiley: "I tried to join the NAACP. It was so dormant, all the middle-class bickering among themselves, that I marched in and said, 'Okay, here I am fresh from Petersburg and I'm ready to go.' I told several of the officers this, and they said, 'Great, great, we'll contact you'—and nobody ever contacted me to do anything. But I was only in Los Angeles eight months and pretty busy at the university, and having a great time socially."

Wiley spent the most carefree summer of his life that year, his datebook filled with the names of young women, tennis games with the university crowd, picnics by the ocean, trips across the desert—and a new, stimulating spiritual quest.

His mother's brother, Alton Thomas, who was then director of the

* Indicative of the attitude of some middle-class black leaders in California was the reaction to King's activist speech in the *Herald Dispatch,* Los Angeles' black newspaper: "This paper submits that Rev. King's philosophy reflects neither the long and stubborn struggle of Montgomery Negroes to end bus segregation, nor the flashing heroism of Negro children braving hostile and jeering mobs in Little Rock."

Urban League in Phoenix, introduced George to the Baha'i' faith, whose purpose was "to complete the messages and aims of all the world's existing religions, and to bring to pass on earth a universal and ideal civilization." In fireside meetings not unlike those cottage prayer meetings of his childhood, he discussed the religions of the Far East, underlining in red pencil the concepts that easily integrated with his form of enlightened, socially conscious Christianity: "All races equal and nonsegregated. Men and women equal. The nations united, as states in a world government. . . . World education; the same chance for education everywhere. Science and religion equally important. Work for all; No idle rich and no idle poor; no extremely rich and no terribly poor. A single standard of right and wrong for everyone. Justice for everyone. The love of God and his Prophets. Prayer. Preparation now for life after death. . . ." And George scribbled across the pamphlet: "This much, at least is true. No movement can possibly capture the heart and conscience of the whole world today unless it claims and demonstrates divine authenticity and authority." In California he pursued a cerebral, idealistic approach to changing the world, while across the country, in Dr. King's church in Atlanta, worshippers clasped hands, singing, "God is on our side. . . . We shall overcome some day."

Through his personal file of newspaper clippings, George was keeping up with the Movement, well aware that southern whites were digging in their heels, offering massive resistance to the Supreme Court mandate for school integration. There was an article also from the *Providence Journal*, that city's major newspaper, in which his father lambasted the hypocrisy of whites in dealing with housing segregation in Providence. But to his colleagues and friends in Los Angeles, George appeared to be following the one word of advice President Eisenhower had for black Americans: "Patience."

It was in Berkeley, where he wrote home ecstatically of a "jeweled city across a big bridge," that George Wiley came closest to passing through the "veil of color" described by DuBois, and in Berkeley that he also began to question his twoness. He was now trying to resolve, rather than withdraw from, the dilemma of how to be both a black man and an American.

From September, 1958, to December, 1960, he was at the top of several worlds: an assistant professor of chemistry on a faculty that boasted five Nobel laureates;* the only black ever hired by that faculty and the most popular young teacher in the department; a faculty advisor known as "Professor Smiley Wiley," who captured student government retreats by leaping up on a table to recite "Casey at the Bat"; a great friend and vicacious companion for his fellow chemists, reveling in the white social world.

* Edwin McMillan, William Glauque, John Northrup, Wendell Stanley, and Chancellor Glenn Seaborg.

William D. Pryor: "George was gung-ho chemistry, as we all were, and California was the zenith. He saw, as the ultimate career, being a research professor at a major Ph.D.-granting university in the United States. That is a tough trick to turn, particularly in organic chemistry. At that time there were only 120 such schools, and to be hired by even the top twenty is very chancy. It takes a lot of luck and ability to wind up at such a place. George had done it."

"He had a very good insight into traditional organic synthetic chemistry, and arguing with George was tremendous fun. He was always popping new ideas, always bantering, yet he never got sore—never at anyone. He was always conscious when anybody's feelings were hurt. The peacemaker, we called him."

Jon Applequist, also an assistant professor then, recalled that George drew his fellow chemists "like a magnet" in gatherings at the dismal campus dining hall, with conversations that would spill over into the classrooms of Old Chemistry, arguing their theories at the blackboards and in the laboratories: "George knew his own specialty very well, and could discuss it in terms that would interest others outside the field. He always strove for a high level of understanding, and wanted others to do so as well."

Bill Pryor: "He had real charisma, in the genuine sense of the word, and great leadership qualities. People looked at him when he came into the room partly because he would be the only black, but also because he had style. He walked with real grace, he spoke and smiled with real pleasantness. And people loved him."

Wiley's buoyancy carried over into another, quite different world from the laboratory, that of the student politics he'd always believed vital to a healthy university life. He quickly became advisor to "Cal One-A," a freshman orientation session at a quiet forest in San Mateo County, where he led California fight songs ("Our Golden Bear" and "Sons of California"), leaped on a table to challenge the freshmen to a volleyball game against the faculty, and devised a skit for the losing team to perform.

Wiley's exuberance never ceased to astonish his friends. How could he be such a serious, productive chemist as well? It was as if there were two separate but equal compartments in George Wiley's life in California. But there was also another compartment, one that they did not share.

George was selected as an *Ebony* "Bachelor of the Year" in 1960—a close-cropped, proper young professor in narrow bow tie, one of two blacks on the 1,575-member faculty of a prestigious American university.

And in the *San Francisco Independent*, a weekly newspaper serving the Bay Area's black community, Professor Wiley offered his advice to black youth: ". . . Go ahead and try, step by step, to accomplish what you are interested in doing regardless of what barriers seem ahead. . . . Somebody must keep thumping on the wall. . . . A Negro has to be not only good, but superior." The reporter who wrote that article was instrumental in the education of George Alvin Wiley.

Belva Davis: "He was the first nonblack black guy I had ever met. In fact, the only thing we had in common was our differences—and our race. He was probing and inquiring, looking for answers. My husband used to say I should charge him fees for teaching him. It was sort of an education in blackness. George was just becoming aware of his own blackness, so 90 percent of our time was spent discussing his growing up in Rhode Island versus my growing up in Louisiana. It was amazing, the things he didn't know!

"At Berkeley, he was seeking the thinking of someone from a very ordinary kind of black family, just trying to make it out of the poverty bracket. In my family I was the first to graduate from high school, whereas his was a family of achievers. He talked a great deal about having been the only black kid in school, and about how in college they tried to pair him up with an African girl, though they really couldn't stand each other. He said he had been unaware of the racial differences in his early years, and when he woke up to them, by the time he was in college, it was sort of unbelievable. He didn't know how to adjust to it—his thinking was really very white.

"All of the incidents, the conditions, the kinds of rejection that come with racism, which all of us grew up with and were accustomed to—those were always surprises to George, and he didn't know how to deal with them. He would ask me questions like, 'If you walk into a place where you are not wanted, how do you know?' And I would explain that you can tell by the way they look at you. There are all kinds of little signals. George was trying to discover what those signals were. Then he would say, 'Do you still feel hurt when people reject you? Do you still feel anger?' He would say, 'Well, now look. If you know, when you go into that restaurant, that they will put you in the back room or next to the dirty dish tray, why would you go in there in the first place? Or why wouldn't you try to close the place down?' And then he would ask, 'Why aren't you involved in doing something about the race problem, since you know so much about it?' I tried to explain that most of us were not doing anything about it. We just learned what the boundaries were, and we were living within them. He could not understand that, either.

"I remember telling him why my family had left the South—about my uncle winning a lawsuit against a major company in Monroe, Louisiana, and the white people threatening to tar and feather him because he won what seemed to them a large amount of money. And we all had to leave town. George just could not understand why anybody had suffered through those kinds of experiences was not out there trying to change things. He was trying to understand why we all were so passive."

Yet even as George Wiley and Belva Davis talked in California, the word "passive" was taking on a new connotation in her native South. A new generation of young southern black students were beginning to fight segregation with a new, dramatic technique—"passive resistance"—inspired by Gandhi's methods against British colonial rule.

On February 1, 1960, four well-dressed freshmen at North Carolina's all-black Agricultural and Technical College simply sat down at the F. W. Woolworth lunch counter and ordered coffee. They sat there unserved until the store closed. Within days, thousands of black students throughout the South followed suit. The spontaneous action of these students, many of whom were spat upon, beaten, or jailed, was at once supported by the major civil rights organizations. The Congress of Racial Equality, which had pioneered similar tactics twenty years before, took the lead throughout the country in organizing picket lines outside Woolworths, S. H. Kress and Company, and other retail chains whose southern stores refused to serve blacks.

In Berkeley, George Wiley had believed that the tiny CORE chapter, with its thirteen white members, was "too radical," and declined to join. But he did join the NAACP, and through that organization began to spend some of his Saturdays picketing the local Woolworth store, handing out protest flyers. On the back of one flyer, he scrawled in pencil:

> While picketing one of the local 5 & 10¢ stores recently, I was admonished by a passer-by to desist from this activity on the grounds that we are all good neighbors here in Berkeley and our activities could only lead to ill will.
>
> Many of us have come to realize that none can be secure in his freedom in one part of the country (or for that matter the world) when these freedoms are seriously abridged in another. Our participation locally in this massive boycott can help to defeat the indignities of a form of segregation. . . ."

He also found that Berkeley students were no longer content with the pleasant freshman orientation retreats and tame campus politics that intrigued him: ". . . I got involved in this ad hoc group of politically active students—all white—some of whom had been involved in demonstrating against the House Un-American Activities Committee hearings in San Francisco. They started raising money to support the sit-ins and they needed a faculty advisor to get recognized on the campus, and somehow they got hold of me."

About 3,600 students had been arrested in the South for sit-ins, pray-ins, read-ins, and picket lines, and Wiley's group of students held a jazz concert which raised a thousand dollars for bail. However, the University of California refused to allow the funds to be used in that way. Wiley suggested as a compromise that the money be set aside for California scholarships to aid some of the 141 students who had been expelled from southern colleges, and he began negotiating with university officials.

George Wiley: "This poor dean of students, who I was convinced was a sincere guy trying to do right by the students, was also trying to work within the administration framework. I was always trying to explain his problem to the students. But everyone said to me, 'You're an Uncle Tom! We can't be concerned about that dean's problem. What the hell do you think the students in the South have? They need that thousand dollars and we want to send it to them, and the dean can go to hell as far as we are concerned.' And the students just butchered him. They won their case, with a special dispensation from the Board of Regents. I would have probably been inclined to go along with the administration, but those guys stubbornly held out, and they got their way. That was very impressive to me."

In July, 1960, he joined the students again for a massive demonstration at the Democratic National Convention at Los Angeles, assembling with more than five thousand civil rights advocates at a rally. George and his picketing friends then wove their way around the convention hall, inconveniencing the delegates to make their point. "That was the first big demonstration thing I had been in," he recalled. "It was really kind of fun, particularly when we stood in the way of the Mississippi and Texas delegations."

And he was impressed with the new tactics of direct action in the South: "My experience in Petersburg was with a very apathetic community that had been unable to move. Picketing and sit-ins really seemed to be a way of involving more people. The action was the thing that let them know that something was going on, that could have some stimulating effect."

Yet George told few of his white friends about his changing attitude, or about his own tentative activities. So far as Hyman Minsky, a white economist, could tell, "George was undistinguishable from any other obtuse chemist in his perception and understanding of social and political issues."

And despite Belva Davis' best efforts, he continued to lead a mostly white social life. "I was always trying to introduce him to black women I thought were educationally on his level," she said. "He had said he could find few with whom he had anything in common, and he was worried. But George had a way like a bulldozer, and some black women are just put off by that."

Wiley was dating a young white schoolteacher he called Marty, yet he kept his friendship with Belva Davis in a very separate compartment. Wiley wanted to marry Marty and considered that the marriage would have more meaning than just their personal relationship. He wrote: "That the majority of Americans have not as yet embraced this idea (racial intermarriage) wholeheartedly should be regarded as an important weakness in our society; a weakness best corrected by some of its strong individuals. To my view, the fact that Marty and I have fallen in love, giving us the singular opportunity of being two of those strong individuals, is an exciting challenge."

Martha Goldsmith Schwartz: "It is very hard to say, if George had not been black, whether I would have married him. Had George not been black, he would not have been George. I had never known anybody quite like him before. It was his whole being—his love of humanity—his vital interest in everything that was going on.

"George was interested in the World University Service, an international relief agency of the 'Y'—it was at the 'Y' that I met him—and he was deeply interested in a group medical practice for poor people in Gennessee County, New York, and in a mountain school in North Carolina. One of his frustrations with me was why I didn't care more about some things. He cared so much about anything that he was involved in, it was hard for him to understand why everyone couldn't care as much as he did.

"He was really involved in his chemistry at Berkeley—always working late at the lab. He felt it was an honor to have been taken on at such a prestigious chemistry department. But there was so much more to his life than chemistry! He felt that he'd had a very limited view of the world in his childhood, and he'd done nothing but work hard ever since. And now he was going to branch out and learn about everything, experience everything. Art. Music. Theater. We went to symphony concerts, to foreign films, classic movies. We played tennis together. We drove around in his sports car—he really loved that car—and we went to beaches."

George was not an extravagant suitor, however. He stretched his $580 monthly salary to the last penny. He lived in a cheap furnished apartment in a black section of Oakland, spent virtually nothing on clothes, ironed his own shirts every Saturday, and invested in a pair of the first, odd-looking "space" shoes, individually fitted to his feet, which were guaranteed to last twenty-five years. Some of the salary went to help pay brother Eddie's tuition at the University of Rhode Island, just as his older sisters had helped with his.

"But he was never a martyr, in terms of not enjoying life when he could enjoy," recalls Marty. "He did enjoy. He had all aspects of life in such good perspective. But his love of people was the overriding thing about George Wiley. He cared about people as individuals. His was such an infectious personality, his smile would light up an entire room. And the laugh that went with that smile! He had a wonderful sense of humor—he could see something light in everything. He would never criticize anyone without saying something positive on the other side. His philosophy was to change what he could, and accept what he could not change.

"He was conservative in many ways when I knew him. He wore stocking caps at night to keep his hair from being too frizzy and curly. However, he certainly didn't have any use for people who were not proponents of civil rights or whatever, but he was so tolerant of them. For example, he never met my parents, who lived in San Francisco, because they would have been horrified at the idea. Why should he have accepted that without any feelings about it? He said, 'Of course, that is the way they would feel. I understand.'

"He was saying that, in his eyes, how nice it was that I cared so much for my parents that I wouldn't impose such a difficult situation on them. And I never doubted for a minute that is the way he really felt."

Yet, he did have feelings, so painful that he could not express them to her. And he was deeply hurt by her rejecting his proposal of marriage on the grounds of her parents' disapproval. He wrote an agonized letter to her mother, scrawled on cheap notepaper, his awkward script growing larger with the intensity of his anger. He ended the letter: ". . . were we to be married quietly and with little fanfare and in the East, you would have no public debasement. The word would get out eventually but with a gradual diffusion of the news of the 'terrible calamity' I do not think your reputation would suffer greatly. Martha's father constitutes the major problem, to which I can offer no solution. I am as concerned as anyone that his physical condition might not stand the shock of the nigger's emerging from the proverbial woodpile to marry his daughter. I believe your love and understanding could save the day. . . ." Marty never knew of this bitterness. George did not mail the letter.

In 1960, the blow of Marty's refusal accompanied another disappointment: he would have to leave his beloved California. His was a "rotating" assistant professorship, by which promising young chemists were placed on the faculty for two years,* and it was due to expire in December. Yet he had dreamed that his work would prove so brilliant, so significant that an exception would be made for him. Wiley's research was praised by his colleagues. He was beginning to publish in scholarly journals and to speak at other campuses as well as at meetings of the American Chemical Society. He was now doing research that would bear his own stamp, studying reactions in the benzonorbornene system. "He was getting unusual results," recalls a Berkeley colleague, Andrew Streitwieser, "but he was able to work out an interpretation using a new theory, and it worked out rather well. So it was a novel result." Kenneth Pitzer, who was the dean of the college of chemistry when George was at Berkeley, remembers that he was a "thoroughly competent" chemist and teacher.

Race was, beyond any question, still a factor in chemistry in 1960. When Dr. James Cason, Wiley's senior colleague in organic chemistry, made a strong recommendation for him to Syracuse University, he felt compelled to add, "Just to be sure there is no unexpected misunderstanding, I should mention that George Wiley is a Negro. The only reason I mention this is because he is the kind of person that it never occurs to you what color his skin is when you are talking to him and dealing with him."

* The last permanent opening in organic chemistry had been filled in 1956; the next would not occur until 1967. This arrangement, similar to that at Harvard, no longer is in practice at the University of California.

Wiley was offered jobs by several universities. He chose Syracuse because it promised him a light teaching load and freedom for research. As George said goodbye to his friends in California, he did not let them glimpse his inner feelings. His best friend, Bill Pryor, described the departure: "Nothing was complicated for George. Things had solutions and everything was easy. Everything flowed.

"I said, 'How the hell do you leave California? How do you leave all of this?'

" 'It's simple,' George replied. 'You get in your car and go.' "

8

Wretha

At Syracuse, just south of Lake Ontario in upstate New York, he once again was the first black chemist, and only the second black on a large faculty. George bounced right in with his usual élan, finding an old Rhode Island fraternity brother to share an apartment, buying a bargain-load of second-hand furniture, and captivating student leaders at a retreat in the Adirondacks, from which he emerged as faculty advisor to the student government. He soon found willing partners in the faculty tennis club, one of whom was Chancellor William P. Tolley. He became an enthusiastic fan of the Syracuse football team.

Syracuse lived up to its promise, providing him his own laboratory where he began his research, and students who "despite the fact that I smashed them extremely hard with problems, long reading assignments, and hard exams dug right in and worked very hard." He was pleased with the status afforded a new faculty member from the University of California whose reputation as an excellent chemist had preceded him.

At twenty-nine, George Wiley was once again conquering new territory professionally and socially. But now he was also purposefully searching for a wife. In one last hopeful taped message to Marty in November, he said: "It doesn't seem that there are very adequate replacements for one Marty Goldsmith, although we have been scratching around. Maybe there is a question of whether there is a suitable one in the world. . . ." Her response was a final tearful message in January ending the relationship because of "the love of my parents and knowing that they would never accept you."

Two weeks later, George found "the ideal woman—a beautiful beanpole of a graduate student from Texas," a six-foot-two-inch blonde named Wretha Frances Whittle.

She had been born in 1935 in Abilene, a town in flat, dry country. Her father was a mid-level manager in an oil refinery, her mother a teacher. The Southern Baptist Church was at the center of her life in Abilene, setting the rules for social life as well as religion. These were very clear, Wretha recalls: "Do not drink, smoke, neck, dance." Playing cards was suspect. She tested the rules, but rarely stepped over the line.

By high school, women were expected to take one of two roles: leader or cheerleader. Wretha was a serious student, always conscious of the pressure to compete. "It might be through brains, beauty, or talent, but compete I must." (In college, she debated in the men's division, "where the better competition was.") She shone as a public speaker and a painter and was offered college scholarship in both areas. She chose debate. In many ways— the religious framework, the fierce need to excel—her early life was not very different from Wiley's.

Wretha describes herself as "an arrogant, intellectual student," in rebellion against the prevailing opinions in Abilene. The high school debate issues were segregation (she was opposed) and recognition of Red China (she was for it). The more she read, "the more discontent I was with the provincial world in which I was living." She argued constantly with her family and friends, and always took the liberal position. Segregation was immoral, she told them, a violation of the teachings of the church and everything she had been taught. Yet the only black people she saw until she went to college were occasional visitors who came to the church to receive a special offering. Not until she went to Hardin-Simmons, a Baptist university in Abilene, did she have any real contact with blacks, and then only through volunteer work in a black community on Friday nights.

She graduated with honors in 1957 and won a two-year Rockefeller Brothers Fund Theological Fellowship to Union Theological Seminary in New York. She chose Union because the radical churchmen Reinhold Niebuhr and Paul Tillich were there. At Union, she was forced to reappraise the Baptist Church and her own upbringing. She never rejected them or their values, but learned how to reinforce them in her own life. In this way, too, her experience was much like Wiley's.

Wretha worked in East Harlem with a group of thirteen-year-old girls on a block that was one-third black, one-third Puerto Rican, and one-third white. "I went in with grand schemes for uplifting them, but they were not interested in any recreation I planned or learning what I thought they should." What they wanted, says Wretha, was "sex education, and how to deal with their fathers and mothers. I thought they were too young to be taught contraceptive methods, and besides, there were Puerto Rican families who would run me out if they knew. But I finally taught sex education, and they educated me. It was there that I found out that my ideas for changing the world and the people in it would not work." Her views about religion and social action turned to pessimism. The role of the Christian, she now believed, was simply to be with suffering people, not to save them by one's own efforts.

In 1959, she went to Syracuse for a graduate degree in English literature. She took an apartment in a black neighborhood. The next spring, at a party, Wretha heard a young chemistry professor describe a new man they had hired:

" 'We just hired our first Nobel laureate,' he said.

" 'You really did hire a Nobel Prize winner?' I asked, impressed.

" 'No, but we hired a guy who is going to have one soon. His name is George Wiley.' "

It was nearly a year before they met. Wretha had no idea her name was on one of George Wiley's lists of "people to contact." His sister Shirley, on request, had made up a list of everyone she knew in Syracuse, including Wretha, the white graduate student who had rented her apartment. She was too busy to see him; he called at Thanksgiving. Again before Christmas. Once more in January. She finally agreed to have lunch with him.

Wretha: "He didn't want to meet me in particular; he wanted to meet everybody. But he would not be turned around. His persistence was a general characteristic. If my name was on a list and he was told he should meet me, he was going to persist in meeting me, no matter what.

"When he came to pick me up, he sat down, started writing out a check, and said, 'I have to shake the money tree before I take you to lunch.' " The first thing they did was cash his check at the University business office. Wretha was impressed. "He was nice and easy, intensely kind, gentle, and honest. I thought he was the finest man I had met in a long time." It was the day before Kennedy's inauguration, and both resented his winning. George had wanted Humphrey because of his civil rights stand; Wretha was for Stevenson. George was more conservative than Wretha, more optimistic. He lived in the middle-class white neighborhood, and she was in the black ghetto.

After January 19, the letters "Wre" or "WW" appeared in Wiley's datebook almost daily.

Wretha: "One of the flattering things about the courtship was his single-minded persistence. He called every day and was very disturbed if he could not get me. On our third date, he said, 'You have to decide. We cannot go out together anymore unless you are willing to marry a Negro.' " Wretha had never been confronted that way by a white man, let alone a black man.

"I didn't like it, but I understood. He was nearly thirty years old. He wasn't going to waste any more time on a going-nowhere relationship."

The question of marrying a black seemed almost irrelevant. "George was so white in my view that I never really saw him as being black." They seemed to have everything in common, most deeply their fundamentalist upbringing, out of which they had refined similar values. Both had shed the outward forms of their childhood religion, but both were still ruled by its injunctions to serve humanity and to love the poor.

Wiley was the man Wretha's mother told her to marry: he had a good profession, he was a man of exceptional integrity—"in all ways he was what I had always expected to marry—except that he had dark skin."

But once they were seen together, they felt the subtle pressures against interracial marriage. Wiley was one of only two black faculty members at Syracuse; he was concerned about dating any student, not to mention a white one. Interracial dating was not acceptable, Wretha recalls, not even among liberals. They said that "it was too bad, but that we just weren't there yet."

"In fact, it was official policy that the Syracuse dean of women would notify the parents of any undergraduate woman living in a dormitory who was seen with a black athlete. Dorm mothers were told to observe carefully which white undergraduate women were dating the few black athletes on campus." The editor of the student paper, the *Daily Orange* wrote an exposé, and there was a mass meeting of students calling for the firing of the dean of women. George and Wretha watched the meeting from behind trees, yards away, not wanting to get involved in an issue they felt had nothing to do with their own relationship.

That spring they were trying to decide whether or not they should marry. "We had awful arguments," Wretha recalls. "The pessimism of my view of man and society was in stark and dramatic contrast to George's optimistic view. After a while, our views seemed irreconcilable, and so we decided not to argue about them anymore. We could live together, ignoring our differences, we thought."

Her parents were horrified; her mother organized all the people in Texas whom she knew had any influence on Wretha, and she got calls and letters from them. The real possibility of a total separation from her family was frightening. George's parents didn't like it either, and told him so, but they did not try in any way to change his mind.

His sister Lucille remembers asking him, " 'What about your children?' George was such an idealist. He said he and Wretha felt they could give their children enough strength to face whatever they had to face. But it was such a giant step. There just weren't that many mixed marriages at that time."

George Wiley's family did accept Wretha as their own. Her parents did not accept George. But she had faith in the bonds of her family relationships. "I'll give my mother two years to come around," she told Will Wiley.

The next hurdle was finding a house. George found a rambling, brown-shingled one in a quiet neighborhood, and made an offer. The owner refused to sell to a black. George insisted on confronting her. It was the neighbors who really objected, she tried to explain. George proceeded to knock on every door in the neighborhood. He announced who he was, where he worked, and explained, smilingly, that the owner "says that you would not want to live next door to me—you would find me objectionable." He was very charming and nice, Wretha recalls; all the neighbors swallowed their feelings and said they didn't object at all. The owner finally had to give in. George had enjoyed the campaign; it was not that he saw himself simply as a pioneer for integration. Wretha remembers his "pleasure and pride of being the underdog, going against the odds and winning."

On June 21, George and Wretha were married in Amherst, Massachusetts, in a private religious ceremony performed by the Reverend Bruce Morgan, a theology professor and friend. For Wiley, the most important racial barrier had now been crossed. He and Wretha spent the first nights of their marriage in a mountain resort in the Berkshires. As they drove back to Syracuse in the little red convertible, they happily sang an old missionary hymn, "From Greenland's Icy Mountains." They were a united, interracial couple, and free. At that point they were not concerned with the fight for integration in the South. They were unaware that fifty Freedom Riders from CORE (led by James Farmer, who would later play a key role in their lives), were singing freedom songs in their cells in a steaming Mississippi prison—an offense for which their mattresses were taken away.

Wretha started to work on the house, which was a mess, and George disappeared into his lab. It was a hard period for both, Wretha says; they "hadn't really talked about how we were going to live. Before we got married, we talked endlessly about how we were going to handle the racial problems—only not to have any. The one thing we had not talked about was the chores and the living arrangements."

Wretha steamed off wallpaper and painted. George brought the second-hand furniture from his apartment; she brought contemporary paintings and sculpture, green plants, and her library of poetry, novels, philosophy, and political science. They rented part of the house to three students. "They assumed that I was the cook," Wretha recalls, "so there was a battle to separate our life from theirs." George was behind in his chemistry, and after having had his constant attention it was hard for her to accept his sudden dedication to the chemistry lab. It was all part of his single-mindedness; whether he was courting or buying a house, he did everything with the same intensity. Now, he became a very serious, hard-working chemist.

9

The Scientist

He was not just an ordinary chemist, teaching what he had learned, performing experiments others had perfected. According to his colleagues, George Wiley's research was innovative, daring, and successful. At Syracuse, he developed new ways to put things together.

Donald Botteron, a fellow chemistry professor at Syracuse: "George created reagents—chemicals that you throw into a chemical reaction to make some sort of change. His reagents did things that were previously undoable."

In Bowne Hall, a large stone building on "Piety Hill," he worked within the structure of minute and invisible molecules, predicting reactions by devising a complicated formula, then painstakingly conducting the experiment itself. He dealt, at the most fundamental level, with the way carbon-containing compounds were put together, and looked for new techniques for tearing compounds apart and rearranging them.

The department took pride in more than the young assistant professor's research. Finding that the laboratories in Bowne Hall lacked the sophisticated electronic equipment he had used at Berkeley, he designed his own lab and went out to cajole private industry into donating the equipment. Then he scoured the country for bright graduate students to assist him, while he directed their dissertations in his field. Finally, he solicited hundreds of thousands of dollars in federal and private grants to finance his research.

There had been great expectations of Wiley, and he lived up to them.

He galvanized the organic chemistry department, through a combination of acclaim for his research, which was being published in scholarly journals; his skill at grantsmanship, which placed the chemistry department in high regard by the university administration; and the quality of his students, who considered him brilliant and imaginative. He impressed his colleagues, including one who had said, "Show me a Negro who can pass chemistry."

The expectations bothered him, however. "He had no illusions of becoming a Nobel laureate," Wretha said. "He knew he was a good chemist, a hard-working, earnest chemist with strong credentials, but he also realized he was a showcase. He felt under pressure to perform." Thus the "twenty-four-hour days."

Jerrold Meinwald of Cornell, now an admiring colleague rather than a senior professor, describes the scientific work to which Wiley had devoted his life: "Molecules are groups of atoms linked together, almost like buildings; they have different sizes and three-dimensional shapes, and you can actually build these molecular structures—like 'tinker-toys'—in the laboratory, look at them and think of them in terms of real, three-dimensional entities."

George had already mastered one important subfield of organic chemistry—structural chemistry, the study of the actual arrangement of atoms within the molecule. How do you determine the shapes of molecules, the structure of molecules? Different numbers and arrangements of atoms give rise to different properties: compare a plastic to perfume to a tree to a person—all made up of organic compounds. At Cornell, George's thesis on thebaine was in the area of structure determination.

Another field of organic chemistry deals with how the reactions work—finding out what is the so-called mechanism of an organic reaction. "When one molecule is converted into another, the arrangement of the atoms changes," Meinwald explains. "During this process, when you build molecules, there are some steps, almost like dance steps, that the atoms follow in getting to their new location to form the new product. So George spent his time at UCLA in that second field, learning how to study reaction mechanisms. At Syracuse, he conducted a critical series of experiments that provided the turning-point in a twenty-year-old argument in the chemical literature regarding the mechanism of a somewhat specialized but theoretically important reaction.

"Still another field of organic chemistry, which George began at Berkeley, then really developed at Syracuse, is organic synthesis—the building of molecules, the actual 'putting them together.' In synthesis, you actually create new molecules, and you reason by understanding the structural features of a molecule and the mechanisms of the reactions whereby one molecule is converted into another. This was the most important work of his career."

Professor Donald Botteron: "One of George's major contributions to synthesis in organic chemistry was the conversion of organic alcohol—hydroxls—into halides, a more rare type of organic compound. Take neopentyl alcohol, one of our standard freaks. Every time you try to remove the hydroxyl, it practically unzips itself; the remaining atoms rearrange themselves, and you come out with a completely different animal. George's reagent was special, since it did the substitution in such a way—it was so active right there where the 'unscrambling' reaction is—that the rearranging didn't have a chance."

Wiley was a stimulating teacher who soon was attracting serious young chemists. His students were important to him, and Wiley made them feel important. The logic of his thinking and the clarity of his explanations captivated his students. David Braddon, who became his graduate assistant, recalls: "George liked to have the fundamental facts of something very, very firmly in mind before he began. Then he would hypothesize from that point forward very clearly. He was a good lecturer—he would do enough preparation to know the fundamentals, and then he would develop the arguments from those as he was thinking. The thought process for drawing a conclusion would just flow out onto the blackboard. There was never any stilted, textbook presentation. He was gifted that way.

"He always had ideas," recounted Braddon. "If you ever hit a low spot he would sit down with you for a few minutes and outline another several months' work without any trouble. Ideas rolled off his mind. If an experiment 'failed' or didn't turn out as planned, he'd say, 'Okay, so what? Do it over.' "

The knowledge that every experiment might fail, the patience to reconstruct every painstaking step, altering an element each time, only to have that step go wrong—this was how scientists operate. "He didn't regard one failure as total failure," Braddon emphasized.

He did experience failures, including one particularly embarrassing one shortly after his marriage. Wiley was so confident of the success of one experiment that he submitted the results in advance of the completed work, as a paper to be delivered at the annual meeting of the American Chemical Society. It was to be a major presentation, of which advance publicity had guaranteed a large audience. But before his work was completed, his laboratory burned down and he was unable to finish the experiment. A bold but worried Wiley decided to deliver the paper anyway, and to jokingly explain what had happened. He made his presentation and at least one listener, the prestigious Dr. Woodward of Harvard, was not amused. Woodward walked out in the middle of the talk, but Wiley's many young friends and colleagues gathered around him afterwards and reassured him. It wasn't a bad paper, they said.*

* "Bridgehead Phosphorous Compounds," paper presented at the 140th meeting of the American Chemical Society, Chicago, September 3–8, 1961.

Wiley quickly learned that the twice-yearly ACS meetings were competitive political arenas as well as settings for the exchange of information and a reunion of old friends. His fellow chemist from Berkeley days, Robert A. Fahey, recalls: "Being with George at a meeting of the American Chemical Society was a lot like being in rush hour traffic in Los Angeles. It might take an hour to go down fifty yards of hotel hallway. It seemed as though every member of the Society knew George, or wanted to."

And Berkeley colleague Bill Pryor: "George had a style in going to those ACS meetings that indicated his commitment to chemistry. If you're an established chemist, the ACS invites you to symposia to give an hour's paper. They also have submitted to them fifteen-minute papers. George would go in the morning, from nine to twelve, and then in the afternoon, from two to five—he'd sit through the whole six hours. All those fifteen-minute papers would become a complete jumble in my mind. But George was so focused on what he was doing that he could go and get something out of every presentation."

Going to the ACS meetings became a ritual pilgrimage which he eagerly anticipated. His research progressed and the big, new laboratory he designed was built like a phoenix from the ruins of the fire. He produced other important papers. But, as Chairman Henry Wirth pointed out, it was the presentation, not the writing, that Wiley liked.

George's enterprise at pulling in money, however, brought pleasure to Dr. Wirth, as well as to Chancellor Tolley. The first, a $10,000 grant, came from the Research Corporation of New York.*

His second acquisition was a spectacular $50,000 piece of equipment from the Bristol Laboratories in Syracuse. It was a nuclear-magnetic-resonance-spectrometer (or spectrophotometer), a powerful instrument developed by physicists which also proved invaluable to organic chemists. With it the scientist could "get a real road map" of what was going on within the molecule.

Wiley next acquired annual National Institutes of Health grants totaling more than $80,000 for his long-range studies in pentavalent phosphorous chemistry. He also received a National Science Foundation grant of $28,400

---

* In a letter to Chancellor William P. Tolley, Sam C. Smith of the Research Corporation wrote:

> From time to time a young scientist-educator is brought to our attention in such favorable terms that some unusual recognition of his potential seems very much in order. Dr. George A. Wiley . . . is one such individual.
>
> It gives me very real pleasure, therefore, to advise you that . . . the Board of Directors of Research Corporation has approved a three-year Frederick Gardiner Cottrell grant of unrestricted nature for use of Dr. Wiley. . . . He should feel free to explore any research ideas which may commend themselves, without attempting to justify his plans before others. No reports on the activities he may choose to undertake are required or expected nor do we wish to receive any accounting for the use of the funds. Also, no time limits of any sort have been imposed. . . .

for "Non-Classical Directive Influence in Addition Reactions" and a PRF stipend of $21,000 for "Synthesis of Bridgehead Arsenic, Antimony, and Dismuth Compounds."

The acquisition of two additional new spectrophotometers, gas chromatographic equipment, a carbon-hydrogen nitrogen analyser, a set of fractionating columns, and a variety of other equipment as a result of George's efforts was cause for celebration at Syracuse. The chemistry department now boasted a very well-equipped laboratory.

At the end of two years, his research was beginning to attract national recognition. Hundreds of requests for reprints of his paper at the 1963 national meeting of the ACS in New York, "Reactions of Dihalophosphoranes with Alcohol"* (G. A. Wiley, R. L. Hershkowitz, B. M. Rein, and B. C. Chung), came from universities around the world.

Jerrold Meinwald: "At Syracuse, he made a substantial contribution to the body of knowledge in organic chemistry. Synthetic organic chemistry is a lot like architecture: You build molecules, so you need a way to join A to B, and a way to join B to C, and a way to join C to D. Even though there are a couple million organic molecules, they are all made of carbon atoms, and only about five or six of those atoms are used in all those millions of molecules. So, if you have a new way to put things together, as George did, that is a very fundamental step which might be useful for any other building problems that come up a generation or two later. He really created some very nice things in the field of synthetic methodology."

Wiley's scientific work has been durable. His major contribution, the conversion of organic alcohols into halides without molecular rearrangement, proved to have an important application. It was timely work: the research had been used as reference in other scientific papers 165 times by the end of 1974, as recorded in *Science Citation Index*.** "For nearly a decade the techniques he worked out were the best available," said Bill Pryor. "His mechanistic studies stand as the first proof positive of the existence of very special intermediate species that occur during the course of some chemical reactions."

At Syracuse, Wiley was developing a very solid future for himself. Dr. Meinwald, who followed his work closely, said, "Out of the thousands of chemists, there are about two hundred academic organic chemists from the

---

* This paper, noted as well in *Chemical and Engineering News*, was subsequently published in the *Journal of the American Chemical Society*, 86, 964 (1964), *Tetrahedron Letters*, 64, 2509 (1964) and *Tetrahedron Letters*, 67, 232 (1969).
** His paper with then graduate student Braddon on the mechanisms of the formation of carbonium ions had been referred to twenty-four times by the end of 1974. It proved the existence of the so-called nonclassical carbonium ion which occurs for a fleeting moment while certain special types of molecules are undergoing chemical change. This is a specialized but theoretically important point. The influential H. C. Brown of Purdue cited the paper and noted: "This observation supports the presence . . . [of these species] . . . and the efficacy of this tool [Wiley's techniques] as a test. . . ."

forty major universities who are first-rate. If you consider what other organic chemists his age were doing in the early sixties, George would easily have been among the most promising half-dozen people in the country."

But during this time, in another area of his life, he had begun another kind of action-and-reaction—one that would employ all his methodology in "putting things together," all his rationalization and applied humanistic philosophy, and, in an era of "Freedom Now," "We Shall Overcome," and fervent hopes of black people to gain equality in American—all his heart.

II

◆

CONFRONTING
THE DEEP NORTH

10

Joining
the Movement

On a snowy evening in November, 1961, eleven graduate students and one chemistry professor gathered in a small student apartment in Syracuse. Sitting on the floor munching potato chips, they posed more questions than answers, and none of them knew quite where to begin. The only common agreement was that they wanted to act. The simmering civil rights struggle in the South had moved them, and they wanted to do something about it, not in distant Mississippi but at home.

The first thing they did was pick Dr. George Wiley as their leader. He was a professor, he was black, and he had shown a willingness to challenge the Syracuse campus on the issue of racism. Two months earlier, the *Daily Orange,* the student newspaper, had published an exposé about racial discrimination in the university's fraternities and sororities. Wiley, faculty advisor to the Greek letter organizations, responded with a one-sentence letter to the editor: "Unless all fraternities and sororities submit in writing to the Dean of Men and Women an anti-discrimination pledge in this year's rushing, I shall propose before the Faculty Senate that all fraternities and sororities on this campus should be abolished."

When George came to Syracuse in 1960, he was bent on enjoying the stimulating but cloistered life of academia. He might have continued on that pleasant track for the rest of his life, but times were changing, and he was slowly enveloped in the change.

While Wiley was busy buying his house, confronting northern hypocrisy on Mother's Day, 1961, fifteen hundred miles away Freedom Riders from CORE were confronting the pervasive, brutal system of segregation in the Deep South.*

The events unfolding in Alabama had little reality to most white residents of Syracuse, a medium-sized community with a small and apparently docile black population of fourteen thousand. The blacks lived in a tightly-packed ghetto near downtown, and if whites saw them at all, it was usually as servants or day laborers. Viewed from Syracuse, the budding civil rights movement seemed far away, a protest against southern laws and customs.

But as the Freedom Rides followed the impetus of the students' lunch counter sit-ins of the previous year, the movement changed the consciousness of millions of black Americans, and whites as well.

When George challenged the Syracuse fraternity system, he was responding to those winds of change. For middle-class blacks, it was a crucial time for deciding whether to get involved. Until the early 1960s, there had been few opportunities for effective protest. The talented and lucky, like Wiley, could feel they were contributing by their own achievements. In the early 1950s, the initiation of George Wiley into Phi Mu Delta was seen as an unusual sign of progress. Ten years later, however, the acceptance of token blacks into white clubs seemed far less important, and their exclusion far less acceptable.

Wiley's uncompromising letter signaled his independence from a white college world he had worked so hard to master, into which only a few "exceptional" blacks were accepted. He was no longer willing to accept that special world on its own terms. He now examined his own status as a token black, watching with some amusement the efforts of white university officials to get along with their two black professors.** Asked by a fellow professor how it felt in 1961 to be a Negro at Syracuse University, he replied:

* The thirteen members of CORE who boarded a Greyhound bus in Washington, D.C., on May 4 attracted little attention as they set off for the Deep South. The purpose of their trip was to challenge racial segregation in bus terminals, declared illegal by the U.S. Supreme Court in December, 1960, but still rigidly enforced in the South. By the time they reached Birmingham on May 13, the country had come to know these self-proclaimed Freedom Riders. As they crossed Alabama, white mobs burned their buses and brutally beat the integrated crew of volunteers, while police looked on, or looked aside. Attorney General Robert F. Kennedy tried to stop their journey, calling for a "cooling-off period." And James Farmer, CORE national director, replied: "We have been cooling off for a hundred years. If we got any colder, we'd be in the deep freeze!"

The courage and persistence of the bus riders and the uncontrolled brutality of the white mobs finally forced President Kennedy into action that spring, dispatching six hundred United States marshals to Alabama. Not since Central High School in Little Rock (while George Wiley was in Virginia organizing black voters) had the civil rights movement produced such a confrontation. Now, it seemed, the time was ripe for a far broader response.

** The other was Charles Willie, in sociology.

"When I first got here, I met Dean Frank Wingate, and in the course of the conversation he said, 'Wiley, I understand you play a bit of tennis. I'll call you sometime for a game.' Some weeks later the dean called and said he'd scheduled a tennis game for 4:00 P.M. that afternoon. He announced with some seriousness that Chancellor Tolley would be joining us. Well, I went to the courts at the appointed hour and there was Wingate, and there was the Chancellor, and do you know who else they had found? They had found another acceptable Negro in Syracuse who played tennis. And do you know what we played? We played 'mixed' doubles."

As an attractive young interracial couple, the Wileys drew to their home blacks and white liberals. Wretha, the more radical, helped organize a chapter of the newly-formed Students for a Democratic Society. "Increasingly," Wretha said, "George found the SDS youths more interesting than his student government crowd, even though he really didn't like them personally and didn't share their radical critique of what was wrong with the country's institutions, or their life style."

When SDS leader Tom Hayden visited Syracuse to seek support for the embattled civil rights movement in Albany, Georgia, he stayed with the Wileys. From activist Hayden, just out of jail and followed by FBI agents to the Wiley home (where they attempted to interview Wretha about Hayden's activities), George and Wretha got their first dramatic sense of an emerging national movement.

There were evenings with the late Eduardo Mondlane, the charismatic black teacher who would soon launch the Frelimo independence movement in Angola. "You could get killed doing that," Wiley said, as Mondlane explained his plans. "I expect to be," replied the African.*

Marriage itself gave them a stake in the success of integration. Some of their friends commented tartly that the Wileys seemed rather self-righteously to think that their own relationship established them as experts on race relations. Integration was the answer, Wiley felt, and it was possible.

That November evening, in the apartment of Bob Blanchard, a white graduate student in political science, the sparkplug was Rudy Lombard, a black graduate student from New Orleans. Only twenty-two years old, Lombard had risen quickly in civil rights to become national vice-chairman of CORE. With his dramatic retelling of experiences in the South,** the mag-

---

* Mondlane was assassinated by mail-bomb, February 3, 1969.
** Lombard earned his spurs as a college student in 1960–1961, organizing a CORE chapter in New Orleans. His group showed repeated bravery, demonstrating in the face of threats not only from the Ku Klux Klan, but sometimes from local police as well. A few months earlier, he narrowly escaped death from marauding Klansmen in Plaquemine Parish, Louisiana, by spending the night hiding in a fig tree. In another incident, he called the Justice Department for help and was told to call the local police. "We're surrounded by the police," he replied.

netic Lombard had moved and inspired the eleven graduate students, most of them from Syracuse's Maxwell School of Citizenship and Public Affairs, and the Wileys.

They discussed whether the direct-action techniques of southern Freedom Rides would work in the North. They didn't know, but wanted to try. They formed the Syracuse chapter of the Congress of Racial Equality, electing George Wiley as chairman.

"We wanted to get something going in the North, where the problems were ignored because there were no laws officially sanctioning segregation," said Blanchard. "We were impatient with the idea that if it didn't exist in the law, it didn't exist."

Most of the founding members at that meeting were white.* "All the people who came to CORE were in rebellion of one kind or another," recalled Everett Makinen, "rebellion against the style of life of their parents, against the atmosphere of the university, against the specific problems of injustice. Several of us held fairly leftist socialist views. Others, however, seemed totally apolitical, or even conservative, except for the racial problem. Many of us were undergoing a lot of self-searching about our own lives. At this point, we weren't taking on the community. We felt we would be doing something worthwhile in CORE, if it became an organization through which at least the people participating in it could improve themselves, lead more just lives."

George Wiley: "By and large, they were not from the mainstream of campus life. They came out of the byways and coffee houses, not the fraternities and sororities, nor from traditional campus activities. The students who participated were involved in a more serious dialogue over the social issues that confront them."

CORE seemed the most effective stage for their activism. Founded in 1942 as an interracial civil rights organization, the Congress of Racial Equality was started by a group of Christian pacifists who belonged to the Fellowship of Reconciliation, the group George had found too "extreme" to join at Cornell. James Farmer and other CORE founders believed that racial discrimination must be attacked directly rather than through the legal approach taken by the NAACP, or by careful cultivation of white businessmen, the method of the National Urban League. Theirs would be the method of nonviolent direct action taught by Mahatma Gandhi.

Thus, CORE would first attempt to convert opponents through negotiation; when negotiation failed, CORE would confront its opponents with picketing, sit-ins, and boycotts, thereby hoping to dramatize the wrongdoing, end the discrimination and, they hoped, embarrass and convert the wrongdoer.

---

* Blanchard was the son of schoolteachers from Rock Springs, Wyoming. Everett Makinen came from a working-class, Catholic background in Detroit. Deborah Neimand was the daughter of a Syracuse rabbi.

The first "actions" initiated by the Syracuse CORE chapter had nothing to do with local blacks. In early 1962, Rudy Lombard led eight CORE members in picketing an apartment that had refused housing to two African students. The owner quickly capitulated, and CORE moved on to challenge successfully the discriminatory practices of all university-approved off-campus housing. They also tested the university's own hiring practices, documenting the fact that well-qualified blacks were turned down for secretarial jobs while whites were accepted. Rudy Lombard and Wretha Wiley negotiated with the university, which grudgingly granted some job concessions. The next project was aimed at stopping the university athletic teams from playing segregated southern schools. Football was king at Syracuse in the early 1960s, and this effort failed.*

George Wiley, nominally the chairman of CORE, took no active leadership role in those early activities. The students found Wiley very much the scholarly, skeptical teacher.

"We wanted to get out and do something," said Blanchard, "but George kept taking the approach that we couldn't act until we got our facts together. Of the two Wileys, Wretha was by far the more activist at first. She was ready to act."

During those early CORE days Wiley often told people, "Wretha is more radical than I am," or, "I lead with my wife."

In his first civil rights involvements, Wiley revealed his modest goals as well as his naïvete about the politics of protest. "Everyone George talked to in that fraternity fight was more political than he was," said Wretha. "He saw it as a simple moral issue of right versus wrong. He was puzzled and couldn't understand how some people dismissed the fraternity issue as insignificant, while others debated involvement only if the issue could be won and then be used as a lever for other, more significant protests. He still believed in the fraternities. They had been good to him. He just thought they ought to let everybody in."

Though he was cautious, George was appalled at the reluctance of university officials to end discrimination on the campus. As he told a student assembly in 1962: "It is a sad commentary on the society and university that only a few students have been free enough from the shackles of conformity to participate in these dynamic and revolutionary happenings.

"Look at your elders and see what approach they are taking to the problem. You don't have to look beyond the confines of Syracuse University to find the kind of complacent attitude that essentially says to you that these problems don't exist. This kind of head-in-the-sand attitude is particularly unpleasant when it would apply to the university community—a place where

* A university athletic official was so detached from the CORE complaint that he thought they were protesting "discrimination" in scheduling the team against hopelessly weak opponents.

the highest value should be placed on the quest for truth and justice, a place where one would hope there would be unusual social sensitivity to human conditions, a place where there should be the greatest amount of ferment toward change and social justice."

And then the black professor who in 1957 had pointedly rejected teaching at black southern colleges in favor of seeking his own success in the élite white university world talked of those same black schools: "It is a remarkably paradoxical sign of the times that some of the most important leadership of the civil rights struggle has come from Southern University in Baton Rouge, from Florida A&M in Tallahassee, from Alabama State College in who-knows-where, Alabama, from Tougaloo College in the backwoods of Mississippi—universities so insignificant that you probably would never have heard of them. Most don't even have a significant football team. And these are the places where the people with the concern, the commitment, the drive toward the correction of these social problems are coming from."*

Wiley felt that Syracuse CORE, too, was now ready to carry its fight against racism beyond the campus and into the community.

---

* As the *New York Times* commented: "The moral leadership of the new generation was established by the Negro students in the South who quietly and courageously began to assert their rights with the sit-in strikes at lunch counters. These were not organized from outside, they came from the Negro youth themselves, and everywhere in the country their example touched the moral imagination of white fellow students who formed groups to support their effort."

11

A Direct-Action
Victory

The two men confronted each other from opposite sides of a long oak table, around which were seated members of the Syracuse Board of Education. At one end of the austere board room stood George Wiley, chairman of Syracuse CORE, and at the other end sat David Jaquith, chairman of the school board. Wiley was there in June, 1962 to demand that the city integrate its public schools.

Syracuse CORE was protesting the system by which most blacks were crowded into three rundown schools in the inner-city slums. The CORE protest, its first outside the university campus, had begun with quiet talks but had grown more intense, until now a dozen CORE members, including Wretha Wiley, marched with picket signs outside the school administration building. Inside, George talked for more than an hour about the cause of black children, his voice growing steadily louder. He charged that black students were segregated not only because of housing patterns, but by a deliberate gerrymandering of school boundaries.

Annoyed by Wiley's accusations and his escalating rhetoric, chairman Jaquith fidgeted restlessly. Finally, his face crimson, he furiously turned his chair to the wall.

Jaquith flatly denied that there was any deliberate segregation in Syracuse, either in the schools or elsewhere. The school board even refused to consider whether there might be a problem. "It would be illegal to make a study," Jaquith said. "State law prohibits us from identifying children by race in school records."

Jaquith, the blunt, hard-driving president of a large industry, was the uncompromising leader of the Syracuse Association of Manufacturers, and the most conservative politician in a staid, conservative city. Four months hence, he would run for governor against Nelson Rockefeller, as the New York Conservative Party's first candidate for that office.

There seemed no meeting-ground between Wiley and Jaquith. The school board refused to consider the matter.

In 1962, CORE brought the civil rights movement alive in Syracuse. The Wileys' living room was the battle station, with reports, CORE literature, and charts spread around among the bright, contemporary paintings which Wretha Wiley also collected. The Wileys were very much a team. Wretha was an indefatigable researcher, organizer, and stimulator of people, with strong ideas and a commitment to action. Only half jokingly, Wiley told CORE supporter Barbara Rumsey, "Wretha is much more of a fighter than I am. I have to hold her back."

Wretha, however, still took a far gloomier view of human nature than did George. "I was pessimistic," she said. "I never expected anything we did would change Syracuse in any crucial way, but I thought it important to do it, whether we won or lost. George was motivated by another vision. He expected a situation in which people in Syracuse finally would be able to live where they wanted to live, work where they were qualified to work, attend thoroughly integrated schools. He was the best of the rational humanists.

"He really did not, at that time, want to change the country in any fundamental way."

The first year of their marriage was consumed by CORE activities. "We were totally caught up in it," Wretha recalls. "We lived, breathed, ate, slept civil rights. George worked at the chemistry department all day, every day. In the evenings, our house would be full—people sprawled all over, several meetings going on at once. George seemed to have boundless energy then, for he literally lived two lives: civil rights and chemistry. Life was a constant rush, full of activism, no time for reflection, for the kind of abstract philosophizing we had done all our lives. But we felt worthwhile, happy."

There seemed to be little time to talk about the child that was due in the fall. The question their family and friends had asked—"But what of the children?"—seemed far less important than the activity at hand. But it was the approaching birth of their first child, and the question of how the child would be educated, that pulled George Wiley into total commitment to a CORE issue.

The citywide debate over integration of the Syracuse school system began when the Wileys read a one-paragraph notice of a proposed school boundary change. Wretha quickly noticed that the boundary shift for the Sumner Elementary School in their neighborhood would change the racial composition of the school from a small percentage of black students to a majority black school. Both Wileys wondered, as Wretha recalled, "whether we had not stumbled upon one of those little municipal decisions that held great consequences."

Could it be possible, Wiley questioned, that a casual realignment of school boundaries every few years served to keep Syracuse's small but shifting black school population confined to a few schools? Was it possible that northern cities, by a series of subtle bureaucratic maneuvers, maintained school segregation almost as effectively as the South did by state law? Wretha showed him maps in which she had correlated census data with school boundary changes.

"As soon as George saw the data, he was off and running," said Wretha. "He did the projections. He really loved it. It was the first issue he took over and made his own. It seemed outrageous to him that no one paid any attention to segregated northern schools while national attention was riveted on desegregation battles in the South."*

"The biggest problem in Syracuse in 1962, as in most northern cities, was that no one would admit that there was a problem," said Albert Ettinger, who investigated the school dispute as a representative of the New York Commission Against Discrimination. "There was a universal denial of discrimination."

It wasn't just the school board. Syracuse was a stolid community slow to respond to new trends. The political leadership seldom was challenged. At a time when most industrial cities had become Democratic strongholds, Syracuse remained a Republican enclave. In 1960, the city had a population of 216,000, of whom only 5 percent were black. Most had come there between 1945 and 1960 as part of the massive migration in which three million blacks left the South seeking opportunity in the North and West.

As they pored over census data, George and Wretha saw that twice as many blacks as white were unemployed. Seventy-five percent of those who were employed worked either as laborers, as menial service workers, or in

* At the time, Mississippi state officials were resisting a federal court order that James Meredith be admitted as the first black to the university. On September 30, President John F. Kennedy ordered a force of 320 marshals to protect and escort Meredith as he enrolled. After a bloody, night-long riot by white mobs battling the marshals, Kennedy ordered in thirty thousand troops. A personal reminder of the Southern fight came in a letter from Wiley's younger brother, Edwin, a recent Rhode Island graduate who joined George's fraternity and was now an Army enlistee. After describing how he had been stoned with rocks, bricks, and Molotov cocktails, Eddie had concluded his letter: "I'm fine so don't worry about me. I've got my rifle and about sixty rounds of ammunition. I can take care of myself—at least there will be about sixty dead rebels before they get me (jest?)."

semi-skilled factory jobs. Black families earned 50 percent less, yet paid twice as much of their income as whites for housing. Blacks actually paid, on the average, as much rent as whites, yet 50 percent of blacks (compared to only 8 percent of whites) lived in housing classified by the census as deteriorated or dilapidated.

Nevertheless, many Syracuse whites thought of their city as having a proud record of race relations dating back to the 1850s, when a group of whites stormed the Syracuse jail to free an escaped slave before he could be returned to the South.* White Syracuse was, in many ways, typical of the white North: ignorant of the Other America, blind to its poverty, and believing in the myth of the North as the promised land for blacks. "After all, we're not prejudiced," wrote a Syracuse editorialist. "We believe that blacks should have their rights."

George Wiley described the situation: "Discrimination in the North is often more genteel, more polite, but nonetheless damaging. The fact is that problems are so cleverly masked and the basic causes so roundly suppressed by the community at large, in a kind of community pride in hypocrisy, that one is often not able to identify who the antagonist is. In the South, there is a certain comfort in being able to have a clear identification of the problem, to be able to fight against it or avoid it as one sees fit. In the North, one does not have this option. The problem is apt to pop out at you in many places. There is no way, essentially, to predict—to protect yourself."

With the refusal of officials to supply information about race in the schools, Wretha, now in her eighth month of pregnancy, supplemented the census data by standing in front of schools in the morning, counting the black and white children who entered. When the Wileys finally compiled their data, this picture emerged: fifty-five percent of all black children attended two schools, while the other thirteen elementary schools all contained few black pupils.**

Scrupulously following CORE procedures, Wiley tried for weeks to negotiate with the school board. When it failed to respond, he picketed, and when that effort also failed he organized a one-day boycott of the largest black elementary school. The boycott, on September 4, 1962, was 95 percent

---

* The next month (October, 1851), Negro rebels smashed into a Syracuse courtroom and rescued another fugitive slave. Negro leaders, acting independently, played a large role in this history. Meeting in Syracuse in October, 1864, Negro leaders organized the National Equal Rights League, and issued an address to the nation calling for the complete abolition of slavery and the granting of the ballot to blacks.

** The Syracuse situation mirrored the national picture, which received little attention in 1962. Seventy-five percent of all black students attended elementary schools with at least 90 percent black enrollment, while 83 percent of white students attended schools that were 90 to 100 percent white.

successful, and more than five hundred people gathered in front of the school to hear Wiley declare: "We have demonstrated today that Negroes in this community have the will and the courage to stand up for their rights. We will keep on demonstrating until the people who run this city hear us, and respond with justice."

The demonstration worked. Pressed by state civil rights officials and embarrassed by growing publicity, the school board agreed to participate in a "study committee." Once again, George Wiley and David Jaquith faced each other across an expanse of oak table and a set of ideological differences which seemed far too wide to bridge. The two men dominated the semi-monthly study committee meetings which began in October, 1962, and continued for eight months. Although most CORE members regarded Jaquith as an implacable reactionary opponent, someone who needed to be steamrollered, Wiley approached him calmly and coolly.

"Wiley," challenged Jaquith, "if you can convince me—which you can't—that there is the slightest bit of educational value in integration, then I will support you."

"I'll convince you, all right," replied Wiley good-naturedly. He quoted the 1954 Supreme Court decision on the harm of segregation to black children, and argued, citing studies by Kenneth Clark, that the damage to the children was the same whether segregation resulted from southern law, northern boundary juggling, or housing patterns.

When Jaquith denied that there was housing discrimination in Syracuse, Wiley told him, "If you are really interested in the facts, I'll show you." On a bitter-cold Sunday afternoon, the two set out to test the situation. Jaquith discovered that the houses and apartments offered eagerly to him were flatly denied to Wiley.

When Jaquith denied that teachers discriminated against black students, Wiley brought him twenty-five documented cases of discrimination and took him to interview black parents and their children. In case after case, it appeared that black children were expelled from school for no reason, that teachers regarded their black pupils with disdain and expressed low expectations of their ability to learn.

When Jaquith argued that the reading disabilities of black children came from their earlier experiences in black southern schools, Wiley showed him that the children had been taught "not to read" in Syracuse. Most persuasive to Jaquith was the fact that Syracuse school records indicated that black children performed better academically when transferred to middle-class white schools.

In his relationship with Jaquith, Wiley practiced the Gandhian tactics of CORE. The CORE "Action Discipline" manual declared that the nonviolent method "confronts injustice without fear, without compromise and without hate." CORE believed that direct action should be accompanied by a spirit of good will toward the discriminator, a frame of mind calculated to change not only his actions but his attitudes as well. As CORE national leader James Farmer explained: "We believed then that truth alone, the transparent justice of our demands, would convert the segregationists, once they agreed to listen."

As the Syracuse study committee members settled into their seats at the first meeting in April, they were surprised to see Jaquith and Wiley enter arm in arm, both smiling. Jaquith opened the meeting: "We have studied this issue for more than seven months and we have heard all the arguments from every point of view. I think our decision is a clear one. The schools of this city should be integrated."

The study committee and school board quickly followed Jaquith's leadership. By the summer of 1963, Syracuse became one of the first northern cities to commit itself voluntarily to a positive program to integrate its schools.

"Wiley turned me around completely," Jaquith recalled. "I started out 100 percent opposed, and I am the one who changed. If you put enough drops of water on a rock, I guess it wears away. George was just tremendously effective in presenting facts. He was intelligent, rational, reasonable. I just could not help but admire the guy."

Jaquith also came to understand the new tactics of the civil rights movement. "When we first met," he recalled, "I told him quite heatedly that his tactics were wrong, that even if his cause was just, confrontation politics would make too many people angry. But he answered me by saying, in effect, 'I don't have any choice. Whoever has power never gives it away voluntarily. The only progress that we are making in the movement and the only progress that is going to be made is on the basis of direct, honest confrontation.'

"In this case, George was right. CORE's confrontation politics alerted people to problems and wouldn't let them ignore them. Wiley made people uncomfortable, but they paid attention. Without dramatic confrontation, there would have been no movement. The blacks had no political power in Syracuse and weren't going to have any. They were too few in number. The community was overwhelmingly conservative on any issue involving race. We were running our own little segregated society."

The Jaquith-Wiley agreement came at an advantageous time. Many northerners supported the righting of obvious southern wrongs, and that good will moved them in their first dealings with civil rights in the North. It was a time when people of good will could agree on theories, and northern school integration was still a theory; it had faced no acid tests in the interplay of human lives.

On October 5, 1962, after a long, difficult labor for Wretha, Daniel Kent Wiley, named for George's grandfather, was born in Syracuse. George, who had gone home to rest up for the next day's school board meeting, was not present at the time. The next few days were shattering.

Wretha Wiley: "The first word was that the baby might not survive. The doctor estimated that Danny had been without oxygen for several minutes. He said that we wouldn't know for twenty-four hours whether he would be all right. George came to the hospital after I regained consciousness, and we were both very subdued. Danny's development prognosis was unknown. We were trying to imagine the consequences, and what it was going to be like, but the worst fear was over. He was alive.

"All during the school boundary fight, we watched Danny. He was a delightful, lovable child, and though his development was slow, he did almost everything he was supposed to. George was immersed in the school board fight and in his chemistry, so it seemed he never took time to worry. He loved this little baby, and he just sat and looked at him, in quiet wonder."

Wretha and her mother were reunited when Mrs. Whittle came to Syracuse to see her grandson. William Wiley, George's father, recalls that visit: "We drove up to Syracuse one day not long after Danny was born, and there was Mrs. Whittle. I don't know if she'd ever had any contact with black people before, but she was wonderful. And we felt sorry for her because George and Wretha were carrying on the civil rights battle all around her, playing records of 'We Shall Overcome' and all the other songs. Neither George nor Wretha spared her one little bit."

When he first arrived at the university, Wiley would charge super-confidently into social gatherings, ready to have a good time, and not adverse to shocking the guests. But as time passed, he became less playful. Gone was the lighthearted, happy-go-lucky fraternity boy. The ebullient partygoer who beamed his way into every group with that "Aren't you glad to see me" smile became more reserved.

"He seemed very cold at first, very unemotional, an academic planner of civil rights activity," said Susan Rice, a white activist in CORE. At social gatherings, Tim Rice, her husband recalled, "He was quite stiff. I remember, at parties he was extremely rigid. He had all his guards up."

He was no longer so much of a "white Negro," anxious to please and succeed in a white world. He was becoming immersed in the black struggle, and he began to judge white people with a newly critical eye. The coolness was also a means of self-control, of coping with an awesome assortment of responsibilities.

Wiley's capacity for leadership was growing rapidly. Ronald Corwin, a Syracuse CORE member and graduate student who wrote his Ph.D. dissertation on the Syracuse school integration fight, recalled: "He set the moral, political, and intellectual tone of CORE. He had a fierce commitment to information and data. He was able to summon the evidence as a researcher and present it clearly and powerfully without being hysterical. He translated to the school board the great frustrations that black families saw in their children's school experience."

Another attribute that served him well in that early civil rights period was the fact that, aside from a belief in simple morality, justice, and integration, he was not loaded down with a lot of political theories. He was not a "true believer" ideologue. He could approach David Jaquith as another human being.

CORE member Sue Rice: "Most of us in CORE would never have even tried to sit down and talk with Jaquith. But George could do that. He believed that if you talked with someone, if you were reasonable, and if the other person had some sensitivity, you could convince them. That gave him the confidence to encounter people in very hostile situations."

The other skills he brought to civil rights had their origins in his organizational work in student government and as a scientist. He could juggle thousands of facts while keeping his eye on the main target. He also could hold together a diverse, loose coalition of very strong-minded people, as well as competing civil rights organizations. Syracuse CORE, like many idealistic organizations, was populated by people with noble intentions, good ideas, and exalted rhetoric. Wiley had a rare knack for applying all those heady ideas in practical ways. He organized picket lines in front of the school board with the same attention to detail with which he put together a chemistry experiment or, in the past, had organized Student Union picnics and dances.

"He was very effective at getting people involved," said Sue Rice. "He was also a tremendous resource of resources, a keeper of lists. If you needed to find people who were mad at landlords, George had their names. Or people who were ready to fight the local utility. Or people who knew how to reach executives in big companies, or people who knew how to put on demonstrations. The list was written down on the back of an envelope or stored in his head, but he could always tell you who to call. And once he had put together a group of people who never would have known each other, they did work together."

He also had developed over the years a distinctive, subtle style of control—an essential talent in the stormy CORE chapter which often seemed on the verge of splintering apart. "He led with a light rein," said poet Philip Booth. "He presented his own case strongly," said CORE member Makinen, "but at the same time was totally deferential and agreeable to any other ideas and the wishes of the group." If Wiley dominated CORE, said Rudy Lombard, "it was because he did the research, the work, and the follow-through. He led by example."

Edwin Day, a graduate student who served as Syracuse CORE's executive secretary: "There are people who will try to lead by aggressively pursuing their own agenda. George did not take that kind of role. He would ask questions and advocate viewpoints of his own, but he did not come off as an advocate. He did an amazingly small amount of talking, and he was a good listener."

"If he was quiet and attentive, it often was because he didn't know what he wanted to say or do," recalled Wretha. "But as the meetings proceeded, he would feel his way along, sifting through other people's ideas, and eventually come up with a plan that made sense to him."

Feeling the strain of too much activity, George and Wretha began to feel the need to get away together. Their only escape had been to conventions of the American Chemical Society, where George was totally absorbed in his other life. "What we need is an island," George said. So they bought one, for three thousand dollars, two wooded acres of land in Devil Lake, in Canada, just over the New York state border and accessible only by boat, with no telephones, no plumbing, no water, not even a cabin—just the water rippling against the rocks and the occasional cry of a loon.

"It was perfect," Wretha recalls. "We would camp there under the stars, away from the entire world. George would go fishing, swimming in the cold water, then lie on his back, looking up at the sky. It would take him about two minutes there to unwind."

They had that idyll together in the early summer of 1963, but there soon was a new reality. The civil rights movement was heating up, and George was drawn for the first time into the lives of poor black people.

12

The Fifteenth Ward

In 1962, 90 percent of Syracuse's black population was crowded together in a dilapidated slum north and east of the downtown business district. A survey showed not only that 80 percent of blacks preferred to live elsewhere, but also that most paid rents high enough to pay for housing elsewhere in the city. Yet, their way out of the Syracuse ghetto was tightly blocked by an alliance of landlords, owners, realtors, and bankers. One mother of five described this dilemma: "We were pinned to the Fifteenth Ward slum. We could not move on the north side of Fair Street, nor the south side of Castle, nor the west side of Salinas, nor the east side of Furman. We lived there paying high rents for bad housing and being very disillusioned because there was nothing you could do about the conditions. You could fight with the landlord, but no one, not even in the building, would back you up. You were alone with your problem."

As if conditions were not bad enough, the city was ripping through the black neighborhoods with an urban renewal program and interstate highway system. More than two thousand families were to be displaced by a process that blacks called "urban removal."* Of the first 250 Syracuse families forced

* Begun as a national "community renewal program" in 1959, with an amendment to the 1949 Housing Act, urban renewal in America's cities had started with the objective of eliminating slums, thereby removing substandard housing. All over the country were springing up massive slum-clearance and building projects—brand-new glass office buildings and modern high-rise

to move, all but seven had been relocated into different parts of the same slum, many into substandard housing.

The employment situation was equally grim. General Electric had never promoted a black to foreman. The Niagara-Mohawk Power Company employed less than a handful of blacks and offered a black college graduate a job as a janitor. In 1963, not a single black man belonged to any of the skilled craft unions. Almost one-half of black families lived on less than three thousand dollars a year, the so-called poverty line, and the gap between black income and white income was growing larger.

Those problems had not touched the band of integration warriors from the university. Aside from the school integration fight, Syracuse CORE had worked on projects that helped only a few middle-class individuals. They had spent weeks helping a black physician find suitable housing. Another time-consuming (and unsuccessful) campaign was directed at a local bank which had blocked the purchase of a house by a black professional man.

Wiley well understood the weakness of his group. In 1962, Syracuse CORE's membership consisted of only eighteen active and twenty associate members. Wiley knew that if his campaign to persuade Jaquith had not succeeded, CORE would have been unable to mount larger demonstrations. He also knew that the few local blacks who did join the school integration fight were attracted more by the first spark of activism than by the school issue itself. Earlier than many northern civil rights leaders, Wiley realized that if Syracuse CORE was going to thrive it badly needed not only troops but "momentum and ideas" from the black community. In the summer of 1962 he set out to find that support.

Originally CORE had not been meant to be a mass-based organization. New members had to serve a probationary period in which they proved themselves in an action project. A two-thirds vote of approval was needed for membership. Those small, tightly-knit CORE chapters could often outmaneuver, outwit, and embarrass their opponents. But opponents who learned that CORE did not have wide support were unlikely to accede to its demands, particularly as these escalated. And CORE's leaders began to wonder whether their efforts really fit the needs of the black poor.*

apartment buildings for middle- and upper-class families, buildings with big picture windows looking out on the newly transplanted "green spaces." But the planners failed to relocate the people displaced by the projects, forcing them out of their dilapidated homes and their neighborhoods into poorer, even more crowded circumstances. By March 1963, 609,000 persons had been forced to leave their homes, two-thirds of whom were blacks, Puerto Ricans, and other minorities.

* If Wiley had been listening to blacks in the Syracuse slums, he would have found that many were far more intent on improving schools in their own neighborhoods than in achieving integration. His sister Shirley, then an education specialist in a special program to enrich the curriculum in a Syracuse ghetto school, found George uninterested in her program. He was bent on "integration."

As early as 1961, James Farmer, CORE's national director, warned that northern CORE groups "can't survive on sympathy for the South." Farmer worried that CORE had neither the following nor the program to combat discrimination in the North. Many CORE chapters, dominated by middle-class whites, had trouble attracting black members.

On a July Sunday in 1962, Wiley delivered a five-minute speech during services at the Missionary Baptist Church. He briefly described the ideals and aims of CORE, and asked anyone who was interested to meet with him afterwards. He had been making the same speech every Sunday for weeks, at any black church that would give him a few moments on the pulpit. Many black ministers refused his request. They regarded Wiley as a young upstart, a newcomer to town, and the leader of a radical, troublemaking organization that would do more harm than good.

But that afternoon, as he stood outside the church door, Bruce Thomas and Anna Mae Williams stopped to shake his hand and ask questions. They became CORE's first recruits from the black slums.

Bruce Thomas, thirty-one, a lean, hard-muscled factory worker at General Electric, seemed to be an unlikely CORE member, much less a man who would become an important influence on George Wiley. A ninth-grade dropout who had served three years in prison as a juvenile offender and spent most of his military service in an Army stockade, Thomas had a reputation as the toughest man in the Syracuse ghetto.

"I sold numbers," said Thomas. "I fought in bars every Friday and Saturday night, drank tons of alcohol, ran women, was known as a street-fighter, and went to church every Sunday and sang in the choir. I was glad to have a job paying $120 a week and was willing to go to jail for maybe rolling some cat, but I never dreamed I would go to jail for civil disobedience.

"When George stood up in that church talking about de facto segregation, I'd never heard of that term before and I'd never heard of CORE. You knew, just looking at him, that he didn't belong in that neighborhood. He was tall, buttoned-down, quiet, smart. He didn't have the anger. He didn't express himself like black people do to each other. He was very white, both mentally and verbally. At the beginning, I thought he was one of those well-educated Negroes who knew nothing about the problem. He did not understand what blacks did to survive."

Nevertheless, Thomas was drawn to "this professor who was trying to stir people up. He was a very open person and he always had that smile. He could win people over. And he was accepting; he accepted me into the group without question. Here was a group that wanted to do something about the problem and they let me, a nobody, take part in its discussions and decisions."

When Bruce Thomas attended his first CORE meeting and then did not return for several weeks, it was Wretha who found him and drew him back. Despite a decent paycheck from General Electric, the only housing Thomas could find was a slum apartment located on a busy, commercial street, where he worried about dangers to his three daughters from roaring trucks and loitering winos. The children had no place to play. Wretha and George, in their house on the hill, listened to his deeply-felt personal concerns. "This hill is not where my people are," Thomas told them. At his insistence, CORE moved its office to the Fifteenth Ward slum.

Friendship between the two men grew as Wiley introduced the streetfighter to the CORE philosophy of nonviolent direct action while Thomas introduced the college professor to his friends in the ghetto. The spirit of CORE rallies quickened as Thomas, an authentic black voice, led the singing of the stirring freedom songs. On late afternoons, as Syracuse blacks stepped off their buses, homeward bound from work, Wiley and Thomas cornered them, trying to interest them in CORE. Their efforts were seldom successful, but they kept on trying.

"George and I grew together," recalled Thomas, "with him learning how to relate to black people and me finding that I was worth something and had some qualities that had not been developed earlier. The first time he put me in front of a crowd, I nearly got sick. There were eight hundred people there celebrating the anniversary of the Supreme Court decision on school desegregation. When I told George I didn't know what to say, he said to just tell them what I felt. Well, I did it. I told them how strange it was that here we were having a big celebration about this famous decision, but the schools here in Syracuse weren't even following it."

Wiley soon stepped down as chairman of CORE, installing Thomas as his successor while he took the lesser title of community relations chairman. Wiley still dominated the organization, but the promotion of Thomas was a measure of his commitment to a different brand of civil rights leadership. Beginning with Thomas, Wiley pushed the new black recruits forward into visible, active leadership roles. Bringing forward indigenous black residents of Syracuse was part of an effort to legitimize CORE, but Wiley believed that poor people must lead themselves.

Wiley also developed a close relationship with Anna Mae Williams. A strong-willed, middle-aged woman, Mrs. Williams had picked cotton in Mississippi from the age of six, then as a teenager trekked up and down the East Coast—part of a stream of migrant workers—and settled in Syracuse in the 1950s, one of several thousand black farm workers who came there in search of a better life. She had divorced her husband, and tried to support five children doing day work as a domestic, living in a rat-infested three-room apartment.

Anna Mae Williams: "On that first Sunday afternoon in church, George gave me a glimmer of what I have been looking for all my life. Even in Mississippi, my grandmother had taught us to stand up for our rights. But when you come to a strange city, what can you do? You don't know where to go unless someone shows you the way. George lit the lamp for me and he stirred up something that has continued to burn."

Mrs. Williams quickly became a dedicated CORE member. On many afternoons, she would leave her job in the suburbs at 4:00 P.M., take a long bus ride home, and an hour later be walking on a CORE picket line.

Virtually all the poor black people Wiley worked with in Syracuse stress that his influence in getting them to act in their own behalf was the key to his leadership. Inez Heard, who lived in a ghetto housing development, remembered how Wiley encouraged her to form a tenant council and organize her neighborhood to fight against relocation of a bus terminal next to her apartment: "George could have put together that protest against the bus terminal, but he thought it would be more meaningful if we did it; after all, it was our children who were going to be run over by the buses.

"When George came to Syracuse, many people were so afraid, or so satisfied with what little they had, that George had to show them that there was more out there in the world. He would give us statistics on how the other half of the world lived. If you wanted a house over on segregated Buckingham Avenue, he would tell you to go over there and get it, and not be afraid of people."

Charles Goldsmith was a day laborer who, like Bruce Thomas, gave up street life to work for Syracuse CORE, and eventually became its president: "George gave us facts and information about our rights. He gave me the confidence to push for myself and get my rights even though I didn't have a very good education. He told me that education was good and that he wasn't going to knock it, but there were other ways to get ahead if you worked hard enough." Wiley helped Goldsmith get into a manpower training program, through which he became a skilled auto repairman.

Wiley and the CORE chapter started an adult education program, which combined basic literacy courses with black history and leadership training. Anna Mae Williams, Inez Heard, and Bruce Thomas all eventually passed high school equivalency examinations. Thomas became a community organizer, Mrs. Williams ran a halfway house for unmarried mothers, and Mrs. Heard became administrator of a job training program. All became leaders in CORE and the black community.

The civil rights movement throughout the North was headed for a crisis because of its failure to mobilize and serve large numbers of the black poor. Still, Wiley had made a beginning. In the case of black women, his low-key manner added to his appeal. As Mrs. Williams said: "He didn't have to put on all those airs and show us how black and strong he was, and that was one of the things that impressed me about him. He had confidence in himself that he knew where he was going, and he instilled confidence in us that we could take on any project and do it."

From its ghetto storefront headquarters, opened in an effort to reach the black community, CORE expanded protest activities in the summer and fall of 1963 in a calculated effort to provoke a confrontation over equal employment and housing opportunity in Syracuse. But first Wiley conducted an informal poll of slum residents. The largest number of complaints were directed at the Hotel Syracuse, which refused to hire blacks for the better-paying jobs of doorman, waiter, bellman, and busboy—jobs that paid tips. Blacks were confined to washing pots and cleaning rooms.

Some CORE members from the university crowd protested that these jobs were too menial and demeaning to be worth fighting for. Wiley, however, wanted to focus on an issue that poor black people felt strongly about. The pay at the Hotel Syracuse might be low, but young blacks and newly-arrived migrants from the South constantly applied for these jobs and were always turned down. Wiley picked the hotel as a target for direct action.

The Syracuse Hotel campaign featured a new demand. By 1963, civil rights leaders throughout the country had learned that "promises" of equal employment opportunity often meant little, as did the hiring of a few token blacks. A favorite tactic of employers was to place the burden on the civil rights group, saying, "We can't find any qualified blacks, but we'll agree to hire them if you can find them," a corporate ploy that forced the civil rights group to spend most of its time acting as an employment agency.

So Syracuse CORE changed its strategy. Promises of nondiscrimination were not enough. Now CORE demanded ironclad agreements by which employers would give jobs to blacks in proportion to their percentage of the population. In Syracuse, only 5 percent black, this was hardly an onerous demand, but the Hotel Syracuse angrily rejected it. Hotel officials complained about demands for "preferential hiring" and "reverse discrimination." Negotiations came to a halt. At this point, Wiley initiated a series of escalating direct-action demonstrations. CORE secretary Ed Day described them:

"George was orchestrating this, and it was a matter of wits, testing them out. First, we just marched in little groups all day long. Then we mounted bigger and bigger demonstrations until the picket lines went almost around the block to surround the hotel. We were getting bolder, seeing how far we could go. Then George led the line into the hotel, through the lobby, and out another door. After another time or two, we just took over the hotel. Every day we would come down and take over the hotel. We had shifts and assignments as to who would take over when."

The hotel restaurant, a fashionable spot for Sunday brunch, was filled with white diners as Wiley led his group of singing demonstrators in and out, around the tables. The diners, like most white Syracuse residents, passively watched the demonstrators. Some, however, lashed out at them.

"We had a lot of young boys on the picket line," said Anna Mae Williams, "and my job was to keep them under control, because we had people call us names, spit on us, and try to provoke fights. It got worse at nights, because they would try to shove us into the streets. George would keep stressing that we had to show that we were nonviolent. I myself am a very violent person, and I would pray, 'Lord, please God, don't let anybody hit me.' "

After six days of steadily declining business and cancellation of a convention, the hotel agreed to reopen negotiations and quickly met CORE's demands for jobs. Wiley had scored another modest victory. Other Syracuse employers, figuring that they might become the next target, began hiring a few blacks as a protective measure. However, as CORE gained new credibility and support in the black community, Wiley worried that his master plan was not working. His disappointment was not that only a few people had gotten jobs. Much larger demonstrations, including those led by Martin Luther King, Jr., in the South, also had yielded only relatively small negotiated gains. The broader objective, however, was to polarize an entire city—or nation—bringing forth a new army of supporters and sympathizers, and creating a situation which would force the community to deal with a whole array of minority problems. The heart of institutional racism was to be attacked and exposed. In this regard, Syracuse CORE had failed.

The business and political community had decided that the best way to neutralize Wiley and CORE was to pretend they didn't exist. The police were ordered to arrest no one. The Syracuse newspapers virtually ignored the hotel confrontation.* Alice Tait, the Syracuse CORE secretary, wrote of the dilemma in a letter to national CORE headquarters: "How does one take direct nonviolent action against opposition that refuses to articulate its prejudices?" But white leaders who thought that by ignoring the civil rights movement they could make it go away were soon to be jolted out of their complacency, for in the summer of 1963 electrifying events in Birmingham, Alabama, would catapult the movement—and George Wiley—into a new age.

---

* Events in Syracuse mirrored what was happening in cities throughout the North. Civil rights leaders experimented with means to produce visible, meaningful confrontation over black grievances; white leaders tried to ignore the protests. In Omaha, Nebraska, for example, the *World-Herald* refused to report a demonstration outside its office, aimed at the paper's own employment policies and its blackout of civil rights news. It took a riot several years later for the white community to become aware of the grievances of Omaha's thirty-five thousand black residents.

13

Baptism

On August 28, 1963, George Wiley, Bruce Thomas, and two other CORE members huddled around a small portable radio at the edge of a downtown lot, where a wrecking crew was tearing down an old gasoline station. The lot was part of the urban "removal" site; Syracuse was going to raze a black slum and replace it with shiny new middle-class housing and modern office buildings.

George listened to the broadcast of Martin Luther King's words as he proclaimed from the steps of the Lincoln Memorial in Washington, D.C.: "I have a dream"—a speech that would become woven into the fabric of American history. It was the day of the "March on Washington," in which 200,000 black and white Americans marched peacefully to protest racial injustice.

It was also a historic day in Syracuse, New York. As King talked of his dream for America, he also urged the marchers to go home to continue the fight. The leaders of CORE had already "gone home." CORE national director James Farmer chose not to spend that day in Washington, but to remain instead in a Louisiana jail. "The historic march on Washington will go on beautifully without us," Farmer explained. "The historic struggle of Plaquemine Negroes might not."

Wiley shared Farmer's view. Although a delegation from Syracuse CORE drove to Washington, Wiley felt the Washington march drew energies away from local work. And so he purposefully picked August 28 to launch CORE's major plan to change Syracuse. His objective was to confront the city with a direct-action campaign to block the downtown urban renewal project.

Switching off the radio, Wiley and his three companions slowly approached the debris-strewn lot and then suddenly clambered onto the bulldozers and power shovels. Almost immediately, Bruce Thomas received a stern initiation into the ways of nonviolence: "I climbed up on a crane, and the operator who was running it picked up an iron pipe and said, 'Get that black nigger off this crane or I am going to break his head.' He stood over me waving his iron pipe. I was very scared, but I just sat there. After ten minutes of screaming and hollering, the worker threw the pipe away, and the next thing he did was to punch me in the eye. I bent over to protect my face, and he started beating me across the back and head until a policeman finally asked him to stop. I felt very good. I felt bigger than he ever could be. I could have wasted that guy, but I didn't. The way I felt then, I could have been walked over, punched, spit on, and I would never lift a finger to defend myself, because I felt that the problems were bigger than me being hurt or degraded. I felt the future generation was more important than me being hurt or abused.*

The new phase of Syracuse CORE's activity, and similar demonstrations by other groups around the country, had been sparked by events in Birmingham, Alabama. On May 3, 1963, Police Commissioner T. Eugene "Bull" Connor unleashed German shepherd dogs and high-powered fire hoses against hundreds of civil rights demonstrators there, many of them children—a brutish action that raised the curtain on what came to be called "the long hot summer." President Kennedy, in response to the "fires of frustration and discord burning in every city," proposed to Congress a bold program of civil rights legislation.**

Blacks and whites throughout the country were stung into action. "When those Birmingham dogs bit those children," said one writer, "every black person in America felt the pain." Before the summer ended, fourteen thousand demonstrators had been jailed in the South alone; Mississippi civil rights leader Medgar Evers had been murdered from ambush; and another violent tragedy in Birmingham provoked even greater black outrage.

* Shortly after being beaten, Thomas asked his minister to speak at a CORE rally. When the minister refused, Thomas quit the church and told the minister, "CORE is my religion now."
** The Civil Rights Act of 1963 called for: 1. a ban on the exclusion of any person on account of his race from hotels, stores, places of amusement, or other public facilities; 2. authority for the attorney general to file suits to speed desegregation of public schools and colleges; 3. a federal Equal Employment Opportunity Commission; 4. a ban on discrimination in all federally-assisted programs and activities, with authority to withhold federal funds in case of violation; and 5. the establishment of a Community Relations Service to help communities through disputes in eliminating racial discrimination.

The effect of Birmingham on Syracuse CORE was electric. CORE veterans recommitted themselves to action. Wretha wrote to the national office requesting more "Freedom Now" buttons, and reported enthusiastically that one hundred new members had joined CORE. George Wiley told them: "Birmingham signals the rise of the Negro everywhere, with a defiance of authority, a defiance of pressure, a defiance of intimidation, and a willingness to stand up and be counted for his citizenship."

Wiley worked over the final plans for Syracuse's biggest, most ambitious direct-action campaign. CORE would attempt to tie up the entire downtown urban renewal project as means of bringing the city face to face with its own racial problems.

Urban renewal was a good target, Wiley reasoned. It dramatized the housing problems of poor blacks; it touched the city's economic power structure, which had the biggest investment in urban renewal. Wiley also hoped that urban renewal would engage more university liberals, who supported the national civil rights movement with rhetoric but did nothing at home. By demanding that urban renewal stop until adequate integrated housing was found for displaced blacks, CORE hoped to force the city to face the enormity of the problem—segregation of most of the city's housing, the failure to enforce housing codes against slumlords, and the totally inadequate supply of low-income housing.

Joined by the NAACP and the civil rights committee of the International Union of Electrical Workers from Syracuse's General Electric plant, Wiley presented Mayor William Walsh with CORE's nine-part action program. It called for construction of low-cost public housing outside the ghetto, relocation of blacks to safe, integrated housing, enforcement of housing codes, and passage of an ordinance prohibiting housing discrimination. Wiley informed Walsh that CORE would attempt to bring to a stop all urban renewal construction unless the mayor agreed to the program. The mayor said he would not negotiate with perpetrators of lawless acts. The scene was set for the largest protest demonstration in Syracuse history.

On the morning of September 13, 1963, CORE carried out its promise to disrupt urban renewal. Several hundred pickets, including Wretha, now in her second pregnancy and carrying baby Danny, marched on the sidewalk while selected CORE volunteers rushed onto the site, again swarming over tractors and bulldozers. Demonstrators padlocked themselves to the construction equipment with heavy steel chains, while others climbed onto the roofs of the apartments which were being smashed with wrecking balls. For the first time, the city struck back; the police swept into action and fourteen demonstrators were arrested.

CORE had finally produced the confrontation. The news media no longer ignored the story. The problem now was to maintain pressure, and to do that they had to find hundreds of people who were willing to go to jail.

Wiley spent a hectic weekend seeking volunteers and raising money for a bail fund. Wretha sat at her telephone with a calendar before her, scheduling and coordinating who would get arrested on which day.

On Sunday afternoon, September 14, the Syracuse CORE leaders were sitting on the grass in Wiley's backyard planning the next day's demonstration. Their conversation was interrupted when a grimfaced Rudy Lombard raced into the yard and announced that four young black children had been killed that morning in the dynamiting of a Birmingham church.

Inez Heard, the black woman now known in the Syracuse ghetto as "Mrs. CORE," recalled her reaction to Lombard's news, a reaction shared by thousands of others who were engaging in disciplined, nonviolent protest: "I wanted to get a machine gun and go down there and shoot that Bull Connor. You can really only stand to see so much and keep on peacefully walking the streets. You begin to feel just like the people who do these things. I felt hatred and wondered whether all our nonviolence programs did any good."

The staying power of nonviolent protest was being put to a crucial test. After the dogs of Bull Connor, the slaying of Evers, and now the slaughter of four innocent little girls, it became clear that advocates of nonviolence, whether national leaders like Dr. King, or local leaders like George Wiley, had to produce tangible results, and quickly. If they didn't, others waited in the wings to act more forcefully.

Until that Sunday, Wiley had seen himself as the backroom organizer, the tactician, the negotiator. Even as he grew more involved, he thought his talents were best used orchestrating the strategy. That day, however, he decided to join more deeply in the struggle.

After a Monday-morning meeting with his doctoral students, Wiley headed for the urban renewal site. Arriving at the scene, he saw in progress the largest demonstration his group had ever mounted. Several hundred pickets, singing "We Shall Overcome" and shouting "Freedom Now," had encircled the urban renewal lots, which were ringed by armed policemen.

Wiley carefully circled behind the policemen and dashed into the center of the lot, shouting "Remember Birmingham." The police, angered by his defiance of the orderly picket line, moved quickly. Three policemen tackled him, twisting his arm sharply as they handcuffed his hands behind his back. Wiley grimaced in pain from the sprained arm as they dragged him by the handcuffs into a paddy wagon.

The dignified college professor's rough handling by police, as shown on television, aroused more new support for CORE in the Syracuse community than had all of his recruitment speeches. For the next three days, the doctor of chemistry whose scientific work was gaining national recognition* chose to

---

* On the day of his arrest, an article in the *Journal of Chemical Engineering* announced the results of his revolutionary method of converting alcohol into halides.

refuse bail and remain in the Willow Street jail, a nineteenth-century dungeon overrun by rats and vermin.

When Wiley emerged from jail on the evening of September 19, he was driven immediately to a civil rights rally in the Grace Episcopal Church, where four hundred excited supporters cheered his arrival. As he walked slowly to the speaker's podium, the audience was stunned to see him ashen and bruised, his arm in a sling. They were even more startled by his words:

> For the last few days, I have had an experience different from any I have ever lived before. I have not sorted it all out yet, but I know that I am closer to the problem than I was three days ago. The problem is a lot more basic than urban renewal or housing discrimination.
>
> I had heard stories about the Willow Street jail, but I thought that people were exaggerating.
>
> Virtually every concept of our system of justice is routinely violated there. No attempt is made to inform prisoners of their rights. Seldom is a person granted the immediate right to call a lawyer. Legal rights are handed out at the whim of the jailer, or as rewards for cooperation—and by cooperation, I mean giving the police whatever information they want.
>
> Detention in the Willow Street jail can only be regarded as cruel and inhuman punishment, even if the people held there for weeks at a time had actually been found guilty of some crime, rather than were just awaiting trial. Let me tell you about it.
>
> You sleep on a board without a mattress or blanket or springs. Your only protection from the cold is whatever clothes you happen to have on your back. Prisoners are fed survival rations and I found people who were extremely hungry and underfed. No exercise is permitted. No books or writing materials are permitted. You couldn't read anyway. There isn't enough light.
>
> I am horrified at how people are treated there. I have been treated as less than a human being and seen others treated that way. Poor Negroes in this community, young men and old ones, are treated that way every day of the year. I talked to them and heard their stories—how they were beaten by the police and thrown down stairs.
>
> People are not only beaten physically but they are systematically deprived of any human respect. There is extreme degradation. There is an effort to reduce human beings to animals. You are stripped of all the little things. You are deprived of basic cleanliness. You can't shave or wash or brush your teeth. There is no toilet paper. It is a conscious effort to degrade people——

At this point Wiley stopped, his voice breaking. He tried to steady himself, but his large body finally gave way, shaking convulsively as he cried openly.

The audience sat silent, sensing that something powerful had happened to George Wiley. When he regained his composure, his voice rose: "We have work to do. What I have seen this week has shown me that urban renewal is only the beginning of a wholesale pattern of discrimination and hostility that goes through the whole system. The issue transcends civil rights. It is a question of human rights."

His followers were stunned. This was the man they had criticized as too cool, too cerebral and unemotional.

Standing in the back of the audience, Bruce Thomas and other young black men who knew the Willow Street jail intimately were surprised to see that Wiley was so shaken by conditions they knew so well. "Shit, they didn't do anything to him," said one. "They treat us worse than that every Saturday night."

George Wiley, the master of self-control, who expressed personal inner feelings rarely, and only with great difficulty, would seldom again so totally lose his composure in public. But he had changed.

Wretha Wiley said that the changes involved George's relationship with black people: "It was a radicalizing experience, not so much in political terms but in terms of feelings that are important. It became part of what he lived and a source of energy. It was an important part of the commitment to things he would later do, and it was an experience that had to be renewed. He said he had never felt so close to anyone as he felt to those people in jail. Up until that point, he had been very cerebral in his involvement in civil rights.

"When I first met George, he would talk with resentment about the chaos with which some poor black people lived. He thought that those people reflected unfavorably on people like himself and made it more difficult for "good" black people to be accepted and get ahead. George was ashamed of their behavior and he wanted to cover it up, not let anyone know about it. This was the first time I had heard him express solidarity, real identification with ghetto blacks, and it was clear that it was very basic. He had made an emotional connection. In that jail he was stripped of everything he had associated with his life. He talked about the tremendous feelings he had, being with the other black prisoners, how personally and emotionally involved with them he was. He listened to their stories. He was appalled at what they had been deprived of in simple dignity, and that they had accommodated."

Wretha believes that George also was deeply affected because of his upbringing: "The chords that were struck in him involved something more than the political civil rights struggle or equal rights for people. It reached way back into his fundamentalist upbringing, to the teachings of Jesus, all those fundamental values. Blessed are the poor and the meek, the humble, and the despised, the prostitutes—'Blessed are ye when men revile you and persecute you.' The jail experience brought all of that back to him, in a very meaningful way." It was, in a sense, a baptism. "He was himself for the first time in the same position as all those miserable poor black people, and he realized how precarious and how chancy were the circumstances which had made him different from them. It stripped away all of the status, all the achievement which had made him feel different."

The urban renewal protest continued for another month, but CORE's efforts had reached a climax with George's jailing. More than a hundred CORE members and sympathizers had been jailed, and CORE was running out of volunteers willing to go behind bars for acts of civil disobedience. The end came in a final meeting at the Wiley home which brought together the leadership of CORE, the NAACP, and other supportive groups. They debated whether to accept the mayor's promises of improvements. Wiley insisted that the campaign could regain momentum only if all groups committed themselves to further acts of civil disobedience. When NAACP president Robert Warr opposed this, Warr and Wiley argued heatedly. At that point, CORE's militant white graduate students, led by Ronald Corwin, urged that CORE leave the fainthearted behind and continue alone. Wiley refused.

"As strongly as George felt, and with all his commitment to direct action," said Corwin, "he would not break with Warr. They had an unspoken agreement to act together and George would not violate their unity." Privately, Wiley knew that Warr would have liked to continue but could not get his NAACP members back into the streets. Both men knew that the black community of Syracuse would pay the price of further disruption. Charley Goldsmith and others already had been threatened with loss of their jobs. Welfare recipients who demonstrated had been warned about losing their grants. The police and community at large would take retribution on local blacks, not the graduate students or middle-class liberals who could walk back into their own comfortable worlds when the fight was over.*

Syracuse was not the South, where wave on wave of determined blacks, led by committed organizers, were willing to keep filling up the jails to produce a decisive confrontation. Wiley was learning that many ghetto-hardened northern blacks reacted indifferently to direct-action protest. Many, who had only recently scratched their way out of the South, were unwilling to endanger what little security they had gained in an effort which seemed too remote from their lives. Some did not understand the urban renewal issue or see that their direct interest was involved. Others did not accept the philosophy or tactics of nonviolence. In the South, it was almost a religion in which southern blacks followed their ministers, but that kind of religion did not have a strong hold in the North.

By the end of 1963, it may have been too late for the use of nonviolent direct action in the North. More and more blacks doubted that nonviolence would produce results, while the limited white tolerance for black protest turned to irritation.

Mayor Walsh and other officials repeatedly stressed that CORE had hurt its own cause and lost many supporters and sympathizers by its resort to lawlessness. Wiley thought otherwise: "I was in Syracuse for two years be-

*Syracuse University officials did threaten to expel students charged with acts of civil disobedience, but liberal university professors blocked this action.

fore we organized any demonstrations and no one ever asked about the problems that affected Negroes, nobody ever asked what kinds of things we wanted done in the community. It was not until there were people down there in the streets, pounding on the doors of the establishment, demanding, protesting, agitating for change, that there began to develop some dialogue about what were the underlying issues. I believe that the movement of people, pressing in a militant and vigorous way around their interests and around their issues is a needed step in the educational and political process."

Martin Luther King, Jr., had made much the same point to white ministers in his famous "Letter from Birmingham Jail." Like King, Wiley knew that there had been gains from demonstrations. The Syracuse city government had responded by establishing a Human Rights Commission and by pledging a program of scattered-site public housing, strengthened housing code enforcement, improved efforts to relocate persons displaced by urban renewal, and tougher enforcement of the state law against housing discrimination. In theory, at least, the city had accepted most of CORE's demands. Wiley also detected changes in attitudes, increased knowledge of and sensitivity to the problems.* Communications opened up for the first time between some blacks and whites in Syracuse. "If we did nothing else, we at least integrated ourselves," said Fern Freel, a white CORE member. Interracial friendships were established, to the lasting enrichment of the community as well as the people involved.

As the weeks passed, however, Wiley's first euphoric assessment faded. It was obvious that the basic problems remained unchanged. Most promises of city officials turned out to be only rhetoric; commissions were created and spouted well-meaning platitudes, but could not effect change. The gains were illusory. "We had mounted tremendous protests and brought people to a serious level of confrontation," Wiley said, "but we could not sustain the pressure on the political system in Syracuse in order to make a relatively permanent change that would have an influence on the lives of the people."

Wiley realized that the problems of employment and housing discrimination were far more deeply ingrained in the fabric of the society than he had understood earlier, but he also saw weaknesses in how civil rights tactics worked in the North. The northern campaigns faltered, in part, because the Mayor Walshes of Syracuse were not the Bull Connors of Birmingham. Instead of total intransigence, northern officials met demands with reasonable-sounding rhetoric. Tension was reduced, and it became difficult to force real change.

*Wiley cited the creation by Syracuse businessmen of a chapter of the Urban League, as well as the many interracial conferences held and committees created by church and civic groups. There was also a revival of the Civil Liberties Union, a critical study of discrimination by the Maxwell School of Government, the formation of neighborhood and community civil rights groups, and the many forums in which CORE and NAACP were invited to participate.

"After the embarrassment of the initial campaign," Wiley reflected, "the city began to resettle into its old patterns; it became increasingly satisfied with the mayor's definition of the demonstrations as irresponsible and lawless acts, which somehow seemed to assuage the need for concern about the immediacy of the social problems at hand." Syracuse officials and editorialists kept insisting that there was a difference between praiseworthy southern black protests against unjust laws and "lawless" northern protests. Wiley failed to see the difference:* "The problems in the North are not different in kind from the problems in the South. Northerners are willing to solve problems in the South, but no one is willing to solve problems at home. The northern white majority say they believe in equality for Negroes, but they will not permit that equality to come at any inconvenience to themselves, at any disruption to what they consider the normal processes of their own lives."

Wretha Wiley and Rudy Lombard, the black veteran of southern campaigns, knew that George's attitudes were shifting: "When George started out," Lombard recalled, "he assumed that people of good will could be convinced to do the right thing. He was very optimistic about that, about the possibility for change. By the end of the urban renewal campaign, he was no longer so certain nor so optimistic."

Wretha Wiley: "During the first years of our marriage, we would have tremendous arguments about our assessments of people. I thought George was very naïve and that he clung to his naïveté with great tenacity. He insisted always on accepting people at face value, while I was always wondering what was going on beneath the surface. I think his naïve attitude came from his early upbringing and his initial relations with white people. It was a protection as a black person to accept white people at face value. The surface relationship was always nicer, more pleasant. I think his was also the orientation of a laboratory scientist, for whom reality is what you see, what is demonstrated. To believe otherwise requires tangible, scientific proof. But by the end of 1963, he was no longer so naïve or so trusting."

The halcyon days of Syracuse CORE had gone; grave troubles were looming, and Wiley had to figure out how to face them. He now realized just how deep were the prejudices that controlled his environment, which he called the "Deep North."

---

*As George's old mentor from Petersburg, Wyatt Tee Walker, who was now King's chief lieutenant, pointed out: "We've got to have a crisis to bargain with. To take a moderate approach hoping to get white help doesn't work. They nail you to the cross, and it saps the enthusiasm of the followers. You've got to have a crisis."

14

Backlash

George Wiley was in his laboratory concentrating on his experiments, an occasional telephone call from the CORE office his only distraction. He left the
lab just before noon for the faculty club, where he had a leisurely lunch with
his graduate students. During lunch, the reports came rapidly from Dallas.
The president had been shot; he was mortally wounded; he was dead. At
mid-afternoon, November 22, 1963, CORE leaders held an emergency
meeting at the Wiley home. Through their shock and sadness, CORE had to
decide how to respond to the assassination: should a planned demonstration
against downtown merchants be canceled? The CORE members wanted to
be respectful, but they also felt that their own plans must continue. Most
black Americans regarded President Kennedy as a friend and champion. But
many civil rights leaders, including Wiley, judged Kennedy as too quick to
ask blacks to compromise their demands and (except during his last few
months in office) hesitant to act decisively to end discrimination.*

*During his campaign for the presidency, Kennedy had said that a stroke of the president's pen
would end discrimination in federal housing programs, yet he had waited twenty-two months
before issuing the promised executive order. He proposed a far-reaching civil rights law, yet administration officials, claiming Congress would not grant as much as the civil rights leaders
wanted, had tried to water it down.

   At a moment of crisis in civil rights protests, the black leaders found Kennedy and his associates too eager to compromise with white southern politicians. More infuriating was the Justice

George drafted a brief public statement: "The Syracuse Council of Racial Equality (CORE) is shocked and stunned by the violent death of the president of the United States. We shall, of course, carry on our nonviolent campaign for racial equality, despite the violent death of this man who we believe was honestly and sincerely dedicated to achieving this goal."

The previous morning, a letter from Wiley explaining a new CORE tactic had appeared in the student newspaper: "Since the urban renewal demonstrations have not transmitted to Syracuse merchants the most elementary facts about the plight of displaced Negroes, we hope that a boycott of their stores will awaken them to a new definition of their community responsibilities."

In the days following, the violent act of assassination was loosely associated in some people's minds with the turmoil attached to the civil rights movement. Stephen K. Bailey, dean of the Maxwell School of Government at Syracuse, declared in a long newspaper article that one could not differentiate between the lawless acts of a Lee Harvey Oswald and the civil disobedience of civil rights workers. Either kind of lawlessness, Bailey said, could destroy the society. He called for a cessation of civil disobedience protests by blacks.

For Wiley, the black struggle was the overriding concern; it could not be slackened, despite the unease it stirred in an already shaken country. In a long, angry letter of rebuttal to Bailey, he wrote: "At a time when the sum total of the experience of my existence cries out for an awakening of the social conscience of America, the principal counsel you espouse would appear to serve the best interests of the comfortable and the complacent."

"Freedom Now" was still a slogan, not a reality. Northern blacks were beginning to question the validity of nonviolent direct action. The mood of the movement shifted from strict adherence to Christian/Gandhian techniques. "Turning the other cheek" to white brutality had worked only so long as white consciences could be touched or shamed. New recruits to CORE and other militant civil rights groups were impatient, less attuned to the more subtle forms of protest. By 1964, protests often escalated quickly into random acts of lawlessness. The movement could no longer be carefully orchestrated by a Roy Wilkins, James Farmer, or George Wiley; it was taking on a life of its own. The movement, conceived years earlier by black in-

Department's inadequate response to complaints about mistreatment of civil rights workers. FBI agents in the South seemed more interested in maintaining their friendly ties with local law enforcers than in protecting blacks in dangerous situations.

Many leaders felt that Kennedy simply did not recognize the changing mood in black America. The symbol of this gulf was a meeting with black leaders in Attorney General Robert Kennedy's New York apartment. As the meeting ended, one black leader told reporters, "He [Robert Kennedy] just doesn't understand what we are talking about."

tellectuals and launched by middle-class activists like Wiley, was generating more candid responses from the northern black masses. As communications with poor blacks increased, civil rights leaders could see that their strategies still did not match the felt needs of the people.

School integration was a case in point. Painstakingly negotiated deseg-regation plans such as the one contrived by Wiley and Jaquith for Syracuse were not working out. Blacks were willing to send their children on buses to white schools, but white parents refused to send their children into black neighborhoods. Syracuse blacks, in turn, repudiated "one-way busing," and the Wiley-Jaquith agreement of early 1963 was a shambles. Answers to dilemmas of race had seemed much more clear-cut when worked out in prin-ciple between two men of reason, character, and good will than when put into practice with fearful whites and proud blacks. Blacks were tired of lis-tening to white platitudes that seldom were borne out in deeds. As Syracuse CORE member Charles Sparks declared at an interracial rally: "White man, I don't want to talk to you anymore. I can say 'Good morning' and 'Good-bye.' Just give me a job."

CORE was redefining its philosophy to reflect this attitude, no longer stressing integration as the magic solution. As more ghetto blacks joined Syracuse CORE, the chapter adopted new issues, reflecting their immediate problems. Black resentment of conduct by the Syracuse police force topped the list of grievances in 1964.

The first case involved a fifteen-year-old black charged with a purse-snatching in which an elderly woman had died. Syracuse newspapers head-lined the arrest as part of a citywide campaign against teenage crime. Members of Syracuse CORE, however, saw it as a police drive against the black community.* The teenager had been seized at his home and held in-communicado for six days, while his home was ransacked by the police. At the end of a bizarre series of events in which the police could not link the boy to the crime, the youth was sentenced to three years in prison for a juve-nile parole violation that consisted of a three-day absence from school. Acting for CORE, Wiley hired Faith Seidenberg to defend the youth. A state ap-peals court, in later dismissing all the charges, criticized the lawless conduct of police and prosecutor.

"Until George Wiley started doing something about it," said CORE member Anna Mae Williams, "this happened every day to our kids. We never knew when they would be grabbed out of school or home or off the street." Other incidents followed: a ghetto youth was beaten in a jail cell by

---

*The movement provided a vital connection between civil rights workers and ordinary black people. Both shared a concern about police lawlessness. Blacks were appalled and angered at how violence against civil rights workers went unpunished. Twenty-four civil rights workers had been murdered between 1960 and 1965; only one murderer had been convicted. Nationwide polls revealed that a majority of blacks distrusted the police and doubted that law enforcement operated with equal justice for blacks.

five policemen, and a black Marine home on furlough was beaten on the street by police. It seemed to Wiley that the police had reacted to civil rights protests by dishing out violence against the black community. CORE attorney Seidenberg was harassed and followed by police, police maintained surveillance of people entering and leaving the Wiley home, and a black stranger driving through town, mistaken for a local civil rights worker, was slapped into jail on fabricated charges.

A young black man told Wiley he had been approached by FBI agents with "a deal." If he would join Syracuse CORE and report on its activities to the federal agents, drug charges against him would be dropped. "George thought the whole thing was insane," recalled Wretha. "He didn't believe such things happened in America." But other members of Syracuse CORE were disturbed at the thought of police infiltration, and the once closely-knit group was splintered, not only by differing aims but by mutual suspicions. "If the FBI had wished to disrupt CORE, it could have planned no better strategy," said Wretha Wiley.

The city council passed an ordinance aimed at CORE, prohibiting demonstrations at city hall. CORE workers who came there on business were swiftly arrested and required to post one thousand dollars bail for charges that carried a maximum fine of only two hundred dollars.*

Heightened northern resistance to civil rights activity came, ironically, just as Congress finally completed action on the 1964 Civil Rights Act, the most sweeping legal advance for blacks since the signing of the Emancipation Proclamation.** Passage of the law was the culmination of one phase of the civil rights movement, yet it had little meaning to blacks in northern cities like Syracuse. Only their expectations had been raised; nothing in their daily lives had changed for the better.

National CORE's primary program in 1964 was the Freedom Summer project, a joint effort of CORE and other civil rights organizations, in which several thousand students and other volunteers were to work in the South, mainly on voter registration. The project began in tragedy. On the second day, June 21, CORE staff members Michael H. Schwerner, a white New Yorker, and James Chaney, a black Mississippian, and white volunteer An-

---

*Stiffened official response to civil rights protest was not confined to Syracuse, but was widespread throughout the North in 1964. For example, CORE demonstrators in St. Louis, protesting job discrimination by a bank, drew one-year prison sentences for unlawful assembly. Political resistance to civil rights activity was defined by a new term, "white backlash," and was reflected in the 1964 Democratic presidential primaries, in which segregationist George Wallace drew substantial votes in Maryland, Indiana, and Michigan.

**The law, introduced by Kennedy, but pushed through by Johnson, prohibited discrimination in public accommodations, thus settling, in law at any rate, the issue which the early southern protests had been fought for. It promised federal action against discrimination by state and local governments where federal funds were involved, and against employment discrimination.

drew Goodman, also a New Yorker, disappeared near Philadelphia, Mississippi. Three weeks later, after a massive search conducted by the FBI, their bodies were found buried in the isolated countryside. They had been ambushed, beaten, and shot to death. A tense, bitter summer had begun. Before it ended, civil rights casualties in the South included four dead, three wounded by gunfire in thirty-five shootings, one thousand arrested, thirty-seven black churches burned, thirty-one homes burned or bombed.

Delivering the eulogy at the funeral of James Chaney, David Dennis, CORE's southern program director, spoke for the soul of the southern movement: "I'm sick and tired of going to funerals of black men who have been murdered by white men. I'm not going to stand here tonight and ask anyone not to be angry, not to be bitter tonight. We've defended our country. To do what? To live like slaves? Don't just look at me and go back and tell folks you've been to a nice service. Your work is just beginning. And I'm going to tell you deep down in my heart what I feel right now. If you go back home and sit down and take what these white men in Mississippi are doing to us . . . if you take it and don't do something about it . . . then God damn your souls!"

Less than a month later, another phase of black protest exploded in Harlem. An off-duty white police lieutenant shot and killed James Powell, a fifteen-year-old black youth who allegedly had lunged at the officer with a knife. On July 18, following a streetcorner rally about the Mississippi slayings, the crowd marched to a police precinct house to protest young Powell's death. That was the trigger. Harlem erupted in the first major race riot of the sixties. The violence raged on for four days; blacks smashed storefronts, looted, and threw bricks at the police, who fought back with great force. The rioting was contagious, spreading quickly to Philadelphia, Elizabeth and Patterson, New Jersey, and Rochester, New York—just ninety miles from Syracuse. The Rochester riot began after police tried to arrest a youth at a street dance. In two violent days, one person was killed, 350 injured, and nearly one thousand arrested. It took four hundred state troopers, reinforced by a twelve-hundred man detachment of the National Guard, to restore order.

The tumult in Rochester seemed about to spread. Syracuse was awash with rumors as blacks gathered in the streets, angry and ready to riot. In a frantic effort to ward off trouble, Wiley and other CORE members worked day and night. On ghetto street corners and in and out of bars were seen an unlikely trio—the tall college professor, accompanied by his white wife and the familiar Bruce Thomas. Black youths told them that they were armed, ready for the police, and not interested in any speeches about CORE. "We were both afraid and didn't know how to deal with that Saturday night scene," said Wretha. "The bars were scary. The whole situation was unpredictable. It was a chaotic mess with a potential, even without the riots, for random violence, the usual knife fights and stabbings."

Still, George kept on talking. Later he explained his job: "We saw our role as trying to prevent the spark which might precipitate disorder. We were there as a stethoscope, listening to the pulse-beat of the community. The main thing we learned was that if there was a spark which would precipitate trouble, it would come from the police. We were told again and again that the police were typically provocative, the police were always pushing. We concluded that if we could keep the police as restrained as possible, and as out of contact with blacks as much as possible, we could reduce danger. Rather than an usual show of force, what was needed was extra-judicious restraint by the police."

Police Chief William H. T. Smith, following Wiley's suggestion, withdrew most police from the black slums in an effort to avoid confrontation. Syracuse almost erupted anyway when six police cars descended on a street corner in response to a call about a bar fight. Within minutes, scores of angry persons gathered. Wiley rushed into a pay phone booth and called the police chief. "Your policemen are about to start a riot," he said. "Get those damn police cars out of here."

The police were withdrawn, Wiley talked the crowd into dispersing, and Syracuse did not riot. Two days after the rioting had ended in Rochester, Wiley confronted Onondaga County Sheriff Patrick Corbett at a community meeting in the Syracuse ghetto: "It's obvious that your overwhelming concern is with public security and keeping the peace. But you don't show the same concern about the underlying problems. If you don't understand these causes, you had better stay up twenty-four hours a day and learn. It's the only hope you've got. By your inaction, you may bring an end to CORE and the NAACP. The people may take the leadership away as they did in Rochester and Harlem. If we leaders don't produce, there will be more trouble. I think we are at that point now."

Sheriff Corbett bounded angrily from his folding chair and demanded: "Do you have any knowledge that anything is going to happen?" Wiley had made the same speech for months. Before the riots his words had fallen on unlistening ears. Now they were taken as a threat.

Officials of the State Commission Against Discrimination reported that Wiley had played a key role in averting a riot. However, he claimed little credit for CORE's two-and-a-half-year program in having eased tensions: "That the presence and vigorous operation of this movement may have given hope to people is a speculative possibility that I dare not embrace. For I do not think that those depressed people at the bottom of the ladder have any confidence that the nonviolent civil rights movement will better their conditions. Syracuse, like every other northern ghetto, sits like an ugly case of leftover Civil War black powder, ready to explode when a careless spark from the police, the ghetto symbol of oppressive authority, becomes too intolerably hot for people to endure any longer."

Along with other militant leaders in CORE and SNCC, Wiley refused to join in statements condemning the riots or calling for a moratorium on civil rights demonstrations during the 1964 presidential contest between Lyndon Johnson and Barry Goldwater: "I'm not convinced that the riots don't help," he said, "though I remain committed to a nonviolent alternative. I think violence does play a role in bringing progress. The riots are a fairly natural response to ghetto conditions. If the conditions under which black people are forced to live existed for any substantial segment of the white community, there can be very little doubt, given our extremely violent American tradition, they would have produced a violent holocaust long before this."

Wiley's forceful leadership of Syracuse CORE had propelled him into national notice. Project 101, Wiley's blueprint for change in Syracuse, had caught the attention of the national CORE office and had been copied by CORE chapters in a number of northern cities. National staff organizer Robert Gore sent a memo to James Farmer: "Syracuse CORE is on the road to becoming one of our better chapters. George Wiley, whom you may know, is furnishing some of the most militant leadership in the chapter." On speech-making visits to Syracuse, Farmer was similarly impressed, as was Bayard Rustin, the movement's intellectual strategist.

Wiley was appointed to the National Action Council, CORE's policy-making and governing board, where, during the summer of 1964, he urged that CORE become involved in partisan politics—a departure from traditional CORE policy. The object of his motion was support for CORE's voter registration effort in Mississippi, which, despite the national attention drawn to the Philadelphia murders, was bogged down by vigorous opposition by white officials. If blacks could not vote, they still could organize politically, Wiley argued, and he asked CORE to support the newly-formed Mississippi Freedom Democratic Party. Begun by blacks and a handful of whites, the group sent its own delegation to challenge the regular Mississippi delegates at the Democratic National Convention in Atlantic City in 1964.

Wiley took the lead in asking CORE to change its policy of avoiding partisan politics: Not only should CORE continue its own protest activities and support the Mississippi Freedom Democrats, but the organization should also initiate political organizing to defeat Republican candidate Barry Goldwater—who already was exploiting the new white backlash against civil rights. Wiley's ideas were approved by the National Action Council. "When George Wiley said something at the NAC, it was usually very much to the point, very well thought out, and very well articulated," said Robert Curvin, the black CORE chairman from Newark.

A case in point was the controversy over Brooklyn CORE's proposed "stall-in," a plan to tie up traffic leading to the 1964 New York World's Fair.

The plan reflected the frustration of militant CORE members with the ineffectiveness of civil rights efforts in the North, particularly in New York. To protest the inattention of the country to civil rights needs, Brooklyn CORE workers planned to stall their cars at key points of access to the fair, disrupting it with a massive traffic jam.

Most NAC members disapproved of the Brooklyn plan but sympathized with the frustration and anger which had given birth to the idea. Dealing with Brooklyn CORE posed a touchy dilemma: how to defuse the plan without betraying the CORE commitment to militant protest. Wiley coolly dissected the proposed stall-in:

> Brooklyn CORE has not attempted to engage in prior negotiations with New York officials, ignoring an important dynamic in the direct action bargaining process. The stall-in does not focus on or dramatize a specific issue of discrimination on which action is demanded. It is not designed to win support or participation from large numbers of Negroes and probably won't. It will interfere with and divert attention from other planned demonstrations in New York, which have a specific focus. Failure to act against the stall-in will lessen CORE's ability to control other runaway operations. Finally, the tie-up will block emergency vehicles which could make CORE directly responsible for deaths and seriously damage the organization.

Wiley suggested that CORE instead mount a demonstration inside the fairgrounds, aimed at the New York state pavillion, with specific demands directed at New York officials. The NAC voted unanimously to suspend Brooklyn CORE, disapproved the stall-in, and held the alternative demonstration. The stall-in fizzled when only a handful of cars participated.

His active participation on national CORE's board of directors gave Wiley a telescopic view of the racial struggle in America in 1964:

> Though conditions in the South are often more gross and extreme, the deep-seated, hard-core problems of the northern ghetto are much less tractable, much more difficult to define and identify, and thus considerably more frustrating. Racism in the North produces far more emotional tension for the person subjected to it. In the South, at least, a person is dealing with a clearly identifiable caste system, which it is possible to identify and to fight. In the North, problems are often subtle, extremely complicated, and difficult to define or identify. It is difficult to have any sense or feeling of progress. In the South, there is at least the illusion that one can escape to the promised land in the North. Once here, and finding himself restricted in his job opportunities, housing, and education for his children, the Negro has nowhere else to run.

After the 1964 riots, Wiley began to state the need for far more basic changes in the society. Writing about the options facing American society, he listed three choices:

We may make the fundamental readjustments in the institutions of our society to bring about a greater degree of social justice for all citizens.

We may continue our present course of actions, which do more to salve our consciences than solve our problems: creating powerless commissions for human rights, launching highly publicized "remedial" and "self-help" programs which seek to give first aid to the victims of social injustices rather than removing the conditions which incapacitate people for full participation in society.

Or we may attempt to suppress protest and contain the problems by more stringent police action.

George Wiley, the lifelong believer in the American dream, was no longer so certain in 1964 that America would choose the right path. "When we started CORE," said Rudy Lombard, "Wiley was a terribly patient guy with everyone and not one to write off the white community as being too hostile to deal with. I think Syracuse, in its resistance to change, has hardened his feelings and led him to consider more radical alternatives to shake the city out of its sense of unreality, to give it some reason to make changes. I think he has gotten closer to the Negro community, and that closeness has shown him the enormity of what needs to be done and the enormity of what it would take to change the community generally. He is less optimistic about that."

Nevertheless, Wiley did not lose his own positive approach to life. A failed experiment was never a failure; the problem could always be attacked from another direction. He also refused to allow his political view of the world to dominate or color his personal view.

Wiley did not pretend to reject material comforts, or the joys of what he considered good life. He enjoyed his sports car and tennis and quiet vacations on the island campsite in Canada. There was a healthy new baby, Maya Devi, in whom he delighted.

He still preferred the style of middle-class liberals to that of the young campus radicals who talked about tearing down a corrupt society. Still wearing his baggy tweeds, narrow neckties and those weird California "space" shoes, he continued to emphasize scrupulous research, then to proceed carefully and pragmatically. He moved easily across a broad range of the Syracuse community, from wealthy white industrialists to rebellious black high school students. In another role, he maintained close personal ties with the seven chemistry students whose doctoral dissertations he supervised. A key to his effectiveness was his simple enjoyment of human comradeship and the ability to tolerate severe stress while switching back and forth from competing demands for his time.

Even while he worked to publish his ground-breaking chemistry research, he was beginning to renounce the competition for status in academia. He also had begun to alter his earlier civics-book view of the functioning of society and its institutions. When Senator-Elect Robert Kennedy came to meet with Syracuse leaders in November, 1964, speaker after speaker called for federal aid for virtually every group in the city except the poor. Finally, Wiley's turn to speak came: "We've heard a lot about federal assistance, which would essentially subsidize the economic development of business and industry in this community. Yet, there is always a tremendous reaction when one suggests the idea of subsidizing low-income families, the ones who are in greatest need. We are told that subsidizing business will improve economic conditions and this somehow is going to filter down to these poor families. Well, I'm here to tell you that there are ten thousand families in this community to whom not very much has filtered down." Kennedy and his entourage came expecting to be embraced warmly and appreciatively by people like Wiley. "We were surprised," said Kennedy aide Peter Edelman, "to find George Wiley so suspicious of us, and skeptical."

Wiley was beginning to define the issue of civil rights in broader terms. In 1964, he wrote:

> Our objective in the struggle for racial equality should not simply be full citizenship for Negroes, but the reshaping of American values in directions which will cure the basic disease of racism and its religious and ethnic analogs.
>
> Peace is the imperative of our time—freedom and social justice are its prerequisites.
>
> People frequently attempt to console my frustration over the condition of Negroes by reminding me that the Irish or Jews or Italians were in similar conditions in the recent past. They assure me that, if we are patient, we will eventually be displaced on the bottom rung of the socioeconomic ladder by some other less fortunate group, perhaps the Puerto Ricans.
>
> As Negroes, our most significant contribution to reshaping of values is to profit from our experiences as a persecuted group and by cultivating mores which reject the notion of financial success, social graces, or the façade of academic degrees as barometers of a person's worth.

After years of struggling to achieve all the symbols of success in a white world, Wiley was reassessing their value, and he was also restating the lessons of his early religious training, which told him that wealth and success meant nothing, that only through a simple, godly life could a man find his own salvation, his own worth. He had begun to place a new and higher value on the dignity and warmth of the poor blacks he met through his work in CORE.

James Farmer, the national director of CORE and one of the most influential leaders of the civil rights movement, called from New York in November, 1964. He asked Wiley to become second-in-command, the associate national director at CORE. "We talked about it for about ten minutes," Wretha recalled. "He said, 'I was offered a CORE job in New York,' and I said, 'Whoopee! When are we going?' Actually, I think he had made a decision to leave chemistry the minute the CORE job was offered."

Wiley took his offer to Henry Wirth, chairman of the chemistry department. A one-year sabbatical from teaching could be arranged, Wirth said, "But I hope you will come back here when it is over." As part of the agreement, Wiley would return to Syracuse four days a month to supervise the work of his doctoral students. Wiley then called Ed Day, who had dropped his Syracuse graduate studies to serve full time as Syracuse CORE's executive secretary at a salary of twenty-five dollars a week. Wiley asked Day to go to New York with him, and Day quickly agreed. Wiley made momentous decisions seem casual, but he knew that he was taking a first step on a long road that might take him away from chemistry forever. He had worked so hard for nine years as a student and for seven years as professor. He was on the verge of promotion and tenure, the guaranteed security of a lifetime job. His research was being published in scientific journals. He still had not abandoned his dreams of becoming a university president. He would be giving up all this.

Wiley's new job would be to run the daily operations of CORE, taking over the administrative duties for which James Farmer had little time or patience. Floyd McKissick, a black North Carolina lawyer who served as chairman of the National Action Council, recalled why he wanted Wiley: "The premium we had in the early days of the movement was courage. Wiley had courage and commitment, but I was looking for a lot of other qualities. He was an organizer, he had intellectual ability, and he had a cool toughness. He could say exactly what he wanted to say and still smile about it. He was one of those guys on the council who could cut you to death, and you would never know it until you saw the blood, because he would be smiling with you the whole time."

Alan Gartner, also an NAC member, and the white president of Boston CORE: "There were people in CORE who had strong program ideas or who had powerful rhetoric, and there were others who were fairly good at administration, but there was no one who combined a sense of what we ought to be doing substantively and of how we might do it. George just stood out as someone who could do that. He had been exerting a strong role in the council that was a combination of programatic militance and a sense of management capability."

Wiley's friends in science, however, argued against his decision. Dr. William Pryor: "I harangued him that this was the wrong choice, that there are lots of folks who could organize some kind of civil rights action of one kind or another, and that black leaders with these kinds of talents weren't that rare. On the other hand, Martin Luther King couldn't have been an outstanding chemistry professor."

"There are at least two hundred good organic chemists," Wiley retorted to Dave Braddon. "On the other hand, there is nobody else with everything I can bring to the movement." Behind Wiley's decision was a knotted mixture of idealism, personal frustration, and ambition. "I was doing chemistry by day and the movement by night, and was strung out really heavily," Wiley told an interviewer. "And it seemed like doing the movement professionally would really kind of get it together and solve this problem. Of course, it sounded like excitement and I thought I would enjoy it."

Wretha Wiley: "The demands on George from CORE increased geometrically from 1962 to 1964. It wasn't anything George didn't want; he got more interested as the campaigns got more complex. But that created serious problems for him as a chemist. Before he got involved in civil rights, he put in fourteen hours a day in chemistry, every day. He was enormously focused and concentrated his energy and attention to his work. But he was burdened by the expectations of his peers. He was viewed as the golden boy. If there had been just normal expectations of him, it wouldn't have been such a problem, but that put him in a double bind. What he did in CORE was unacceptable to the larger community, and pressure was put on the university to bring George Wiley into line. Many people at the university were looking over his shoulder, demanding production because they were defending him against those who wanted to kick him out.

"A lot of the administrators and professors did not like one bit what George was doing, and they let their displeasure be shown, directly and indirectly. George had earlier enjoyed the life style of an academic. Now he was the renegade, the rebel, and the good campus life was only an echo from the past. We thought that by moving somewhere else, we could rearrange our lives, have more time together, more time to enjoy the kids and take quiet trips to our little Canadian island.

"George also saw his civil rights contribution in Syracuse as coming to an end. The chapter was falling apart, and it didn't look as if we could wring any more concessions out of the city. George thought that new approaches had to be found, and those were more likely in New York, on the national scene, than in Syracuse."

In the long run, ambition did inform his plans for the future. Wiley accepted the national CORE job after gaining an understanding from James Farmer that he would support Wiley as his successor if he, Farmer, were to leave. The civil rights movement was heading into a chaotic time, and the thirty-three-year-old professor of chemistry was determined to help shape it during that period of change.

III

◆

CRISIS IN
THE MOVEMENT

15

Crisis of Victory

"The movement is changing direction," James Farmer announced to the reporters and cameramen gathered in CORE's conference room in New York
City. "We are moving toward a more meaningful militancy of community organization and political action." Farmer's resonant voice rolled on, explaining
the new direction in which he was leading CORE: "Direct action and demonstrations won us the right to eat hamburgers at lunch counters; direct
action is winning us the right to vote. But direct action has not basically affected the lot of the average Negro!"

As reporters pondered on November 23, 1964, whether the CORE
leader might be admitting the failure of the civil rights movement in the
light of black riots, Farmer spelled out his "more meaningful militancy":
"Under our new programs of community action, we hope to have block-by-
block influence, the ability to rally entire communities to protest—not
merely our own members. . . . We will organize rent strikes, form cooperatives, and participate in local politics. We will develop and harness the
strength and potential of the Negro vote."

Standing in the national headquarters, which had been the focus of
media attention since the day in 1961 when he first announced the Freedom
Rides, Farmer then introduced his new associate director: "Dr. Wiley com-
bines the militancy of the past with the new directions of the future. As
number two man, he will serve as chief administrator, to help tighten

CORE's central control, and will have responsibility for implementing new programs for community action."

Wiley hardly fit any conventional picture of the militant civil rights leader. The boyish face, looking younger than his thirty-three years, the close-cropped hair, the very narrow bow tie and engaging bright smile gave the appearance of a studious graduate assistant. When he spoke briefly, there was no angry rhetoric but rather a quiet, academic analysis in which he did not underestimate the new challenge facing CORE: "The ultimate battle-ground of the civil rights movement will be the urban centers, North and South. The problems are very complex. The solutions require major institutional changes in society."

Less than two weeks after moving into his new job, Wiley joined leaders of all the major civil rights organizations in a crucial meeting entitled "A Summit on Race." With Farmer away on a trip to Africa, Wiley, representing CORE, received a quick initiation into the complexities and turmoil facing the entire movement. Those two days of summit in New York dramatized not only the problems but the absence of unity or any plan of action.

A. Philip Randolph, the white-haired patriarch of civil rights and chairman of the Negro American Labor Council, opened the meeting: "The civil rights revolution has been caught up in a crisis of victory, a crisis that may involve great opportunity or great danger to its future fulfillment."

The opportunity was to continue the unparalleled progress in which blacks had scored greater gains in four years than in the previous fifty. One danger was that the country would assume that the black American had won full equality with the passage of the 1964 Civil Rights Act. A white backlash already had begun as blacks continued to push militantly for change. White support, in terms of money and volunteers, was diminishing. Whites, including some early civil rights supporters, had started admonishing blacks to stop demonstrating and to concentrate instead on "earning" the fruits of their newly-won rights.

A different danger was that the assembled leaders could not move successfully to the next stage of the revolution. The great masses of poor blacks, particularly in northern urban slums, had scarcely been touched by the victories over official southern segregation. Great expectations had been aroused, however, and with hopes far exceeding results, many blacks felt new bitterness and despair, as indicated by the 1964 riots.

Roy Wilkins, veteran leader of the NAACP, urged moderation. Blacks could best achieve progress by working within the existing structures of society, he said, and should concentrate on enforcement of the 1964 Civil Rights Act, which outlawed discrimination in public accommodations and employment.

The Reverend Andrew Young, speaking for the Southern Christian Leadership Conference (SCLC), urged that the movement ignore the Civil

Rights Act and push instead to mount larger direct-action demonstrations, dwarfing even those of Montgomery and Birmingham. Young represented SCLC while Martin Luther King, Jr., was in Selma, Alabama, mounting a direct-action campaign around the issue of voting rights.*

Kenneth Clark, a psychologist whose writings had influenced the 1954 Supreme Court school decision, said that blacks' primary aim should be upward mobility into the middle class, a status best achieved by pushing for the increased opportunities which black children could gain from integrated education.

Bayard Rustin, the movement's strategist, warned that the Johnson administration's War on Poverty, by overpromising and pitifully underdelivering, was "leaving a trail of despair" in the black ghetto. Rustin urged a national legislative drive for a multi-billion-dollar public works program which would serve the black poor with schools, hospitals, and community centers while at the same time providing jobs and job training.

James Forman, the fiery leader of the Student Non-Violent Coordinating Committee (SNCC), chastized the other leaders for their middle-class mentality. Forman represented the militant ideas and growing bitterness of many young blacks who had carried the brunt of front-line work in the dangerous southern campaigns. "The movement must now meet the black poor on their own terms," he said.

Speaking for his organization, George Wiley described CORE's plan to switch away from the sit-ins and freedom rides and concentrate on community organizing for political power. Listening closely to the proceedings, Wiley engaged in his first high-level debate over this new series of issues. His immediate concerns, however, were the mundane but critical matters that beseiged the CORE national office.

Along with other militant groups, CORE had mushroomed in size as the civil rights movement expanded. Between 1959 and 1965, it had grown from a seven-person staff operating on a sixty-two thousand dollar-annual budget to a sprawling national organization with a ninety-two-person staff spending almost one million dollars annually and serving more than 150 local CORE chapters.** The spontaneous growth, the constant shifting of direction to meet new emergencies, and now the diminishing white financial support, had created an administrative quagmire.

Ed Day described the scene he and Wiley found in January, 1965, at CORE's national headquarters on 10 Park Row: "The place was in absolute

---

* One of the persons marching in Selma was George Wiley's sister-in-law, Jeane, his brother Alton's wife.

** The national office's income for the seven months ending December 31, 1964, was $547,000 —down from almost $605,000 for the same period a year earlier. (The NAACP as well was in debt; its income was down $327,000 from the year before.

chaos. CORE was $200,000 in debt and didn't even know it. The bookkeeping was more than a year behind. Communications within the organization were often nonexistent. No one knew what anyone else was doing. Hundreds of gasoline and telephone credit cards were issued, but no one knew who had them. We had twenty cars in the South but no one knew where they were. Every other telephone call was from a creditor demanding immediate payment. The clerical help had organized into a union and were demanding higher salaries, when we couldn't even meet the payroll. We were delivering thousand-dollar checks by messenger to the telephone company on Friday afternoon to keep them from turning off the phones."

After a hasty assessment of the financial chaos, Wiley bluntly informed the National Action Council: "It has been practically impossible to do anything beyond caretaker activities. The most significant accomplishment I can record is that we have met payroll, and with a little luck we should make it again today."

CORE's problems in 1964 were not simply the result of management inefficiency. The organization faced the dilemma of a "mom and pop store" that had grown overnight into a multi-million-dollar business, but CORE was not really comparable to a business. It was a volatile "movement" that had rapidly mobilized thousands of people into a series of often uncoordinated actions. This movement had a life of its own which would not conform to any amount of advance planning.

The field workers in the South who earned $12.50 a week or served as volunteers were not trained administrators, nor did they have time for administrative niceties such as filing reports. The national staff tried to plan strategy and coordinate actions but its attention was concentrated on servicing those workers in the field, who constantly phoned in with emergency needs for lawyers, bail bond money, and quick infusions of manpower to meet new problems and opportunities as they arose.

CORE had reached the point where it sorely needed management skills and a functioning administrative bureaucracy. At the outset of 1965, it was unclear whether groups such as CORE could become viable organizations, whether the movement could become a permanent, rational institution. This was the challenge Wiley faced, armed with little more than his own ingenuity, his capacity to learn quickly and to handle many jobs at once.

With Day's assistance, he launched an administrative crackdown. He demanded that each field office file an immediate report detailing its activities and telling how it would cut spending. He hired a new bookkeeper to bring the records up to date. He canceled hundreds of credit cards and set up better internal controls on spending. He canceled meetings of the NAC Steering Committee when precious dollars were better used in other ways. He reorganized the membership department, getting a more accurate listing of chapters and members. He learned how to carry on a half-dozen conversations at one time, fending off an angry creditor on one phone, conferring with Farmer at a Mississippi demonstration on another, getting answers to the director's questions on still another phone. He reveled in the action and the little gains from improvisation, in making do with sparse resources. Within four months, Wiley had consolidated and stabilized, at least temporarily, CORE's debts, slightly easing the financial crisis and bringing some order to the organization.

Robert Curvin, the scholarly NAC member from Newark, was encouraged: "We began to get a much clearer picture of where the organization was financially. Things began to be done in a more prompt and efficient way. For that period, I think George really turned the organization around. He gave the organization a sense of stability and the potential began to be created for CORE to survive, in some way."

In his first days in office, Wiley encountered the poisonous atmosphere in which CORE was forced to deal with the federal government. Cartha DeLoach, associate director of the FBI and one of J. Edgar Hoover's most trusted aides, met with Farmer and revealed that the FBI was carefully monitoring CORE's activities and its workers. DeLoach claimed that a midwestern CORE official was a subversive with Communist associations. He told Farmer that national security considerations required that CORE fire the man immediately. Farmer assigned Wiley the job of firing him, and Wiley reluctantly complied.

As Wretha Wiley recalled the episode: "There was a stormy meeting. Farmer argued that the man must be fired. Farmer was afraid that the FBI was going to destroy CORE. George argued against the decision. He had heard this man was a valuable, effective worker. Nevertheless, George followed orders and carried out what, for him, was a most distasteful assignment. George was very unhappy in this new role of hatchet man."

Wiley now knew what others had suspected in Syracuse. The FBI threatened the movement and undoubtedly infiltrated it at all levels.

Professors August Meier and Elliot Rudwick, in their definitive history of CORE, wrote of Wiley's administrative role:

> By far the most important change at the national office [in 1965] was the appointment of George Wiley to function as CORE's primary administrator and as representative of the national organization in the absence of the director. . . .
>
> With Farmer on the road most of the time, Wiley handled staff placements, determined allocation of funds to a great extent and made most of the day-to-day decisions.
>
> Both by the virtue of his position and the force of his personality, Wiley performed [these] functions. . . . He worked hard at "keeping on top" of what CORE was doing, and he made special efforts to exchange ideas with staff and chapter leaders around the country. At the same time, he attempted to see that the NAC (National Action Council) was better informed than it was previously.

Wiley's days were filled from eight in the morning, when he and Ed Day boarded a bus together and headed downtown, conferring on the way about how to allot the limited hours, until late at night, working in the East River apartment building where the Days and Wileys lived. During those late-night sessions, after Wretha put the children to bed, she also participated, writing speeches and pamphlets and helping the two men sort out the conflicting loyalties and intense jealousies which permeated the CORE office staff. There was little time for the relaxed time together, the evenings of concerts and theater of which Wretha had dreamed. George was too busy trying to master a new job. And he was not content with administrative duties. He was determined to play a larger role in CORE.

16

Lessons from
the Deep South

CORE's aim was to concentrate on northern urban problems, but its money, manpower and vital energies were still heavily deployed in the Deep South. In 1965, despite the new Civil Rights Act, even the desegregation of public facilities was still far from reality. Most southern blacks still could not register to vote, and the South massively resisted efforts to dent its economic system, in which rural blacks were often virtual serfs.

CORE's summer plans were shaky. Half the national field staff and budget were focused on four specific areas: the Fourth Congressional District in the wooded countryside of central Mississippi, the Seventh Congressional District in northern Florida, several rural areas in South Carolina, and the isolated southeastern section of Louisiana—targets among the toughest segregationist strongholds in the Deep South. They were largely rural and isolated, light years away from comparatively moderate and progressive cities like Charlotte or Atlanta. The rural southern blacks were among the poorest in the country; they desperately needed outside support to seize any benefits of the new civil rights era.

The major organizations, CORE, SCLC, SNCC, and the NAACP, in an attempt to coordinate some activities, had joined together in the Council of Federated Organizations (COFO).* CORE took responsibility for those four

* COFO had operated forty-seven freedom schools and almost that many community centers— and had collected a burden of grim statistics: one thousand arrests, thirty-five shooting incidents,

southern regions, though there was great disagreement about exactly what
CORE should do.

On January 22, 1965, Wiley flew to New Orleans. He had to decide
whether CORE should again sponsor a summer project such as that of the
turbulent previous year. There were serious disagreements between the national office and the southern workers, and he was expected to be the media-
tor.

The southern CORE field workers, crowded into the New Orleans
regional office, made George Wiley apprehensive; he was new on the job, he
knew most of these fabled freedom fighters only by reputation, and he knew
they were very angry with the national office. The southerners were also dubious about Wiley, wondering whether he was another northern "armchair
general," ignorant of the South. They had already received an initial report
from Richard Haley, the southern regional director, who had met Wiley in
New York a few weeks earlier, and was somewhat dismayed by his first encounter.

"There he was," recalled Haley, "in his college professor clothes, pad-
ding around all over the New York office in his socks. And I said to myself,
'Well, here's another one of those casual eastern professors who has come to
give us six months of his expert advice.' He came across to me as very cool,
very cerebral, impersonal, and academic, without any feeling for or knowledge of the southern problems. He also seemed very white in his percep-
tions and his mannerisms. I was not impressed."

It was not a promising advance notice. Nor was the tension eased when
the southerners poured out a torrent of complaints about CORE. Wiley listened quietly to these angry black men. There was Haley, a professor fired
by Florida A&M for supporting the sit-ins, who then devoted himself full-
time to the movement; James T. McCain, a South Carolina schoolteacher
who had given up his limited security to start a career in civil rights; Dave
Dennis and Ronnie Moore, young Louisianans who joined the first CORE
demonstrations as college students at Southern University and regarded the
movement as a sacred cause.

These veterans told Wiley they believed the day of the nationally
orchestrated, direct-action demonstration was over. Southern blacks needed
to organize for change in their own communities, they emphasized. What
did it matter if CORE got credit for organizing in Bogalusa and Ferriday,
Louisiana, or statewide in Mississippi? It was the Bogalusa Civic and Voters
League, the Ferriday Freedom Movement, and the Mississippi Freedom
Democratic Party that needed recognition. About the battle for prestige and

resulting in three injuries, thirty homes and buildings bombed, thirty-five churches burned,
eighty persons beaten and at least six persons murdered.

power between their own national organization and SCLC, or SNCC, or the NAACP, they cared not a whit.

They had little patience with national leaders like King and Farmer, whose descent for two-day demonstrations attracted nationwide publicity, but whose departure left local blacks with few tangible gains. Such tactics once may have served a vital purpose in arousing the nation, but the struggle was entering a new phase; they argued that local organizing efforts were the only way to change the South.

As Ronnie Moore put it: "If the community wants to have a sewage service above everything else, then we must organize them to meet that need. The organization can then work to reach long-range ends. By doing what the community wants, community leaders automatically will emerge. When these leaders come forward to work for the community, it's our responsibility to take a back seat and advise such community leadership. This is the only way we can permanently build self-supporting community units strong enough to stand on their own to solve their own problems."

Wiley told the southern staff that he shared their commitment to local community action. But he also warned them that their zeal might cloud their appreciation of CORE as a unifying national organization. "Some issues have to be fought out on a national level," he said, "and CORE needs national visibility in order to raise the money to support your local activities."

The dilemma endemic to all organizations seeking radical change would trouble Wiley throughout his civil rights career. How can you balance the central coordinated leadership you need to effect broad institutional change, with the grass-roots autonomy you must preserve for the sake of the movement's vitality? Can you institutionalize verve, commitment, and democratic self-renewal? Wiley's experience in Syracuse had convinced him that the civil rights movement could not move on unless large numbers of poor blacks were engaged directly in the struggle.

At first, he had not worried about the elite leadership style of his own CORE chapter. It did not matter that only a handful of CORE members, who met privately, spoke for an entire black community. He was afraid, in the early Syracuse days, that a grass-roots neighborhood approach would become mired in parochial issues such as garbage collection, and would overlook the central problems.

Wretha Wiley described his changing viewpoint: "His thinking progressed slowly, starting with a dawning awareness in Syracuse. Then he went to New York where he found that national CORE was so elite, that local community organization was an absolute necessity. CORE headquarters was just a laboratory in the consequences of elitist power. The National Action Council tended to be dominated by prima donnas, many of whom did not even represent a local constituency, competing for money, resources and power. George now saw that the local organizations were a necessity for undoing the bad national organization and for getting anything done.

"He also was very attracted to the local leaders and field workers who organized in Bogalusa and places like that. He warmed personally to those people. They were a relief from the people on the national staff who were destructive and cutthroat. And he began to see that local organizing was important for people's individual growth and development. It was clear to him that something happened to people that was good for them when they participated fully and had a clear stake in their own programs."

The requests for help from the southern staff had a monotonous and depressing similarity: CORE headquarters, usually in a church or private home, had been fired upon or burned down.

In Klan-dominated Rankin County, Mississippi, CORE-led efforts at voter registration ran into a stone wall. George Raymond, the CORE leader, was arrested, the home in which CORE workers lived was fired at, and five black churches, the sites of civil rights meetings, were burned. Wiley responded by dispatching additional workers to reinforce the effort.

In West Feliciana Parish, Louisiana, blacks attempting to register to vote were charged with perjury for making mistakes on their voter registration forms. Wiley searched for and hired lawyers to defend them.

In Ferriday, Louisiana, Frank Morris, a black CORE sympathizer, was burned to death in his dry-cleaning shop. Wiley pressed the Justice Department, demanding federal intervention to protect the lives and civil rights of local blacks and CORE workers.

Community organizing often failed, and, even when it was successful, it seldom produced dramatic or immediate results.

• In 1965, CORE supported the Mississippi Freedom Democratic Party's challenge to the seating of the Mississippi congressional delegation. This failed, as did attempts to elect MFDP candidates to state and local office. But Wiley correctly perceived the Mississippi effort as laying the groundwork for future victories.

• In Gadsden County, Florida, the CORE organizing effort gave local blacks sufficient strength to demand successfully that white officials install street lights and to pave roads in black neighborhoods.

• In several Mississippi counties, CORE helped black farmers vote for the first time in the election of members to the county agricultural and stabilization committees, which traditionally discriminated against black farmers in the distribution of crop support payments. Wiley pressured the Agriculture Department to supervise the elections and to nullify an election in which black voters were excluded.

• In South Carolina, Jim McCain developed grass-roots political organizations and conducted a statewide voter registration campaign, with Wiley setting a goal of defeating segregationist Senator Strom Thurmond in the 1966 election. Although Wiley later conceded this was "pretty unrealistic," blacks for the first time elected precinct committeemen and delegates, and would help elect a more moderate senator in the next election.

But the focus of CORE's southern organizing campaigns in 1965 was in Bogalusa, an isolated Louisiana lumber town. Civil rights protests won the appointment of a black deputy sheriff, O'Neal Moore, who promptly was murdered. Wiley and Farmer brought pressure on the Crown Zellerbach Corporation, the town's largest employer (with a giant paper mill), to end the firm's discriminatory practices and also to shame it into providing a moderating force against the Ku Klux Klan. CORE support helped the Civic and Voters League develop lasting organizational strength. Again, the results seemed paltry compared to the blood and sweat of the effort, but two black policemen were hired, the public schools began to desegregate, and federal, state and local officials were forced to deal with the local black leadership across the bargaining table.

On Wiley's trips to Bogalusa, he would be met at the New Orleans airport by A. Z. Young or Robert Hicks, the Bogalusa leaders, and a member of the Deacons for Defense and Justice, a group of armed black men who protected civil rights workers and discouraged attacks on them by firing back at attacking white terrorists. The Deacon, a pistol on the car seat at his side, would drive through desolate swamp country to Bogalusa, while Wiley and the local leaders planned their activity. Throughout his stays there, George knew his life was being protected by armed black men. The gut awareness of real danger was changing his mind about passive resistance. In Bogalusa, where homes in which black meetings were taking place were daily fired upon, George appreciated the need for self-defense.*

The southern campaigns instilled in Wiley a deep appreciation for the southern workers; it was reciprocal and was sealed by a fierce loyalty. Even CORE southern director Richard Haley became a Wiley friend and ally: "I finally decided," Haley said, "that George did learn about our problems in the South, and he was genuine in his commitment. I admired him for having given up his professional status at a time when blacks had a first chance to get ahead in the universities, and devote himself to the struggle. A lot of black professors and teachers could never make that choice, although they did a lot of talking and wringing of hands. George did it."

James McCain, the South Carolina organizer: "Wiley helped CORE change directions and become more involved in black communities. Many of us on the staff had wanted to do that but in the past had been blocked by the

---

* Wiley often spoke of the time he and a carload of white CORE workers had driven out into the country for a meeting in an isolated house, to talk with the homeowner, a black man, when they realized the house was surrounded. It was a new twist, however. Their host's black neighbors, seeing so many whites entering his home, had arrived with their shotguns.

NAC and by the national office. Farmer didn't have much personal contact with the staff. Even when he came South, he made a speech and left. George did everything possible to stay in touch with staff members in the field."

Dave Dennis, the young director of southern programs, said that Wiley did more than anyone in CORE to bridge the differences between the national organization and the rebellious southern staff: "He just worked harder than anyone else in attempting to learn and to relate to people. He had a good sense of organizing and what it took to do it. He had a good sense of other people's feelings. He didn't look at his position as being that of higher than anyone else but as just another person who had a particular job to do. He was always available. He worked with people to help resolve problems. He really made us work harder and have a stronger commitment to the national organization."

The historical high point of the southern civil rights movement arose in the small city of Selma, Alabama. For three months, Dr. King had been leading demonstrations, seeking the right to vote. The campaign reached a climax on March 7, 1965, when Alabama state troopers and sheriff's deputies, mounted on horseback, mercilessly beat five hundred blacks seeking to cross the Edmund Pettus Bridge on a voting rights march to Montgomery. A stunned national audience watched Sheriff Jim Clark shout "Get those god-damn niggers" as his men mauled the blacks, who were fleeing to safety in a black church. Before the Selma demonstrations had ended, three more civil rights workers had been murdered, President Johnson had gone on national television to pledge "We shall overcome," and congressional passage was assured for a tough voting rights law, which finally would guarantee southern blacks their right to vote.

CORE's Selma role was limited, partly because of rivalries between civil rights groups and partly because southern CORE workers thought it more important to concentrate on their own local community organizing. Wiley's role was to organize a sympathy demonstration in Washington, D.C., in which fifteen thousand persons gathered in Lafayette Park, across from the White House, to protest federal inaction in Selma.

Two months later, in Jackson, Mississippi, Wiley was in the thick of things. Members of the Mississippi Freedom Democratic Party were picketing a special session of the state legislature, which sought to subvert the proposed federal voting rights law. Within three days, 726 demonstrators had been arrested and confined in a makeshift jail in the state fairgrounds. On June 16, 1965, MFDP leaders telephoned Wiley in New York, begging him to focus national attention on conditions at the fairgrounds, where prisoners were being beaten and denied medical treatment.

Wiley was on a plane to Jackson that same night. The next day he led the first wave of demonstrators to the state capitol. Within a few minutes he was arrested. He scribbled notes with a pencil stub describing the experience (later he added to the notes in a tape-recorded account and in an interview with FBI agents):

> We were lined up against the wall and frisked. They made us stand facing the wall with our hands high over head against the wall for over one-half hour. Arms felt very numb and weak.
>
> We were joined by others who were arrested attempting to enter the Baptist Church headquarters across the street from the capitol to make an appeal for the right to picket on their property. Some others were arrested handing out leaflets in residential neighborhoods. About eight hundred are now arrested.
>
> Prison is the industry pavilion at the fairgrounds. It is a large cinderblock building, about one hundred by three hundred feet with wooden arching roof, concrete floor, no furniture.
>
> The officers were a combination of sheriff's deputies, Jackson police, highway patrol, and game wardens. Highway patrol and police were most hostile and menacing.
>
> After processing we were brought into the industry building to the wild cheers of the occupants. We were the first new people they had seen that day.
>
> I began interviewing prisoners. On first day, police had beaten the prisoners rather wantonly. They were made to run a gauntlet of highway patrolmen to get from the reception area into the pavilion. They were clubbed about the head and body. The whites were attacked most vigorously. Smith had bad cut on head, closed by eight stitches. Inside the pavilion they were encircled by highway patrolmen who harassed them, mostly by jabs to the ribs and stomach with the end of clubs. In this melee, Chris Dixon was beaten. Still in pain. He was singled out for wearing SNCC button. Cop took button, threw it on the floor, crunched it under foot, then told him to pick it up. When he bent over, a trooper struck him in the small of the back from behind. Two officers struck him several times with their clubs. Beatings stopped the third day when news media showed up.
>
> Saturday morning word of a meeting was spread and people began moving toward center of compound. Police came out, clubs at the ready and formed a ten-foot corridor between the black and white groups to keep them segregated. This placed police in a crossfire of exuberant songs, chants, and speeches. Prisoners' morale was at a high level. The whole time of continuous exposure to the police tended to build our self-confidence and reduce fear of police. Now the police seem rather intimidated.
>
> Bob Smith, MFDP organizer, said, "Let's march across this line and integrate this jail." Stu House and I moved toward the line, and rallied others. Black and white groups moved toward each other. Police with extended clubs pushed us back. I tried to move through a hole in the police line. The officer who appeared in charge grabbed me by the shoulder and threw me back, causing me to fall. Then I was dragged by one arm and one foot by two officers a distance of about twenty yards towards the exit of the compound. They then took me from the fairgrounds compound and put me in the city jail.

The detective typed notes as he questioned me about trouble in the compound. He asked what I was trying to do. I said we were trying to integrate the jail. He asked what else. I said we were trying to walk across the line between blacks and whites. He growled that I was trying to lead a prison break.

I was bailed out by the Lawyers Constitutional Defense Committee about 5:00 P.M.

Annie Devine, a MFDP leader, later thanked CORE for its intervention in Jackson: "If CORE had not come into Jackson, there would have been a massacre in the jail. We made a cry for help; you answered it." George was inspired by the poor Mississippi blacks who were joining the movement. And, as in his Syracuse jailing, Wretha said, he felt renewed by the experience of being in jail with common black people.*

George, who as a teenager wrote that he did not want to be "saved" in the Metropolitan Church, was "saved" in jail. Miller Tarkes and Mr. Riles, two aged, deeply religious black men he met in Jackson, reminded him of his early lessons in Sunday school—of St. Paul's experiences in jail and of the Beatitudes: "Blessed are ye when men revile you, persecute you, and say all manner of evil against you." The meaning of those early church teachings about prison and its relationship to salvation, and ministering to persecuted early Christians, came back to him. George Wiley was now finding his own ministry.

By midsummer, 1965, the COFO coalition of major civil rights groups was disintegrating, its energy drained in feuding over philosophy and tactics. Selma had seemed almost an anachronism, the last great passion play which produced an outpouring of national sympathy and concrete results in the form of voting rights legislation. White financial support continued to decline, as did the summer shock troops of white volunteer workers. The idealistic white students were turning their attention to protests against the Vietnam war.** Other whites left because they were rebuffed by CORE and SNCC militants who were determined that blacks should lead the movement and felt the northern white volunteers were too often insensitive to local black communities.

---

* As James Farmer noted of the "baptismal" qualities of the jail experience in sustaining the fervor of the movement: "Most people want at some time to have the jail experience—it's become such an important part of the movement." It was Wiley's third civil rights jailing. Earlier in the year, in New York, he had been arrested leading a protest at the Chase Manhattan Bank against its loans to South Africa.

** In April, 1965, the first mass protest against Vietnam brought out twenty thousand young men and women at the University of Wisconsin. During the summer President Johnson had escalated the war to 150,000 American troops—whereas there had been 5,000 U.S. military advisors a year earlier. The universities, whose young idealists had turned south for five years, now threw themselves into protest against a war they felt was sapping their own generation.

The southern campaigns settled into a series of localized guerrilla actions. Extricating southern blacks from the bonds of serfdom proved much more difficult than desegregating restaurants. George saw that the painstaking work of local grass-roots organizing would be a slow, agonizing process, if indeed it worked at all. Blacks would soon have a potent new weapon in the 1965 Voting Rights Act, which would in time dramatically alter southern politics. But the evidence of 1965 told George that the struggle would be long and difficult.

17

Failure in the North: Division in CORE

The idea for "a reverse freedom ride" was conceived as Farmer and Wiley struggled with the intractable problem of how to organize poor blacks in the northern cities.

Their plan called for a group of black people from Selma, Alabama, fresh from their victory over Governor George Wallace and Sheriff Jim Clark at the Edmund Pettus Bridge, to travel by bus to the Deep North to dramatize the plight of blacks in Syracuse, New York. It was a frantic attempt by CORE to inject life into the northern movement.

There were few signs of successful northern activity. Cincinnati CORE had organized a rent-strike and a march against whites-only building trade unions, and had carved out a role in partisan politics; New York CORE worked at forming tenant councils; Baltimore CORE organized the Maryland Freedom Union to help black employees in laundries and other small businesses; Boston and Rochester CORE had some success in organizing poorly-paid hospital workers. But many chapters were rapidly losing membership or becoming entirely moribund. Chapters argued over whether to concentrate on school integration or organizing the black community and ended up doing neither.

Wiley prepared material and held training sessions around the country to equip local chapters for community action. Community organizing was the most expensive and sophisticated type of civil rights activity, requiring full-time organizers working in a community over an extended period of time. However, most of CORE's dwindling funds already were committed. The choice, Wiley had to report, "is to transfer the resources in from where we've got them in the South, or get some new resources." When a few thousand dollars were raised, Wiley had to decide whether to pay off creditors, meet southern obligations, or invest in new northern programs.

Wiley's own Syracuse chapter suffered from the entire range of northern problems and was struggling to survive. Blacks finally were taking over Syracuse CORE, but whites who had time for volunteer work and who possessed important skills were leaving. Also, echoing a pattern found throughout the country, talented blacks were drawn away from CORE by jobs in the Johnson administration's antipoverty programs. These programs gave blacks much needed jobs and a first opportunity to play a role in the system. But Wiley and other CORE officials felt that the programs were co-opting the civil rights movement. And the poverty programs themselves, with an emphasis on education and job training, did little to fill the immediate needs of poor blacks for jobs, adequate housing, and money. However, the main malaise of the northern CORE chapters was a failure to find issues which would mobilize the black community.

In a last-ditch effort to mount a meaningful program in Syracuse, the chapter spent six months demonstrating against Niagara Mohawk Power Company, the giant public utility which employed only six blacks—as janitors—among fifteen hundred Syracuse employees. CORE had modest demands—eighty jobs over three years so that the utility's employment figures would reflect the percentage of blacks in the Syracuse population—but the utility refused to negotiate.

Wiley decided to make Syracuse a dramatic test case which would reveal northern hypocrisy and resistance to change. James Forman, the SNCC executive director, agreed to support the new campaign, "Freedom Ride North," in which Alabama blacks would join Syracuse CORE in demonstrations against Niagara Mohawk. If the Syracuse effort proved successful, the planners hoped for similar protests in other cities.

There was a symbolic showing of solidarity in Syracuse as the Selma blacks took their places on the picket line outside Niagara Mohawk's chain link fence and stayed there for more than two weeks. But there was no solidarity within the Syracuse black community. To Wiley's surprise, participating daily supporters numbered several hundred at most, and usually not more than several dozen.

Niagara Mohawk refused to budge. Syracuse Mayor William Walsh, who had praised the voting rights campaign in Selma, now lamented "this attempt to embarrass Syracuse," and the *Syracuse Herald American* questioned whether uneducated Alabama fieldhands were qualified to solve problems in Syracuse. As the demonstration lost momentum, CORE was forced into a desperate tactic, one Wiley had rejected at the New York World's Fair a year earlier.

Wiley assistant Ed Day returned to Syracuse and planned a "stall-in." Wiley rented six cars, and, at 6:00 A.M. on May 3, Day and six other volunteers drove the cars to the Niagara Mohawk plant and locked them in positions blocking the entrance gates. They then bound themselves with heavy chains to the axles beneath the cars.

Hundreds of cars soon backed up in Syracuse rush-hour traffic. Two hundred CORE members and sympathizers picketed outside the gates, as horns blared and furious white Niagara Mohawk workers began rocking and beating on the cars underneath which Ed Day and the others were helplessly pinned. Day felt the car being pressed down upon him, threatening to crush his chest. A diabetic, he had fainted from insulin shock by the time police pulled the workers off the car and firemen cut the heavy chains. Day was charged with resisting arrest and an assortment of felonies that could have sent him to prison for forty years, charges that were reduced only after the demonstrations were halted.

Despite the stall-in, Syracuse CORE still could not mobilize more than a few dozen blacks into either direct action or community organizing around neighborhood problems. A few months later, the CORE chapter which Wiley had created was dead, a victim of internal dissension and apathy.

Wretha offered a postmortem: "Too many people went to jail from Niagara Mohawk, and this time, they did not get out easily. We were arrested many times before but always got off and got out. But the charges began to stick in Niagara Mohawk.

"When we had started out in Syracuse, we had taken people by surprise. The system was not really equipped to deal with us, but by 1965, the system was learning. We had used up people's good will and patience—which was not enormous in the first place. People were tired of us and were ready to clamp down by any means necessary."

Angry white reaction and tough official action was setting a pattern throughout the North. Chapters picked tougher and more ambitious targets, the demonstrations had lost their dramatic appeal, fewer sympathizers offered support, CORE chapters became smaller and weaker, often torn by black-white dissension and disagreements over strategy and goals.

Wiley summed up the dilemma: "Basically, the need was to build a substantial network of grass-roots, community-based organizations to deal with the political structure and mount a direct assault on problems of poverty. Our people were professional, middle-class, very activist . . . but they didn't do that job."

Ruth Turner, an articulate black NAC member from Cleveland, said that the CORE chapter members, who had known how to expose racial discrimination through direct-action demonstrations, now lacked the skill and patience to organize ghetto residents for dealing with complex socioeconomic problems.

Even with popular support, the vehicle for organizing had to be just right. For example, Wiley had great hopes for organizing tenants around the issues of housing conditions and abuses by slum landlords, but his plan turned out to have serious defects. In Detroit, a tenant-organizing effort at first showed signs of progress but then collapsed as tenants were evicted or sent to jail, and landlords who were forced to make repairs raised the rents, pricing the housing beyond the means of the tenants. Even when a rent strike succeeded, the end result was often failure as landlords simply abandoned their buildings.

All of the problems facing the movement came to a head as CORE held its 1965 convention in Durham, North Carolina. More than a thousand CORE delegates were warmly greeted by the Durham Chamber of Commerce. Where less than five years earlier the sit-in students had been spat upon and arrested there, hotel and restaurant banners now proclaimed "Welcome CORE." But there was little rejoicing in the dismantling of Jim Crow laws, for the issues which would eventually destroy CORE menaced the 1965 convention. The old problems of money and strategy still were unresolved. "If we don't raise $130,000 in the next six weeks," Wiley reported, "we have to forget everything and may have to put ourselves on a subsistence basis."

On the "New Directions" program of community organizing, Farmer reported: "If we are honest, we will admit we have failed." The admission of failure set the tone for the next debate: Should CORE seek to build an integrated society or create political and economic power for a self-sufficient black community?

Blacks in one wing of the movement were increasingly alienated from American society and its institutions. They saw a repressive, inhumane, white racist society grudgingly yielding only token concessions. They believed that meaningful progress for blacks required revolutionary change. At the opposite end of the spectrum, other CORE members believed that real gains had been made through the passage of civil rights laws and that future progress was possible within the existing framework of society. These fundamental differences informed two other hotly-debated issues: the role of whites in the movement, and the maintenance of nonviolence as a cardinal precept.

The shift of views within CORE was dramatized by the appearance for the first time of a Black Muslim as a convention speaker. His message was: "All whites are created evil." The convention called for black control of CORE chapters. Many wanted to ban white participation entirely, while others merely wanted to restrict whites to lesser jobs. The desire for black control of the movement was fed by several sources: by growing black pride, confidence, and strength; by disillusionment with the response of most whites to black demands for equality; by black separatist ideology.

The question of violence or nonviolence was extremely troubling to Wiley. It was hard to define terms—between nonviolence as a way of life or nonviolence as a movement tactic; between violence as a weapon of self-defense or violence as an attack against whites. Years of civil rights battles had worn thin the patience and sharpened the instincts for survival of the movement workers. The CORE convention nearly adopted a resolution canceling CORE's commitment to nonviolence; it was turned back only with the help of Louisiana's Deacons for Defense leader Ernest Thomas, who said that CORE should pursue nonviolence as a tactic and that the Deacons would provide the protection, imperative after the slaying of thirty civil rights workers. Farmer drew a careful distinction between CORE's rules of nonviolent direct action and the constitutional right of self-defense.

The final divisive convention issue was the war in Vietnam, against which Martin Luther King, Jr., had just spoken out strongly for the first time. The convention approved but then, at Farmer's urging, rescinded a resolution condemning the Johnson Administration's "immoral policy of racism abroad" and demanding an immediate withdrawal of American troops.

From its outset, Wiley personally opposed U.S. involvement in Vietnam. He encouraged Wretha's work in one of the earliest antiwar groups. He was sickened at the killing of black youths in a meaningless war while a crucial one was being fought at home. He was depressed at the drain of volunteers away from the civil rights movement to protest the war, at the diversion of national resources from antipoverty programs to the war. But in 1965, many civil rights leaders, Farmer included, thought it tactically unwise to mix the issues of civil rights and Vietnam. In their view, taking a strong stand against the war simply weakened their movement, splitting away some of its pro–Vietnam war supporters and incurring the wrath of President Lyndon Johnson, when CORE had enough problems pressing the president to move faster on civil rights.

Wiley still dreamed of an integrated society, but he did not think that ideal was inconsistent with his commitment to building black community organization. He now knew that his earlier hopes in Syracuse for integrated housing and schools had been too optimistic and simplistic. If blacks were ever to have those options for integration, and if they were to overcome poverty and powerlessness, Wiley said, they first needed sufficient power to bargain with and make demands on society.

Many CORE members welcomed this concentration on community organizing as a turning away from integration and toward black nationalism or separatism. Wiley did not. That black people acquire the political power to change things, to better their lives, was more important to him than deciding in advance what kind of changes blacks should seek once they gained some power. Separatism to him was impractical, as well as alien to his own philosophy. At a time of weakness in the movement, he could not understand why blacks would purposely drive away white support. He wanted blacks to amass power through community organizing, but he did not believe that blacks could ever get enough collective power to make it alone in America. Wiley agreed that blacks must lead their own movement, yet he was unconcerned that two of his key aides, Alan Gartner and Ed Day, were white. He trusted them as brothers and considered them as committed as himself to the movement.

He was equally pragmatic on the issue of nonviolence. As much as he loved the action of demonstrations, Wretha recalled, he was sickened when they disintegrated into bloodshed. Yet he thoroughly appreciated the role of the Deacons for Defense. They had given him personal protection and a sense of security in Louisiana. As the nonviolence issue was debated endlessly at a NAC meeting, Wiley said: "I think we should consider nonviolence as a useful tactic, and not get hung up in a lot of philosophical arguments."

Less than two months after the CORE convention, on August 11, 1965, black violence erupted in the Watts section of Los Angeles. An estimated ten thousand blacks participated in burning, looting, and attacks on whites to shouts of "Burn, baby, burn." When the five-day spasm of rioting had ended, thirty-four were dead, hundreds were injured, and thirty-five million dollars in damage had occurred. After Watts, Wiley wondered whether Wretha and he could still walk together through a riot zone, as they had in Syracuse a year earlier. His earlier dreams of an ideal society in which interracial marriage signaled the advent of equality had never seemed further from fulfillment.

In an interview with *Time*, Wiley said: "Negro revolts are not simply expressions of frustration. They are angry retaliations against the long and continuing oppression of blacks by white people in America. We may look forward to the grim prospects of more disciplined and selective attacks upon whites so long as the subtle but pervasive racism that dominates our culture persists. The passage of token civil rights measures and a War on Poverty that lightly brushes over some problems—won't do." Wiley's private views were far more complex. He was sickened by the rioting and thought it was largely counterproductive. But he kept these thoughts to himself, as did many black leaders who wanted to make common cause with the angry black masses. And so when he spoke about the riots, Wretha said, "he gave out the party line."

The issues dividing the movement were further exacerbated by Watts and a second summer of riots. Even the timing of Watts seemed ominous. It was just five days after the historic 1965 Voting Rights Act was signed by President Johnson that Watts went up in flames. The concurrence of the historic legislative victory and of the most destructive race riot in American history* seemed to symbolize the fact that not much of the dramatic, hard-won progress of the 1960s had meaningfully reached the life of the black urban slum-dweller. As Martin Luther King, Jr., walked through Watts with Bayard Rustin, he found that many there did not know who he was and that others regarded him with scorn.

Civil rights leaders again were face to face with the issue that A. Philip Randolph had posed seven months earlier. There had been one more great legislative victory, and then Watts, and still "a crisis of victory."

---

* As white America watched Watts burn, and began to equate civil rights demonstrations with destructive riots, President Johnson issued a warning: "To resort to terror and violence . . . strikes from the hand of the Negro the very weapon with which he is achieving his own emancipation."

18

Total Immersion

During one two-week period in the summer of 1965, George Wiley led a demonstration in Mississippi, called an emergency meeting to repair the splintered COFO alliance, planned details of CORE's national convention, made four speaking trips to support northern organizing efforts, and met with a dozen millionaires to seek money for CORE's depleted treasury. Meanwhile, he ran the day-to-day operations of CORE and made biweekly trips to Syracuse to supervise his Ph.D. students.

Alan Gartner, Boston CORE president, who had joined the national staff as Wiley's key aide on policy issues, was struck by his fierce determination to do all things: "Requests would come in for a speaker, and at first, no one ever thought of George. He was perceived initially as the quiet, non-speech-making professor who ran the store. But George wanted to do more. He half-agreed, at first, that he wasn't capable of making the speeches or leading national demonstrations, but he forced himself to do it, and he learned how to do those things with some success. After all, he came to CORE as an administrator, and he didn't really have any experience at that either. But he was confident he could learn. I don't think I've ever seen anyone who went at challenging new jobs with that kind of perseverance. With all that mild manner, he was a man with no small sense of himself, and if someone insisted that he couldn't do a certain job, he insisted, 'I am the associate national director, and if you don't think I can do something, I am going to learn how to do it.' "

Wiley's ego was so tightly controlled that none of his closest associates believed that he meant to become national director of CORE. Rudy Lombard and others close to him said his work was effective partly because he seemed "selfless" and did not engage in intra-CORE personal politics. In Wretha's view, however, George thought he could get to the top "simply by performing and working harder than anyone else."

One new activity was fund-raising. Whites had cut down their contributions, so Wiley set out to capture new financial support. He sought advice from Anna Rosenberg, a dynamic former assistant secretary of defense and one of the country's shrewdest public relations advisors. She put him in contact with the wealthy who agreed to give money to a new fund-raising appeal. He virtually apprenticed himself to professional fund-raisers who volunteered help to civil rights organizations.

The ability to deal openly with all types of people, cultivated in Berkeley and Syracuse and stretched even further at national CORE, now served him well. In the course of a day, he could charm the middle-class liberals who feared black militants, and then move back to an easy working relationship with the militants of SNCC, including executive director James Forman. Was he simply a man for all seasons who, chameleon-like, reflected the views of whomever he happened to be dealing with, or did he have his own coherent philosophy? Lombard thought the latter was true. Underpinning everything Wiley did was "a basic seriousness of purpose, a trust that he could be relied upon to do exactly what he said he was going to do, and a basic moral commitment, which was communicated to others."

Wiley was a pragmatist whose flexibility was a function of his lack of narrow ideological intensity. He was pragmatic in his effort to bridge the differences among the COFO alliance, which was collapsing with the withdrawal of the NAACP and the rejection of SNCC and CORE militants. At COFO meeting to mend the alliance, Wiley wrote out his own thoughts:

> Bringing about desirable social change requires a variety of strategies, approaches, and tactics. Recognizing and respecting the wide range of individual capabilities, technical competencies and interests, the civil rights movement needs to efficiently tap the available resources of a variety of organizations. The movement must provide opportunities for a broad spectrum of degrees of involvement. The likelihood of a single civil rights organization being able to provide simultaneously the requisite variety of opportunities for participation is infinitesimal.
>
> Against the need for a variety of organizations stands the need for coordination and communication among organizations to avoid divisive conflict, needless duplication of effort, confusion and misunderstanding. However, the dynamic character of the movement requires a variety of coalitions.

Just as he did not allow ideological differences to distort working relationships, he also refused to let personal friendships color his judgment of issues. NAC member Curvin: "The guy just had enormous integrity, and he never got swept away in the politics that were involved. He had the unusual ability to say or do the right thing regardless of personal friendships or whose side you are on or that kind of thing. I think that is one reason he was so good." NAC chairman McKissick: "The schism came in CORE because many liberals didn't understand the conversion of the colored man to becoming black and a first-class citizen. We were going through many changes. George was one of the few who was able to maintain an identity with both sides— white and black, including the black poor."

In his work relationships, he seemed the same relaxed, smiling man who always had to pay attention to others. But there was a change in him that could be seen clearly only in his own home. The late hours, the constant field trips and speaking engagements, the compulsion for self-improvement, the self-imposed discipline required to deal with so many different people, the adrenalin highs induced by coping with daily crises—all these took a toll in other ways. Driving with Ed Day to a CORE meeting in June 1965, Wiley suddenly remembered that he had forgotten his wedding anniversary the previous week. The man who for years had meticulously kept a book with the dates of important family occasions—and always celebrated them with a present or a note—no longer took time for his own family.

Wretha Wiley: "He was just totally absorbed in CORE. He was always choosing. He always had to say 'no' twice to every 'yes.' The demands were too great, and they came from so many different quarters that he was always trading off one thing against another. George was very tired when he came home, and many times he was sick. He had an ulcer. He had his worst time with it during his student days at Cornell, but he was still troubled by it, and it began to flare up again in New York. I only have a couple memories of him that year."

His relationship with Wretha had changed. In Syracuse, she had at first been both an intellectual and a spiritual force, leading the way. In New York the battlefield was bigger, and Wretha, occupied with two small children, could no longer share in the far-flung activities that kept Wiley on the tread-mill. "I was very resentful," Wretha recalled. "In the office he was super-charged, full of tremendous energy and vitality, and he rose to every crisis, even sought them out. But at home he was exhausted and preoccupied. He didn't even focus on what he was eating, much less on his family. The only time we really communicated anymore was when we were working together in civil rights."

There were still strategy sessions held in their apartment, in which she participated. She wrote speeches, drafted position papers, and served as a confidante and sounding board for thoughts which George did not want to reveal to others. He confided to her his dismay at the growing issue of black separatism. They were both sensitive to the implications that the black-white split in the movement had for their own lives.

In chemistry, Wiley had felt driven, in part, because he thought others expected too much of him and overrated his abilities. But in civil rights it was his own desire to prove himself that drove him relentlessly. He had grown up in relative comfort and detachment from the most difficult problems of being black in America. He had dues to pay, and he was working alongside others who had paid their dues many times over.

In CORE, at this juncture, he set about the task of trying to help define a future civil rights policy for the country.

19

Seeking New Ideas

Not only CORE but the entire civil rights movement needed an infusion of new ideas. Wiley set out to find them, following a familiar pattern. He got hold of new mentors.

His first recruit was S. M. Miller, a sociologist who had been a fellow Syracuse professor and CORE supporter. At Wiley's urging, Miller brought together a group of men who soon became CORE's Research Advisory Committee. They were all white academicians: Frank Riessman, a manpower specialist; Herbert J. Gans, a city planner and sociologist; and William Ryan, a Boston psychologist. Other participants included Richard Cloward, a Columbia University sociology professor; Robert Schrank; and Sumner Rosen. At least once a week, the professors met at CORE with Wiley and Alan Gartner and, when they were available, Farmer, McKissick, and other leaders. The seminars often went on long into the night.

S. M. (Mike) Miller: "The atmosphere was quite different from the usual meetings in which academics meet with activists. Usually, the academics come in; they present their own favorite ideas of how to solve the problem; they then write a report which is filed away and forgotten. If you organized meetings like that with Martin King, you always had the additional difficulty of people making lectures to King, trying to influence his behavior. Well, that never happened with George. You had the feeling that George was someone in the group who was participating in thinking about the issues.

We sensed that George was searching for new policy directions and new strategies."

As McKissick described it: "George was playing an intellectual role, throwing up good questions and documents and papers as to where we were going. CORE was at the crossroads. We had reached a point in the movement where we had to deal with who we were and what we were going to do. The days were over when you could concentrate on direct-action demonstrations."

Wiley used the meetings, Professor Miller thought, to help him lessen a problem that has traditionally hampered radical activists in America: "Radicals in this country haven't had an experience which has prepared them for what they are doing. It hasn't been a gradual education process. There isn't a body of radical literature, and what there is is hard to distill, with conflicting material in it. And most of the time, the leader doesn't have time to study it. The people who lead movements are self-taught; most of their learning is taking place in direct experience, often an enormous amount of experience in a short period of time, and they haven't been able to absorb it, to do anything with it. In this situation, there is a terrible feeling that the activist leader either reacts by being very arrogant that he knows what to do, or he relies on one or two advisors, or else he becomes terribly indecisive.

"George's way to deal with this was to call together that group of academics to help him assimilate what had happened when he moved from being a Syracuse professor to a national civil rights leader. George would pose issues, very general problems, like: What do you do about poverty? How do you organize people? How do you move from civil rights issues to economic issues? He was taking big problems and operating on the assumption that they could be seriously thought through, that slogans weren't the last line of thought. George was a learner; he was open to experience and thinking about it. He wanted to be practical and get things done but he wanted to have a context for what he was doing. Not many leaders of the sixties and seventies had this twin perspective. He was a chemist of action, seeing things in flux and movement rather than fixed and unyielding."

The Research Advisory Committee meetings had an immediate, pressing objective. President Johnson announced that a White House conference would be held in November, where the best minds in America would assemble to outline the next steps in civil rights progress. The conference even had the clarion title "To Fulfill These Rights." Wiley's academic committee was preparing CORE's blueprint for change, which would be presented at the conference. At the same time, they were pressed to deal immediately with a controversial government document which became known as the "Moynihan Report."

Daniel Patrick Moynihan, another academic friend of the Wileys from Syracuse who was serving in 1965 as an assistant secretary of labor, had confronted the civil rights leadership with his own strategy for future action. The seventy-eight-page report, "The Negro Family: The Case for National Action," had influenced President Johnson, who suggested that it should be a focal point of the forthcoming White House conference. The report soon created a storm in the civil rights movement, and Wiley felt that CORE had to answer Moynihan.

Moynihan wrote that the next national priority in civil rights was to remedy defects in the structure of the poor black family. He said the weakness of the black family was shown by its instability, its proclivity for producing illegitimate children, and its matriarchal structure. He cited statistics on the number of illegitimate children, the divorces and desertions, and the absence of fathers in poor black families. The report concluded:

> At the heart of the deterioration of the fabric of Negro society is the deterioration of the Negro family. It is the fundamental cause of weakness in the Negro community at this time. Unless this damage is repaired, all the effort to end discrimination, poverty and injustice will come to little.
>
> Three centuries of injustice have brought deep-seated structural distortions in the life of Negro Americans. . . . The cycle will be broken only if these distortions are set right. In a word, a national effort toward problems of Negro Americans must be directed toward the question of family structure.

Wiley was troubled by the report, but was not certain why, at first. He knew and liked Moynihan, and considered him a friend of the movement. At the time of Wiley's marriage, Moynihan and his wife were the first of the Syracuse faculty to invite the new interracial couple to their home to toast the marriage. Moynihan had solicited Wiley's views on the report early in 1965. As he first studied it, Wiley agreed with its stress on the importance of a strong, stable family. After all, he and all his brothers and sisters had been the beneficiaries of just such a family. He, too, was deeply troubled by what he saw of lower-class black life styles—the brawls, the promiscuity, the lack of family stability.

But Wiley finally realized that what troubled him about the Moynihan report was its timing and sense of priorities. The political and philosophical overview that Moynihan propounded came at a vulnerable moment for the civil rights movement. It would be read by many, he felt, as blaming the victim for the crime. In preparing for the White House conference, Wiley wrote out in longhand his own reactions to the Moynihan report:

> The civil rights movement has been, as much as anything, a drive on the part of Negroes for recognition, dignity and self-respect. After having managed to survive nearly 350 years of slavery, segregation and multiple forms of humiliation and injustice, and after having waged an uphill struggle for most of these years for a chance at a decent life, it is more than most Negroes can bear to hear

that the major emphasis now should be placed on inadequacies of the Negro family.

I am willing to admit that there are major social problems which confront Negro families and communities as a consequence of the destructive economic and social conditions which Negroes have endured. But I would regard the Negro family in its present state as the most positive adaptation possible under the conditions which American society have forced upon it. Neither Moynihan nor anyone else has produced any compelling arguments that the black family is not basically an adaptive mechanism. If there is a pathology of the Negro family (a question debated by scholars) the removal of the adverse social and economic factors is the most fundamental aspect of the cure.

The basic difference between the administration-Moynihan approach to civil rights and that of the civil rights organizations lay not in a quarrel over whether the Negro family is deteriorating, but over the next steps necessary for Negroes to achieve equality as a fact and as a result.

Civil rights groups are all too painfully aware not only that Jim Crow is still very much alive in the South, but that token integration is becoming institutionalized in federal policy under a façade of progressive pronouncements. Thus, while the Johnson Administration waves banners to rally civil rights workers for at best a quixotic assault on the illusory "Negro family," Negro children are beaten and harassed for attempting to integrate southern schools, federal action is miniscule to enforce voting rights and desegregation of schools, segregation in northern schools has hardened, residential segregation grows worse, ghetto housing conditions remain untenable, and above all, the employment situation, particularly of Negro men, remains acute.

It should surprise no one that we regard the first order of business of a White House conference to be the mobilization of a massive assault on these problems.

"The more I studied the report and talked with Moynihan," Wiley recalled later, "the more I saw the report as a political document drafted by a politician, traveling under the guise of an academic. I came to view both the report on the black family and the War on Poverty programs as efforts to seek political consensus. Namely, whites might support a program which sought to correct defects in black people and poor people, but would oppose a program which said the defects were in white institutions which left millions unemployed and underemployed, in slum housing, and without adequate medical care."

Wiley wrote:

Moynihan admits that he has no interest whatsoever in changing the system which produces the poor and that he is perfectly happy with a War on Poverty working to change the poor. He says that we have the best social system the world has ever seen, though he admits it can be improved.

We in the civil rights movement, on the other hand, far from focusing on a drive for political consensus, have sought at every turn to sharpen and focus at-

tention upon the basic issues and obstacles which proscribe the freedom of
Negroes in America.

As Wiley labored over these thoughts, redrafting them three or four times,
he was struggling to elucidate a critique of American society, calling for
nothing less than massive social change.

The White House pre-conference planning meeting convened on November 17 as one hundred of the nation's top civil rights leaders, academics,
and Johnson administration officials gathered in a Washington hotel. Farmer,
McKissick and Wiley presented CORE's proposals for fulfilling black rights.
The George Wiley who spoke that day was a different man from the young
Syracuse professor who had admired America's institutions and believed they
functioned well enough to make life better for blacks:

> The White House Conference must reject notions which demand that the
> Negro change himself and accept the requirement that the society itself must
> change. . . .
>
> More than any other word, "tokenism" characterizes America's treatment of
> the Negro. With little more than "tokenism" an array of laws has been passed,
> each in turn heralded as "the answer" to "the Negro problem." Often with con-
> siderably less than "tokenism" these laws are being enforced, or frequently and
> more precisely, not being enforced. . . .
>
> If this is the vaunted "breakthrough" in the areas where a "legal frame-
> work" for equality has been established, in the areas where no framework has
> been established, there is as much retrogression as progress. Negro unemploy-
> ment, approximately equal to that of whites a generation and a half ago, is now
> twice that of whites. In the last decade the median income of Negro families
> compared to white actually dropped and is now only 53 percent of white family
> income. Northern schools are at least as segregated as they have always been, if
> not more segregated. Housing segregation was higher in 1960 than in 1940.
>
> It is now fashionable in some circles to proclaim that the major problems of
> giving to the Negro equality in American society have been solved and we now
> must deal with the individual deficiencies of Negroes to make them "ready." To
> mask the fact that the economy has failed to generate a sufficient number of new
> jobs, we attribute the Negro unemployment rate to the Negro's failure to train
> himself. To excuse the failures of the public school system, we ascribe the
> Negro's lack of success in school to the "fact" that he is "culturally deprived." To
> cover the inadequate supply of low-cost housing, we invent the attribute of the
> "untenable" nature of Negro families. And most recently, in a new and all
> embracing canard, we hear about the pathology of the Negro family instead of
> the sickness of American society. . . .
>
> The problems which face us, today as yesterday, are deep-seated and struc-
> tural in nature. They demand bold and imaginative rethinking and reshaping of
> many of the institutions of our society. They will not be solved by seeking to ma-
> nipulate the individual Negro, seeking to have him "shape up" and "clean up,"
> or, as some would have him do, join the Army.

The CORE delegates proposed a list of sweeping actions to change society. These included:

• a $25 billion public works program to provide the jobs and fill the public service needs of schools, libraries, hospitals and recreational facilities;

• one million public service, nonprofessional jobs in teaching, recreation, hospitals, etc.;

• a two-dollar minimum wage to cover all workers;

• a guaranteed annual income or negative income tax for those who cannot work or those society is unable to employ;

• six million new housing units for low- and middle-income families;

• new civil rights laws to desegregate housing, to protect persons exercising their civil rights, and to eliminate discrimination in the judicial system.

The administration and militant civil rights leaders were now at loggerheads. The heyday of the civil rights movement, and of major federal actions in response to it, was over. Yet, for Wiley, the planning that had gone into the White House conference was not wasted. He was thinking out the next stage of the movement.

As Professor Miller recalls the issues: "We were all concerned about the temporariness of what we were doing in the movement. You had mobilized people for an event and it dissipated. There wasn't any continuing power that came out of it. How could you jump the gap between local problems and the omnibus economic and political issues that had to be treated on a national level? That was the key unanswered question. You can mobilize people about the local issues, but you can't resolve those issues locally. You have to get national action. And that tension between trying to get people to have broader perspectives, but being involved in things that mean a lot to them, is the chronic difficulty facing organization. After a while that became the theme of the group."

It was hard to conceptualize how national issues could be linked with local organizing. Some academics grasped issues but were ignorant of organizing strategy. Some civil rights leaders tried to place organizers in the field first and worry later about the issues which might rally local communities. Wiley's training as a chemist, Miller thought, would help him conceptualize what Miller called "the interconnection of elements."

Miller and other professors on CORE's Research Advisory Committee worked overtime for Wiley. They wanted to advance their own ideas, and they were also committed to the movement. But there was something about Wiley which drew support. As Alan Gartner says, Wiley made "people feel part of the enterprise, full participants." It was a quality of leadership very hard to define. He was never the obvious "glad-hander" or pep leader. "That quality of attracting help was in those days, largely unconscious," said

Wretha. "It was the winning smile, the winning manner." Said Gartner, "If George manipulated people, and I think not, it was the most extraordinary, masterful, subtle kind of manipulation."

Towards the end of 1965, there was a new reality. Not only was the federal government not going to deal seriously with the economic problems of the poor, there were signs everywhere that the government and politicians were backsliding on the commitments already given to equal rights.

The telephones on the wall behind Wiley's desk rang incessantly as CORE workers phoned in reports from around the country. In South Carolina, officials still refused to register black voters. From Chicago CORE came word that the government had backed off from its plan to cut off federal school aid if Chicago officials refused to implement a school desegregation plan. From Washington Wiley learned that the White House had drafted new regulations to limit the role of the poor who served on policy-making boards for the antipoverty programs.

Congress, after the spurt of social legislation in 1964 and 1965, had turned to attack some of the new programs. Lyndon Johnson's attention was on winning a tax increase to finance the growing military operation in Vietnam. And in his pocket the president carried the results of public opinion polls recording white fears and resentments against the pace of civil rights.

Disturbed by reports of federal backsliding, Wiley flew to South Carolina in December, 1965, to review the situation himself. He found that blacks were denied the benefits of antipoverty programs, that local officials refused to implement school desegregation and voter registration plans, and that federal officials failed to enforce the new civil rights laws. CORE's field workers were more bitter than ever before, and many were quitting. Some hinted that black people would have to seek their own remedies in their own ways. Wiley returned to New York deeply shaken.

At Wiley's urging, Whitney Young of the Urban League induced Attorney General Nicholas Katzenbach to hold a meeting to discuss lagging civil rights enforcement. Seventeen leaders of the four major civil rights organizations, accompanied by white allies, met with Katzenbach and John Gardner, the secretary of Health, Education, and Welfare, who shared responsibility for enforcing the Civil Rights Act.

Wiley spoke of his visit to South Carolina and tried to convey the despair of local civil rights workers and of poor blacks. Gardner refused to change policy: HEW would continue to advance federal funds to schools and hospitals without first requiring complete civil rights compliance. If states and cities were later found to violate the law, then, and only then, would the federal government move to get its funds back. Such a procedure would take years to implement, Whitney Young protested.

"Negroes are going to consider it a white man's trick to pass these laws and then not enforce them," said Joseph Rauh, general counsel of the Leadership Conference on Civil Rights.

"When you passed the voting rights law, the nation expected results," said Martin Luther King's aide, Harry Wattel. "The results have been pathetic."

And then Wiley clicked off statistics: "You have received complaints on voting rights violations from over a hundred counties in the South, but you have only thirty-two registrars in the entire area—only thirteen in Mississippi, one of the worst states."

Katzenbach and Gardner acknowledged that they did possess legal authority to go further. What they left unsaid was clear to all: Katzenbach and Gardner had received their instructions from President Johnson. The president was now listening to Mayor Daley of Chicago, who wanted no federal interference with his federally funded antipoverty program and his de facto segregated schools. And he listened to the generals in the Pentagon, who assured him that they could win the war in Vietnam if he would only give them more men and supplies.

The meeting ended unhappily. The Johnson cabinet officers made no promises, and the civil rights leaders came away empty-handed. The lack of response and the inertia of the Johnson administration would itself be a factor in provoking new crises—in civil rights and over the war.

The year 1965 ended gloomily for CORE, but there was promise for Wiley's own future. On Christmas Eve, George and Wretha were sitting on the living room floor of their New York apartment, wrapping presents for Danny and Maya, when Alan Gartner telephoned with a stunning piece of news. James Farmer was resigning as national director of CORE. Farmer's departure would heighten the crisis at CORE, but it would also offer a unique opportunity to Wiley.

20

Defeat: Remembrance
of Things Past

Farmer had promised to recommend him for the job, and he had strong support on the NAC and on the staff. As the National Action Council convened on December 28 at New York's Belmont Plaza Hotel, Wiley presented a detailed plan to rebuild CORE.

"Farmer's resignation is being used both subtly and explicitly to confirm the death of the militants in the civil rights movement," Wiley told the NAC. "Public confidence can be restored only by launching a major program aimed at the urban centers and a tight, efficient national structure to pull it off."

Wiley proposed a "major program thrust into the North," an attempt in four cities to test the strengths and weaknesses of four different approaches to community organizing:

> a large-scale political organization aimed at a specific goal such as electing a major official;
> a bootstrap social services operation which attempts to turn the corner into protest/political activity by organizing welfare recipients;
> an Alinsky-style organization,* seeking to organize around the felt needs of the local community;
> a community-owned center such as CORE operates in Columbus, Ohio.

* Saul Alinsky developed methods of organizing neighborhoods and communities around local issues.

To support the efforts, "flying squads"—teams of experts from the national office—would go to a community to help with fund-raising, public relations, legal assistance, and the actual organizing.

Wiley's plan included strengthening the national office, expanding the regional offices, forming of a research department, opening a Washington lobbying office, and developing "Friends of CORE" to raise money among whites and middle-class blacks. "An effective national communications network" would, he said, require a revived CORE newsletter, an internal house organ, and a national WATS telephone line. Last on Wiley's long agenda was a national legislative program focused on "job creation and a living wage."

The Wiley plan was a distillation of his five-year experience in CORE, a synthesis of theory and practical action, a blueprint for linking a national organization with people at the grass roots, and a guide showing how the civil rights movement could turn itself into a movement for social and economic justice.

Wiley's grand design, however, was not what some NAC members wanted. They were looking for a leader to rally the black masses, one who would himself personify black identity and the newly re-emerging belief in black separatism. CORE leaders like Floyd McKissick, Ruth Turner from Cleveland, Lincoln Lynch from Long Island, Wilfred Ussery from San Francisco, and Will Bradley from Los Angeles no longer saw integration as a feasible answer. If the federal government were to renege on its commitments to civil rights laws and antipoverty programs, if the white majority would only grant grudging, token gains to blacks, then black cultural and political unity was the only salvation. Blacks must no longer have to depend on white liberals and white institutions.

The budding separatists had their own candidate in their board chairman, Floyd McKissick. The selection of a national director of CORE turned into a contest between him and Wiley.

McKissick had been a pioneer in civil rights since he carried a picket sign as a twelve-year-old in Durham, North Carolina. He was one of the first black students admitted to the law school of the University of North Carolina and had fought in all the early integration battles. He and Wiley shared common views on the need for black community organization, but McKissick had begun to stress black independence. More important, although he was a polished lawyer and sophisticated businessman, he came from a family that had included ministers and could affect the speaking style of a "down home" country preacher—a style Wiley could not manage. The contest was a personality conflict and a struggle for power between the staff (aligned with Wiley) and the NAC. At stake was control of CORE jobs. But, in the end, the real issue was the "blackness" of George Alvin Wiley.

As part of the final selection process, the NAC summoned each candidate to a hotel conference room and cross-examined him.* Wiley knew in advance what some board members wanted to hear him say, but he was unwilling to endorse the separatist line. He was asked how he proposed to lead poor blacks in the ghetto. "We are often too bound by mythology as to what it takes to relate to the black community," Wiley replied. "People want advice, help in cutting through their problems. The same quality of leadership that we want and need is what the people want and need.

"I don't see myself replacing Jim Farmer's qualities. I would hope that my principal identity would be as head of an organization, not as the organization itself. Other spokesmen for CORE must be developed. The qualities that are needed to do this job are organizational ability, ability to direct, think, and deal with complex problems, and to articulate them so that the fundamental racism of our society might be brought out."

Wiley still was committed to nonviolence, for "tactical and humane reasons. The tactic of nonviolence distinguishes this movement from its enemies." The major key to solving many ghetto problems was at the federal level, Wiley said, and thus political instruments were necessary to effect change. As for black nationalism: "I believe that blacks should lead their own movement but I don't think we can make it alone. We are a small minority and we need allies."

Nor was Wiley ready to renounce white financial support. "CORE needs a diversified fundraising approach," he told the NAC. "Money does not come that easily from the Negro community. We still need white money." And finally, "Being 'nitty gritty' is not necessarily the quality that will inspire people."

McKissick told the NAC that he would stress black awareness. He called for a concentrated fund-raising effort through the black church community, a program of Negro history that "must be incorporated throughout CORE from top to bottom," and for the development of black economic cooperatives in both the North and South.

Wiley and McKissick then left to await the decision in their own rooms at the Belmont Hotel, while the NAC members debated.

Ruth Turner organized support for McKissick: "McKissick, as the result of long experience and deep roots in the Negro community, understands the idiosyncrasies, institutions, and relationships. At this point in our history, we need this badly if we are not to become irrelevant."

Ruth Turner later explained: "There was never any question that George was a very competent administrator and attempted to put some order into what was a very chaotic situation. Yet, in terms of basic focus, he

* Candidates were considered "in light of the following criteria: sensitivity to the needs of the ghetto, ability to reflect ghetto needs in carrying on a dialogue with the nation, charisma to stir enthusiasm, sound programming and administrative ability, and ability as a public speaker."

appeared to desire to participate in a society as it is rather than developing our resources and power to change it.

"George and I were in agreement in support of the thrust for community organization, but with one major difference. I felt that focusing on the black community necessarily forced you to deal with the question of blackness and what the black community meant. George's commitment to community organization led him in a different direction—organizing for economic benefits without an emphasis on race. He was talking about a community of like interests, and some of the rest of us were talking about a community of like culture and experience and tradition, which necessarily in a society that was racist, dealt with questions of race.

"I think that George would have been the perfect choice to head up an effort to deal with economic issues irrespective of race. The only problem is that I don't think, in the American context, you can ever dismiss race or you can ever treat it as a secondary consideration.

"There was a perception in any kind of conversation with him that George was a middle-class guy who was not picking up on black culture in the broadest sense the way other people were at that time. The fact of his 'middle-classness' couldn't be the problem in itself because we were almost all from that background in varying degrees. But George had a white wife, and that had to be taken into consideration. His associates and friends tended to be white. He seemed to be a little bit uncomfortable with the process by which we were all getting reacquainted with our black culture.

"You could see it in use of language, just basic style. At the time when even the most conservative had at least one daishiki in their wardrobe, I suspect George didn't. It was a journey that he didn't seem to be quite willing to take. But it's difficult to define. Certainly not just a matter of dress. It is more a matter of cultural tastes. Floyd McKissick was a great blues lover and all of us from time to time would, in a social setting, loosen up and enjoy music that was popular in the black community. And you always had the view that George would feel more comfortable if Mozart was being played."

Although Ruth Turner led the attack on Wiley, it was James Farmer who became the deciding factor. In the NAC debate, Farmer spoke to "the question of empathy and ability to articulate the feeling of the ghetto." Aside from this consideration, he "felt that other things were more or less equal." James Farmer: "I had to do a lot of soul searching to choose between Wiley and McKissick. Obviously, Wiley had a sounder intellect than Floyd, a better mind, and he was probably a better organizer. But I felt then that George was still the professor, in both manner and dress, with his suits and narrow ties.

"The kids were starting to relate to African dress and styles. They were talking ghetto language. Floyd talks that down-home language, you know, splits his infinitives and everything else. He can give a real rabble-rousing speech. He's a Baptist preacher at heart, he can have them rolling in the aisles. At that time, that was Floyd's talent. And others felt with some justice that maybe that charisma was about all he had. I don't know."

To Wiley's surprise, Farmer made a speech endorsing McKissick. "I do not know yet whether I made the right decision," Farmer said, "but it was an honest decision. I searched for the thing to do. I said that in this stage of the organization's development, if CORE was to maintain any of its status in the movement, we required someone with mass appeal and real grass roots, who could talk to the washerwoman and the guys in the street and the little people. Later, I was pleasantly surprised when George demonstrated in the welfare rights movement that he could work with such people."

Yet the militant blacks on the southern staff, who might have the most compelling reasons for mistrusting whites, did not question Wiley's blackness. David Dennis, CORE southern program director, recalls the leadership fight: "Those charges against George were crazy. The southern staff was black and he related to us. He related okay with black people. Other than the Black Muslims, no one in the national organizations had been able to relate well to what's happening in the ghetto. The Black Panthers couldn't do it too well either. At that particular time, orators were a dime a dozen. Every organization had orators who could stand on the street corner and talk. George could do that, too. I just think that in terms of running the organization at that particular time, George was the better person."

One of Wiley's strongest supporters was Robert Curvin, a black man who was the chairman of Newark CORE and a professional social worker: "In retrospect, I think that Ruth Perot and those people's claim was right, that there is a certain kind of gut response that some people have about blackness because of their experience. But where do you place that in the hierarchy of skills that you want for an organization? Do you deem that response as being more important than intelligence? The people who supported George argued that the organization needed competency, needed business and management intelligence, and that George could do all the other things. He was committed and courageous.

"I think it is kind of interesting that some of our people would place so much importance on the role of the national director as personally organizing the masses in the South. It almost typifies the northern condescension that we have about southern people, that they aren't really going to be able to get it together unless we have a Martin Luther King speaking to them.

"George could be challenged on his blackness. It depends on how you define it. The things that were being questioned were not things that were picked out of the air. They were things that were real issues in the minds of black people in this country. There was the feeling that intellectualism alienates blacks from the masses. A professor is not of the masses. There are things that affect your style of life, your attitude, your stimulation, everything.

"It makes a difference to many people, for understandable and I think justifiable reasons, whether a man is married to a white woman or a black woman. It is more than a sociological fact. It tells us that a man has made a certain kind of choice. In George's case, it meant to me that he had grown up in a situation different from most blacks, with more options available to him, and he had chosen some of them. So far as I was concerned, he had overcome all of those disadvantages, except he could not change the color of his wife.

"But it was also a political fight. People really were concerned about that, how in fact the reward system would work after George or Floyd took office. And George just would not wheel and deal for votes. He would not promise jobs in exchange for support."

Politics had shaped James Farmer's reasoning, however: "Administratively, George was doing a very good job. I thought it was first-rate, with the help of Ed Day, who had a unique kind of organized mind. And they worked excellently as a team. But it soon became apparent to me that it was not my team. The organization was becoming hydra-headed. It had two poles of power in the national office—the director and his people, and the associate director and his people. Their loyalty was to him."

Wiley's supporters had diverse backgrounds and experience. Marlene Wilson, whose Columbus, Ohio, CORE was a model for community organizing in the ghetto, later wrote McKissick her reasons for supporting Wiley:

> The questions that were posed of George when he came before the NAC were designed to show that George would not be accepted by the black community—he has a white wife, he is an intellectual, and he lives near Park Row; that he is not committed to the need for black leadership—he has no confidence in the ability of Negroes and has surrounded himself with whites and therefore thinks white; he is not strong enough to make decisions about staff where his personal relations were concerned.
>
> It was an underhanded and unfair attack. First, everyone knows that CORE is not accepted by the "black community" and it is not because of any kind of CORE leadership—even though Farmer has a white wife, lives on Park Row and is about as intellectual as you can get—and I used to be very proud of that. And you, Floyd, are a "prominent attorney" earning $20,000 a year, and are president of a couple of corporations. The problem is that CORE's members are so busy interpreting and devising slogans about "the black community" and "the man in the streets" that they have convinced themselves that they are the experts on the "ghetto," and have neglected to get out and do a job. . . .
>
> The "New Direction" has been too long in coming, but NAC members talk of the "ghetto" as if there was something romantic, glamorous and exciting about it, and it is almost becoming fashionable and sort of a status symbol in CORE.
>
> But those of us who have really experienced the life of the poor, uneducated, exploited Negro (exploited by blacks and whites) and who really know what it means to hate all whites (and blacks who have "made it") will tell you that this life is not glamorous or exciting—it's very painful and dehumanizing. And

that it is a mistake to try to identify with the man in the streets by trying to become like him.

Rudy Lombard, despite his own deep disillusionment with whites and with integration, had no doubts about George Wiley: "He was unusual. He had a house in an integrated neighborhood. He was the one black in the chemistry department. He had a white wife. But having all that did not make him insensitive to discrimination. He never sat idly by and said I've done a good job, I've got a good house, I don't need to do anything. His obsession was that something had to be done. So what compelled him, if he didn't have a sense of being black? The people who said that were a lot more superficial than George, because he never felt it necessary to be anything other than what he was, and you can't be any blacker than that. He was confident of his blackness. He didn't have to worry about his accent or his dress, or whether he could talk street language."

Gregg Harris, the CORE publicity director, recalled: "The entire idea of turning the whites out of CORE was repugnant to George and me. Damn it, a hell of a lot of white people put blood, sweat, and tears into this thing in good faith and with good heart. If you were talking about equality, decency, and fairness, that applied to human beings across the board. Just because it had been denied to us for centuries, George and I couldn't see where you accomplished anything by turning around and denying it to other people. But we recognized that there was an opposite point of view. George was sensitive to the reasons for black separatism. He was, to a degree, sympathetic with it, but he seemed to view it as being both impractical and immoral."

It was hard for Wretha, who knew that she was in the center of a storm, yet worked night and day helping George in the leadership fight: "George got completely into community organization for blacks with his heart, his mind, and his soul. But he never got with, and didn't know what to do with, the black nationalist current that was running at the same time. Those two things merged, but they diverged, also. It was somewhat confusing to him, because the black separatists tended to be the elitists in CORE.

"During the course of 1965, George was concerned about what he thought were stupid analyses in the NAC. For the most part, he would come home complaining about how unrealistic that was, that blacks already were a tiny minority and they needed cover, not more exposure. They needed allies that would bring them closer to whatever their goals were. They did not need more separatism. That was his sense of what was politically necessary to change conditions for blacks, and he did not believe that the country would do it for blacks alone. He thought that action by blacks alone would just make them the object of more brutality and would not get them anything.

"In terms of his own identity, he was still identifying as an American, period! The hardest abuse he took in CORE was because he wasn't black.

And it hurt, because he knew there was an element of truth to it. He knew that he had struggled to be accepted by the white world and that he had competed successfully in a white man's world. That gave him something that everybody responded to, but he knew that what he traded off in that process was his racial identity. He separated himself from his blackness to do that. That was the trade-off. He had chosen white and chosen the white world.

"His feelings about blackness were really to some degree separate from his strong outrage at what black people and poor people were subjected to. He was for the underdog, he was morally repelled by racism and the cruelty inflicted on blacks and the poor. But that didn't mean to him that he had to identify exclusively or primarily with blackness. His close friends were still white.

"It took him that year at CORE headquarters to become aware of the current of black power. That year, we were both very defensive. Partly, the defensiveness was in relation to the political struggle within CORE. He saw the black power thing fueling the other side. George learned to understand the feelings and the philosophy, but he just disagreed with it. He never stopped being an integrationist in the pure sense, in believing that race should be irrelevant to the primary basis of human relationships."

On January 3, 1966, the NAC finally voted for a new national director. It would be a black decision; of the twenty NAC members present, only one was white. McKissick won, receiving twelve votes to eight for Wiley. McKissick urged Wiley to stay on in his old job, but Wiley said he would resign in a month. Outwardly, Wiley was serene in defeat. He had just lost by four votes a job that would have made him one of the "Big Five" of the civil rights movement.* He would automatically be in a national spotlight, be consulted by presidents, and have a chance to try out his ambitious new plans.

Then the meeting turned nasty. Ed Day renounced Farmer for having broken his earlier agreement to support Wiley. "CORE is dead," Day shouted. He was fired on the spot by Will Ussery, before he could resign. Wiley took his white friend by the arm and, admonishing him to "take it easy," led him from the room. "George was very calm," recalled Day. "That's how he appeared to everyone in CORE, but on the inside he was seethingly angry and very unhappy. But he wasn't going to let that show, he wasn't going to let them get him on that. In the crisis, he was keeping cool. He also didn't like to burn bridges. He wanted to make the best of the situation."

At home with Wretha, he let loose his emotions: "The anger lasted for days. He felt he had been betrayed by Farmer. He was furious with Ruth Turner. He didn't know how he had made such an enemy of her. He was

* At that time, they were: Farmer of CORE; Martin Luther King, Jr., of SCLC; A. Philip Randolph, Brotherhood of Sleeping Car Porters; Roy Wilkins, NAACP; and Whitney Young, Urban League.

extremely hurt by her comment that he 'smiled too much' and that this is not the image she wanted as a leader.

To Farmer, McKissick, and Turner, George behaved like a professional. He organized a testimonial dinner to honor Farmer and raise money. He tapped rich white contributors for funds without telling them he was leaving CORE within a few days. He prepared a detailed memorandum for McKissick, alerting him to items that would require his priority attention. He wrote a soothing open letter to CORE about his resignation. For reporters who sensed a bitter split in CORE and were looking for a story, Wiley offered no help. He said only: "I have great respect for Mr. McKissick. I feel my best contribution to the civil rights movement could be made in ways other than continuing as associate national director of CORE."

In a later interview, Wiley recalled his thoughts on the defeat: "I was fully intending to go back to the university, but when I woke up the next morning and thought about it, it seemed there were probably a lot of things out here to be done. And I had enough money saved up so I could live for a couple of months without income. I decided to look around." In his pocket he carried a plan—the one he had presented to the National Action Council. Now he had to find a way to use it.

IV

◆

BIRTH
OF A MOVEMENT

21

Finding a
New Strategy

As he debated his next step, Wiley went back to Syracuse in January, 1966, for an unusual meeting, "The Poor People's War Council on Poverty." Grassroots leaders and community organizers from federal antipoverty programs throughout the country, as well as local civil rights leaders, were meeting there for a first national protest. The rhetoric of the War on Poverty and the legal language of the Economic Opportunity Act called for "maximum feasible participation" of the poor in community-action programs. The people at the Syracuse meeting took that language seriously. By 1966, however, politicians—from President Johnson down to ward leaders—were sorry the phrase had ever been written into law. Poor people were complaining; indeed, they were laying down the law, to city halls, county courthouses, and local "community chests"—the organizations that traditionally decided what benefits were granted to the poor, and how those benefits should be dispensed. The traditional power-holders reacted vigorously, and the Johnson administration was clamping down on participation in antipoverty programs. The Syracuse program, for example, was losing its federal funds because it had fought city hall too hard and too often.

Wiley went to Syracuse to make new contacts with grass-roots organizers. He met old friends from Cesar Chavez's United Farm Workers' Organizing Committee; he had marched with them in Sacramento as CORE supported the grape boycott. He renewed acquaintances from CORE chapters across the country, and he met disciples of Saul Alinsky, who had organized poor black and white neighborhoods in Chicago. He met welfare recipients from Cleveland and from New York's Lower East Side. And he met with two people who would shape his future, a black welfare mother from New York named Beulah Sanders who had been able to organize welfare recipients, and a white professor at the Columbia University School of Social Work, Richard A. Cloward.* The encounter was pivotal.

George Wiley: "Cloward got me off in a corner about midway through the meeting and pointed out to me a curious fact. Here was a meeting of poor people from all across the country, but there was not a single workshop on welfare—despite the fact that most of the people at the meeting were on welfare, and were having trouble with the welfare system. He attributed that omission to the middle-class values and orientation of the organizers who set up the conference. But he began to elaborate to me some of the problems of the welfare system that he had uncovered in his studies, and to outline a strategy that he and Dr. Frances Piven had been developing, that they felt gave significant promise as source of political power for welfare recipients and other poor people."

Cloward and Piven were academicians who liked to test their theories in the field. A pioneer in studies of juvenile delinquency and poverty, Cloward joined with Piven, a political scientist, to study the welfare system in 1961, when he was research director of Mobilization for Youth, a foundation-funded antipoverty program on the Lower East Side.

Richard Cloward: "We became aware of families who were on welfare but who had severe financial troubles. We discovered that they were not getting the full benefits to which they were entitled under the law. A subsequent systematic study uncovered these two problems: huge populations of eligible but unaided people, and massive underbudgeting of benefits among those on the rolls. Our final conclusion was simple: that for every person on the rolls there was another who was eligible. That was a very conservative estimate."

As Cloward and Piven saw the civil rights movement foundering in the North, they thought about how a mass movement of poor people might be organized. The answer was through the welfare system. In the fall of 1965, Cloward and Piven drafted an article: "We observed that a welfare organization drive would surely make a substantial dent in the hunger, malnutrition, and poverty problem in the United States. But, more than that, we also suggested that were such a drive to reach sufficient magnitude, were enough people able to get on the welfare rolls, were enough people to get their full legal entitlement, something approaching a fiscal crisis would begin to occur

---

* Wiley had known Cloward from the days when he served on Wiley's CORE advisory group of professors.

in the big cities of the nation, where the poor were increasingly concentrated.

"And we thought that this crisis, in turn, would make governors and mayors and other political leaders at the local level turn with increasing anxiety and apprehension to the federal government, demanding that it should intervene and reform the welfare systems, possibly along the lines of a national minimum income. Organizing the poor around welfare was a twofold idea: You could get immediate relief for a great many people, and you might even get a more far-reaching reform that would result in a permanent income floor to protect the poor from the worst ravages of poverty."

As they distributed the article to people in the civil rights movement, they made another discovery. Frances Piven: "Nobody knew anything about welfare, and nobody wanted to know anything about it. Even among radicals and organizers, the American values toward welfare prevailed, so that everywhere we turned, we got no help. We met with Whitney Young, director of the Urban League, and he gave us a long speech about how it was more important to get one black woman into a job as an airline stewardess than it was to get fifty poor families onto welfare. We went to Bayard Rustin, but he said, 'If you have an idea that takes two hours to explain, then you don't have an idea.' And then we turned to George Wiley.

"George took our theory and immediately saw the possibilities. He had his own plan in his pocket. 'The time is ripe,' he said, 'for issues that affect people at the bottom, especially in northern cities.' But he didn't as yet have any concrete organizing handle. He knew absolutely nothing about welfare, but he was sufficiently interested to set up a series of meetings with us to learn."

Wretha Wiley: "George came back from Syracuse very excited about the Cloward-Piven theory. Nobody had ever described an idea to him that he accepted so quickly. The plan met all his criteria for revitalizing the movement: more grass-roots organization, more poor blacks, more substantive, immediate benefits for involvement. He was intrigued by their idea of organizing welfare recipients and potential recipients, but he wasn't limited to the concept of welfare as an issue. He still felt that poor people could be organized around housing, education, jobs—and welfare could be a first step."

During the next few weeks, Wiley followed a familiar academic process. He organized a seminar. In a series of evening meetings in the Lower East Side apartment he and Wretha owned, he brought Cloward and Piven together with civil rights activists and other academics—including Ed Day, Alan Gartner, Marvin Rich, Robert Curvin, and Bruce Thomas from CORE, and sociologist S. M. Miller.

Cloward: "First we just laid down the data and established the magnitude of the eligible but unaided population. Then we ran down the reasons why they didn't get on relief. People were either ashamed or afraid to apply, or if they did apply, there were various ways in which the welfare system managed to turn them down. Then the discussion turned to various ways in which to challenge the welfare department for denying eligibility.

Piven: "George spoke up for direct action. He said, 'Once you start demonstrating and picketing and sitting in, you can break through a lot of that stuff.' There was excitement about his direct-action ideas. The issue was whether you tried to get action started all over, or whether you concentrated on a few major cities, and literally tried to bring them to the brink of bankruptcy. We argued for that approach. Welfare was such an unpopular issue we were skeptical about the ability to mobilize resources and raise money to do this thing on a nationwide scale. But George saw it—the nationwide possibility. He only needed a base from which to operate."

Even before he found a new base, Wiley burned his bridges as a research chemist. Syracuse wanted him back, and had promoted him and granted him lifetime tenure while he was on leave of absence at CORE. After his defeat at CORE, he had asked Chancellor Tolley to extend the leave for another year. When Tolley refused, Wiley resigned: "I don't see how I could in good conscience give up my active involvement in the civil rights movement at this critical point in its history," he wrote.

George Wiley was leaving university life just at the time when opportunities for black academicians were being opened up by Civil Rights Act enforcement. Members of the "Talented Tenth" had never had wider horizons. Wiley's parents and older sisters urged him to take advantage of the new climate, to not waste the years he had invested in science. But his direction had changed, and permanently. Convinced now that only a network of powerful grass roots organizations could deal with the economic issues, and believing that the nation's capital was the place to coordinate them, Wiley sold the New York apartment in February 1966; he and Wretha packed up four-year-old Danny and Maya, now two, and moved to Washington.

At first Wiley tried to sell his plan to a promising new organization, the Citizens' Crusade Against Poverty, a private liberal-establishment group which sought to ensure that the government's War on Poverty programs lived up to their promises. Wiley took a job with the Crusade as national action coordinator, and tried to encourage organized political protest by the poor. The first issue he chose was a minimum-wage bill pending in Congress. The bill would help millions of the black poor who worked in laundries, restaurants, and hospitals, on farms, and in many other jobs excluded from minimum-wage coverage.* The effort put Wiley in contact with local

* A less comprehensive bill than the one Wiley favored became law in 1966.

poor people's groups all over the country. Meanwhile, he studied Cloward and Piven's proposal for welfare organizing.

In April, Wiley handed the Crusade an ambitious proposal for an "Action Center" to coordinate militant, grass-roots action on welfare as well as other issues. "The Center would be ideally equipped," he wrote, "to coordinate the Cloward-Piven welfare crisis strategy, spearheading the drive for a guaranteed minimum income." Wiley made it clear that he would leave the Crusade if his plan were not adopted. His constituents, he wrote, were "deprived Negroes at the bottom of the social and economic ladder. I don't feel I can be happy working for the Crusade unless I can continue to be an activist."

The response came in mid-April, 1966, at the Crusade's annual meeting in Washington. The board turned down his proposal, as Wiley had anticipated. He did not, however, expect the poor people present to rise in protest against a conference which was supposed to be serving their interests. At that meeting, R. Sargent Shriver, director of the Office of Economic Opportunity, delivered an "upbeat" speech, sprinkled with success stories from the War on Poverty, and received a rude surprise. Sixty poor people representing local organizations began interrupting him with hostile questions and angry speeches. They were the new and, in some cases, self-appointed spokesmen for the poor. "Tell us where the poor are being helped," they demanded, and as Shriver doggedly continued his prepared speech, they shouted, "He's lying," and "Stop listening to him." Startled by this reception from people who were supposedly his own constituents, Shriver stalked out, saying, "I refuse to participate in a riot."

The disruption was embarrassing for Wiley, who had recruited some of the people who broke up the meeting. But he also saw in those angry, forceful, and often well-informed people a potential for grass-roots leadership. He collected names and addresses of people from Mississippi, Chicago, Cleveland, and other places. One who particularly impressed him was Johnnie Tillmon, a black welfare mother of six from the Watts section of Los Angeles. "The poverty program is a laugh," she told the meeting. "When all the money is spent, the rich will get richer and I will still be receiving a welfare check."

That afternoon, Wiley told Wretha that the Crusade had turned down his plan. "The poor are developing a voice," he said, "and if they can get together, somebody is going to have to listen to them. We may just have to do it alone."

"Why not?" answered Wretha. The Wileys had lived frugally, and they had three thousand dollars in savings. George rented a two-story row house around the corner from their new home near Dupont Circle for an office. Wretha placed Danny in nursery school, hired a sitter for Maya, and went to work as a temporary secretary, and then as a proposal writer for a company operating antipoverty programs. Her role would be to support the family financially while George started the new venture. For the first time since their marriage, the Wileys began to lead separate lives.

George Wiley's office at 1730 R Street, N.W., was called the "pink house" because of the color of its peeling stucco exterior. Installing a telephone, a decrepit duplicating machine, and canvas director's chairs for rudimentary office furniture, Wiley, true to his lifelong habit, sat down and made a list.

1. Decide upon name. Poverty/Rights Action Center (P/RAC).
2. Secure Interim Steering Committee of 3 to 5—by Tuesday, 5/10.
3. Design and print stationery by Tuesday 5/10.
4. Secure office and telephone no. by Mon. 5/9. Done!
5. Secure seed money. $5 to 20 thou.
6. Decide name and relationship of advisory groups.
7. Build staff.
8. Apply for grants.
9. Build Board.
10. Build advisory committee.
11. Revise and distribute proposal. Done!

Cloward and Piven kept telephoning, urging him to tackle the welfare issue. Wiley made notes of the conversations: "Cloward is concerned about getting someone to take over the overall direction and coordination of a nationwide project around the welfare issue. He was concerned about the problem of having a very piecemeal and uncoordinated effort if someone did not pick up the ball and run with it."

At first Wiley had doubted whether the conditions Cloward and Piven described in New York were duplicated nationally. He needed more data, and, in short order, Ed Day brought it to him. Day traveled to Baltimore, Chicago, and Los Angeles. Everywhere, he found a majority of eligible persons were not receiving welfare benefits. And Day made another important discovery. Small local welfare recipient organizations were springing up in a number of cities. There was JOIN in Chicago, ANC Mothers Anonymous in Los Angeles, and several groups in New York City, Cleveland, and Baltimore.

The idea of welfare organizing was boosted by the publication of the Cloward-Piven strategy on May 2 in *The Nation*. The magazine was flooded with requests for reprints. Activists around the country, discouraged by the splintering of civil rights groups and the diffusion of antipoverty efforts, were looking for an idea. The welfare strategy looked like a good one.

When Day returned from his exploratory travels, Wiley asked him to join him in his new venture. Ed Day: "Just like the decision to leave Syracuse and join CORE, P/RAC was a major decision, seemingly made very casually. George said, 'Here is something that might work out.' He was fascinated by the possibilities of organizing. And I said, 'Okay, we'll do that.' "

The names and addresses of contacts he had made through CORE, the Crusade, Cloward and Piven, and of new people from Ed Day's trip, made an enormous master list. There was only one question: where to begin? The answer came before Wiley had had much time for reflection.

On May 21, the University of Chicago School of Social Services Administration held a conference on "guaranteed income," a little-known idea in 1966, although one Wiley and others had advocated at CORE. Main speakers were Richard Cloward and Robert Theobald, a young economist who said a guaranteed annual income was needed in a rapidly automating society which was eliminating forever many jobs traditionally held by the poor.

Wiley and Cloward seized the opportunity to get together some of the people they had identified as potential organizers. They arranged a second meeting with forty of those people in a conference room at the Chicago YMCA. There were representatives of welfare recipient organizations from Chicago, New York, Detroit, Cleveland, and Ann Arbor. Anna Mae Williams came from Syracuse. Some begged and borrowed money for the trip. Others used federal antipoverty funds to pay for their transportation.

It was informal. People introduced themselves and told what they were doing. Edith Doering, a white welfare recipient from Cleveland, told about a 150-mile protest march that her group planned from Cleveland to Columbus on June 30 to dramatize cutbacks in the Ohio welfare budget.

Ed Day: "People in the room became very excited and were going to join the march from all over. Then, after about ten minutes of bubbling enthusiasm, it dawned on everyone that nobody had any money to bring large groups of people to Cleveland, Ohio. But then George suggested that they all ought to do local demonstrations on the same day. The enthusiasm built up again. And then someone turned to George and said, 'Well, you've been telling us about this Poverty/Rights Action Center. You organize it!' George agreed. The nationwide march would be coordinated by the Poverty/Rights Action Center in Washington, D.C." The excited group at the Southside YMCA didn't know that P/RAC did not yet exist. It was still on a piece of paper, and in George Wiley's mind, but he boldly grabbed the opportunity to organize.

This meeting in Chicago was very different, in style and substance, from the academic gathering at the university the day before. George T. Martin, then a University of Chicago graduate student, attended both: "The meeting at the university was held in the law school auditorium, comfortable surroundings, plush seats, and an aura of very intellectual conversation. Robert Theobald conceptualized in the most complex language how automation would eliminate jobs. It was all talk about theory, in the most esoteric of terms, by very comfortable academics, some of whom were interested only in theory; others, particularly the students, also wanted to express their ideals for a better society.

"The meeting the next day in a seedy conference room at the 'Y' was not intellectual at all. There was no talk about theories for a guaranteed annual income. People were concerned about where their next meal was coming from, how they were going to get rid of the roaches in their collapsing apartments. There were poor welfare mothers, frustrated activists, and just a smattering of intellectuals like Cloward and Theobald."

Wiley meant to bring bring the two worlds together, to act without losing sight of ideas. He had a theory and a plan of action.

Ed Day: "We had talked at the meeting like our organization already existed—and now it had to, and in a big hurry. We raced back to Washington very excited. We had a telephone and a lawn chair in this house on R Street, and we flew into action. George got a five-thousand-dollar loan from Irving Fain, an industrialist in Providence, to get us going. We got an old broken-down mimeograph; we pulled in Nancy Steadman, who had been Farmer's secretary at CORE; Faith Seidenberg, our brilliant CORE lawyer from Syracuse; and George Wiley's father, who is quite a writer. And we jumped in to start this nationwide demonstration. We had twenty-five days to put it all together.

"It was fun. It was exhilarating. We ran through our repertoire of civil rights people, and some of the emerging poverty people, and we just pulled the plugs and started calling all over the country. No one had any time to do any planning to speak of. We managed to send out two or three mailings.

"We got on the telephone, called up people all over the country, most of whom we had never talked to in our lives. We told them about this event in Ohio, this 150-mile walk for decent welfare, and asked whether they would participate in a simultaneous event on June 30. An awful lot of them said yes. People were ready. We knew we had something."

22

Birth

of a Movement

"We are on the eve of an historic occasion. We are about to witness on June 30 the first concerted action of a new movement. It is a movement of the poorest of the poor in our nation. Welfare recipients of more than twenty-five cities across the nation will raise their voices in unison to cry out against the terrible injustices and shameful inadequacies that uniformly characterize welfare systems in every state of the union."

—George A. Wiley, Cleveland, Ohio, June 29, 1966

The Ohio Steering Committee for Adequate Welfare, formed in March, 1966, consisted of welfare recipients supported by church groups and social workers. They wanted Governor James Rhodes to convene a special session of the legislature to raise grants at least to the state's own minimum "standard of decency."*

On June 20, 1966, the Reverend Paul Younger and welfare recipient Edith Doering began with one hundred marchers on the 150-mile walk from Cleveland to Columbus. Bystanders yelled at them, "Why don't you get

---

* Their protest was spurred by the state legislature's passage of a welfare reorganization act. At first glance, the act was innocuous enough, centralizing the complex relief programs spread among eighty-eight counties. It seemed a rational administrative reform. Yet, the new assistance payments provided only 78 percent of the amount the state itself mandated as minimum standard for health and decency. In welfare payments for families with dependent children, Ohio, fourth wealthiest state in the nation, ranked thirtieth among all the states. A woman with three dependent children in Cleveland or Cincinnati was expected to support her family on only $150 a month.

Since 1958, local groups in Ohio had protested inadequate payments and periodic cuts in

jobs?" Others along the way provided meals and overnight housing. Some jeered and shouted racial epithets; a cross was burned near a church in Creston.

The marching welfare mothers sang:

> We feed our children bread and beans
> While rich folks ride in limousines.
> After all, we're human beings,
> Marching down Columbus Raod.

By the time they arrived at Columbus on June 30 the band numbered two thousand. There were labor, church, civil rights, and political leaders, and George Wiley. "We are the vanguard and cutting edge of a new movement," he told the marchers, "in which the poor and the underdog are rising and declaring—on their own terms—the war on poverty." Comedian Dick Gregory, standing on the steps of the Ohio State House in the sweltering sun, said to the crowd, "This is bigger than civil rights—this is human rights."

Welfare groups in twenty-five cities across the nation, organized and orchestrated by P/RAC, held similar demonstrations that day. They were not particularly large—in the entire country only about six thousand turned out—but Wiley was jubilant at the coordinated local protests. They had marched or picketed in Louisville, Baltimore, Chicago, Philadelphia, San Bernadino, and other cities.

• In New York City, demonstrators met with city welfare commissioner Mitchell Ginsberg, who promised them a special clothing allowance (a provision called for by law but seldom implemented) and his support of their demand for an increased budget.

• In Boston, there was a rally on the Common, then a march to the state house. The group asked Governor John Volpe and Attorney General Edward Brooke for the right to supplement welfare checks with some earnings and for confidentiality of welfare application interviews, and requested that the word "illegitimate" not be used to describe their children.

• In Philadelphia, 150 men, women, and children staged a "sleep-out" at a state office building to demand that AFDC payments be raised 30 percent to the level required by a ten-year-old law.

• In Louisville, one hundred demonstrators, led by Hulbert James of

---

aid, but seldom got any attention. In 1962, a group of three hundred welfare families petitioned President Kennedy to "let the country know that in fertile Ohio, families on relief have been sentenced to hunger." They got no response. In 1963, Ohio State University professors protested cut in Columbus' welfare budget reducing payments to 50 percent of the state's minimum standard.

the West End Community Council, demanded that the federal food stamp program be instituted for the poor of Jefferson County.

The June 30 demonstrations hardly created a national sensation. But the *New York Times,* the *Washington Post,* and two of the three television networks covered them, giving some credibility to Wiley's fledgling movement.

The news media, however, were far more intent on the Vietnam war protests and other civil rights activities—Martin Luther King's first direct-action campaign in the North and the dramatic new battle cry of black separatism. Wiley, King, and the separatists were pursuing three different strategies.

On June 6, James Meredith* was shot from ambush and slightly wounded as he set out on a march across Mississippi to symbolize the black man's right to move freely about the Deep South. Civil rights leaders from all over the country rushed to Mississippi to continue his walk. They promptly began bickering. King, who still believed in integration and non-violence, quarreled openly with McKissick of CORE and Stokely Carmichael of SNCC, the proponents of separatism. The split in the movement was now out in the open. On June 15, Carmichael used the phrase that would wreck what unity was left in the movement and give opponents new ammunition for terrifying the white majority.

At a rally in Greenwood, Carmichael said: "I've been arrested twenty-seven times and I ain't going to jail no more." Then he started the chant, "Black power. We want black power." The cry swept the nation. Most advocates of "black power" meant nothing more violent than consolidating black voting and economic blocs; black power here was about as sinister as "the Catholic vote" or "the labor vote"; it was a conventional way for a group to get its share of the pie. Most whites, however, feared that "black power" was a war cry for vengeance and saw only more cities going up in flames.

CORE and SNCC endorsed the black power slogan, while King and the moderates of the NAACP and Urban League denounced it with the warning that violence or separatism would mean total defeat for the black minority. The Watts riot of 1965 had forced King to admit that the movement had ignored poverty and racism in the North. He hoped his new campaign in Chicago would produce a dramatic confrontation leading to reforms in the North, just as Selma and Birmingham had led to the laws against discrimination in voting and public accommodations. However, in Chicago King was using techniques that Wiley and other northern civil rights leaders had already tried and abandoned. He concentrated on housing, trying to open up white neighborhoods to blacks. He called for a crackdown on slum landlords, development of scattered-site public housing, and enforcement of a city or-

---

* In 1962 Meredith was the first black admitted to the University of Mississippi.

dinance against housing discrimination. Little attention was paid to the fundamental economic conditions underlying the problems of black housing.

After eight months, King learned—as Wiley had learned in Syracuse three years earlier—that the North was not the South. Mayor Daley was not an accommodating, simplistic antagonist like Bull Connor or Sheriff Jim Clark. To each King salvo, Daley issued a grandiose press release, promising to end slum housing, eradicate poverty, and bring the good life to all. King learned also that northern whites' sympathy with blacks fighting southern sheriffs and southern lunch counters evaporated when their own immediate interests—their neighborhoods, their labor unions, and their jobs—were at stake.

The Chicago campaign, despite King's magnetism, drew little participation from the black community. And for very understandable reasons. Few Chicago blacks had the money to move into higher-priced white neighborhoods, even had they been welcomed with open arms. "Open housing" meant no more to Chicago's black poor than had Wiley's "scattered-site public housing" in Syracuse. King now did see that the movement must turn to economic issues. The main difference between King and Wiley was that King believed that the old style of dramatic, nationally-focused direct-action demonstrations was the best instrument. Wiley believed that well-organized local groups were the starting-point for achieving economic justice.

Wiley agreed with Stokely Carmichael that black people would have to build their own power base. The disagreement was that Wiley thought the initial power base should include all poor people, not just the one-third who were black. "I felt, in 1966," Wiley said later, "that the basic issues confronting black people were going to be economic issues, and the failure of the United States to deliver to blacks the forty acres and the mule, the piece of the economic pie which would grant us a measure of dignity and independence.

"We very consciously chose welfare rights as the battleground for our struggle. First, it was a very repressive nationwide system geared to disseminate economic benefits to large numbers of people, but it operated totally out of conformity with the Constitution, with the Social Security Act under which it was supposed to operate, and, most strikingly, with its own rules and regulations. Second, if the system were forced to deliver anything like the amounts of cash benefits to which poor people were legally entitled, that system would collapse of its own weight.

"Those facts were important for two reasons. First, any movement that hopes to capture the interest of poor people at the grass roots throughout the country is going to have to deliver to them tangible benefits and rewards very early and very continuously. The return of cash money benefits would be an essential ingredient. Second, the welfare system was one which was sponsored and operated jointly by all levels of government. When recipients confronted it in their local community, that could start them on the path of politicalization which led them first to the local welfare department, then to the state welfare agency, then to the state legislatures and governors, and eventually to HEW, the Congress, and the president of the United States."

The June 30 demonstrations emphasized two of Wiley's central themes. First, a series of coordinated marches was chosen rather than one massive demonstration—and lack of money for transportation was not the only reason. Wiley was positive now that the mobilization of people in their own communities was the essential first step. The second theme was the interracial character of the new movement. "The Poverty/Rights Action Center," Wiley wrote, "seeks to unite the efforts of people of all races and ethnic backgrounds into cooperative action against poverty and injustice."

"This is for all people, not just Negroes," echoed Mrs. Lilia Calloway, a black Washington welfare recipient.

Stretched out in the aluminum lawn chair in his spartan office, Wiley pasted clippings on the June 30 demonstrations into a scrapbook he entitled "Birth of a Movement," which he xeroxed and distributed to his mailing lists. And then he plotted his next move, knowing full well that a one-day demonstration is not a movement.

23

Impossible Mission

The experts said it couldn't be done—the people at the bottom layer of society, the *Lumpenproletariat,* could not be organized. Karl Marx had written that the unemployed poor, because they had no relationship to the means of production, no central workplace, were incapable of launching a political struggle. Nearly a century later, scholars still followed that theory. Social scientists such as Edward Banfield attributed to the poor of America attitudes of fatalism, apathy, and passivity, as well as a general sense of hopelessness. One would certainly not expect recipients of Aid for Families with Dependent Children to become politically active. AFDC recipients were generally female heads of households. In the words of another social scientist, George T. Martin, Jr., "It is reasonable to speculate that such individuals are too harried by the daily exigencies of life to have any time or energy with which to participate in political activities"—an educated understatement to describe the lives of women who were barely surviving on the fringes of society.

American social history seemed to confirm the academic view that protest movements by the poor would fail, or at best win fleeting success or minor victories. Throughout history, blacks had staged periodic isolated rebellions. These usually were crushed quickly. A "Back to Africa" crusade by Marcus Garvey* in the 1920s attracted enthusiasm and aroused black pride,

---

* Garvey rallied thousands around "black is beautiful" rhetoric and also spoke against middle- and upper-class blacks.

but had little lasting effect in organizing the black poor or solving their problems.

Nor did uprisings by the white poor in the twentieth century offer great hope. The labor union movement had scored great successes, but labor unions were successful, at least in part, because workers were already gathered together in specific workplaces where they could bring pressure to bear on employers. Poor people, without jobs, had no such focal point for action.

Several protest movements of the 1920s and 1930s hinted at the possibilities of organizing, but these were ultimately defeated. Writer-activist Upton Sinclair had organized the End Poverty in California (EPIC) program, but it fizzled after Sinclair waged a losing campaign for governor. The Bonus Marchers, World War I veterans suffering from the Depression, marched on Washington to seek relief, but the U.S. Army, on President Hoover's orders, drove them out of the city. Dr. Francis E. Townsend, who claimed two million members for his Townsend Plan for pensions for the elderly, also faded into obscurity, though he contributed to the passage of the 1935 Social Security Act. Townsend's followers, however, were not the hopeless poor, but basically middle-class citizens, who had been struck by a combination of old age and Depression economics. Huey Long, the demagogic, populist governor of Louisiana, formulated the "Share the Wealth" plan, but he died of an assassin's bullet before his idea could be tested. The most promising effort of protest politics during the Depression was the Workers Alliance of the unemployed led by David Lasser, an engineer and writer. Its vigorous efforts helped force the Roosevelt administration to create various work relief programs, including the WPA. But the Alliance splintered when one wing was captured by the Communists and preparations for World War II eased the unemployment crisis. By 1941 the Alliance was dead. But, again, the Workers Alliance drew its support from solid working-class and middle-class people temporarily injured by the Depression. Finally, there was now the inability of the civil rights movement to organize the poorest of the black poor.

George Wiley was not an historian nor a sociologist. The poor people he knew and admired—the Inez Heards and Anna Mae Williamses—led him to believe that the poor could mobilize to help themselves. His own failures had only stiffened his determination. He now knew what didn't work—not that nothing would work. Poverty would not be swept away by proposing a law to end it. Wiley believed in the nuts-and-bolts, step-by-step approach. The civil rights movement and antipoverty programs had trained hundreds of potential organizers; the rhetoric of the sixties had given the poor a ray of hope. In 1966, George Wiley saw himself as a connector—a social chemist who was combining unknown elements.

He studied the welfare statistics to learn where his army was to be found: 8.6 million people were receiving welfare benefits—of whom 2.1 million were aged (Old Age Assistance), 85,000 were blind (Aid to the Blind),

583,000 were disabled (Aid to the Permanently and Totally Disabled), 649,000 were on general assistance, and the largest group, 4.6 million, were mothers and their dependent children (Aid to Dependent Children, or ADC).* It was this last group, of whom millions more were eligible but not getting benefits, that became Wiley's target.

When Congress approved the Social Security Act of 1935, it established these four programs as temporary expedients to take care of the unfortunate who could not qualify immediately for regular Social Security benefits. It was hoped that, with the growth of the social security system, virtually all needy people would be covered. The Roosevelt administration and Congress liked to think of the typical ADC recipient as a West Virginia mother whose husband had died in a mining accident—she was "God-fearing, white, Protestant, and rural."

For the first twenty years, the program attracted little public attention. The ADC rolls grew very slowly and, at times, even decreased. There were 372,000 women and children, almost all whites, on ADC by 1940, but wartime prosperity led to a reduction to 274,000 in 1945. After World War II, the rolls grew again to 651,000 in 1950, as men returned from the war and many women lost their temporary place in the working class. The number of welfare recipients had dropped back to 602,000 in 1955. Then came a curious development. Although the country was jolted by two severe economic recessions in the middle and late fifties, the ADC rolls, considering the hard times, grew relatively little—from 602,000 in 1955 to 803,000 in 1960.

The ADC statistics from the Deep South tell a revealing story. In 1940, nine states, five of them in the Deep South, each had fewer than 1,000 families on the welfare rolls. Texas had a total caseload of 85, and in Mississippi, the poorest state, only 104 families got ADC assistance. In seven southern states, the proportion of blacks among those accepted for the ADC program was even smaller than the proportion of blacks among all children. In Georgia, for example, 38 percent of all children under age fifteen were black, but only 11 percent of all children receiving ADC were black.

The figures revealed a pattern of racism and disregard of the law in the way the states and local governments operated the ADC program. (Aid to Dependent Children was administered by state and local governments which, in theory, operated under some rules and regulations from the federal government, which supplied one-half or more of the money.)

In 1966, the Department of Health, Education, and Welfare's Advisory Council on Public Welfare concluded that millions legally entitled to benefits were denied them, and declared that "large numbers of those in desperate need, including many children, are excluded" from receiving public assis-

---

* Later named "Aid to Families with Dependent Children" (AFDC).

tance benefits. State and local governments—using a variety of strategies often winked at or overlooked by the federal government—kept people off the welfare rolls and the grants small.

When Wiley's early efforts pushed the federal government to investigate further, HEW discovered that thirty-nine out of fifty states operated their welfare systems out of compliance with federal regulations. The system was operated in most states so as to grant the least possible money to the fewest possible people. Occasionally, a brave federal official attempted to force the states and counties to comply with federal laws and court orders, but these efforts usually were lost in the paper shuffle.

The mass urban migrations of the 1950s and 1960s put enormous pressure on the system. The industrialization of agriculture, particularly of cotton in the South, sent millions of unskilled farm workers and their families to look for work in northern cities. The work was not there. The number of unskilled jobs was shrinking, and factories were leaving the cities. Inner cities were jammed with thousands of poor people who could not begin to cope with the complexities of urban life, let alone support themselves. Racial discrimination in employment made things even tougher for black immigrants. Divorce and desertion became a fact of life as men could not support their families, and thousands of women, both black and white, struggled in an alien environment to feed and clothe their children.

Yet the welfare rolls still did not expand significantly. In the fifties and early sixties, most of the women coped as best they could, with irregular jobs as domestics or low-paying service jobs, or by leaning on relatives. Contrary to popular notion, the black immigrants did not come North to get on welfare. They came in search of work. Studies showed that most women receiving AFDC benefits had lived in the North at least several years before they applied for welfare. It was a last resort, one reluctantly chosen and, even then, not easily achieved. Most northern welfare departments made it difficult to get welfare. In the early sixties, welfare departments in New York and other cities gave destitute new arrivals a one-way bus ticket back home, but this cruel device was no answer. Planters no longer needed low-paid help for hand-picking and weeding of cotton, and as the displaced blacks moved north their one-room shacks were bulldozed.

The expansion of the AFDC welfare rolls finally began in the 1960s as the civil rights and antipoverty movements emboldened the urban poor to seek welfare. Antipoverty workers, including legal service lawyers, were beginning to help the poor apply for benefits and fight their way through the bureaucratic maze. When northern cities erupted in riots, officials sometimes responded by easing entry to welfare for people who for years had been eligible for benefits.

For the first time, politicians and the public began to worry about welfare. Although more than 50 percent of AFDC recipients were still white, the image of the welfare recipient was no longer the white coal miner's widow. The rolls were increasingly filled with black mothers who had been deserted or had not been married at all.

Wiley hoped to turn the growth in the rolls into a welfare explosion. In a 1966 interview, he talked about his hopes: "A lot of us who have come out of the civil rights movement have been quite frustrated about finding significant handles for bringing about some substantial change in the living conditions of people in the northern ghettoes. The potential for major economic pressure through trying to encourage people to gain their rights in the welfare system is one that has had an immediate response, and has been enormously attractive to activists working in urban areas.

"For millions—particularly people who can't work, the aged or female heads of households—just encouraging them to assert their rights is a very attractive thing. I think that this strategy is going to catch on, and be very important in the time ahead. A crisis strategy has been the only one that has really produced major successes in the civil rights field. The potential here is enormous for getting the people involved in demanding rights as human beings from a system that doesn't treat them as human beings."

With one victory behind him, Wiley moved quickly. He fired off invitations to a "national welfare rights meeting" which would, he said, be "the next step in the development of this new movement." When this second meeting convened on August 6, 1966, at the South Side YMCA in Chicago, Wiley was surrounded by 136 people who had come from twenty-four cities and represented seventy-five different organizations. It was a motley group—civil rights workers, SDS members, social workers, community-action agency employees, organizers, academics, and a large group of unknown and very angry welfare mothers.

Wiley was determined that this was not going to be another "cadre" movement with educated, middle-class professionals trying to lead the masses like sheep. The poor had to be involved in all stages of the process, including planning meeting agendas. Wiley sensed also that the newly militant poor who were rising as leaders in their neighborhoods and local communities were no longer in a mood to be told what was good for them by professionals, no matter how pure their motives.

Hulbert James, a young black community organizer from Louisville, Kentucky, said that one of his strongest recollections of the meeting was the tension between professionals "with very precise ideas about what they wanted to do" and welfare mothers "who were not going to get into something where the case worker types told them what to do." To be successful, the movement would have to blend carefully the talents of the professionals with the interests of the women.

Wiley's plan for the meeting, drafted with two welfare recipient leaders, called for general meetings to exchange ideas and workshop training sessions to discuss organizing strategies and tactics, to plan national goals for immediate and long-range welfare reform, and to discuss national strategy for the next steps in a nationwide action for welfare rights.

Mrs. Tillmon, the president of Los Angeles' ANC Mothers Anonymous, described the meetings: "People just started talking. We found out that all over the country the attitudes of the general public and the welfare departments were the same toward anybody on welfare. The people from New York got treated by the social workers and the other people the same as they did in Mississippi. The only difference was money.*

"It was very exciting. Most of us had never been anywhere before, never met other people outside our own cities, never had an opportunity to talk about ourselves, our organizations, or our community. There was discussion all the time—a buzz, buzz, buzz—from the time we got there Friday night. People felt something they never felt before. They knew they weren't alone in the situation. Everybody was suffering from the same problems.

"It was a very different experience. In the past, most of us had been so ashamed that we were on welfare that we wouldn't even admit it to another welfare recipient. But as we talked to each other, we forgot about that shame, and as we listened to the horrible treatment and conditions all over the country, we could begin thinking about the idea that maybe it wasn't us that should be ashamed."

At the training sessions, welfare mothers from New York City and Cleveland explained how they had learned the welfare regulations, discovering that they were entitled to benefits they weren't getting, and then described how they had started demanding their rights under the law. Wiley's constant repetition of the word *rights* got through to the women. Most of them had been led to believe that they didn't have any rights under welfare, not even the right to look at the welfare manual to find the rules and regulations under which they received the dole. The message of the meeting was that they not only had rights, but that if they acted collectively and had the nerve to demand their rights, they could actually get them.

At the final meeting all agreed to go home and launch a three-month organizing drive, either to build up their own small welfare rights groups or to start new ones. Finally, the future form of the movement came up for discussion. There was an uproar, as the women disagreed about how soon a new organization should be formed, and who should belong to it.

Despite the pressure for immediate formation of a national welfare rights organization, Wiley prevailed with less ambitious plans for an eleven-

* Welfare payments for a four-member family in 1966 averaged $32 a month in Mississippi, $208 in New York, and $146 nationwide—all far less than the $270 which would bring a family's income up to the official government poverty line.

member national coordinating committee, with one member to be elected from each state represented at the meeting. The new coordinating committee would meet to plan the next steps of national action. Wiley and P/RAC would hold a series of regional meetings to train people in the techniques of organizing.

Ed Day: "It took a great deal of diplomacy on George's part to turn that around. We were not hell-bent on forming another national organization, with P/RAC as headquarters. We were too embryonic, we had been through paper-tiger organizations, and we were worried about locking ourselves into a structure which would later inhibit us. We envisioned ourselves as a headquarters for this sort of thing, a servicing center.

"Welfare was not going to be our sole activity. It would be case study number one. There was going to be a welfare rights organization, and then an old people's organization, a tenants' organization—a whole variety of grass-roots organizations, each doing their own thing. And eventually, they would be brought together under one giant umbrella of a national poor people's organization."

The meeting produced one major document. It embodied their vision of a more humane, just society, and enumerated both the long-range and immediate objectives of the new movement. The statement began:

> Our rights are not for sale. We are not willing to sell our rights as American citizens, our rights to dignity, our rights to justice, our rights to democracy—to obtain the food, clothing and shelter which our age, our disability, the absence or death of our family's breadwinner, our lack of economic opportunity, our society have made us unable to provide.
>
> Our goal is: jobs or income now! Decent jobs with adequate wages for those who can work; adequate income for those who can not work."

And then came four general goals which would become the "bill of rights" of the movement:

> 1. Adequate income: A system which guarantees enough money for all Americans to live dignified lives above the level of poverty.
> 2. Dignity: A system which guarantees welfare recipients the same full freedoms, rights and respect as all American citizens.
> 3. Justice: A fair and open system which guarantees recipients the full protection of the Constitution.
> 4. Democracy: A system which guarantees recipients direct participation in the decisions under which they must live.

Except for a guaranteed job or income, most Americans took these rights for granted—for themselves, but not for the welfare poor. In 1966, the legislatures, the courts, and public opinion in general held that the welfare poor received their dole at the mercy and sufferance of the state. For welfare recipients, the assertion of these basic rights was revolutionary.

The statement then listed specific complaints against welfare departments. These were an indictment of the system itself. They called for the end of:

> Midnight raids, and other searches and seizures without search warrants.
> Giving recipients smaller grants than the law says they should be getting.
> Not giving recipients "special grants" for heavy clothing, household furnishings, etc. which the law says they should get.
> Illegally cutting people off welfare.
> Threatening, scaring, or intimidating recipients.
> Discriminating against families with so-called illegitimate children.
> Discriminating against large families.
> Racial discrimination.
> Forcing recipients to accept social services in order to keep their grants.
> Not informing recipients of their rights of appeal.
> Making friends or non-legally responsible relatives pay child support.
> Forcing mothers with young children to take jobs.
> Forcing recipients to live in segregated or substandard housing.
> Illegally rejecting applicants for welfare.

These demands were not theoretical ideas from academics who had taught Wiley about the welfare system. They came out of the general meetings at which the welfare mothers spoke out.

The statement then outlined short-term goals for improving the welfare system. These told more trenchantly than any study how the system had failed:

> Recognition of welfare recipient organizations as representatives of welfare recipients, including the rights to pass out information at welfare centers and to be with recipients at interviews and fair hearings.
> Making public to welfare recipients, their organizations, and anyone who wants to know, all the rules, regulations, and policies of welfare departments rather than hiding these public documents.
> Full budgets and welfare grants based on current cost of living standards, rather than, as in many states, cost of living standards of the 1950s.
> Full budgets and grants for all recipients, rather than the practice in many states in which recipients receive only a percentage of the state's own grant standards for minimum health and decency.
> Fair hearings, immediately, with free lawyers for recipients who believe they have been treated illegally or unfairly by welfare departments. Many states do not provide the fair hearings called for by federal regulations.
> Direct representation of welfare recipients' organizations on all welfare policy-making and advisory boards.
> Clearer and simplified welfare regulations, policies, and procedures.

Property maximums for welfare eligibility set at equal to one year's income at the federal poverty line, rather than at such low levels that persons must give up their homes, cars, and even small cash reserves to qualify for welfare.

Clerical and sub-professional jobs in welfare departments for recipients who are able to and wish to work.

Getting rid of special investigation units in welfare departments.

Allowing all recipients to earn some money without deducting it from their welfare grants.

Ending all liens by welfare departments on welfare recipients' property.

Making all banks cash welfare checks.

Providing child care for welfare mothers who are able to and wish to work.

Providing real job training and actual jobs for recipients who are able to and wish to work.

Finally, the statement listed long-range goals for reform of the nation's welfare system. It was only in this area of government reform that Wiley and the other professionals added their own ideas:

National federal grant minimums set at or above the federal poverty line to replace the fifty state minimums, which varied widely.

Ending the various categories of assistance (Aid to the Disabled, Aid to the Aged, Aid to Families with Dependent Children) and having only one category for assistance—need.

Welfare grants for all people in need who have incomes below grant levels, including people who are employed.

Wiley and the women had identified the problems, written their declaration of independence and their bill of rights. Now they had to fight the war.

24

Putting the
Pieces Together

A national apparatus had to be created. Grass-roots organizing had to begin in dozens of neighborhoods and communities. Organizers—smart, energetic, and motivated—would have to be found and trained to do the job. There would have to be a cadre of welfare recipients who could assume leadership roles in the movement. The local groups would have to be merged into larger groups and, finally, a national organization. An education and public relations campaign was necessary. Funds had to be raised to do all these things. Finally, Wiley had to coordinate the whole complex operation.

He was a whirlwind of activity, yet he did not give the impression of being a driven man. He was amiable and easygoing with everyone—hostile government officials, rivals for power, rich philanthropists, temperamental organizers, angry welfare mothers. Details rarely escaped him, but his mode of organization defied rational explanation. He switched his attention quickly from one subject to another. And he instinctively went for the main chance, seizing whatever opportunity he could. The first one came when he returned to Washington in August, 1966, from the second Chicago meeting.

When civil rights and local community-action program leaders met in New York to protest cutbacks in the federal antipoverty programs, Wiley again volunteered his fledgling organization for leadership, directing a Poor People's March on Washington. After a month of frantic work by Wiley and

Day, the march came off as planned on September 27, despite a soaking rain, more than two thousand poor people participated. Thirty-one delegations, from communities as disparate as Harlem and McComb, Mississippi, marched to the Capitol and then tried to visit with their congressmen. Wiley led a small group to meet with House Speaker John McCormack and Senate Minority Leader Everett Dirksen.

But the experience convinced Wiley that seeking to move on the whole broad front of poverty issues was a useless dissipation of resources. By 1966, the War on Poverty and the federal Office of Economic Opportunity were under severe attack. News accounts daily reported chaos in OEO programs, misuse of federal funds, political infighting for control of programs. Many felt left out; it was said that the programs concentrated too heavily on the black poor to the exclusion of other minorities and poor whites. As for the middle class, they believed too much was being gained too fast, no matter for whom. There was legitimate criticism of high-sounding programs which did not address the primary needs—for food, housing, jobs, and money. The election of November, 1966, swept out of Congress the huge Democratic majority, which had passed the wave of social legislation. Wiley decided that little progress would be made trying to improve the OEO programs. In late 1966, he began to concentrate exclusively on the welfare issue.

At the pink house on R Street, Wiley and his small staff geared up to get a welfare rights movement off the ground. There was Ed Day, associate director for research and program development; Doris Castle, community relations representative; Nancy Steadman, secretary and administrator, who had done a similar job for James Farmer at CORE. Tim Sampson, a California social worker, moved to Washington at a big cut in pay to join the group. They kept the mimeograph hot, the telephones ringing, and the airlines well supplied with business as they worked up mailing lists, ground out promotion and information materials—red, white, and blue banners and slogans proclaiming "More Money Now." They adopted an emblem of two linked circles that symbolized the "uniting of the civil rights and antipoverty movements into a strengthened link in the cause of human freedom." The pamphlets, inexpensively printed on colored paper, were crucial. They described clearly and simply how to set up meetings, how to organize local actions, and how to promote these actions with the news media.

The office ran on enthusiasm. It had to—there was never enough personnel or money. The initial funds amounted to the five-thousand-dollar sixty-day loan from Irving Fain from whom Wiley had solicited funds for CORE. Fain was impressed by Wiley's ideas of self-help for the poor, by the reputation of the Wiley family in Providence, by George's presentation, and by the fact that the loan was repaid promptly. He advanced more money, and Wiley was launched on a fund-raising effort. The initial kitty was about fifty thousand dollars.

Wretha Wiley said George was most excited by the welfare recipients: "He saw so much in their potential for building the kinds of local organizations it would take to create a movement. I remember his talking about those women: 'very strong, articulate, shrewd, smart, savvy, manipulative, cunning, very effective.' They were very direct, and as a teacher, he judged they would be very quick and good students."

Wiley's next job was to get the women back together again, to train them, and begin to make a union out of the tiny, sporadic welfare protests that erupted randomly around the country. He might see potential in the women, but he had not yet proved either himself or his idea to them. The next step would be a meeting of the National Coordinating Committee, created in Chicago last August. It would meet in Pittsburgh on December 21 to take the next steps to transform itself from a paper organization to a functioning one. Merely bringing the women together again was a problem. Wiley borrowed some more money, told the women how to raise their own, and pleaded with them to get to Pittsburgh.

Wiley had planned carefully for the meeting. But what he didn't count on was the joy the women, all strangers before Chicago, would have at seeing each other again, and the electricity that joy would generate. None of them, it seemed, had really believed they would ever see each other again. Wiley had the women up at 6:00 A.M. and crammed the day with training sessions. He taught them how to study welfare regulations, how to prepare organizing campaign literature, and foremost, how to learn about their opponents in advance, and to avoid scrupulously any improprieties, since they would be under constant surveillance from the FBI.

As George Wiley sat around the table at the Central Avenue YMCA with the eight women from the National Coordinating Committee,* he was struck by one thing. Beneath their rough language and their gropings to understand the complexities of welfare law, there was a great similarity between what these welfare mothers wanted and his own mother's aspirations and activities in Rhode Island. They wanted better lives and opportunities for their children. And they wanted an organization. They wanted a group of their own, with officers and conventions and elections.

Out of his own political philosophy as well as his desire to follow the wishes of the women, Wiley began to see prospects of change through a formal organization. Militant tactics, yes. But he saw that the poor might pry their way into the system, taking a place as another power bloc in the traditional democratic process. In only a few months, the number of groups in

---

*Etta Horn, Washington, D.C.; Dovie Coleman, Illinois; Edith Doering, Ohio; Kate Emmerson, Michigan; Marian Kidd, New Jersey; Margaret McCarthy, Maryland; Alice Nixon, Pennsylvania; Johnnie Tillmon, California.

the welfare rights network had doubled, totaling 170 in sixty cities in twenty-three states. The membership, now estimated at more than four thousand, had doubled, too.

At Pittsburgh the leadership structure of the organization was shaped, as was Wiley's role in it. During their talks about officers and duties, one of the women proposed Wiley as chairman. A majority of the eight women present seconded the idea. "No," Wiley replied, "the officers of this group should be the welfare recipients themselves, representatives of the local groups." His suggestion was accepted. He truly thought that the most effective, legitimate leaders of the poor should be the poor themselves. Yet he was, and would remain, ambivalent about his own position of power. He wanted prestige. He wanted to run things. But he chose to seek that personal gratification through his role as teacher and coordinator.

Some of his aides argued that the movement needed a single dramatic, charismatic leader. It would be most effective for Wiley to seize the singular leadership role; it would be easier for the news media to focus on one person. In the end, there was a rough sharing of power between Wiley and the women. The National Coordinating Committee officially designated the Poverty/Rights Action Center as the national headquarters of welfare rights groups. Wiley was to be national director. His job, to coordinate welfare rights groups.

Back in Washington, Wiley concentrated on three things: a newsletter which would let groups around the country exchange information; the formation of new local groups; developing a staff and technical materials for training the grass-roots leaders. The *Welfare Rights Newsletter* reported encouraging news:

• The West Side Organization in Chicago had processed more than one thousand welfare grievances and set up a dues-paying system, organizing recipients into a primitive union.

• The Welfare Recipients League of Patterson, New Jersey, staged two weeks of picketing at welfare department headquarters, protesting for emergency winter clothing allowances and mattresses, so that children would not have to sleep two and three to a bed. The county government agreed to negotiate their grievances and to correct violations of state law.

• In Cleveland, the Welfare Grievance Committee, after a summer of struggle, had won the right of any welfare recipient to see the departmental regulations on request, and the right to represent welfare clients before the welfare administration.

• In Wiley's home city of Providence, a group of welfare recipients called Welfare Improvements Now published a manual on welfare problems and won a hearing from the Mayor's Commission on Human Relations.

• In California, thirty-two groups linked together into a Welfare Rights

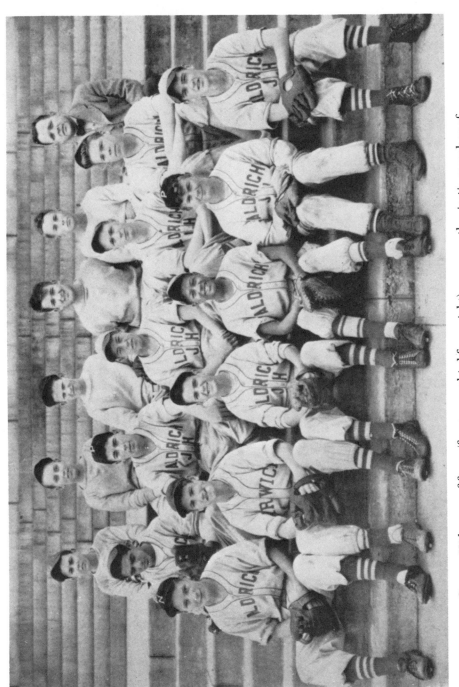

George Wiley, age fifteen (front row, third from right) was an enthusiastic member of the Nelson Aldrich Junior High School baseball team.

Wiley as a college student at
University of Rhode Island.

William Wiley, the proud father of two ROTC cadets at the University of Rhode Island. George (left) and Alton (right).

Wiley (far right, standing) began a long career of "always the first black, the only black" by crossing the racial barrier in his college fraternity, Phi Mu Delta, in 1950. (He was named, posthumously, to the national fraternity's Hall of Fame.)

Assistant Professor "Smiley Wiley" drove his beloved Austin-Healy from California to Syracuse in 1960, arriving with "a foot of water sloshing around" because he loved to drive with the top down.

Honeymooning with Wretha in June, 1961. Wiley and his bride had spent "hours discussing how to handle discrimination problems because of their marriage—only to have none." The problems would come later, when a white wife was considered a liability.

Daniel Kent Wiley was born in October, 1962, during the height of Wiley's fight to integrate the public schools of Syracuse, New York.

Danny, left, and Maya, George and Wretha's children.

The quiet college professor, always in white shirt and bow tie, became a militant leader in Syracuse CORE, the first step toward changing the direction of his life.

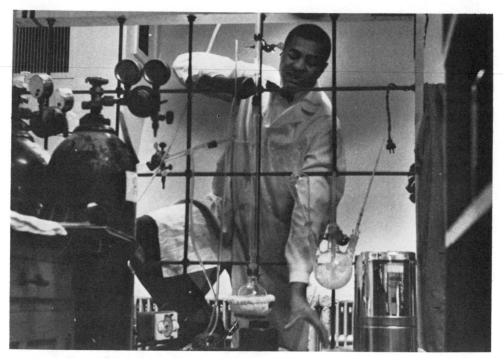

From Syracuse, Wiley sent friends a photo of "the mad professor" in his chemistry lab. From 1960 to 1965, his research and teaching made inroads in the field of organic chemistry.

Wiley, as associate national director of CORE, leads a 1965 civil rights rally in New York City.

Wiley often spent hours at a time on the telephone, sometimes conducting several conversations at once on different phones, as he tried to direct the widespread activities of the NWRO.

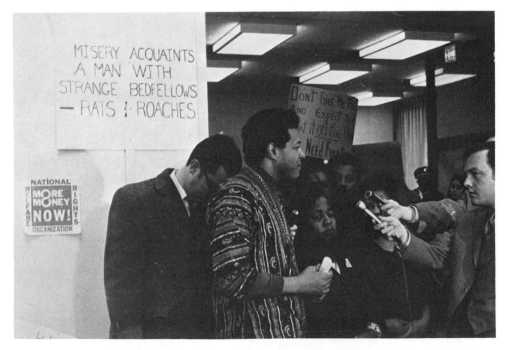

Wiley leads a protest at a New York City welfare center.

Johnnie Tillmon, NWRO chairman, along with Beulah Sanders and Eliza Williams, testifying at a congressional hearing on welfare reform.

While NWRO chairman Johnnie Tillmon holds her grandchild and listens, Wiley tells Dr. Martin Luther King, Jr., about the realities of the welfare system at a tense 1968 meeting.

Wiley and the Reverend Jesse Jackson, leaders of the 1968 Poor People's Campaign in Washington, urge on their supporters at a hearing on Capitol Hill.

NWRO members picket in front of the Cuyahoga County Welfare Department office in Cleveland on September 3, 1969. The demonstrators later took over the building.

Welfare mothers from Connecticut join hands with Wiley to encircle Connecticut Welfare Commissioner Harder.

Wiley meets with activist Dick Gregory, an early and consistent supporter of NWRO, and attorney Barbara Williams.

Wiley and NWRO members at a seminar explaining welfare rights.

Wiley and Ruby Duncan, NWRO chairman in Las Vegas, enlist the support of entertainer Sammy Davis, Jr., for a Nevada march protesting welfare cutbacks.

Wiley leads a march in Las Vegas protesting a state action which cut thousands off welfare.

Wiley addresses a NWRO national convention.

Organization and won a protest campaign to get better and more accurate processing of medical identification cards, after the death of a baby who failed to receive prompt care because of a bureaucratic mishandling of an ID card.

• The League for Adequate Welfare, a collection of neighborhood groups in St. Louis, won larger grants, an end to midnight raids, elimination of residency requirements for welfare aid, and a special clothing allowance for school-age children.

These represented only a sampling of local efforts. From New York City came the biggest success story of all. Five welfare recipient groups on the Lower East Side banded together to form the Emergency Council for Winter Clothing. Hundreds of recipients invaded welfare centers with forms for the clothing allowances, to which they were legally entitled but which they seldom received. After several days of protest, the applications were processed and several hundred families received checks for from fifty to a hundred dollars to meet their emergency clothing needs. Wiley and the Washington office had helped. They designed a do-it-yourself kit which welfare recipients used to challenge their local welfare offices. The kit, called "More Money Now," was a model for similar guides distributed all over the country.

The "basic needs campaign" reached a culmination on June 30, 1967, the anniversary of the Ohio march. The "basic needs form" distributed from Washington was used to organize protests and marches on welfare offices throughout the country. More than five thousand people participated in forty cities, and some groups successfully filed their requests for greater welfare assistance.

All this activity, reported in the newsletter, generated new ideas and new actions. It was just what Wiley had hoped for. The success of his work became clear on February 5, when the National Coordinating Committee held its second meeting, this time in Washington. Wiley had expected seventy-five people to show up, but instead 375 came. Many had to sleep on the floors and couches of the Wiley home and those of other staff members.

The Washington meeting was another success. For help here, Wiley again turned to the university world. His most important new contact was Edward V. Sparer, director of the Columbia University Center on Social Welfare Policy and Law. Sparer was considered the nation's most original thinker in the area of welfare law, the attorney who figured out a variety of techniques to challenge the inequities of the welfare system and went to the courts to win rightful benefits for the recipients.* Equally important, Sparer

*Sparer assisted Carl Rachlin, who served as NWRO's first attorney, solving legal problems for the new organization.

was willing to work on issues which would help recipients not only to gain benefits but to organize. Unlike many public service lawyers, he was willing to let his client, the movement itself, establish the legal priorities.

Sparer's first contribution was a simplified welfare rights handbook and an analysis of federal regulations most pertinent to local welfare offices. Those booklets were handed out to the 375 women who jammed into the Sunday School rooms of the Washington church. Sparer's basic handbook was the model for others by which welfare recipients could understand their rights. Sparer would lead the way in winning a dozen Supreme Court decisions establishing the rights of welfare recipients; the preliminary work for those lawsuits was being laid out at that Washington meeting.

For three days the women attended seminars on welfare law. They learned the procedures of filing appeals. There were meetings on the concept of a guaranteed annual income. Other sessions concentrated on organizing and showed how various local groups had built their membership by applying for and winning legal entitlement.

The question of leadership was still unresolved. If other antipoverty meetings at this time were any example, the scene was programmed for chaos; groups often split into angry factions, including black caucuses and white caucuses which fought bitterly for control. Wiley's group was not a gathering of middle-class clubwomen or professional men, whose political struggles were settled through well-defined institutional arrangements. It was a group of poor, uneducated women unfamiliar with power and Robert's Rules of Order, and highly suspicious of the professionals who sought to guide and, they feared, to control them. There was an initial struggle over who should control the meeting—the women or the young professional organizers, most of whom were middle-class white radicals. The women from Massachusetts decided that "Whitey" was still running the show and walked out in protest.

Most of the women did not know Wiley; they didn't know or trust his motives, either. Just who was this light-skinned college professor with the New England accent? What was his game? The welfare women were suspicious of many black male leaders, who, they felt, ignored them, exploited them, and sometimes degraded them. Johnnie Tillmon: "George had told me he was from CORE, and my only comment was that I didn't like CORE, and he said, 'Well, why don't you like CORE?' And I said, ' 'Cause CORE is not interested in no integrating; those CORE leaders are interested in intermating.' And George cracked up laughing." Later, after Johnnie Tillmon met Wretha Wiley, she joked with another welfare mother, "Why in the world didn't you tell me that George Wiley was white?"

It didn't matter to Johnnie Tillmon and to many of the other black welfare women that Wiley was married to a white woman. Everything about his manner, his personal relations with them, his public conduct of meetings assured them that he was not an exploiter of women, black or white. Also, the welfare women did not share the rigid anti-white, black power ideology. The early women leaders of NWRO wanted an integrated movement of poor people. Welfare recipients, nationally, were 53 percent white.

Ed Day: "Stokely Carmichael and some of those other black power guys were running around openly laughing at George, because at this time we were starting an interracial organization. But that was our cornerstone. We weren't about to cut out and lose a chance for support from one half of the country's welfare recipients, who were white. The black power guys were also disdainful of George because he was organizing women. Black men at that period were very intent on freeing themselves from the image of a maternalistic, matriarchal black society, and here we are out organizing black women, and white ones too. Everybody was going one way and George was going another, all by himself."

But Wiley's personal manner and style forestalled any acrimonious splits. Johnnie Tillmon: "He was calm; he had a very good sense of humor, and he had come to get a job done. He made a very brief speech and then he spent the rest of the time just listening, and putting things together. He had no hang-ups, no middle-class attitudes of disdain about us welfare mothers. And he wasn't the kind of person that flaunted his educational background in your face. Oh, he would argue his point, all right, but mainly he would sit and listen."

The conference was also salvaged from chaos by the emergence of Mrs. Tillmon as a leader. The members of the National Coordinating Committee elected her to chair the conference. She recalled the experience: "I was put in a position where everyone was looking to me for leadership, but I had no more ability to be no leader than they did. It turned out very good because those other folks didn't know any more than I did. We were like feeling our way along, and learning together. It was just like a classroom and George was teaching."

Wiley's attitude toward the women and toward the chaos of the meetings was realistically premised on working with people as they are. He knew by then that poor people were angry, disorganized, disrespectful, sometimes unruly, and even irrational. He accepted them the way they were. He had come to work with them.

The conference concluded its private business by expanding the National Coordinating Committee to twenty-five members (providing representation to new states with welfare rights organizations) and by adopting a clear set of legislative goals for the Ninetieth Congress. The next day was spent in coordinated lobbying efforts on Capitol Hill. Each member of the National Coordinating Committee visited her congressman to push for welfare reform, including a guaranteed annual income.

The lobbying group then turned its attention to the Johnson administration. The White House ignored a telephone request for a meeting. When John Gardner, the secretary of Health, Education, and Welfare (HEW), also refused a meeting, the women grew angry and prepared to march on the White House and HEW. Wiley advised further efforts at negotiation and finally arranged a meeting with Joseph Meyers, HEW's deputy commissioner of welfare. To the astonishment of HEW officials, seventy-five women piled into Meyer's office, sitting on his desk, the chairs, and the floor. They found a sympathetic listener.

Meyers agreed that many states flouted federal welfare regulations but said that the federal government had neither the power nor the inclination to push the states into compliance. The women poured out hundreds of complaints, many of which Meyers acknowledged, but suggested that he was powerless to act without higher authority and public support. The meeting was significant because Wiley and the women learned that there were civil servants in HEW who cared about their problems and would try to help. In the thirty-one-year history of the Social Security Act, which had established the welfare program, no such meetings with the poor had ever taken place. A new avenue had been opened.

The mimeograph machine in the back room of the pink house ran night and day as Wiley, Day, and Sampson prepared the booklets that would educate their growing constituency. Each budding welfare rights group around the country received a steady barrage of "how to" books, telling about their legal rights, how to organize, how to raise money, how to get publicity, how to lobby, how to file lawsuits.

Meanwhile, Wiley began a series of cross-country flights, scurrying from city to city to raise money, seek out volunteer organizers, and to settle arguments between rival groups. At each airport stopover, he was on the pay telephones, making new contacts and checking on operations in Washington.

He took some of the women on a cross-county fund-raising trip and spoke before groups of federal and local antipoverty program employees, urging them to support the movement. He testified before the House Agriculture Committee in March, 1967, describing in detail to unsympathetic congressmen the defects in federal food aid programs, defects that Senator Robert Kennedy and others would soon discover and turn into another new crusade. And he met regularly with middle-echelon federal bureaucrats to press complaints about abuses in federal welfare and food aid programs.

In trying to knit together a national movement, Wiley had to convince a lot of people to alter their own agendas to make room for the issue of welfare rights. Mrs. Tillmon says he was successful because of his manner with all sorts of different groups: "He never pretended that he knew everything. He never gave nobody the impression that he was God's gift to poor people. He didn't say he was going to come in and save the world or change the entire system. But he had some ideas on how some of it could be done. He listened to the other people. I think he respected folks and he also demanded respect in return."

He was moving at a furious pace, some would say a reckless one for a man who wanted to conserve his energies and his life. (For example, on a trip to San Francisco with Mrs. Tillmon, driving in a rented Volkswagen, he discovered he was going the wrong way and made an abrupt U-turn in the middle of a fast-moving, crowded freeway, nearly causing a mass collision.) And in the process of building his organization he was taking even less time than at CORE for his own family.

Wretha Wiley: "In Syracuse, and to some extent in national CORE, we had worked together as a team. In Washington, we no longer did. At first, it was a necessity. We needed a steady, reliable income, and so I got a job. George didn't want me involved in welfare rights, and I became busy with my own professional life. I spent every spare moment with the children. He was consumed by the movement. Home became a rest stop, and when he came home he was totally exhausted." He would collapse at home for a day or two of rest and be on his way again.

Wiley was hatching the next grand step. He thought the "movement" was ready to become a formalized national organization.

25

Convention:

The Founding Mothers

The creation of a National Welfare Rights Organization versus a free-form protest movement had from the outset been a subject of debate between Wiley and Cloward and Piven, the original theorists of welfare organizing. Cloward and Piven objected to a formalized national organization. They intended to bring about welfare reform by overloading and breaking the system.

Some of Wiley's aides feared that the Cloward-Piven approach, which they described as "disrupting and praying," was more likely to provoke repression than inspire positive change. They still leaned to the traditional technique of building an organization that could capture power politically. Ed Day, on the other hand, saw the same pitfalls in a national organization as had befallen CORE. A national superstructure would merely waste energy and would end by devoting itself to self-preservation. Still others predicted different complications. "The ladies," as aides began to call the leaders on the National Coordinating Committee, were untutored in the ways of government. They were not "ready" for a national organization, which would thus be little more than a paper tiger.

Wiley saw the points of each argument, but he had a variety of motives for forming a national organization. He sympathized with welfare recipients yearning to be part of the American system—which meant PTAs, clubs, committees, honorific offices. The ladies wanted to belong, to be involved, and they wanted all the trappings of middle-class social life that mirrored a world from which they were excluded. Wiley saw nothing wrong in the poor joining the middle class.

But the heart of the argument between Wiley and Cloward and Piven was over which method might bring about real social change. Cloward and Piven recalled elements of the discussion, ranging from deep philosophical differences to George's own very human drive for power and recognition.

Cloward: "George believed that poor people had been manipulated by movement leaders. When the leaders had achieved their purpose, they moved on and the people were left alone. So he believed that poor people needed not only an organization, but an organization run by them. Not by the Wileys, not the Kings, not the Abernathys. But actually run by poor people themselves."

On another point, Cloward recalled: "George said the only way he could legitimize himself as the leader was to have a clearly marked out constituency of welfare recipients who acknowledged him as the leader. So that when he went to the press or to a foundation or to Congress, he could say, 'We are the Welfare Rights Organization.' Without that kind of legitimization, he questioned whether anybody would pay attention to his leadership or his ideas."

On the question of social change itself, Cloward remembers long discussions: "Frances and I said: 'George, when was there ever a time in this country when poor people had effective electoral influence? You don't understand the influence of money. You don't understand the nominating process and all of the other ways in which the system is controlled by other groups that have infinitely more important resources for influence than you have. All you have is those bodies, and you don't have that many of them. So what if you have twenty-five thousand dues-paying members, or even get a hundred thousand, or even if you could mobilize all twenty million poor people? This is a country made up of middle-class people.'

"George would reply that we were too cynical. George began to sense the possibilities for electoral influence—that they could be a factor in influencing state legislatures and even the damned Congress. In this sense he had in our opinion a very straightforwardly conventional view of political influence, namely that you mobilize a constituency, and through the promise of their supporting votes, or the implied threat of their voting defections, you influence political leaders. We argued that overloading the system was the way to get influence. Then, when New York was faced with welfare bankruptcy, Mayor Lindsay and Governor Rockefeller would become your lobbyists for change in Washington, not Johnnie Tillmon and Beulah Sanders."

At first, Wiley did think that he could flood the welfare rolls and build a traditional political force, both at the same time. At times he would agree with the two professors and tell them that he was going to do exactly what they had planned. Their continuing debates would be crucial much later, when Wiley was forced to decide irrevocably how to use his limited resources. But in August, 1967, he was optimistic; he thought he could accomplish everything.

The details of how the new organization should work had been carefully planned by Wiley and his aides and then approved by the National Coordinating Committee.

Wiley and Sampson had designed "a national membership plan" as a cornerstone to involve people at the grass-roots level. For recognition as a National Welfare Rights affiliate, each group would need at least twenty-five dues-paying members. Dues would be one dollar to join and one dollar a month. Half the membership fee and 20 percent of the dues would go to support the national organization. A majority of members in any group would have to be persons who were on welfare. Others could qualify for membership if their incomes fell below the official government poverty line, then thirty-five hundred dollars a year.

As the promotional literature put it, "Your group gets hooked up with all the welfare rights groups across the country working together to change the welfare system." Each group would be entitled to a full voting member in the National Welfare Rights movement at its convention. Additional voting strength would go to groups with more than twenty-five members. "You get a vote in the movement" was the slogan. Ed Day and Tim Sampson designed a "packaged, simple way to build your group's membership, collect dues, and make your group independent and strong." The package included materials for rosters, membership cards, and a guide for dues-collecting and distributing.

Each detail was carefully considered. Ed Day: "We thought that financial participation by the membership was critical. It would permit us some operating money, if all the liberal money dried up. But we thought financial participation, no matter how meager, was critical to developing the identity between the organization and the membership.

"The formula for deciding eligibility for membership and what constituted a qualified welfare group was carefully designed to insure that we would truly have an indigenous group of poor people. We didn't want these groups to be taken over by church people or social work people or other do-gooders. The civil rights cadre organizations disappeared because the middle-class members just walked away and did something else.

"The apportionment of voting power was another critical issue. Many groups, including Johnnie Tillmon's in California, were quite small, and if we were going to have a true democracy, we had to devise a representational plan in which the truly big groups, like those already formed in New York, would have voting power. If we didn't do that, the big groups wouldn't have stuck around for five minutes.

"And we also spent a great deal of time working on developing paraphernalia so people could feel they were a part of something. That is why there was such an early priority on printing up all those banners, buttons, and stickers that people could wear, wave, or put on their windows."

A month before the national convention, Wiley presented his action plan to the National Coordinating Committee, meeting in Cleveland at the church of the Reverend Paul Younger, an early movement leader. Tim Sampson: "I remember the feeling I had as George led the people through that plan. First was the very open way George did it, which inspired confidence on the part of the leadership, but also evoked their participation. The ladies were quick to attack him, not holding him in any awe at all. It was part of their style. They were always testing, testing. And George inspired confidence because he was such a secure man. He could listen to criticism and even abuse, and remain calm and seemingly very secure.

"I think he had respect for the women's ideas and respect for them as people. He also recognized that our ideas were being acted upon and he tried to create a situation where the ladies could express their ideas without whacking at his. There was always a normal, healthy tension then between the staff and the elected leadership, tension in terms of people's relative levels of sophistication. We knew a bunch of stuff that they didn't know. But George accepted them and they accepted George."

To some observers, the August 1967 founding convention, held in Washington, D.C., was pure chaos, but to Tim Sampson, "It was an orderly convention. It was run by the welfare recipients and they did a good job. The non-recipients, the organizers, and the staff sat on the sidelines where they belonged. The ladies ran a good show." Ed Day recalled the opening: "It was frightening. We had three or four hundred angry people who were very critical of our running of this operation. We were just absolutely flying by the seat of our pants, despite all the preparations. And at some point, Wiley stood up and said, 'If you think you can do it better, then you do it.' And then Wiley said, good-naturedly, 'It's a marriage between us and we can make it work.' It was kind of a put-up or shut-up situation and they finally shut up, and somehow we survived that meeting."

Wiley and Day knew that Johnnie Tillmon probably held the key to what the recipients might do. They knew that there would be a power struggle and that Tillmon would be in the middle of it. Ed Day: "The big question in our minds was whether she was going to pick up the organization and run with it for her own benefit. Was she going to use it as a stepping-stone to something else, or was she going to really be dedicated to the organization? It worked out pretty well, over the long haul, but we were scared."

Johnnie Tillmon also remembers: "It was pouring down rain that evening. People began to pour in, including Jennette Washington from New York. And Jennette says, 'You just watch your step. I'm here to observe. You better watch yourself 'cause New York got some shit for you.' Jennette was right—they had some, but it could have been worse.

"As temporary chairman of the convention, my job was to set up committees. And there was a nominating committee, a platform committee, and a constitution committee. I had made a decision there was going to be eleven people on the nominating committee and that's all.

"The New York people came in the next morning, ready. They had their stuff together. It wasn't just black folks raising hell. They had some whites and some Puerto Ricans. They told me they didn't know what was going on in the nominating committee and they wanted more representation on it.

"Next I'm accosted by about thirty Mississippi folks 'cause they wants to get on the nominating committee, but I told them, 'I done closed the nominating committee and I'm not going to open it for anybody.' Then the Californians descended on me with the same complaint, saying there was so few Californians there 'cause it was too expensive to make the trip.

"A heavy-set man from New York comes up and says, 'Mrs. Tillmon, you are going to elect yourself chairman, and if you deny that, you are a liar.' And I said, 'Mister, I ain't even running.'

"Pretty soon I was sitting on a step, surrounded by about thirty people, and the only thing you could see of me was one white shoe sticking out of that crowd. George saw all those folks standing over me and he came rushing up the hill. Well, when he gets there, I'm laughing and talking with folks so he keeps on going. He thought I was being killed.

"I was so busy talking to these people that I didn't even know that the elections had taken place until a young girl comes up to me and says, 'Congratulations. You just became chairman of the organization.' " If Mrs. Tillmon was surprised, no one else was. She was in fact a masterful, shrewd manipulator of the convention proceedings. She was a tough-minded politician, a strong leader who could be inspiring and autocratic if needed.

It was a new day for welfare recipients, as their leaders showed they could play old-time power politics as roughly as anyone from the established institutions. The nominating committee was stacked with Mrs. Tillmon's allies from the National Coordinating Committee. The women who had been at the meeting a year earlier had gotten in on the ground floor, and they managed to preserve most of the power for themselves. At this point, Wiley had to face a fundamental problem—what do you do if your grass-roots, democratic organization acts undemocratically?

Ed Day: "George had worried about this. He was going to leave it up to the people; the cards were not going to be stacked by the staff. But George knew it was wrong for the National Coordinating Committee to give themselves this power and not share it. He advised them to come out with a multiple slate of candidates and then let the convention choose. But they didn't follow his advice, and all hell broke loose, and he simply didn't know what to do. The result was about ten hours of total turmoil. Finally, at our urging, the nominating committee compromised, and several people nominated from the floor were elected to lesser offices. Members of the nominating committee got all the higher offices."

Wiley was upset, but he tried to be philosophical. He had witnessed democracy of a sort, the kind of rough and ready democracy that prevails in most organizations from national political parties to the League of Women Voters. Wiley had to go along. The women who seized power had the toughness which he knew the organization needed.

The women elected were: chairman, Johnnie Tillmon of Los Angeles; first vice chairman, Etta Horn of Washington, D.C.; second vice chairman, Beulah Sanders of New York City; third vice chairman, Carmen Olivio of New York City; treasurer, Marian Kidd of Newark, New Jersey; financial secretary, Dovie Coleman of Chicago; recording secretary, Edith Doering of Akron, Ohio; corresponding secretary, Dorothy DiMascio of Rochester, New York; and sergeant-at-arms, Alice Nixon of Pittsburgh.

Of the nine, six were black; Mrs. DiMascio and Edith Doering were white; and Mrs. Olivio was Puerto Rican. Each had fought in the front lines of the movement. Each had organized other welfare recipients. Each was on welfare and had a large family. From them would come the organization's leadership in the years ahead.

The next day, the delegates, joined by two thousand other welfare recipients, made an all-out, one-day lobbying effort in Congress. The movement was taking on an aura of legitimacy. The principles enunciated by Wiley a year earlier in Chicago were incorporated into the platform. NWRO stood for adequate income, dignity, justice, and democracy. The convention closed with the adoption of a resolution:

> That the present welfare system has driven 8.5 million Americans to fifth class citizenship and makes it impossible for us to live with decency and dignity.
> The present welfare system castrates and destroys our family life and family unity.
> The present welfare system condemns the future of millions of our children.
> Whereas, the welfare recipients of America deserve, need and demand justice, dignity and adequate income.

For Wiley the convention had served its purpose.

26

The Ladies

"Those women are strong, I tell you. By the time they came to welfare rights, they had been through so much they had to be strong to survive. And they used that strength to lift us all up."

—Faith Evans, the only male member of the National Coordinating Committee

At a 1967 hearing of the Senate Finance Committee, Senator Russell Long of Louisiana was expounding the popular wisdom about welfare. He couldn't get anyone to iron his shirts, he complained to his witness, Johnnie Tillmon, while welfare recipients were living high on the hog. Tillmon, who had ironed shirts for eighteen years, noted that when she was too sick to iron and had to go to the hospital, she couldn't get anyone to feed her children.

The women who emerged as welfare rights leaders in the late 1960s had paid their dues. Anyone who bothered to listen to them talk would learn how the welfare system operated in fact rather than theory. None of the women had wanted to go on welfare, and none ever enjoyed any part of it. Even worse than their shame was the welfare allotment itself. It was not a matter of spending unwisely; there was just not enough to spend.* In 1965 a national study by the Agriculture Department showed that only about 25

---

* In 1966, the average AFDC payment for a family of four was seventeen hundred dollars a year. No state's payments approached the thirty-five-hundred-dollar figure which the government defined as the minimum income to avoid living in poverty.

percent of the poor could be adequately nourished on the department's "low-cost food plan," on which many state welfare budgets were based.

The story of welfare is a tangled one in which myth often prevails over facts. Rivers of misinformation have obscured a profound national problem, as prejudice and preconceived notions about the life of the poor have shaped popular views of welfare recipients. The optimistic vision of America as the land of opportunity does not allow for people who cannot survive on their own. Of course, few middle-class Americans knew people like Johnnie Tillmon. As Wiley came to know and respect them, their experiences worked on him. As the strength and example of his grandmother, his mother, and his wife had molded his ideas, the women of NWRO taught him new lessons about life, work, and poverty.

Johnnie Tillmon was born in a little town in Arkansas. Her father was an itinerant sharecropper and as a child she hoed and picked cotton along with him. At eighteen she set out on her own to Little Rock with $1.75 in her pocket. An aunt found her a job as a maid for $2 a day, a sum that seemed magnificent. But by the second day, when she was given only an onion and tomato sandwich for lunch, and relegated to the back porch with a dog, Johnnie Tillmon "promised myself, God, and Moses that I was through working in anybody's kitchen but my own." She worked as a dishwasher, a sandwich girl, a short-order cook, inspected bomb fuses in a war plant, and when that closed after VJ Day she went to a laundry. Then she married James Tillmon and had five children; but things didn't work out, "so I just went on my way, raising the children by myself," ironing shirts to support them. In 1960 they all went to Los Angeles.

She ironed shirts at $1.50 an hour and became a shop steward in the local laundry workers' union. A woman of irrepressible energy, she was also active in a group that had been set up to beautify the public housing project where she lived but that branched out to help residents with food, rent, and welfare problems. Until she went to the hospital with acute tonsilitis and had to stay in bed for a month, she never thought she'd have to go on welfare. Even when she had only $20 left, she resisted. She had heard too many people "talk down" to welfare recipients. But she was unable to go back to work, and there was simply no alternative. The first welfare check was for $177 a month, not "half as much as I made with ten-hour days at the laundry. When I went down to the grocery store to cash my first check, I was very ashamed. I just didn't want anybody to see me cashing the check because I didn't want anybody to know that I was on welfare."

Tillmon is a born fighter, and soon her natural feistiness conquered her shame. She went to the manager of the housing project, a competent and sympathetic man, to outline the grievances of the welfare mothers and to ask for help. "I told him how the detectives came and they would go in the dirty clothes hamper, they would look in the refrigerator, they used to wake up the kids with the flashlights in all the bedrooms checking under the beds and in the clothes closets and tell you that they looking for men, full-grown men. Then there were the women who needed to go back to school to qualify themselves for decent jobs, but couldn't get any money from the welfare department for baby-sitters or transportation. I knew very little about organizing but I'm telling him there is a need to do something." The manager, Mr. Griggs, told her to find five other women who thought as she did, and before long they had the beginnings of a welfare organization.

They wrote a letter: " 'Dear Mrs. Jane Doe: You are requested to come to a certain place, a certain time, a certain day at a certain hour to discuss your check and your housing lease.' Mr. Griggs signed it. We got the man who is the principal of adult schools there in Watts to run it off. He donated us some stamps and paper. Mr. Griggs got his secretary, who had access to the files, to type the names and addresses of the clients on the letters that had been signed by him." They sent out five hundred and set up an interview schedule for the women who responded.

And the response was amazing, Johnnie Tillmon recalls: "Well, when the people got their letters, boy—everybody came! 'Cause you know why, everybody was concerned! About their check, about their lease. And they come on in and look at us, and they thought, 'Well, who in the hell are you?' Some of them thought we were working for the welfare department. I always did talk fast, but I learned to talk faster. We were able to really calm them down and they got real cooperative. So in three weeks we had covered the first two housing projects in Watts. We had two more to go. We decided that we were going to become an organization and so we had our election that night, and we elected us some officers. We called ourselves ANC Mothers Anonymous—we got a dictionary and found *anonymous* meant 'nameless.' We understood that what people thought about welfare recipients and women on welfare was that they had no rights, they didn't exist, they was a statistic and not a human being. So we thought that would fit us very well."

For over a year the little group worked quietly, afraid of an investigation by the welfare department. "In those days there was no such thing as organizations that were geared to the need of the recipient," says Tillmon. "They used all kinds of things to disqualify people on welfare or to keep them from being put on welfare. The social workers and the department had gotten the word about us and was worried, because normally welfare mothers didn't do anything but stay at the house, watch the children, cook and wash and iron and watch television, and that seemed to be the thing that the department would like for you to do. But we came along and we're saying, you know, cooking is all right, you're supposed to cook for your children, and you can have a day for washing and ironing, but then you can also do something else that's also beneficial to you and the children. You can participate in voter's registration, voter's education, you can work in some political campaigns or civil rights demonstrations because that'd benefit us, too."

Some attempts were made to stop them. Tillmon's own check was stopped, once because, as the welfare department told her, they had found out that her husband was not the father of all her children. "And I said, 'I never told you he was the father of all of them. You didn't ask me that. The question was, what is your husband's name and where does he live, and that's what I give you.' "

Johnnie Tillmon: "ANC Mothers Anonymous tried to help people being evicted, people not being able to get all their aid, people being cut off for whatever reason. We began finding out that we could appeal. A lot of people were afraid to. We encouraged folk, if what you need are not met, then these are the places that you write to. And then we found out that we could go with the recipient to ask for a fair hearing. We developed some resources where we could contact a person, maybe in the board of supervisors, or a person in the top administration, because most of your trouble comes from down at the bottom. And the people down there, the social workers, don't never see top administration.

"We felt like we was isolated, that there was maybe a conspiracy, to maybe keep us where we were. We didn't want to be where we were and maybe we didn't really feel that it was the entire country or people like John F. Kennedy trying to keep us there, because we didn't have any contact with those big folk. The people we had contact with were the social workers, and of course you strike out at whatever is close to you."

Throughout 1964 and 1965 Mrs. Tillmon's group grew, became more effective, and emerged from "under cover" to join with Tim Sampson's group in the California Welfare Rights Organization. From there Johnnie Tillmon was nominated to attend the meeting in Chicago in 1966, where she met George Wiley and changed his life as he changed hers.

Like Johnnie Tillmon, all the founding mothers on Wiley's board of directors had worked hard and had known humiliation. Their contacts with the young welfare rights movement gave all of them a pride and sense of accomplishment they had never known before. Etta Horn, the first vice chairman, had helped organize the Barry Homes Welfare Committee, a Washington, D.C., group like Mrs. Tillmon's. Beulah Sanders, the second vice chairman, organized welfare clients in New York City in 1964. (She was fired from her job in the antipoverty program because of her welfare rights activity.) Edith Doering, the secretary, helped organize the 1966 Walk for Decent Welfare from Cleveland to Columbus which foreshadowed the birth of the new nationwide movement. A mother of five, she was not on welfare but lived on an income below the poverty level. Marian Kidd, the treasurer, a mother of eight, had broken new ground by helping another woman apply for welfare in Newark after she was illegally refused aid. She also started a food-buying co-op for welfare recipients. Wiley and his staff called them "the ladies," and the women loved it. They brought to NWRO a wealth of knowledge and solid experience with grass-roots groups. They had been effective. They confirmed Wiley's faith that democracy would work.

There was Jennette Washington, the fiery New York woman who challenged Johnnie Tillmon's power play for leadership at the founding convention. She had fought the system long before she met George Wiley. A factory worker, she had held seven jobs in one year, and with recession-year layoffs she was forced into one hotel room with her three children. "I decided I was going to move in on the welfare department. Take the furniture and the kids and just move to the welfare office because I was angry that this society was playing games with people's lives."

Once in welfare rights, Jennette Washington was also an irrepressible activist, and she started to organize groups with Beulah Sanders. "We sat down and looked in the welfare manual and it said there were minimum standards," she recalls. "I remember the first meeting I had with George Wiley in 1966. I told George that people like myself didn't want to be used anymore. We didn't want to be manipulated and played games with, and we wanted him to be honest with us. I told him I was willing to commit myself to do what was necessary to further the black people's struggle and poor people's struggle for economic and social change in this country. It seemed to me that George was in some way saying that it was not him we had to put our trust in as much as we had to put trust in our own selves."

Like George Wiley, the black women guiding the new organization believed that NWRO, though its roots were in the civil rights movement, must include whites—women like Shirley Dalton, who lived with her husband, Darris, and seven children in a West Virginia hollow and was managing to scrape by until Darris lost his job working on the roads. Shirley Dalton: "I went to Morgantown and asked the welfare for coal. They wouldn't give it to me. They gave me a seven-dollar food stamp for the nine of us. Now, that's what we lived off of for one month. I had one loaf of bread to divide between the nine of us. We chopped wood to keep a fire going. The worst part was having to see the kids go hungry." With the help of an anti-poverty worker in the VISTA (Volunteers in Service to America) program, Shirley Dalton formed a small welfare rights group, teaching proud mountain people that they had rights and need not be ashamed to claim them.

As NWRO grew, a few women took on responsible jobs in the movement, working on national issues. But most, like Shirley Dalton, kept on working in their own communities. In Houston, Texas, for instance, Bertha Hernandez never finished the sixth grade, and never had a chance to do anything but laundry work. Her husband drifted in and out of the house, and only occasionally contributed the few dollars he earned moving furniture or digging ditches. She raised three sons by working seven days a week, earning thirty to forty dollars when business was good. "I was too proud to go near a welfare office," she said. (Applying for welfare would probably have been a futile effort anyway. Texas, with over a million poor people eligible for benefits, managed to keep its rolls lower than almost any state in the country, and discriminated against its large Mexican-American population.) Her married status (although her husband did not support her) was also grounds for disqualification.

But she met an NWRO worker who was organizing welfare recipients in Houston and who helped her apply for welfare. She received a check for $154 to support her family of four, of which $70 immediately went to pay for rent and food stamps. She attended her first welfare rights meeting, timidly wearing an apron, but her ideas soon changed. Although she didn't look the part, she was transformed into a community leader, "to help people get the right to a decent life, to be proud and not ashamed." Soon she was sitting on three community boards, helping other poor people get on welfare, campaigning for higher benefits.

Thousands of other women from working class and middle-class backgrounds were forced to turn to welfare. Terry Szpak, who became an organizer in Boston, found herself padlocked out of her apartment because "my husband just walked out and left, and I couldn't pay the rent. I had no living relatives, nowhere to go." Pregnant with her fourth child, and with one of her children running a high fever, she went to the police station, from where she was taken to the welfare department. "I was given a welfare form to fill out and told to come back in thirty days, when they would decide if I was eligible for welfare. And I said, 'But what am I supposed to do? Where am I going to stay with my kids, and how am I going to feed them?' The welfare worker replied, 'Well, that's the way the regulations work; that's the way it is.'

"That experience made me very, very angry. I had no income, no money. I was out on the street and I just couldn't understand them turning us away. How could anyone possibly be that cold and heartless and do that to my kids? I had read about 'Mothers for Adequate Welfare' in the paper and how they were starting to do things. I wrote to them and asked how I could start one of their groups in Waltham. I had a lot of friends, and we asked for the use of a church, and a hundred people showed up. I had expected maybe two or three. I didn't know what to do, but somehow we managed to start a group."

These women were among George Wiley's star pupils, but he learned from them, too, and knew the force that drove the movement. George

Wiley: "It is the power and motivation of mothers who are driven by love for their children, mothers who are determined to see to it that their children will have a chance to grow and to develop to their potential, mothers who are motivated to take a risk, mothers who are motivated to act, to struggle beyond all odds."

As he learned more about their lives, he realized how deeply rooted were the myths about welfare in America. Even his own family subscribed to them. Only as he came to know welfare mothers as individuals did he learn just how great was the disparity between myth and reality.

His own feelings were supported by solid data.* Larry R. Jackson and William A. Johnson showed that husbands desert their families not so that they can qualify for welfare, but because they cannot support them. Leonard Goodwin in his book *Do the Poor Want to Work?* analyzed thousands of interviews (mostly of welfare recipients) and reached the same conclusions as Wiley about welfare recipients' strong attachment to middle-class values and the work ethic.** If women on welfare prefer work to welfare, then why are they not working? Some of the answers are obvious: ill-health, lack of jobs or of steady jobs that provide a minimum income needed to support a family and provide child-care. But Goodwin also found that failure breeds more failure. Women on welfare who went through job training or "work experience" programs and still failed to find work were far more willing to accept welfare. He also found that women on welfare inculcated a strong work ethic in their children. If failure bred more failure, participation in the welfare rights movement gave the women a feeling of achievement. Success bred more success, and many welfare rights activists were able to move off welfare.

When Wiley launched the movement in 1966, about 1.3 million mothers and their 3.5 million children were on the AFDC rolls. Government studies show that death of the male breadwinner was a minor cause for their going on welfare. Physical incapacity of the principal breadwinner was a more significant cause, not surprising in light of the health care available to the poor. But the two principal causes were desertion of the husband and illegitimacy. (These same studies show that among the very poor who cannot afford the legal rites of divorce, alimony, and child support, the dissolution of the family usually takes the form of desertion.)

* In particular, *Protest by the Poor* by Jackson and Johnson (New York: New York City Rand Institute, 1973); *The State of Welfare* by Gilbert Steiner (Washington, D.C., Brookings Institution, 1972); and *Regulating the Poor* by Cloward and Piven (New York: Pantheon Books, 1971).

** "Evidence from this study unambiguously supports the following conclusion: Poor people, males and females, blacks and whites, youths and adults, identify their self-esteem with work as strongly as do the nonpoor. They express as much willingness to take job training, if unable to earn a living, and to work even if they were to have an adequate income. They have, moreover, as high life aspirations as do the nonpoor and want the same things, among them a good education and a nice place to live. This study reveals no differences between the poor and nonpoor when it comes to life goals and wanting to work."

In the popular mythology about welfare recipients' presumed moral depravity, illegitimacy has been a red flag. About 30 percent of the children on the rolls were born out of wedlock. Until abortion laws were changed in the early 1970s, the poor could not afford this option, and they also lacked proper birth control information and apparatus, which until recently were barred from federal and state antipoverty programs. But it is undeniable that some women, blacks more often than whites, chose to have children without benefit of marriage. (Illegitimacy was on the rise nationwide, and although still far higher among blacks, the rate is actually declining among blacks and rising among whites.) Joyce Burson is one example.

Burson came from rural Virginia, the only child of a black sharecropper who left his wife when Joyce was three. Her mother scraped by as a maid until Joyce was nine, then moved to New York. Joyce Burson: "My mother preached to me what most black folks do, that I had to get an education, finish school, and be a nice person." She dreamed briefly of becoming a dietician but never graduated from high school. She worked for four years, first as a keypunch operator, then in a jewelry factory. Her highest salary was sixty dollars a week. "I chose not to get married," she recalled. "I never wanted to. I also didn't want to have kids, but they happened." Her first child was born when she was twenty-one, her second a year later.

When she first applied for welfare, the welfare office refused to deal with her because she didn't know where to locate the father of her oldest child. She asked the minister who had christened her baby for help, and he went with her to the welfare office. "The minister just sort of sat there, and finally the welfare worker said, 'I told you not to come back until you could produce the father.' And I said, 'I don't know where he is, but I need help bad for these babies.' So he said, 'Well, we can't help you,' and he took the application that I had filled out again and threw it in the waste basket. At that moment, I think he realized this man was with me and asked who he was. The minister handed him his card, at which point the welfare worker's attitude changed completely and he was ready to deal with me. And that's how I got on welfare. I was very angry, very upset, and very ashamed. I didn't really believe that I was entitled to welfare. I had grown up being told by my mother and others that welfare was terrible and that people on welfare were terrible." She hoped to get a job but then found out she was pregnant again. "It was too late then to do anything but have the baby. So I just resigned myself that I was on welfare, and would have to be until the kids are old enough for babysitters, or at least going to school all day."

One day in 1966 Burson left a ghetto grocery store and was handed a leaflet inviting her to a welfare organizing meeting. She went, timidly, and her life changed. She went to work as a volunteer three hours a day, helping other recipients at the welfare office. Eventually, she became president of the Brooklyn Welfare Rights Action Council, which had two thousand members. She became the first recipient hired to work on the NWRO national staff in Washington. "I guess the thing that I valued most about my involvement in welfare rights was that I began to relate to other things than to my little family, and to the survival of other people. I never thought about those things until I got involved in the organization."

27

Organizing

In Washington, Wiley set up an organizing plan, a network that enlisted raw recruits in the struggle. Often they were kids, like Wade Rathke, a twenty-one-year-old redhead who dropped out of Williams College to work in the antiwar movement. He heard George Wiley speak on the Boston Common and promptly went to work for NWRO as an organizer. He hitchhiked to Springfield, the third largest city in Massachusetts, with fifteen dollars in his pocket, a packet of NWRO organizing material in his backpack, and the names of two people he was supposed to ask for help. According to the mimeographed sheet he carried in his pocket, NWRO was building the largest poor people's organization in the country. He knew little more than that.

Within a few months Rathke managed to build a powerful welfare rights organization in Springfield comprising twenty neighborhood groups of whites, Puerto Ricans, and blacks, with more than two thousand members. They won several million dollars in benefits for their members from the welfare department. They forced the city to face squarely the problems of welfare, and their example encouraged hundreds of non-NWRO members to apply for welfare; they mounted large-scale demonstrations, including one that deteriorated into a riot. Rathke's work in Springfield was part of an explosion in the welfare rolls, spurred by the civil rights movement and the antipoverty program and impelled by Wiley and the NWRO. To many Americans the increase in the rolls was a national scandal, but to Wiley the fact that many poor people were finally getting long-denied legal benefits was a reform.* Equally important was the fact that the poor were uniting and working in their own behalf.

Wade Rathke's work in Springfield exemplified one approach to organizing welfare recipients. He walked through all the poor neighborhoods of the city and soon found six neighborhoods that seemed ripe to be organized. He decided that blacks, Puerto Ricans, and whites had to be organized simultaneously. "If you brought in the blacks first, then you probably couldn't get the whites later, or the Puerto Ricans." Then he looked for potential leaders. He found four—a white woman married to a Puerto Rican, a young Puerto Rican who lived in a large housing project Rathke pinpointed as a principal organizing target, a black woman, and a white woman on welfare. Rathke and his four recruits, equipped with material from the national and state NWRO offices spelling out furniture allowances and children's clothing allowances, were ready to knock on doors. In Springfield, few recipients had ever received any of those benefits or had any idea they were entitled to them.

The organizers developed a standard pitch. They walked into an apartment and asked: "Where is your second chair? Do you have a chair for everyone in your family? Where is your couch? Do you have four bedsheets per bed, two pillows, and two pillowcases?" Nobody ever did. "These things are your rights," they'd say, and leave a flyer describing a forthcoming meeting. A large number of welfare recipients were attracted by the "special needs" issue. Rathke estimates that they got 90 percent of the Puerto Ricans, about 45 percent of the blacks, and 25 to 30 percent of the whites.

At the meetings, the need forms were filled out, the recipient trainees translating into Spanish and helping people who couldn't read or write; everyone had to fill in a membership form and pay the one-dollar NWRO dues. Then the women got into buses and headed for the welfare office. The welfare commissioner was confronted with sixty women who had properly filled out legal forms specifying what they were entitled to. "The ladies did the talking," Rathke recalls, "and told him they would be back in exactly two weeks to pick up their checks. A lot vented off steam and complaints, but I pulled them out of there before the director had time to recoup his senses and deal tough, or find out that he was dealing with sixty people who'd never met each other until that day, half of whom didn't speak the same language, and some of them didn't even know what was going on because the conversation was in English."

* The nation's welfare rolls in the Aid to Families with Dependent Children (AFDC) program grew by 107 percent between December, 1960, and February, 1969. (In the fifteen-month period from February, 1969, through October, 1970, an even greater explosion took place—a 55 percent increase—with another 1.5 million families added to the rolls. The total number of women and children on AFDC was then more than ten million.)

The next day another busload arrived, and within two weeks word spread in the housing developments. Several hundred more women filled out forms which were again delivered to the welfare office. On the appointed date, the welfare recipients again got onto buses and were on their way back to the welfare department. Wade Rathke: "We appeared there and we must have had at least four hundred people. And, by God, if we didn't get the checks for the children's special clothing allowance! It was like a hell of a great day for some of those recipients who were walking out of there with checks for a hundred, two hundred, or three hundred dollars. People could see that they had won through organizing and being with NWRO and Springfield Welfare Rights. We were already talking about the next campaign to get furniture."

Within a few weeks, four more groups were organized. The demands were similar; they would be back in two weeks for their furniture checks. On the promised date everyone walked out with a check, some for as much as four or five hundred dollars. Several million dollars in benefits were collected in practically no time. "By then, those people didn't think they could lose," says Rathke. "You had to keep going back and keep having campaigns to keep the organization developing and the leadership active. So there was a third campaign for winter clothing for kids. And we won that, too."

But the need "to keep upping the ante" backfired when Rathke launched a drive to get winter clothing for adults. This time the welfare commissioner, who had found that there was no legal provision for winter clothing for adults, was prepared. The welfare building was locked and guarded by police, but as the crowd grew restive an NWRO leader unlocked a door from inside and hundreds of recipients flooded into the office. Rocks were thrown at police cars and mass arrests resulted. There was a two-day riot in Springfield. Fires were set in slum neighborhoods, and many citizens were angered or terrified by the "welfare riot."

Rathke had to rebuild his organization from scratch. This time he focused on the issue of free school lunches for poor children, which had been mandated by federal law under the National School Lunch Program for thirty years but never implemented properly. Again he was successful, but the major result of his work in Springfield was indirect. Hundreds of new people were emboldened to apply for regular benefits. The welfare rolls nearly doubled. But the glory days of the Springfield Welfare Rights Organization were over. After Rathke left, it functioned as a series of small neighborhood groups which did valuable but less dramatic work in helping recipients solve their individual problems with the welfare department.*

* "People went to meetings because they heard they could get school clothing, because they were lonely, or because their neighbors were going," Rathke recalled. He had learned valuable lessons which he would use to advantage several years later when he worked with Wiley in an effort to organize on a much broader scale.

Wade Rathke was one of a number of NWRO organizers who had been trained by Bill Pastreich, developer of the "Boston Model" of welfare organizing. Wiley had a great talent as an "organizer of organizers." In 1967, he enlisted Pastreich, a wiry, energetic white man who had studied organizing in a Syracuse University training course based on the methods of Saul Alinsky in Chicago and had worked briefly for Cesar Chavez's United Farm Workers. Wiley told Pastreich he could go anywhere in the country. Wiley had gotten Pastreich a hundred-thousand-dollar grant from a National Council of Churches–related program to support civil rights and poor people's activities (beating out Alinsky, the master, to get the money). His only stipulation was that Pastreich get permission to organize from the local recipient leaders. Pastreich picked Massachusetts, designed his campaigns around the issues of school clothing and furniture, and soon had dozens of functioning welfare rights groups.

At that point Wiley was "not interested in lobbying or anything except organizing welfare recipients and helping them raise hell," says Pastreich. "He just wanted me to build large organizations." Soon Pastreich had twenty full-time paid organizers and fifteen volunteers working in the state. Only a few were paid by NWRO. Most, like Wade Rathke, "lived off the land," or the antipoverty programs or local community groups. In Boston, Pastreich spent four thousand dollars from his own savings in the first year.

Wiley gave his organizers almost total freedom and intervened only when he had to. In Massachusetts there was a fight for control between the old leadership and Pastreich's new leadership. The old leadership demanded that George remove Pastreich. He came up to a meeting, Pastreich says, "and stood there, taking unbelievable abuse from the original leadership, and he took it in a way that most national leaders would not. Finally, he said that we had to have both the old leadership and the new leadership, and the new leadership was now in a majority and they wanted me to stay, so I was going to stay.

"And he could come in and supply charismatic leadership for a big demonstration when you needed it. He had a sense of the dramatic. In one demonstration, an Army guy grabbed one of our NWRO flags from the other side of a fence, and George knew enough to climb the fence and get back the flag. He knew that was going to be the press picture. He had a good sense of how to do those things.

"Wiley was not inhibited by a lot of cautious middle-class attitudes," said Pastreich. "He understood that recipients wanted a lot. At the end of one of our campaigns, some people wanted to ask for bright-colored bed sheets. So far as George was concerned, that was all right. Poor people wanted the same things that other people had, even colorful sheets."

As a recruiter Wiley was casual and disarming. Rathke recalls his first serious conference with Wiley, a luncheon meeting to decide whether he would succeed Pastreich as chief organizer in Massachusetts. "He asked me how much I wanted to make and needed to make. I told him I had a wife to support. And he said, 'Well, you can make it on five thousand dollars a year.' I argued that I wanted to be paid whatever he paid his top organizer. He kind of giggled and changed the subject to something else. And I didn't get mad. It was just difficult to look at George and really get mad, even when he did stuff that really pissed you off. I told him exactly what I wanted to do, and he kept talking about other things. Finally, we were walking back to the office, and he said, 'Well, if that's what you want to do, that's the way we'll do it, and we'll pay you five thousand dollars.' And I went along with it. It was not his smoothness so much as his lack of it."

Although Wiley financed Pastreich in Massachusetts by capturing a big grant, organizing was usually done on a shoestring. One device was to recruit students at the schools of social work; another was to plead for help from employees of the antipoverty program agencies, particularly VISTA volunteers and community-action agency employees. "All these training programs and so forth are fine," he would say, "but people need to organize to get some power and money now. Help them get it!" Hundreds of antipoverty program workers did, either overtly or covertly, at the risk of losing their jobs.

And at last Wiley was learning to be an effective, even rousing, speaker. His deepening involvement in the lives of the women on welfare inspired a new passion in his speech-making. The great arching slogans of the civil rights movement could no longer serve as rallying cries, he said.

In a 1968 speech, Wiley said: "I am not at all convinced that white, comfortable, affluent, middle-class Americans are going to move over and share their wealth and resources with the people who have none. But I do have faith that if the poor people who have the problems can organize, can exert their political muscle, they can have a chance to have their voices and their weight felt in the political processes of this country—and there is hope.

"We are organizing around simple issues of whether you get a pair of shoes to send your children to school; the issue of whether you have to pay forty dollars to get your gas turned on in Detroit, Michigan; the issue of whether you have a bed for every member of your family to sleep in in New York City. The issue of whether you have to starve for ninety days, while you wait for a hearing because the caseworker decided she didn't want you on welfare; the issue of whether a state should be required to pay 100 percent of its own defined standards of minimum need, rather than 50 or 60 percent. Simple issues, but very basic issues.

"Hope rides with those small bands of welfare mothers and the possibility of developing other organizations like them, of people who still have the hope, who still have the faith, and who still want to make the try at making America the kind of country where everybody can live together with a sense of dignity and respect as a human being."

"Organization does not come out of an immaculate conception," Saul Alinsky insisted. "It takes a highly trained, politically sophisticated, creative organizer to do the job." Wiley completely understood that need for professionalism. Daniel Patrick Moynihan wrote of Wiley, once his friend and often his foe: "Einstein is on record stating he'd only in his life had two ideas. In that sense, George Wiley had only one. . . . It was a Gandhian idea, to take a group thought to be powerless, whose only strength lay in numbers, and to assert a moral rather than a political point about its condition. It was, very rightly, a revolutionary idea."

Wiley was a pragmatist. Ideology was not important in NWRO. The goal was simply to organize the poor, black and white, and, as he noted, the most effective method "is to concentrate upon specific benefits the organization can bring to recipients, like winter clothing, when it's needed. We're kind of afraid of becoming separated from the people, if we get too ideological." The archtypical organizer, Saul Alinsky, espoused no political ideology. His fundamental belief was in the value of organizing per se. Once the people were organized for power, they would decide what to do with it. Wiley did formulate a specific goal. Power and a voice in the system were nice theoretical goals, but a guaranteed annual income was what he particularly sought. And in this he went beyond Alinsky, who never attempted to organize on a national scale. Still, Wiley's plans included conflicting ideas that he never resolved. How could you allow your local groups and organizers to be free and autonomous and build a permanent national power bloc at the same time? Did you need to stress long-range goals and a guiding ideology to sustain the organization?

Pastreich's Boston organizers, for example, did not outline an ideology, or a blueprint for a future society. They subscribed to the vague notion of "power for the people" and devoted most of their time and energy to turning out new groups, almost on a production-line basis. Wiley himself had no fixed ideas about how organizers could best use their time. Should there be rapidly organized, ad hoc campaigns to get furniture and clothing, for instance? Or would welfare advocacy be more effective—the time-consuming approach of helping people qualify for welfare benefits and improving their benefits on a case-by-case basis? He tried to do both—mass campaigns, and the painstaking casework with individual recipients. He felt he could maintain the fragile balance between local organizing techniques and national goals.

Neither his words nor his actions clarified his complex views. In one speech he would say that NWRO was not a revolutionary movement but sought a gradual transition to a system of a more adequate income maintenance system for all; in the next breath he would quote Stokely Carmichael, the militant black separatist, and say, "If we don't get our rights, ain't nobody going to have peace in this country." In the early stage of the movement (1966–9) Wiley was willing to go along with anyone who was able to produce results. And events were running away with him. He had created this tiger of a movement; now he had to ride it.

In 1968, the movement looked as though nothing could stop it. Special benefit drives in New York City alone yielded ten to twelve million dollars a month in special grants for NWRO members, compared to three million the previous year. In New York, Wiley installed as his chief organizer Hulbert James, a twenty-four-year-old black man. Soon NWRO claimed more than eight thousand active, dues-paying members in New York City alone. By August 1968, fifty local groups had separately launched special-grant campaigns, precipitating a welfare crisis in the city. The *New York Times* described how "bands of organized clients descended on welfare centers demanding special grants for items provided under the law but in practice rarely given out. The demonstrators have jammed the centers, sometimes camping out in them overnight, broken down administrative procedure, playing havoc with the mountains of paperwork, and have been increasingly successful. . . . They have thrown the city's welfare program into a state of crisis and chaos."

As the city resisted the special-needs campaigns, NWRO's tactics grew tougher and Wiley and James lost control. Angry recipients destroyed case records and made a shambles of welfare offices; demonstrations turned into riots. NWRO's tactics in the cities seemed to suit the times. The day of the peaceful, nonviolent march was over. Blacks were rioting; so were students on college campuses; and anti-war demonstrations turned into riots. The destruction of property by welfare recipients outraged voters and government officials, and in the backlash that inevitably came, the first to be "put back in their place" were Wiley's welfare warriors.

The basic needs of most welfare recipients were going unmet. In Ohio, in 1968, for instance, AFDC children were allowed an average of eighty-three cents a day for clothing, school supplies, carfare, and all other requirements, and these statistics were echoed in states across the country.* But the mass campaigns for special grants were less and less successful. The backlash was too strong. Before the movement was two years old, both New York and Massachusetts dealt NWRO a stunning defeat by passing laws abolishing the special-grants provisions.

At first NWRO tried to fight the ending of special-need benefits; new loopholes were sought in the state welfare laws. Welfare recipients withheld their rent and utility payments to protest the inadequacy of grants for food

---

* A survey in Detroit showed that less than one-half of AFDC families felt they had the means to feed their children adequately. A Cleveland study found that two-thirds of AFDC children were undernourished because of inadequate food allowances. A Detroit study found that "nearly eight out of ten school-age boys owned only one pair of shoes, that half the children had no boots or rubbers of any kind, and that nearly three-quarters lacked raincoats of any description."

and clothing. An NWRO bulletin urged tougher action: "Harassment, giving ultimatums, overwhelming centers is our greatest tactic. If welfare can disrupt our lives, can harass us in centers and where we live, then we have a right to disrupt their lives and to disrupt them where they live."

There was a debate in NWRO over the "Boston model," the production-line assembly of groups by professional organizers. Quick victories were won, but strong, stable organizations were not developed. It was a hit-and-run tactic that left Wiley uneasy. The tactics of the Boston-style organizers defied a fundamental Wiley principle—that NWRO should be a grass-roots organization run democratically by and for the recipients. Pastreich's Boston model was founded on the idea of control by outside organizers. The recipient leaders resented the way Pastreich operated. Wiley was always uncomfortable with the dominance of outside organizers. "He was much more comfortable with the recipient leader-organizer," says Pastreich, and "with organizers like Bruce Thomas or Hulbert James, who had more legitimacy because they were not white middle-class, but were black and poor."

Other organizing techniques were successful. The Brooklyn Welfare Action Center (B-WAC) worked out methods NWRO proposed as alternatives to the organizer-dominated "Boston model." The Brooklyn leaders were Rhoda Linton, a white ex-missionary; Andrea Kydd, a black ex-social worker; and Joyce Burson, a black welfare mother. All were committed to training recipient leaders who would sustain a long-term, functioning poor people's organization.

Rhoda Linton: "I was very insistent that the welfare recipients themselves should make the decision whether I was going to work for them. They should make all the decisions and I should give them technical help. And George was very casual about it, saying, 'Oh, yeah, you wanna work in Brooklyn; fine, you go to work in Brooklyn.' " Linton had exploited special-needs campaigns to build twenty-five neighborhood groups but soon realized that getting money easily at the outset undermined the building up of a long-term organization. "Once people saw they couldn't get any more money," she says, "they didn't participate anymore."

'The Brooklyn group focused on training local leaders. They taught people welfare law and set up shop in the fourteen welfare centers in Brooklyn to help recipients with their problems. Linton also emphasizes that it was an organization of women run by women. "A lot of the men organizers in NWRO were very much macho and talked down to the 'ladies.' " Linton and Burson were mild-mannered women who disliked demonstrations and were incapable of loudness and aggression—qualities which, as Linton notes, "don't necessarily get leadership which is good for the development of the organization." Burson points out that the Brooklyn group was unique because "the clients did all the work and made the decisions. I was firmly opposed to manipulating our people, and I worried that all organizations eventually manipulate people."

Andrea Kydd, who took over when Linton went to the national office, was also opposed to using outside organizers. "We tried to make democracy work," she says, and for practical reasons. "It made no sense to plan an action unless the leaders were able to turn out their troops. At meetings, no staff person ever spoke. The staff did the leadership and the training, but when we went into meetings the recipients didn't need us to do the talking because they were prepared. That was the key to the strength and the longevity of our organization. Still, the staff was always tempted to map out elaborate strategies and plans and push them through without respect for the membership. And when we did that, it was a myth to say that NWRO was an organization run by poor people for poor people."

The raucous big-city campaigns captured the headlines but were not typical of NWRO groups around the country. In Appalachia, in southern plantation country, and in middle-sized midwestern cities the chapters were smaller. There was more case-by-case filing of grievances, and many small victories were won. The organizers and the organizations came in all shapes and sizes: Johnnie Tillmon's Los Angeles group was a stable neighborhood organization, provided basic services and companionship, and occasionally played a significant role in local politics; Shirley Dalton's group in the isolated West Virginia hill country won for the first time basic welfare benefits that had traditionally been handed out only on the basis of local political patronage.

As the special-grant campaigns petered out, Wiley scouted the far-flung welfare rights groups for new ideas. Some of the best came from Roxanne Jones, a black woman who led the Philadelphia group. She had been a dancer and a waitress, had been deserted by an alcoholic husband, and was stung into activism by the way the welfare department had tried to shuffle her off to the Salvation Army. "The social worker made me feel like I had committed murder when I first asked for help," she recalled.

Aside from the traditional organizing drives that focused on clothing and furniture, Jones found other issues. One was the failure of the city health department to stop ghetto stores from selling rotten food. Her group was successful in getting some action out of the health department, "and that drew members to our organization." They also successfully challenged the telephone company policy of requiring welfare recipients to pay a thirty-five-dollar deposit in order to get phone service, while residents in middle-class neighborhoods paid a ten-dollar deposit or none at all.

Every time Roxanne Jones scored a new victory she would excitedly call Wiley, and he would pass her ideas around the country. Her great coup was obtaining credit from major department stores, an idea Wiley would turn

into a nationwide campaign. Welfare recipients, who could not open accounts at big stores, were forced to pay exhorbitant prices and interest rates
to slum merchants. The Philadelphia campaign was launched when scores of
NWRO members filled out credit applications at Lit Brothers and Gimbel's;
all but one were denied credit. Lit's sent a form letter telling the women to
continue shopping at the store and taking advantage of their wonderful
bargains.

Supported by a middle-class Friends of Welfare Rights group, whose
members marched down to the stores on demonstration day and turned in
their credit cards, the Philadelphia group picketed the stores. Demonstrators
carried signs reading, "Don't shop here. Lit's won't give low-income people
credit but they want our cash dollars." The women were tying up business
outside the store, and the manager finally agreed to a negotiating session. He
would have to check with national headquarters, he told them. The women,
after a vote, replied that they weren't leaving until they got a decision. "It's
all up to you," said Roxanne Jones. "Do we leave here with a credit agreement, or do we stay?" One hour later they had negotiated a credit settle-
ment.

It was a modest but significant victory. "We weren't stupid in what we
asked for," says Roxanne Jones. It was only fifty dollars worth of credit to
begin with, and NWRO members had to present a membership card and letter from the organization. As they paid off the fifty dollars, members could
gradually increase their credit allowance.

Soon NWRO's New York chapters directed a successful campaign at a
major store in Brooklyn, Abraham and Straus. First they went to Korvette's,
the store's competition across the street, and jammed it with welfare women
who made purchases, then blocked the cashier aisles by refusing to pay.
"Charge the goods to the welfare department," they said. Korvette's would
not yield, but A&S, sensing that it was the next target, negotiated an agreement, as did stores in other cities.

Wiley then mounted a nationwide campaign against Sears Roebuck. The
purpose was to help recipients as well as lure new members with the promise of credit. The campaign went on for months with no success. Tactics
ranged from disruptive demonstrations to private negotiations between
Wiley and Mrs. Marion Ascoli, a financial backer of NWRO and a member of
the family that owned America's largest retail business. Wiley was finally
given a hearing at a board meeting, but Sears executives still refused to
help.*

* The sympathetic intermediary who had arranged the meeting suggested that Wiley would
make a better impression on the board if he wore something other than his shiny, worn-out suit
and space shoes—"Dress like a serious businessman." Over Wretha's objections, George and an
NWRO staff member who knew what was fashionable bought George a stylish but conservative
$150 suit, a shirt, and a tie to wear to the meeting. At a recess during the meeting, a Sears board

A similar campaign to get discounts from Proctor and Gamble for its manufactured items also failed. But there was a payoff. Executives at Montgomery Ward saw a chance to score a public relations coup as well as to attract business from inner-city residents. Ward needed no demonstrations; the Sears disruptions had already made the point. Wiley, again comfortably dressed in his old baggy suit, met with Ashley DeShazor, Ward's national credit manager. They agreed that Ward's initially would extend credit to two thousand NWRO members in selected cities who would each be able to charge purchases of up to one hundred dollars. NWRO chapters would collect the applications and take them to the stores; if the pilot plan worked, DeShazor pledged, it would be expanded.

This, too, was a modest victory, but Wiley embraced any technique that would build NWRO and bring in new members. (Borrowing an idea from Cesar Chavez, he also talked with insurance executives about getting low-cost policies for NWRO members, although this never worked out.) DeShazor was so impressed that he offered Wiley a job with Montgomery Ward. To a national corporation under federal pressure to hire blacks, particularly as executives, Wiley would have been a prize. But the days were long past when Wiley got any satisfaction from being the first black through a big white door.

How good an organizer was Wiley? NWRO staffers argued the point endlessly. There was one story Johnnie Tillmon liked to tell, as did Wiley himself. As his own special project Wiley decided to organize poor black men, the winos who hung out on the street corners around NWRO's Washington headquarters, sometimes sleeping on the street. He would create a "D.C. Unemployed Men's Organization." He first brought a handful of the men into the building to cook lunch for a meeting of the NWRO executive board. They tried to cook a chicken dinner, but the meal was inedible; the women choked on it and made fun of Wiley. Tim Sampson, discovering a ledger pad on George's desk, learned what his "organizing" campaign really amounted to. George was lending the street men money, in sums of one to three dollars, keeping a careful record of the day the money was loaned, and when—if ever—it was repaid.

Wade Rathke: "George used to joke that he was not an organizer, that his only credit was his collection of drunks, the D.C. Men's Unemployed Association. That was not true. To be a successful organizer, one must be able to walk with one eye two inches from the ground and the other hundreds of feet into the clouds. George knew that route and could walk it without stumbling. He did it with NWRO."

member approached the nattily-attired Wiley and said: "I'm looking at you and how expensively you are dressed. And you claim that you represent poor people?"

28

Shaking
the Money Tree

Raising money for the National Welfare Rights Organization would have been a demanding full-time job, challenging the ingenuity of the most skilled professional fund-raiser. The cause was not popular; few volunteer contributors stepped forward; each dollar of aid had to be coaxed. For Wiley, fund-raising was just one task of many, yet without his skill at soliciting money the movement would never have gotten off the ground. He personally raised the bulk of NWRO's funds, three million dollars between 1966 and 1972. Yet the money was never enough.

Wiley chronically borrowed from Peter to pay Paul and put on a financial juggling act that amazed, and often appalled, the lawyers and accountants who were supposed to keep NWRO's books straight. But while the other radical civil rights groups were sliding towards bankruptcy, Wiley was building a financial base for NWRO. He built NWRO's national budget from $63,000 in 1967 to $232,000 in 1968, $457,000 in 1969, $535,000 in 1970, $650,000 in 1971, and more than $400,000 in 1972. These funds were only part of the total Wiley amassed. Another several million went directly to local NWRO groups throughout the country. The greater portion of NWRO money came from church and foundation grants, but without Wiley's ability to elicit support from the rich at the outset, the fledgling NWRO would never have taken wing. He was more than a supplicant. He became close friends with the heirs to some of America's largest fortunes, and made them partners in his plans to overhaul the society that had created their wealth.

Once again Wiley became an apprentice. To learn the art of raising money, he went to Seymour Facher, Irving Workoff, and Alan Terestman. They worked as professional fundraisers, mainly for Jewish charities, but they had donated their services to the civil rights movement * and had met Wiley in CORE. In 1966, he began to meet with them regularly. They taught him how to ask people for money, and they told him whom to approach.

Facher says that Wiley was the boldest of all the civil rights leaders with whom they had worked. "If we said to Jim Farmer, 'You should ask someone for five thousand dollars,' Farmer was frightened stiff of asking for five thousand dollars. Amounts didn't frighten George. George's response was, 'Why five thousand? Why not ten thousand?' And we would have to explain to him that if you ask for ten thousand, you might not get anything, but if you ask for five thousand, you might not get that, but you would come away with something."

Facher, Workoff, and Terestman taught George a simple mechanical system, a key ingredient to successful fund-raising. On five-by-seven cards they compiled a dossier on hundreds of wealthy contributors: their family histories; their likes and dislikes; a detailed record of their gifts to various causes, including times and places and circumstances. It was nothing less than a *Who's Who* of charity, a political genealogy of New York's wealthy class. Soon Wiley had his own packet of cards which he guarded closely, often carrying them in his coat pocket. He was designing his own road map to the very rich. "George took to fund-raising like a fish takes to water," said Facher. "After about a year of working with us, he knew everything we knew, and in some respects he had outstripped us. He had entree in places that we didn't. We may have helped launch him but he made it on his own."

Wiley also went for help to two wealthy businessmen, John Marqusee and Robert Ostrow. Marqusee was then president of a mortgage banking company and Ostrow was his expert on law and accounting. Both men had been active in civil rights, and Marqusee had helped bail Wiley and hundreds of other CORE demonstrators out of that Jackson, Mississippi, fairgrounds jail in 1965. They had set up a tax-exempt foundation, "Misseduc" (Mississippi Education Foundation), for civil rights work. In mid-1966, Wiley met them for lunch, where he laid out his plans and his needs, including a tax-exempt vehicle to receive contributions.

"I was very critical," recalled Ostrow, "and I was brutal. I said it was a great idea to add to all the many others that were so crazy that they could never get off the ground, and that he would never raise his initial sixty

* Workoff had raised money for SNCC and Angela Davis, and had organized the party that conductor Leonard Bernstein gave for the Black Panthers, which Tom Wolfe made notorious in his scathing article on "radical chic."

thousand. And his reaction was very calm and interesting. He acknowledged the possibility of failure.

"He wanted Misseduc, which was defunct anyway, and we gave it to him, agreeing to change its charter. But what he was most interested in was an accountant and a bookkeeper and a tax expert and a corporate expert. And two or three days later he called me and asked if he could come by the office and show me some stuff. He showed up at the door carrying a shoebox which I soon discovered was stuffed with enough accounting and legal problems to keep a corporate lawyer-accountant busy for weeks."

That afternoon began a friendship to which Ostrow would donate hundreds of hours. He created a bookkeeping system for NWRO, filled out tax returns, set up tax-exempt foundations and record-keeping systems that would show both foundations and the Internal Revenue Service that NWRO was applying tax-exempt funds to legitimate charitable and educational purposes. Soon Ostrow was traveling to Washington to instruct a succession of low-paid, not very sophisticated NWRO bookkeepers. And, in an emergency, he would arrange bail for arrested NWRO demonstrators.

While Ostrow built up the legal framework, John Marqusee gathered seed money to help NWRO get off the ground. Marqusee contributed more than twenty thousand dollars himself, in gifts and loans, and donated art from his own art business for NWRO benefit auctions. Like other whites who had staunchly supported the civil rights movement, Marqusee no longer felt comfortable or welcome in the movement's new black nationalism. He liked NWRO's interracial character. In addition, Marqusee and Wiley were both Cornell alumni who spoke the same language—a middle-class manner that had nothing to do with race. "Despite the fact that he was black," says Marqusee, "I saw in him the same kind of 'do-gooder' that I was." This feeling that Wiley was a kindred spirit drew many white liberals into becoming his loyal supporters.

While other radicals were either embarrassed, inept, or ideologically opposed to seeking support from wealthy individuals, Wiley moved with aplomb in the orbit of the very rich. Irving Workoff, who sometimes accompanied him, was astonished: "I have been in this business a long time," he says, "but I would never walk into a house and ask for a cup of coffee. George would be so relaxed and at home, he would say to perfect strangers, 'Do you have something cold to drink?' or, 'Could I have a cup of coffee?' " He always seemed happy to meet anyone. For example, at one party at Ethel Kennedy's home, Hickory Hill, Wiley seemed exuberant and carefree, chatting with many attractive women. But at the same time he was recruiting sponsors for an NWRO art sale. By noon the next day, all of the women had been called by Wiley's secretary to confirm their offers of help and to let them know the time and location of their first meeting. The auction brought in more than fifteen thousand dollars.

What seemed to come so naturally to Wiley in dealing with the rich was not easy for others. Cloward could not veil his hostility, nor Tim Sampson his anger. Neither could Dr. Kenneth Clark, the black psychologist, when Wiley invited him to speak at an NWRO fund-raiser at a lush Westchester home. "It was just a hell of a setting in which to be talking about the problems of welfare, amid all the wealthy people, this beautiful home and conspicuous consumption," Clark recalled. "It got to me. All I kept saying were very bitter, negative things. We were there to raise money, and I ruined it." Wiley never made his rich contributors feel defensive or guilty. He dispassionately set out the facts and figures. He ticked off how little welfare recipients actually got and explained how they could be taught to get a little more from the system. Then he invoked the excitement of building a new movement.

"He made you a participant," says Laura Rockefeller, the daughter of Laurence Rockefeller, and herself a social worker. Aside from emergency loans for specific NWRO activities, loans which were unfailingly repaid, Laura Rockefeller contributed thirty thousand dollars to NWRO in its first four years. Wiley established more than a business-supplicant relationship with her and with his other wealthy supporters. Laura Rockefeller: "Sometimes he would appear at the door, with a smile on his face, without much notice, fully expecting to be invited to dinner and to spend the night. There was about George an instant sense of familiarity and ease that seemed bilateral—a trust in others. You felt as if he were someone you had known since childhood, even after a very brief contact with him. He would solicit our thinking about what he was doing. And he would listen very intently when I talked about my ideas. You could ask him about almost anything, and his answers were straight, not just what the consumer wanted to hear. If it was a 'sell' on his part, it was the softest sell in the world."

Wiley met Laura Rockefeller at a Cambridge dinner party given by Anne Farnsworth Peretz, an heiress to the Singer sewing machine fortune. At first, Anne Peretz was dubious about a welfare recipient organization and didn't give him any money. But Wiley was persistent. He contacted her ten more times, each time making a note on one of his index cards. She was finally persuaded. Anne Peretz: "It was very concrete, and I think that's what appealed to me. People were benefiting in specific, tangible terms." She and her husband Martin extended some large loans to NWRO. "A lot of people just conveniently forgot that they owed us, but he never did. He always paid us back." In addition to the loans, Anne Peretz gave an estimated forty thousand dollars to the National Welfare Rights Organization.

The deepest and most enduring of Wiley's friendships with his financial supporters was with Audrey Stern Hess, granddaughter of Julius Rosenwald, the founder of the Sears Roebuck empire. He met her through Trude Lash, a dynamic social worker and the director of New York's Citizens Committee for Children, on which Mrs. Hess served. Audrey Hess was at once his mentor, his student, his sponsor, his constant benefactor. Her elegant townhouse overlooking the East River was his New York headquarters. He nestled into the luxury of her home with its stunning collection of modern paintings, where the butler served him tea after a long day of hustling in New York.

When they met in 1967, Audrey Hess was critically ill, and Wiley was hesitant to ask her for money. But despite her apparent frailty, she was a tough-minded woman. She summoned him to her hospital bedside, where she wrote her first check to NWRO, for four thousand dollars. Over the next five years, Mrs. Hess and her husband Thomas, and their children, contributed fifty-one thousand dollars to NWRO. Mrs. Hess led Wiley to other sources of money—beginning with her own family. She introduced him to her aunt, Marion Ascoli. Mrs. Ascoli was more conservative than her niece, and she was distressed by some NWRO tactics. In 1969 she wrote to Wiley expressing her "reservations about supporting an organization that places so much emphasis on picketing Sears Roebuck." Her father had founded the company, she pointed out, and she was herself a major stockholder. Nevertheless, a month later she contributed seventy-five hundred dollars to NWRO from the Marion Ascoli Fund.

The bulk of NWRO's funding came from churches and from foundations, ranging from the gigantic Rockefeller Brothers Fund to an assortment of small foundations which had actively supported the civil rights movement in the early 1960s.* Wiley soon learned he had to work against the conservative tendency of most foundations to invest in safe projects, to make "brick and mortar" grants for hospital or school buildings. Furthermore, many foundations were increasingly disenchanted with militant civil rights causes or worried about government investigations of their grants to activist groups.**

He first went for help to S. M. Miller, his colleague at Syracuse and advisor at CORE, who then held a key position at the nation's richest fund, the Ford Foundation. Miller helped Wiley draft a proposal, and when the Ford Foundation decided to spend several million dollars on public welfare, Miller was confident he could get George and the NWRO some money. But on the day Miller was scheduled to make the NWRO presentation, a big

---

* These included the Stern Family Fund (also based on Sears Roebuck money), the Field Foundation (based on the Chicago department store fortune), the New World Foundation, the New York Foundation, the Norman Fund, the Irwin Sweeney Miller Fund, the DJB Foundation, the William Whitney Foundation, the Carol Buttenweiser Loeb Foundation, and the Foundation for Voluntary Service.

** Conservative opponents in government wanted to cut off tax-exempt aid to radical causes. The government was also concerned with foundations which were little more than tax shelters and served no real philanthropic purpose.

welfare demonstration in New York erupted. A welfare office was invaded. "It was all over the papers," Miller recalled. "The comments at the Ford staff meeting were devastating. The NWRO grant request was killed on the spot."

After his Ford experience, Wiley decided his chances were better at the few smaller foundations, which were more willing to experiment and take risks. Some of the executives who ran the small foundations were themselves veterans of the civil rights movements; they were sympathetic to the welfare rights movement. But the directors and boards of these foundations supported NWRO in large part because of their implicit trust in Wiley.

"He was not glib," said Andrew Norman, a publisher who also presided over his family foundation. "He did not pretend to have all the answers. He was aware of the complexity of the issues." The Norman Foundation gave NWRO more than forty thousand dollars over several years. Norman also helped by inviting leaders from the small foundations to a meeting with Wiley and the welfare recipient leaders.

Andrew Norman: "They were very tough dames, very impressive. Jennette Washington was there. It was quite beautiful the way they lit up the room with their passion and conviction. It was the beginning phase of the movement, before any competition or pettiness set in. The reaction of that group of foundation executives was very favorable." Using his detailed file cards on contributors, Wiley timed his requests carefully. As Norman noted: "When George asked for money, when he was really desperate, I had the instinct that if I said, 'Okay,' he wouldn't make a habit of it—and he didn't."

Another early ally was David Hunter, executive director of the Stern Family Fund, which administered the multi-million-dollar philanthropy of the Stern branch of the Rosenwald family. David Hunter: "Our ethos at Stern was that we will give you seed money to get started, but then you have to get your money elsewhere. But because of George's persistence and his personality, and his contacts with members of the family, we probably bent the rule and gave a little more support and continued it longer than we otherwise would have.

"My most vivid memory of George is seeing him coming into my office, a big guy with a big smile on his face. Many times, I'd start out thinking, 'Oh, God, here's George again,' but then I would end up being very glad to see him. He was a beautiful guy. He was persistent, he was relentless, he kept coming in there with his good humor and that smile on his face. He was without any personal hostility. He was tough, but never, as some others, in the sense of a black man threatening a white man. There is no question that George had an advantage in his intellectual middle-class behavior that made it easy for a lot of foundation types to relate to him—he was just one of the boys." The Stern Family Fund never waivered in its support, even when some of its own board members, connected with Sears Roebuck, were furious at Wiley's attacks on the nation's largest retail business. Over a five-year period, the Fund gave NWRO more than seventy-one thousand dollars.*

The largest consistent support came from the Field Foundation, which, under the leadership of Leslie Dunbar, aided the most controversial antipoverty and civil rights programs. Dunbar, a white West Virginian who had been a pioneer civil rights worker and director of the Southern Regional Council, liked to take on projects the big foundations were afraid to touch.

Leslie Dunbar: "The whole idea of organizing because you were on welfare was a most radical idea. The movement didn't make welfare dignified; it didn't make it a good way of life, but it did allow people to respect themselves and it did force some attention from the rest of us. You had to take George seriously. George talked to me like I was somebody who had a job to do and he was somebody who had a job to do, and let's get down to it. Foundations intimidate some people, but they didn't him. He never even a little bit bent his knee as he came through these doors. He dealt straightforwardly." During the course of a four-year period, the Field Foundation contributed $128,000 to NWRO.

Wiley's biggest foundation coup was eliciting a $150,000 grant from the Rockefeller Brothers Fund. This story began in 1966 when Wiley approached John Heyman, a wealthy New Yorker who headed the New York Foundation. He gained the long-term support of Heyman and of one of the Foundation's staff, Tom Wahman, who later moved to the Rockefeller Brothers Fund, where he was an advocate for Wiley's cause. At the outset of their relationship, Wahman was cautious. "A cynical side of me was never certain that there wasn't a little hustle in George," he recalled. "That smile of his, those eyes sparkling like crazy. But in the end, I always knew that the commitment was there."

Wiley stressed that American institutions would never change unless poor people gained a voice in the system. Other applicants for funds said the same thing, "at least they had the rhetoric," said Wahman. "But Wiley introduced us to the real people in need. In contrast to many applicants, we didn't feel we were dealing with some distant intermediary."

Wahman arranged a meeting for Wiley with the senior staff and some of the trustees. Tom Wahman: "They were impressed, but they were also very sensitive to the fact that in a week or so he might be leading a demonstration against one of our board members, namely Nelson Rockefeller, the governor of New York.** The board was sensitive to this, and to the increasingly critical

---

* Another member of the family, Philip Stern, an author and philanthropist, gave six thousand dollars in 1966 to educate welfare recipients in the nation's capital about their rights.

** Wiley had been jailed in 1965 for leading a CORE demonstration against another board member, David Rockefeller, after first negotiating unsuccessfully with Rockefeller to get the Chase Manhattan Bank to stop doing business with South Africa.

scrutiny of the foundation by conservatives in Congress, but the board decided to make a grant anyway, and we got no flack, even when he started attacking the governor with some regularity." The two-year grant was handled discreetly, using the National Urban Coalition as a sponsor for $100,000 of the money. Carl Holman, president of the Coalition, likened Wiley to the legendary Bob Moses, a Harvard-educated black easterner who had become a charismatic southern leader in SNCC. "Bob Moses and George Wiley had the same rare ability to work closely with very poor black people," said Holman. "It came from the deep respect they had for people as human beings."

NWRO's single largest source of money was the churches. Wiley's link with church groups was another black leader, the Reverend Lucius Walker, who had served as a community organizer and CORE activist. In 1967 Walker established, in conjunction with the National Council of Churches, the Interreligious Foundation for Community Organization (IFCO), which distributed funds from various Protestant denominations to groups working with blacks and the poor.*

IFCO funneled more than $500,000 into the National Welfare Rights Organization, and Lucius Walker managed to obtain emergency grants when Wiley was in desperate need of money to pay long-overdue bills. Walker had persuaded the IFCO board, which was top-heavy with white church people, to support the principle of maximum feasible participation of the poor, and to include in its membership Wiley and other people from organizations which would be asking for IFCO funds.

Lucius Walker: "At that time, the white church world was bent toward the Saul Alinsky approach, that community organizing should be concentrated strictly in the local community around community issues. George and I had to turn them around. We made the rounds of the various church denomination offices—we really pounded the pavement—arguing and convincing them of the NWRO approach—seeking to expand community organizing." They were remarkably successful, with local Protestant church groups as well as their national headquarters. In several urban dioceses, the Catholic Church also provided major support.

The Reverend John T. Walker, bishop coadjutor of the National Cathedral in Washington, D.C., was a black Episcopal churchman who helped Wiley raise funds and offered some pointed advice: "I told George he should press as hard as possible while there was a feeling of guilt in the land, because the guilt wouldn't last nor would the contributions."

---

* At this point, James Forman, former SNCC leader, began his demands that white churches pay "reparations" for past injustice to blacks. He was accused of blackmail by many whites, but he also spurred contributions to IFCO. Despite conflicts about black nationalism, Forman still saw Wiley, and recommended NWRO as one of the few organizations that deserved "reparations" from the churches.

Wiley sought money where he could get it. He tried the labor unions, but only the Teamsters, United Automobile Workers and the American Federation of State, County, and Municipal Workers responded. Not everyone got the famous Wiley soft sell. At a National Conference on Social Work convention in 1968 he staged a demonstration demanding thirty-eight thousand dollars from the social workers. The NWRO women barricaded the meeting and refused to let anyone leave without making a contribution.

In a truly audacious maneuver in 1968, Wiley asked the Labor Department for a $400,000 grant to assist a work-training program for welfare recipients funded by a law which NWRO had vigorously opposed in Congress. Wiley reached back twenty years to an old college friendship to find some strings to pull. He called the late Steve Wechsler, who had been a friend at the University of Rhode Island and was Senator Claiborne Pell's legislative assistant. Wechsler called the under-secretary of labor, and the grant was approved.

Wiley also dreamed up some disastrous fund-raising schemes, notably a rock concert organized by an ex–professional football player he had met on a train. The concert flopped, as did periodic efforts to raise funds through mass mailing campaigns or full-page newspaper ads. Middle-class Americans would not respond to the cause of welfare the way they would to ecology, consumerism, or a Common Cause effort "to reform Congress."

Wiley made intense, though only sporadic, attempts to involve his staff in the art of fund-raising. At one staff-training session he advised: "Never ask for money on the phone, unless you have already built a clear relationship with the person; you can, however, ask for urgent bail bond money on the phone. Don't tell people it's money you want to see them for. Tell them you want to talk about programs, ideas; you need their expertise. When large sums are at stake, staffers must bring in the top leadership. People want to feel they are dealing with power."

Wiley's financial records were usually sheer chaos despite the best efforts of Robert Ostrow, and a young public-interest lawyer, John Ferren. Wiley knew the law—the 1969 Tax Reform Act stated that tax-exempt funds had to be carefully segregated and could not be used for prohibited purposes, especially lobbying. There is no doubt that he bent the law, using every dollar he could lay his hands on to meet expenses during chronic emergencies. Even normal expenses almost always ran ahead of money received, requiring an intricate Wiley juggling act. "George was aware of the tax laws, and he tried to keep his foundations out of trouble," said Ferren, "but he was more interested in how he could accomplish certain results." When it was apparent that the Nixon administration was going after the radical organizations by challenging their tax-exempt devices, George did his best to keep his house in order, but he just laughed about being a target on a then mythical Nixon "enemies list."*

Wiley consistently followed a practice known as a "float"—that is, he borrowed money with the expectation that a large grant several months ahead could be used to pay off the debt. If the government audited one of his tax-exempt vehicles—for instance, Misseduc—then he would run the contributions through IFCO. "When the Internal Revenue Service tried to break the back of IFCO," said the Reverend Lucius Walker, "they used NWRO as the main hammer. IRS spent three years examining our books. They practically lived in our office and disrupted our work. But they didn't find mismanagement or dishonesty. They found that poor people's organizations didn't have the ability or resources to keep the same kind of fancy books that the IRS does and expects big business to have."

John Ferren spent hundreds of hours trying to straighten out NWRO's fund-raising books, records, and tax returns. "I could give him advice, but if he didn't follow it, and got in trouble, I knew he would never turn on me. I was just willing, with my eyes open, to do twice the work the next time. He was just a magnetic guy whom I liked. I guess he did with me what he did with everybody else. He took me for granted in the best sense. He would dignify you by just taking for granted that you wanted to do all you could for him and his cause. And because of that basic trust and confidence, people like me ended up giving far more."

* As it turned out, Wiley and NWRO were on an official Nixon White House "enemies list" as well as a White House–inspired list of organizations to be probed by the Internal Revenue Service.

29

"Don't Mourn for
Me. Organize!"

In early February, 1968, Martin Luther King, Jr., was coming to Chicago to meet with Wiley and his executive board—at NWRO's demand. It promised to be a showdown. King was planning a "Poor People's Campaign" for Washington, D.C.—a tactic born in desperation, as the civil rights movement was in shreds. King had failed, during the previous two years, to solve the riddle of further effective action against northern racism and poverty. The new campaign called for thousands of the poor to encamp in Washington, dramatizing the issues for Congress and the country. The campaign needed foot soldiers. Wiley had them–ten thousand paid members in one hundred functioning chapters—and felt that King was trying to divert NWRO members to the Poor People's Campaign without any recognition of NWRO and its own purposes, program, and strategy.

When King walked through the lobby of the downtown Chicago YMCA on February 3, 1968, he was immediately surrounded by admirers—a crowd seeking to glimpse or touch the famous, charismatic leader. He moved upstairs, with his lieutenants—Ralph Abernathy, Andrew Young, Bernard Lafayette, and Al Sampson—to a meeting-room where Wiley and his thirty-member committee sat waiting. There were place-cards around the big rectangular table so that Johnnie Tillmon would be seated in the center, with Wiley on her right and Dr. King on her left. King would be separated from his lieutenants, who were surrounded in each corner by the welfare-recipient leadership. Tim Sampson characterized Wiley's seating arrangement as "a grand piece of psychological warfare."

To the ladies, King and the SCLC's Poor People's Campaign was a threat. They were angry that King's lieutenants had moved around the country contacting local welfare rights groups, asking them to join the banner at the cost of abandoning their own welfare-organizing efforts. "The women's concern was that they had a major constituency organization," said Sampson. "They had created it with their blood, sweat, and tears, and it was something magnificent to them. Not to be recognized was an attack on their very being. And to have it taken away was unthinkable."

While Johnnie Tillmon presided, holding her grandchild in her lap, King waited quietly until each woman introduced herself. He then began to describe the purposes of the forthcoming Washington campaign. "We need your support," he concluded.

Then Etta Horn opened the barrage: "How do you stand on P.L. 90–248?" Puzzled, Dr. King looked toward the Reverend Andrew Young, his executive director. "She means the Anti-Welfare bill, H.R. 12080, passed by the Congress on December 15, and signed into law by Lyndon Baines Johnson on January 2," interrupted Mrs. Tillmon. "Where were you last October, when we were down in Washington trying to get support for Senator Kennedy's amendments?" Beulah Sanders held up a copy of the NWRO pamphlet *The Kennedy Welfare Amendments*.

King was bewildered by the technical discussion of the new law as his staff tried to fend off the women's hostile questions. Finally, Johnnie Tillmon said, "You know, Dr. King, if you don't know about these questions, you should say you don't know, and then we could go on with the meeting." "You're right, Mrs. Tillmon," King replied. "We don't know anything about welfare. We are here to learn." The NWRO members proceeded to bring Dr. King up to date on the history of what they saw as welfare repression in Congress and the nation.

Since their founding convention in August, 1967, when two thousand welfare mothers stayed in Washington to protest congressional action on welfare, the women had studied the politics of welfare. A bill approved by the House Ways and Means Committee called for freezing federal welfare payments, denying help to the increasing number of people (drawn in part by NWRO's vigorous activities) now applying for benefits. The bill also would have required work and training for all welfare mothers and their children older than sixteen who were out of school. It was an "anti-welfare bill," reflecting growing conservative thinking in Washington and the country.

To Representative Wilbur Mills (D., Ark.), chairman of the Ways and Means Committee, and many conservative Americans like him, there was somehow a dangerous link between soaring welfare rolls, militant black demands, and the rioting which had ripped through American cities for the fourth straight year. In the summer of 1967, welfare did touch off the disorders. The Mothers for Adequate Welfare, demonstrating at the Grove Hall Welfare Office in Roxbury, Massachusetts, drew angry police whose actions touched off a devastating weekend riot in southeast Boston. The next week, Newark, New Jersey, burned, a reaction to the arrest of a black cab driver; twenty-seven people were killed and ten million dollars in damage done. Detroit exploded the following weekend, leaving forty-three dead, seven thousand arrested, and more than five square miles burned to the ground. In all, 114 cities in thirty-two states were struck by riots during that summer. Punctuating the riot coverage on television was the rhetoric of SNCC leaders Stokely Carmichael and H. Rap Brown, and CORE director Floyd McKissick, who proclaimed that "the day of nonviolent resistance is over."*

In that climate, Wilbur Mills drafted the bill which Senator Robert F. Kennedy called "the most punitive measure in the history of the country—they seem to punish the poor because they are there and we have not been able to do anything about them." Mills demanded an investigation of the soaring welfare rolls in New York City, as though they were the result of a criminal conspiracy. In 1962, Congress had passed a welfare reform bill which prescribed more social services as the medicine for welfare ills. Five years later, the proposed solution was to freeze funds and force people to work.

Against this background, Wiley and the NWRO founding mothers had asked to testify before a Senate committee considering Mills' bill. They were refused. Instead, following their 1967 founding convention, they had marched down Pennsylvania Avenue on a hot August day to demand a meeting with HEW Secretary John Gardner. Tim Sampson described their reception: "The doors were locked. There were guards behind the doors and men with guns on the roof, and that was a moment of awakening for me. The welfare recipients of this country could come to their capital and want to meet with the secretary of health, education, and welfare, and this supposedly liberal John Gardner would not only *not* meet with them, but they would lock the doors and point guns at us."

When NWRO was granted a hearing on the bill on September 19, 1967, with the Senate Finance Committee, the climate was not much better. Senator Russell Long (D., La.), the committee chairman, listened to the first few minutes of testimony by Johnnie Tillmon and then left the room, followed quickly by all the other committee members except Senator Fred Harris (D., Okla.). When Harris recessed the hearing at 12:55 P.M. the women were furious. They had traveled so far, to be received with such lack of interest by the men who would write the Senate's version of the welfare-freeze

---

* J. Edgar Hoover's latest report to the attorney general had warned that "the increasing power of the black power concept has contributed to a climate of unrest and has come to mean to many Negroes the power to riot, burn, loot and kill."

law. The frustrated welfare mothers staged an angry sit-in in the committee room, demanding to be heard, an unprecedented event in the Senate Finance Committee. Chairman Long, equally furious, returned in the afternoon and slammed his gavel to adjourn the hearing.

There was little doubt about the senator's own feelings. He dismissed the welfare mothers as "brood mares" who "if they can find time to march in the streets, picket, and sit all day in committee hearing rooms, they can find time to do some useful work. They could be picking up litter in front of their houses or killing rats instead of impeding the work of Congress." Angered and disgusted that anyone would call his fellow human beings "brood mares," Wiley was at first perplexed that no one in Washington challenged Long on his cruel statement. He appealed to Carl Holman at the Urban Coalition to get someone to answer Long.

Carl Holman: "George was shaken because he expected that some of the black civil rights leaders would rise in holy anger at someone calling our people 'brood mares,' but it didn't happen. So I called a couple of people to urge a reply, and they said it was the wrong tactic to get in a verbal battle with Long, that we should fight on issues that are important; that you don't answer Long if you're trying to be effective behind the scenes. Some even said it was ill-advised for those women to be there anyway. It was a devastating commentary on those people who ran organizations supposedly concerned about poor people and black people. But there was also reflected a reaction to a new organization, NWRO, fear of a new group that would be competing for money and influence—a real selfishness on the part of the established groups."

The sit-in against Long did give the "punitive" provisions of the bill some national publicity. Robert Kennedy, on October 27, introduced amendments to eliminate its more brutal provisions, particularly the freeze of payments. Wiley used the bill to rally welfare rights chapters across the country. In its first national lobbying campaign, NWRO staged demonstrations in forty cities during November as local chapters collected signatures to present to their senators. Some of the Kennedy amendments were approved by the Senate, but when the bill went to a conference committee, with Wilbur Mills from the House and Russell Long from the Senate at the helm, the anti-welfare provisions were restored. On December 15, while Senator Kennedy was lining up support for a liberal filibuster against the Conference Committee bill, Senator Long brought it to the floor, and it was passed with only three senators present. Wiley and other liberal leaders petitioned President Johnson to veto the bill, but on January 2, 1968, he signed it into law.* Appropriations for the Vietnam war depended on the good will of Congressman Mills and Senator Long.

* The new law did contain several reform features proposed by the Johnson administration. Welfare recipients were allowed to keep some earnings from jobs, and states were required to update their welfare standards of need.

For more than an hour at the Chicago YMCA, Martin Luther King, Jr., listened to the NWRO mothers give the history of that welfare freeze. The women leaders explained to him that their 1968 Washington strategy was to lobby for repeal of the new law and to demand that the Johnson administration enforce state compliance with other federal laws or regulations guaranteeing the rights of welfare recipients. King agreed that NWRO's demands would become part of the Poor People's Campaign agenda and reassured Tillmon that NWRO's own organizing efforts would be respected. Dr. King shook hands around the table, saying, "We have a date in Washington, April 22," and the group dispersed.

The meeting dramatized the differences between factions of the civil rights and antipoverty movements in 1968. Andrew Young,* King's chief aide, remembers how hostile the women were: "It was almost as though they were saying that we had no right to do anything for poor people—that poor folk were their property. And they jumped on Martin like no one ever had before. I don't think he had ever been that insulted in a meeting. But I think he understood. In a way, they were testing him. Just to deal with those kinds of women took a hell of a lot of energy and a particular kind of person, which George Wiley had to be. Not many black men could have done that. George had everything he could handle riding herd on those strong black women. Martin King could not have done it, for instance."**

But more than differences of style separated King and Wiley and their two organizations. King, who could captivate a nation, still was seeking another dramatic event that could change the course of history. In late 1967 and early 1968, he was floundering and he knew it. The emotional, moral, and religious appeal of King and his lieutenants, which had so stirred blacks in the South and Americans of all colors, had brought down the walls of legal segregation. Economic issues, however, did not seem to yield to the old magic. Yet King, bombarded by pleas for dramatic action, agreed to the Poor People's Campaign. He had to do something to keep the issues alive.

Wiley was on a much narrower track. His dream was to concentrate on and master a single issue—welfare—deeply affecting the lives of masses of poor people. He saw that King's inspiring rhetoric did not yield much in the way of tangible gains. In late 1966, for instance, King had issued a statement, announcing with great fanfare that he would be leading demonstrations in

---

* Elected in 1972 as Democratic congressman from Georgia, appointed ambassador to the U.N. in 1977.

** Young explained: "We had a hard time with domineering women in SCLC because Martin's mother, quiet as she was, was really a strong, domineering force in that family. She was never publicly saying anything but she ran Daddy King and she ran the church and she ran Martin, and so Martin's problems in the early days of the movement were directly related to his need to be free of that strong matriarchal influence. This is a generality, but a system of oppression tends to produce weak men and strong women, and George somehow was a particularly strong man and really took on the task. I don't know how he did it, but he at least survived."

northern cities to secure "a guaranteed annual income." Not a single demonstration ever took place. King had, in effect, merely issued another press release. Wiley, on the other hand, played down the idea of a guaranteed annual income—even though that was in fact one of his goals. Society would not change merely because you preached high ideals and spoke of grand new concepts. You changed the country, Wiley thought, by working on one thing at a time, achieving concrete gains, and welding people into an organization that could exert power. One-shot national demonstrations were an outworn strategy.

Andrew Young, King's aide, credits the welfare rights movement with turning the civil rights movement significantly toward economic issues: "Civil rights in the sixties was public accommodations, social questions, or voting rights. In some sense, we [SCLC] were afraid to tackle welfare in the South. Everything we did was considered Communist, and I think almost to survive we tended to phrase everything in religious terms and to avoid issues that smacked of economic change. Religion was the language the South understood, and there was an almost calculated avoidance of any economic questions. When we did turn to economic issues, there is no question we chose to concentrate on hunger, improving government food-aid programs rather than welfare. We tried to put things in terms that southern whites might accept, and they might accept hunger as an issue, but certainly not welfare. Not that we were anti-welfare, but it seemed to us you didn't go asking for welfare. I guess in the back of all our minds we felt that asking for welfare was tactically unsound. You asked for jobs, you asked for food. You might get something. If you asked for welfare, you might not get anything."

King's basic constituency and the one Wiley pulled together were different, Young points out. "In SCLC we were working with college students, with independent business people. The civil rights movement, up until 1968, anyway, was really a middle-class movement. There were middle-class goals, middle-class aspirations, middle-class membership, and even though a lot of poor people went to jail, say for the Voting Rights Act, it was still essentially a middle-class operation. Cesar Chavez and George Wiley had poor people's movements."

Wiley understood how difficult it was for SCLC to join the welfare issue in the South, but he also saw middle-class blacks in general shrinking from the issue. As he told a group of black students: "I find so frequently that black students aspire to greater things than dealing with the welfare issue. I'm often told: 'We don't want to deal with welfare; people should get off welfare. We want to get away from that.' But the point is that the mass of our people are down there, and we have to recognize where people are now, and if we're going to get up there, we've got to start from where we are, start dealing with the realities that a lot of our folk have to struggle just to get enough to eat, and to get clothes and decent housing."

There was a profound difference in style between NWRO and SCLC, between the southern movement's religious emphasis, with its Baptist rhetoric and evangelical fervor, and the belligerence of the welfare rights leaders. Andrew Young: "I think their whole NWRO style, the whole aggressive cussing folks out and banging on the table, hell-raising approach was based on a theory that you had to make the poor aggressive and they had to express their hatred and frustration against the system to keep from expressing it against themselves. I think our approach was better and far more indigenous to the black community."

But no one had any magic prescriptions. Some movement people pinned their hopes on the 1965 Voting Rights Act and worked on electing blacks to public office and thus building power within the system. At its 1968 convention the NAACP was split, divided between those satisfied with the significant gains of the black bourgeoisie and the young Turks dissatisfied with the lack of progress of the black masses. Whitney Young was attempting to move the Urban League into a more militant posture; the League should renounce its traditional role as a "power broker" and concentrate on building power in the ghetto, he said. But in 1968, the militant black nationalists held the spotlight. Floyd McKissick was pushed out as CORE national director by Roy Innis, an even stronger advocate of black separatism and nationalism. The names in the news were H. Rap Brown and Stokely Carmichael of SNCC and Eldridge Cleaver of the Black Panther Party.

Two weeks before the King-Wiley meeting in Chicago, Carmichael organized a meeting in Washington that was supposed to create a militant "Black United Front." The effort failed; Wiley attended but still was not impressed with the notion of blacks going it alone. And even as King and Wiley met, sensational national publicity focused on H. Rap Brown's arrest for violation of bail.* Factionalism in SNCC, the pioneer southern organization of the militant young in the early 1960s, had reduced it to a small, fractured cadre which was unsuccessful in transferring its activities to the North, and finally SNCC went out of business via a largely symbolic merger with the Black Panthers. Moderate black leaders, including King, complained that the news media had blown out of proportion the role of the revolutionary, nationalist, and separatist black left. The violence that marked the year was foreshadowed by events in Orangeburg, South Carolina, in February, just four days after the Wiley-King meeting in Chicago. Black students from South Carolina State College protested discrimination at a local bowling alley; there were provocative moves by both the students and local police and National Guard, and then bloodshed.**

* An earlier charge against Brown, which attracted far more publicity than early announcements of the Poor People's Campaign, was the illegal carrying of a handgun on an airplane flight between New Orleans and New York.
** Four black students were killed in an event which Jack Nelson and Jack Bass later recorded in a book entitled *The Orangeburg Massacre* (New York: World, 1970).

In an effort to bridge the diverging concerns of activists, Wiley joined in a March 22 meeting outside Chicago of "New Left" white and black civil rights leaders. There was clearly to be no mutual accommodation. The blacks, including Wiley, left unsatisfied, convinced that the agenda was a white-dominated, white middle-class concern about Vietnam, with only perfunctory attention to the needs of blacks or poor people. The white energy that had once helped fuel the civil rights crusade now worked against the war, or for presidential candidate Eugene McCarthy.

NWRO planned a token representation in the Poor People's Campaign, but the organization's emphasis in 1968 was still on organizing at the grass roots. Hulbert James, then the NWRO staff director in New York, said, "We left that meeting with King and threw ourselves completely into our spring organizing effort in New York, which was our biggest one in the history of the movement."* In the NWRO plan, May and June were designated "key" months for building membership, with June 30, the third anniversary of the Ohio March, set as the "Brood Mares' Stampede." There would be actions at the homes of public officials and demonstrations at the welfare departments. Wiley planned a lobbying program in Washington to be coordinated with Senator Kennedy's promised fight to repeal the welfare freeze.** But in March, after Eugene McCarthy's Democratic primary victory in New Hampshire, welfare rights champion Robert F. Kennedy entered the presidential race, leaving the repeal fight in Congress without a leader. †

On March 31, Dr. King came to Washington to preach in the National Cathedral, vowing that he would bring thousands of poor people to the capital on April 22 to "establish that the real issue is not violence or nonviolence, but poverty and neglect." Afterward he announced that President Johnson or Congress could persuade him to call off the march if he were given "a positive commitment they would do something this summer to aid the nation's slums." The president, however, had other matters on his mind. That evening he announced his intention not to run for re-election.

* See Chapter 28 on organizing.
** The welfare rights movement was given a boost when the president's National Advisory Commission on Civil Disorders warned that "white racism" was chiefly to blame for the explosive conditions that sparked riots. The Commission, headed by Illinois Governor Otto Kerner, scored the welfare system, saying that it "saves money instead of people" and tragically ends up doing neither. Wiley sent to his members the Commission's recommendations (March 11, 1968).

President Johnson, his eye on the forthcoming New Hampshire primary and the anti-welfare feeling sweeping the country, had little to say on the Commission report. However his new secretary of HEW, Wilbur Cohen, criticized the report, saying the Commission put too little emphasis on how the poor can lift themselves up by their own bootstraps.

† In a letter to Ethel Kennedy, Wiley added a note: "P.S. You may tell your husband that I am personally very much in favor of his candidacy though I do not think it is possible for NWRO to take a position on the election. It's not clear either that NWRO public support would be particularly helpful.

Meanwhile, Wiley concentrated on organizing new NWRO chapters. He was at this task in Dayton, Ohio, on April 4 when he received the news that Martin Luther King, Jr., had been murdered in Memphis. Throughout the night Wiley conferred with NWRO leaders around the country. The next day, in a speech to a largely white student audience at Kent State University, he poured out his frustrations: "It is not possible for me to talk to you today without the sense of anger that I have in my heart. I was for seven years a university professor; I have been in the privileged class of black people, and I might say there are many people in upper-middle-class circumstances, such as myself, who have become so disenchanted and so disillusioned with the phony promises, with the phony pledges, that they are going to completely identify at least emotionally with that thrust that is going to tear this country down if it does not deal with its problems.

"I am not going to be throwing the bombs and shooting people, but I am here to tell you today that George Wiley is not going to be out there trying to cool people off so that you folks can be more comfortable in your apathy—that George Wiley is not going to be out there trying to sell out those black folks by making moves to help the power structure ameliorate the rage and anger that there is in this country. There are many of us—and I speak for our welfare rights leaders—who are not the least bit interested in protecting your security or your comfort or those in your family.

"In some respects, I think that I am a dinosaur—because of my commitment to work within the channels, within the institutions, to use protest, to use direct action, to use the courts, to use the democratic process, and I intend to go down with that, but I have no confidence at all with that approach succeeding. It is a period of great ambivalence for people like myself, whose guts identify with those people who are going to be tearing down your cities, who are prepared to cheer secretly when people are planting bombs in Macy's and in Gimbel's and the department stores, who decry violence and don't want to see their families brutalized, but at the same time can't stand to see the kind of things that have gone on in this country tolerated any longer."

Wiley was torn. He followed his bitter words at Kent State with an explanation that NWRO was a dedicated multiracial organization which needed and welcomed support from middle-class "friends' groups." Yet at the King funeral in Atlanta he brusquely turned down a request from John Marqusee (his wealthy white financial supporter and close friend) to march with the NWRO contingent. "I would rather you didn't. Do you understand that, today?" Wiley said. He was angered by the way the funeral was exploited by white politicians, as the Rockefellers, Humphreys, Kennedys, and Nixons occupied the front pews. It was "business as usual," he said in his newsletter, "the rich white folks up front and the poor black folks in the back." Wiley's outbursts of disgust with white liberals, some of whom were among his best friends, were signs of a new pessimism.

The voices of moderation and conciliation were drowned in the wave of violence following King's death. The murder of the apostle of nonviolence triggered a spasm of rage in black communities across the nation; two hundred thousand were arrested and forty-three killed. Wiley immediately proposed that Congress legislate a living memorial to Dr. King by repealing the welfare-freeze law of 1967, enacting a national guaranteed income of four thousand dollars for a family of four, and appropriating federal funds for at least three million jobs. But he knew that this was merely rhetoric. His emphasis could be found emblazoned on the cover of the April 9, 1968, NWRO newsletter. Underneath a picture of Dr. King were the words, "Don't Mourn for Me. Organize!"* Wiley wrote:

> Martin Luther King is free at last, but when will poor people be free? . . . How many deaths will it take before Congress will pass a welfare rights bill guaranteeing all people welfare and jobs now?
> We may be angry, we may be sad, but we must follow Mrs. King's courageous example. We must continue to organize and to struggle for bread and justice now.

Wiley seized the chance to focus the first Poor People's Campaign activities on NWRO. On April 22, when King had planned to present his demands to Congress, Wiley led a group of choir-robed NWRO women to an all-night candle-light vigil in front of the Capitol. They were all arrested before the night was out. The second event was a May 12 Mother's Day Protest March, held simultaneously in Washington and in dozens of other cities where NWRO was active. The march in Washington was dramatic; Coretta King, along with Ethel Kennedy and the women leaders of NWRO, led seven thousand women through the burned-out streets of Washington, where rioting had broken out after King's death. At the Cardozo High School Stadium, Johnnie Tillmon and Coretta King spoke about the abuses of the welfare system, but it was Mrs. Perlie Mae Bynclum, a welfare mother from Lamast, Mississippi, who summed it all up: "I done everything—and I got nothing to show for it."

Within weeks, tragedy again struck the poor who had placed their hope in a few heroes. Robert Kennedy was murdered just after he had won the Democratic presidential primary in California. On June 8, Wiley again marched with a delegation of NWRO women in a funeral procession, this one to Arlington cemetery. "Most people will remember Robert Kennedy for his boyish smile, his engaging manner, and his clever wit," he said, "but eight million welfare recipients will remember him most as the man who tried to return a measure of sanity and decency to a welfare program afflicted by the consequences of the racism, hatred and paranoia of our society."

The Poor People's Campaign was a failure. The mass of poor people

---

* These were the last words of Joe Hill, the martyred early-twentieth-century labor organizer.

mired down in the mud of "Resurrection City" on the Mall in Washington inspired only negative feelings. The Johnson administration and the country resisted granting any major concessions, and in any case, the organizations of the poor could never agree on which issues they should emphasize. But Wiley, always ready to concentrate on specific problems, achieved some results during the campaign. A process of regular negotiations was begun with middle- and upper-echelon HEW bureaucrats, and this led to action by HEW in attacking welfare abuses by the states. And HEW agreed to several important rule changes. Welfare recipients no longer could have their grants terminated without prior notice, and states were required to act on welfare applications within thirty days. (It was a common practice in some states to ignore them for months.) Those victories eventually led to real improvements in the lives of thousands of welfare recipients. When the Poor People's Campaign finally ended, as park police swept through and destroyed Resurrection City, Wiley reflected that the entire operation had only hindered NWRO, sapping time and money from grass-roots organizing.

Militant NWRO organizing activities expanded in 1968. There was a peak of activity in New York City, and chapters sprouted in black urban ghettoes as well as areas of white rural poverty in Virginia, Indiana, and West Virginia, and in Mexican-American communities in the Southwest. Throughout the summer, Wiley crisscrossed the country from Nashville to Lansing, from Miami to San Francisco, speaking, organizing, raising money. NWRO protests won long-denied welfare rights or increased benefits:

In Michigan, NWRO chapters successfully demanded and received school clothing allowances, as well as winning the support of Governor George Romney to ward off cuts in welfare grants; in Denver, a delegation marched on the state welfare board, demanding (and eventually gaining) representation on the board; in Kentucky, white mountain women and black urban mothers joined together in a petition to set up an emergency-assistance program. The protest and organizing activities varied in character. Some were lawful, peaceful assemblies, others militant actions—invading the governor's office in Delaware or taking over the state legislature galleries in Wisconsin.* Wiley tried to give the campaigns a national theme; NWRO would outline a "winter clothing campaign," a "spend-the-rent campaign," or a "Mother's Day protest."

Wiley also was trying to change welfare law through the courts. He spent countless hours planning legal strategy with a small group of lawyers led by Edward Sparer. NWRO won seven important Supreme Court decisions striking down provisions under which states could treat welfare recipients as less than full citizens. The first major court victory came on June 11,

---

* For details of the scope of NWRO activities, see Appendix A.

1968, when the Supreme Court nullified Alabama's "man-in-the-house rule," which denied welfare support to dependent children whose mothers maintained relationships with men not their fathers. In a series of decisions, the federal courts struck down a whole series of devices, including state residency requirements, by which states sought to restrict their welfare rolls.

When Wiley met with HEW officials to discuss guidelines for implementing the court rulings; he was an amiable negotiator, calm and articulate. But he could also chase HEW Secretary Wilbur Cohen outside the Capitol shouting, "Are you going to enforce the Supreme Court ruling?" Press microphones were shoved in Cohen's face. "I am," the secretary answered, tight-lipped, and pushed the microphones away. Wiley had learned to perform for the press; he could capture a bank of microphones with the same agility he showed in commandeering a bank of telephones at Penn Station.

NWRO's withering attitude toward national party politics in 1968 was exemplified by a cartoon in its October newsletter titled "The U.S. Political Jungle." It featured "scorpion" Richard Nixon, "spider" Hubert Humphrey, and "snake" George Wallace, all reaching out for welfare mothers' votes. NWRO held its own convention at Barat College in Lake Forest, a suburb of Chicago, at the time of the violent 1968 Democratic National Convention. Wiley and the leaders of NWRO went through the motions of testifying before the Democratic Platform Committee, but the real convention battle was over Vietnam, and it was a matter of white versus white, divorced from the issues of race and poverty. Black organizations stayed away. Etta Horn and some of the NWRO leaders got swept up into a convention street battle while on a sightseeing trip in Chicago's Old Town, and immediately voted to go home.

Many civil rights movement people, disgusted with traditional politics, scorned any involvement. Between Humphrey, who, amidst all the year's horror, called for a "politics of joy," and Nixon, who had made a pact with southern segregationists to slow the pace of integration and phase out the antipoverty program, there seemed little choice. In a fitting climax to a grim year, Republican vice presidential candidate Spiro Agnew said, "If you've seen one ghetto, you've seen them all," and most of the country agreed. According to the Gallup and Harris polls, only 3 percent of Americans found poverty a key issue of national concern.

Despite the dispiriting events of 1968, even as others were too saddened or disheartened to continue the movement, Wiley kept working with a single-minded dedication. NWRO more than doubled its contributions and its membership, and finally forced its way into a place at the bargaining table of American political power. It was an insecure seat at best, but three years before there had been no organized voice for the welfare poor. Now these voices were being heard and were making some impact on public policy.

There is a great capacity for self-delusion in the world of political Washington, but Wiley saw progress in the fact that NWRO was now being greeted not only at HEW but at the White House. Daniel Patrick Moynihan had been appointed as President Nixon's chief advisor on domestic affairs. And one of Moynihan's first acts in early 1969 was to invite Wiley to his office. Wiley insisted on bringing his recipient leaders with him. Moynihan wanted Wiley's support for welfare reform and recognized that NWRO now had sufficient strength to count in any forthcoming debate. Wiley was cautious. Grand plans were fine things to talk about, but he wanted something specific, a meeting with the new HEW Secretary Robert Finch. Moynihan arranged the meeting.

Wiley wanted HEW to enforce a 1967 law requiring state welfare departments to raise their welfare standards to meet current costs of living. No longer would it be possible, for instance, for the welfare budget of the District of Columbia to be based on a 1958 standard of living (and even then pay only 75 percent of what the 1958 standard called for). The states were now required to come up with more realistic standards; this would inevitably make more people eligible for benefits and in some cases actually lead to an increase in benefits. Finch, a moderately liberal Californian and a personal friend of the new president, was interested, and pursued enforcement of the law with some vigor.

The February 9, 1969, NWRO newsletter compared the icy reception from the Johnson administration in 1967 and the warm reception from Republicans in 1969. "What made the difference?" wrote Wiley. "In 1967 there was no NWRO. In 1969 the nine welfare recipients who went to the White House last week were your elected officers. They represent the more than thirty thousand NWRO members across the country. The Nixon administration met with us because we are organized and because our organization is starting to have some political power. We must continue to organize so that our voices will be heard and our issues addressed." Wiley was still no political ideologue. If a conservative Republican administration took any positive steps on welfare issues, he would welcome them.

Late in 1968, Governor Nelson Rockefeller of New York called for a federalization of welfare that would provide uniform benefits across the country. Rockefeller was responding to the economic predicament in which New York found itself. The New York City welfare rolls had doubled to more than a million people between 1966 and 1968. New York City and New York State could no longer afford their share of the costs. To some extent, the Cloward-Piven theory was beginning to work. At least one governor, overwhelmed by the NWRO-encouraged surge onto the welfare rolls, was calling for an overhaul of the system. NWRO and Wiley now had a new opportunity and a new responsibility.

30

A Thorn in the Side
of Washington, D.C.

On August 8, 1969, before a packed press conference in the Indian Treaty Room of the Executive Office Building, next door to the White House, Daniel Patrick Moynihan announced the Nixon administration's plans for "the most far-reaching new domestic legislation since the New Deal." The president, he said, that evening would propose to Congress and the nation legislation totally overhauling the welfare system, particularly the AFDC program. (Privately, Moynihan claimed that the Nixon program represented a real breakthrough for a guaranteed annual income for all Americans.) Primed with elaborate graphs, charts, and copies of computerized data showing costs and numbers of people affected by the proposed legislation, the presidential assistant was bubbling with enthusiasm, until three reporters insisted, during the question period, that the proposed elimination of food stamps in Nixon's new plan could leave millions of welfare recipients worse off than they were before. The reporters had been briefed earlier in the day by George Wiley, who was fast learning the secrets of Washington—timing, political intelligence, press contacts. Wiley knew in detail what the proposal contained and had his attack ready before the program was announced. Moynihan was startled by the question on food stamps. "That is just simply impossible," he declared, and deftly steered the dialogue back to a lofty historical view: this was the first meaningful presidential initiative for welfare reform in thirty years, he noted, and it was coming from a Republican administration.

But Moynihan was wrong about the loss of benefits. After a week of political stuttering, the White House backtracked and said that food stamps wouldn't be eliminated after all. (As John Kramer, director of the National Council on Malnutrition, critically pointed out: "It is the arithmetic, not the rhetoric, which affects poor people's lives!") During the next three years Nixon administration experts would err repeatedly about how their complicated proposals would affect the lives of poor people, particularly the nine million women and children already living on welfare. For Wiley and NWRO those details were all-important. As in most matters of national legislation, welfare reform became a complex political power struggle. But this particular one was different, because a new interest group with its own "experts" was engaged. At every turn in the debate, Wiley showed how legislative proposals would affect the actual income or legal rights of welfare recipients.

Discussions by economic theorists about welfare reform and a guaranteed annual income were fueled in the early 1960s by a variety of concerns. Economist-futurist Robert Theobald thought a guaranteed annual income was necessary in the job-eliminating computerized economy he predicted. Conservative economist Milton Friedman came to the idea as a means of replacing all bureaucratic, socialistic welfare support programs with one simple system of minimum support through a negative income tax. George Wiley and others from the civil rights movement came to the issue as they discovered the persistence and depth of American poverty. Moynihan and others saw the idea as an alternative to the Johnson administration's "Great Society" programs, which they believed had largely failed.

Political pressure for reform also came from several other directions. In the wake of five years of black urban rioting, the National Advisory Commission on Civil Disorders reported: "Our nation is moving toward two societies, one black, one white; separate and unequal." The Commission strongly recommended a reformed, generous, federalized welfare program. President Johnson had appointed a commission which reported favorably on the idea of a guaranteed annual income in 1969. Other pressures for reform came from the explosion in the welfare rolls; during the first five years of NWRO's existence, the number of families receiving AFDC payments more than doubled. State governments, which shared the costs of the program with the federal government, pressed for reform in the form of a federal takeover. For conservatives, however, "reform" meant reducing the welfare rolls. NWRO had contributed to the movement for reform. The organization had been founded with a principal goal of gaining a "guaranteed adequate income" for all Americans. NWRO's organizing drives and victories to open up the welfare rolls to those eligible for assistance helped swell the rolls, both by emboldening the poor and by making it easier to obtain assistance.

Until 1969, Wiley had concentrated primarily on organizing poor people to secure their legal rights and to get some share of power in the immediate processes that affected their lives. Lobbying in Washington for a guaranteed annual income seemed premature. But when the Nixon administration unexpectedly moved on the issue, Wiley took on a new challenge. For assistance in devising his own program, he again turned to academics, including economists Leonard Hausman of Brandeis University and Ben Okner of the Brookings Institution. From Okner he got the theoretical underpinnings of NWRO's own welfare reform plan, as well as detailed, computerized analyses of how various other income redistribution plans would work. "Somehow, George cajoled a lot of talent free," Okner said. "Here was a guy who was working within the law. He had taken the time and trouble to read the fine print, he had gotten out and organized the mothers. Everyone was moaning about how awful welfare was, yet George was doing something concrete. He was a salesman who sold me on the idea that there was good reason for me to provide him with information."

"You promised us in January to involve us in the planning," Wiley accused Moynihan as the Nixon plan was announced, "and you have handed us a fait accompli. You say this is for poor people. Where were the poor people?" Wiley and Johnnie Tillmon then fired off a letter to President Nixon: "You must tell honestly how much money it takes for people to live. Government research indicates that a minimum adequate income for a family of four is $5,500 a year. The federal government must take leadership in establishing adequate income for everyone as a national goal. . . ."

The Nixon plan called for a basic federal payment to families of four of $1,600 a year, if the family had no other income. As income rose, the federal payment would decline and then stop altogether once the family reached $3,920 a year, which in 1969 was the government's definition of the "poverty line." The poverty line itself was a debatable statistic. Devised by a government statistician in 1964 as a guideline for the War on Poverty, it began with the Agriculture Department's cost of an emergency diet, which the department stressed could sustain a family only during brief periods of distress. By 1969, *poverty line* had been worked into the economic and bureaucratic vocabulary so thoroughly that few stopped to consider the figure's relationship to reality. Wiley's figure of $5,500 a year came directly from the Bureau of Labor Statistics. It included $2,237 for food, $1,402 for housing, $784 for clothing and personal care, $312 for medical care, $484 for transportation, and $322 for insurance, recreation, schoolbooks and supplies, and the rest.

Wiley's deepest criticism was that the sixteen-hundred-dollar Nixon figure, aside from being ridiculously low, was an arbitrary number which did not even pretend to relate in any way to the cost of living. At the least, Wiley thought, any welfare reform plan worthy of the name should set a future goal of an adequate income and bear some relationship to the real cost of living. The Nixon Family Assistance Plan, however, broke new ground with two very important principles. First, the proposal called for a uniform federal payment that would place a floor underneath the income of all American families. Second, it included the "working poor" among the families to be aided—intact, two-parent families who earned less than a poverty-level income but under present law did not qualify for AFDC welfare payments. Wiley—and almost everyone else interested in helping the poor—heartily approved.

A uniform minimum federal benefit would move toward modifying the wide variation in state welfare systems.* Aid to the working poor acknowledged the inadequacy of the bottom end of the American wage structure, and might help poor families stay intact. Despite those two innovations, however, much of the old system remained. The plan did not replace the present system in which states and the federal government share responsibilities for welfare payments. Nor did the Nixon plan offer any meaningful change for most of those nine million women and children already receiving welfare. In fact, the proposed new federal floor—sixteen hundred dollars for a family of four—was set so low that welfare recipients in all but six southern states already were able to receive more in benefits with a combination of welfare and food stamps. Their present welfare income—set at far below the poverty line in most states—depended on the states continuing to pay part of the cost of welfare. Moreover, female AFDC recipients would be required to work at less than the minimum wage or take job training—or else lose part of their welfare check. Wiley's initial opposition to the Nixon plan centered on three key areas: the inadequacy of the benefits, the loss of hard-won legal rights, and the entire concept of work—who should be required to work in American society and under what conditions and at what wages.

Did the Nixon plan represent a "foot in the door" toward welfare reform? Once passed into law, could liberal amendments be tucked in over the years, raising benefits toward a truly livable minimum wage and offering a chance, within the law, for that family to survive until that wage could be achieved? Many liberals argued in favor of the "foot in the door" theory, but Wiley was dubious, particularly since the bill made no provision for future increases, even to match rises in the cost of living, and did not protect the rights of present welfare recipients.

Moynihan and Wiley were deadlocked. Their different visions of the responsibilities of American society to its poor were as far apart now as they had been in 1965, when they clashed over the nature of the black family and

---

* State welfare payments for a family of four in 1969 ranged from a low of $480 a year in Mississippi to a high of $3,000 in New Jersey.

the ills of American society. Moynihan talked of his plan as bringing dramatic change, but Wiley, looking at its details, saw that Moynihan still subscribed to the traditional political-economic arrangement, in which the poor were kept securely in place at the bottom of the ladder, where they were required to perform the dirtiest jobs in the society at the lowest pay, and in which their troubles were still blamed on the instability of the black family. It was society itself which needed drastic overhauling, Wiley said, so that people who could not work would receive adequate income and people who could work would have decent jobs at decent pay. In Wiley's view, Moynihan was just tinkering with the system. Wiley wanted to radically overhaul it.

"Support us," Moynihan pleaded with Wiley and others who pointed out shortcomings in the plan. "This is a breakthrough which later can be expanded." The argument was persuasive—especially to those who saw even sixteen hundred dollars a year and aid to the working poor as going a long way toward changing conditions in the poorest southern states. At first Wiley, too, was inclined to compromise, although he protected his singular role as critic. "George took two positions," recalls Hulburt James. "The public position of being against FAP and pointing out its defects, and the private position of seeking a compromise, a decent bill."

Tactically, Wiley began to pursue a variety of strategies to dramatize the inadequacies of the Nixon welfare plan. He launched with staff aide Tom Glynn a "Live on a Welfare Budget" campaign, in which church members and other middle-class American families were urged to live for a week on the fifteen cents per person per meal that would be permitted by Nixon's sixteen hundred dollars a year in welfare benefits. The campaign was dramatic and effective. Respected citizens described in their local news media how difficult—or impossible—it was to live on FAP's welfare standards. In Washington, the campaign drew support from a dozen prominent congressional wives, led by Jane Hart, the independent-minded wife of Senator Philip Hart of Michigan, and Joan Mondale, wife of Senator Walter Mondale of Minnesota.

When Wiley moved into the halls of Congress to formulate alternative legislation, he found, to his surprise, a void on the liberal side of the issue.* Liberal Democratic politicians, stunned by Nixon's initiative, did not try to develop an alternative, more generous measure. Welfare, after all, was a politically unpopular issue. No politician, especially one with national ambitions, stood to gain much by urging more generous treatment of welfare recipients. Welfare was also an issue that most congressmen had generally

---

* The only prominent liberal legislator to pose a more generous alternative was Senator Abraham Ribicoff (D., Conn.) and his intentions were suspect by NWRO. A few months earlier he had suggested that New York welfare recipients be given brooms to sweep the streets of New York. In introducing his own plan, he rather weakly suggested he would accept the Nixon plan if his was defeated.

avoided as too complicated. Therefore, for years, as political scientist Gilbert Steiner pointed out, welfare legislation and policy were left to a very small group of academics and government bureaucrats. Congress paid very little attention to what was going on—that is, until the welfare explosion of the late 1960s.

The Nixon Family Assistance Plan was introduced in Congress in October, 1969, where it found an unexpected ally in NWRO's old nemesis, Representative Wilbur Mills of Arkansas. Mills, the master manipulator, immediately scheduled hearings in his House Ways and Means Committee and indicated a commitment to move some legislation forward. The author of the 1967 "welfare freeze" had by no means become a sudden proponent for the welfare poor. His professed interest was in a bill that "would have the fewest possible people on welfare for the shortest amount of time." The "work provisions" of the bill appealed to Mills—those requirements that welfare mothers must take almost any available job at any salary. As his intricate draftsmanship soon revealed, he also was interested in inserting fine print which would curtail those legal rights of welfare recipients which Wiley and NWRO had slowly and painfully won. But Mills did support the two new innovative concepts—a federal floor, albeit a very low one, under family income, and assistance to the working poor.

This time, Wiley was allowed a hearing before the Ways and Means Committee. Testifying in November, 1969, Wiley stressed: "The Nixon proposal fails even to tell the country what adequate income is, what people need to live. NWRO believes that as a necessary first step, an adequate income level must be defined and a national goal set to provide that adequate income to all Americans." Wiley protested the plan in the streets as well ("ZAP FAP" was the new NWRO battle cry), but "at the same time," recalled Don Green, NWRO's staff lobbyist, "he wanted to be at the bargaining table. He really believed that representational, traditional democracy could work, and that his people should be included in. While he didn't like the numbers (in the Nixon plan) he felt that he could get those numbers raised by working with our supporters in Congress."

So Wiley continued to play it both ways—to kick in the front doors in protest and then come into the back rooms and negotiate. "There was an obvious need for NWRO to continue vigorous, militant protest activities," said Green. "That was the chief means of organizing and winning gains at the local level and forcing the system to pay attention to welfare recipients. He couldn't give up the militant role because there was no one else to play it. Lots of people were willing to serve as the negotiator."

By this time, Wiley had established a recognizable physical image as a "militant." An NWRO member from New York, sewing daishikis to raise funds for her chapter, had presented him with one of the colorful African shirts. He found it so comfortable that he soon never wore anything else in public. Ironically, this was when the style was fast fading for fashionable black men. His "ladies" kept him well supplied with daishikis thereafter, and he grew his hair long in an exaggerated Afro to complete the picture. The rumpled professor in tweeds and narrow tie had disappeared into memory.

In December, 1969, Wiley pulled off a dramatic coup, in the kind of move that was beginning to win for him national notoriety while it also gained some liberal support for more generous welfare reform. In a daring display of militant tactics combined with skilled negotiating, Wiley and NWRO virtually took over the White House Conference on Hunger and Malnutrition, held in Washington's Sheraton-Park Hotel.

Wiley, in a daishiki, and his members, some in overalls and jeans, appeared at the hotel, bristling for a fight. They marched up and down the hallways, sporting buttons that proclaimed "$5500 or Fight." As the meetings got underway, however, and Wiley began politicking in the caucuses and seminars, he sensed a substantial amount of support for a more generous welfare bill. Although the conferees were meeting to discuss specific problems of hunger, they knew the real reason poor people suffered from hunger was that they didn't have enough money.

Despite White House protests, Wiley persuaded the entire conference to come together in two special sessions at which the now radicalized conferees informally voted approval of a series of resolutions, including support for NWRO's "guaranteed adequate income" plan—fifty-five hundred dollars for a family of four. "The White House conference was a turning-point," said NWRO official Hulbert James, "because we gained a lot more support for our position. The conference gave us confidence that we could be effective on the FAP issue."

The dramatics worked with only one kind of audience, however—citizens of good conscience who were willing to be maneuvered into a more generous position. Wiley's confidence at the hunger conference was misplaced. You could take over the Sheraton-Park Hotel, he discovered, but you could not take over the House Ways and Means Committee. Wilbur Mills took the Nixon welfare bill, added a few restrictions of his own to the rights of welfare recipients, and marched the legislation straight through his committee in March, 1970. Wiley was stunned by the swiftness of the move and, once again, by Mills' impressive power in Congress. Mills shuttled the bill through the House of Representatives, where it passed on April 16, 1970, by a vote of 243 to 155. Noting that the House-passed FAP provided $2 billion for welfare while a defense bill provided $20 billion, including a $2 billion contract for Lockheed and one of $1.6 billion for General Electric, Wiley said: "It is clear that this country can afford welfare. The question is whether we will have welfare bills for the people instead of the war profiteers!"

As the welfare legislation moved into Senator Long's Finance Committee for consideration, Wiley moved his troops into the streets three blocks away, in front of Washington, D.C.'s central welfare office. It was a militant protest demonstration, a special-needs campaign demanding furniture for the capital's welfare recipients. The campaign had a double-barreled objective: Wiley hoped to attract national publicity, helping to stimulate NWRO organizing efforts around the country. At the same time he was sending a message to Congress and the administration: NWRO was strong and tough and prepared to fight. Under local welfare law, the protesters were entitled to receive furniture; the battle cry of the campaign came from a black welfare mother, who shouted: "How come this country has enough money to send a man to the moon,* but can't afford to get my child up off the floor?" The D.C. welfare department resisted, and eventually there was a confrontation. NWRO's angry mothers stormed the welfare offices and were thrown in jail. It was exactly the kind of demonstration to alienate potential supporters in Congress.

Senator Long's Senate Finance Committee now attacked the House-passed welfare bill as a wildly extravagant giveaway filled with loopholes which, as Long saw it, would allow some ingenious poor person to collect a whole parcel of government benefits, far beyond the "poverty line." At this point, the course of welfare reform took on a new direction. Under attack by conservatives on the Senate Finance Committee, the Nixon administration made a series of revisions in the bill—changes which would severely restrict benefits for large numbers of current welfare recipients.

Wiley fluctuated in his tactics as he sought to play a wide variety of roles. One week he would be lobbying effectively on Capitol Hill, winning crucial support from Massachusetts Senators Edward Kennedy and Edward Brooke against the Nixon bill; the next week he would stage a sit-in in the office of HEW Secretary Robert Finch, hoping to dramatize the need to change the bill's current provisions, but principally to invigorate NWRO around the country. It was that sit-in, more than any other action, that turned the liberal tide against Wiley. Along with Johnnie Tillmon, Beulah Sanders, and a dozen of his board members, Wiley camped in Finch's personal office for an entire day, until all the protesters were evicted and arrested at nightfall. The next morning's *Washington Post* featured a large photograph of a grinning Wiley leaning back in Finch's chair, his feet, in those outrageous ten-year-old shoes, propped up on the secretary's desk. The picture was picked up by the wire services and appeared in papers across the country. To the general public, it was a portrait of the ultimate in arrogant disrespect. NWRO's phones began to ring as some supporters chastised him; others dropped their backing.

Although many veteran activists now found these tactics unproductive, Wiley continued to believe in them as a necessary tool for engaging poor

---

* Each of the fifteen Apollo moon shots cost approximately half a billion dollars.

people, whose principal resource was the commitment of their own bodies.

Even at this point, Wiley still felt he could play the militant protester as well as the behind-the-scenes negotiator. It had begun to wear on him, though. "It was very difficult for George to play the two different roles," said his aide Don Green. "He was such a peaceful man, such a big bear of a loving man, he really had to psych himself up for what we called an 'action,' a direct-action confrontation. But he knew he had to lead those actions, if the women were going to follow him."

Wiley's legislative posture was settled in early November, 1970, when the Nixon administration made still further concessions to the conservatives on Long's committee. Unless the bill were radically revised, Wiley would try to kill it. On November 10, 1970, Wiley issued an ultimatum—NWRO's minimum requirements for an acceptable bill: "A minimum federal payment of $2,464 for a family of four, with the elimination of food stamps; a step-by-step timetable to reach adequate income; a guarantee that no welfare recipient would lose present benefits; no forced work; decent jobs at living wages for those able to work; protection of the constitutional rights of welfare recipients."

As Congress drew closer to adjournment, the fate of welfare reform was far from certain. A bill might conceivably be passed if liberals and moderates reached a compromise with the administration. A group of lobbyists representing labor unions, citizens' groups, the League of Women Voters, and church groups began working toward such a compromise. Organizing the strategy was former HEW Secretary John Gardner, who now headed a new citizens' group called Common Cause. Gardner scheduled for November 20, at Common Cause Washington headquarters, a meeting in which Nixon's new secretary of HEW, Elliot Richardson, would meet with representatives of the liberal special-interest groups to explore compromise.

When Wiley heard of the meeting, he immediately summoned more than one hundred of his welfare-mother leaders to town. He contacted Common Cause official Lowell Beck, and requested that they all be permitted to attend and that he be allowed twenty minutes to make a presentation. The two men argued on the phone, with Beck complaining that a large delegation of welfare recipients would interrupt the meeting, and Wiley insisting that the group most affected by the legislation should be present. If the issue had been veterans' legislation, Wiley said, he was certain Beck wouldn't exclude a delegation of veterans. The conversation ended with Wiley citing a cardinal NWRO precept: "When poor people are excluded from the process, we disrupt." The meeting never took place. Common Cause refused to permit a large NWRO delegation to attend; Wiley threatened to protest outside the building; and Common Cause canceled the meeting. Influential liberals thereafter blamed George Wiley for destroying any chance for compromise on welfare reform in the 1969–70 session of Congress. (The *Washington Post* editorially praised John Gardner as the most helpful proponent of reform and accused George Wiley of being its worst enemy.)

Carl Holman of the Urban Coalition, who attempted unsuccessfully to negotiate between Wiley and Common Cause, had another view: "It is true that George was playing political brinksmanship, but I don't think he wanted to kill the meeting. He wanted to participate. The only constituency most of those other folks represented was themselves. And here was one party [NWRO], clearly the party of interest, which would have been the least represented group there. One of the things that incident illustrated for me is that people who never have to deal face-to-face with poor people have very little understanding or concern for the role of the man in the middle. They see only one half of a George Wiley—only the profile that's facing them, not the one that must face his own angry constituents."

Holman represented a minority view. Wiley and his articulate, outraged women leaders had become not only an enemy on which the conservatives could focus but a thorn in the side of the liberal establishment. Yet Peter Edelman,* a vice president of the University of Massachusetts, who helped Wiley with the lobbying effort, agreed with Holman: "Wiley challenged the totally paternalistic, encrusted bureaucracy, and the condescending bureaucracy of do-gooders who thought they knew better what the welfare mothers needed than the mothers themselves. The mothers had been hammering on the door for their own rights, and if John Gardner didn't like it, that was too bad."

Wiley and the welfare mothers finally found a highly unusual public forum, from which they may have helped seal the fate of FAP in 1970. As was expected, Senator Long refused to let them appear before the Senate Finance Committee. But one of the committee members, Eugene McCarthy of Minnesota, held dramatic, though unofficial, hearings in the U.S. Senate committee room on his own. For two days, on November 18 and 19, NWRO mothers from all over the country testified before McCarthy and ten other senators. "It was the first time welfare people had been permitted to speak for themselves," said McCarthy. "Previously, we always heard from some welfare worker or county commissioner. The women's assertion of rights was really pretty overwhelming, pretty powerful. They were saying, 'We are not asking you to give us anything. We are telling you what our rights are and how we ought to be treated.' You could sense they were intelligent people, sensitive people. Many of them were overweight and oversized, but God, the spirit they had in them was something."

* Edelman, as a legislative assistant to Senator Robert F. Kennedy (D., N.Y.) in 1967, had worked against the welfare freeze.

One by one, the women unfolded their personal stories, telling how the bill would affect their lives. Then attorney Ed Sparer meticulously filled in the details of how the revised Mills and Long version of the Nixon bill would hurt welfare recipients and deprive them of their constitutional rights. "This is not a first step for welfare reform," Sparer concluded. "It is a trading off a number of the poor against hopelessly inadequate benefits for the working poor—and guaranteeing that those working poor stay in place in those sweatshops of industry." Testifying in support of NWRO's position were two influential, moderate black groups, the Urban League and the National Council of Negro Women, which until then had supported the Nixon plan. Wiley had turned them around. Speaking to a small group of influential blacks in Urban League Director Whitney Young's office, Wiley described how the House Ways and Means Committee and Senate Finance Committee teamed up in conference committee at the end of the legislative process to produce punitive welfare legislation. "Here we are, coming in with a compromise we know is less than right, knowing full well they are going to cut into even that," Wiley concluded. "Why should we do the cutting for them?"

On November 20, the day following the conclusion of Senator McCarthy's unofficial welfare rights hearings,* the Senate Finance Committee held its crucial vote. The Committee voted ten to six against the bill as drawn by the Nixon administration and modified to suit the committee conservatives. Three liberal Democrats, McCarthy of Minnesota, Fred Harris of Oklahoma, and Albert Gore of Tennessee, joined seven conservatives to defeat the bill.

Moynihan, in a book recounting the fight, contends that by pushing the three liberals into joining the conservatives Wiley killed welfare reform. Wiley believed he had persuaded them to kill a bill that was bad for poor people.

President Nixon vowed, in January, 1971, that welfare reform would be his number one domestic priority. FAP was to be resurrected. Congressman Mills whipped out a new bill, symbolically designated as House of Representatives Bill Number One—or "H.R.1." But "reform" still had different connotations for different people. When Nevada Governor O'Callaghan sent the conservatives his message by slicing the state's welfare rolls in half, Wiley geared up for a major NWRO offensive there. When the courts upheld NWRO's plea and Nevada benefits were restored, Wiley was jubilant. "We've turned back the anti-welfare tide," he announced. But he was wrong. A conservative tide was running strong in the country, and it would markedly affect the welfare legislation.

---

* And the day on which the Common Cause compromise meeting had been scheduled to take place.

The Ways and Means Committee had been meeting privately with officials of the Nixon administration to draft a new welfare bill. What finally emerged was a much sterner measure than the original FAP proposal of 1969. The money ante was basically the same. A family of four would receive a basic federal payment of twenty-four hundred dollars—but no food stamps.* To Wiley and NWRO, there was one devastating change: states that now paid benefits higher than the new minimum could lower their benefits to the proposed federal "standard." Most of NWRO's members were concentrated in those states, and the cost of living was on the rise. Ninety percent of welfare recipients stood to lose money if the states chose to stop paying part of the cost of welfare. In addition, Wilbur Mills' fine print in the bill** outraged George and sent him to the halls of Congress to resume his lobbying role.

Again, he found himself at odds with other liberals: the "lib-lab lobby" of labor unions, Common Cause, League of Women Voters, and other groups held to the idea that the Nixon bill, with a few liberalizations, still could be a "foot in the door" toward welfare reform. Let it pass the House, they argued. We can improve it in the Senate. Wiley disagreed. He had watched the Mills and Long surgical techniques far more closely than they had. His three friends on the Senate Finance Committee, McCarthy, Harris, and Gore, were gone.† Rockefeller in New York and Reagan in California, reflecting the new conservatism, were shaping plans to cut welfare benefits in their states, and President Nixon himself now described his legislation as a much more hard-line approach. As he sniffed the political wind and looked toward the 1972 election, the president emphasized that the bill was designed to get at welfare cheaters and make lazy welfare recipients work at whatever jobs were available, including emptying bedpans, a job he said was just as honorable as his own.

"We've got to go for a better bill in the House," Wiley told the liberals as he began a virtuoso lobbying performance that won't be soon forgotten on Capitol Hill. On a single day of the debate, three welfare reform proposals were introduced, each offering larger benefits and more protection of rights than the Nixon plan. Wiley was the public author of the fifty-five-hundred-dollar NWRO plan and the secret author and initiator of the other two—a four-thousand-dollar plan backed by allies he had won in the National Coun-

---

* In the first version, a family of four with no other income could receive $1,600 cash and be eligible for $864 in food stamps.
** One requirement would cause some people who lost jobs to wait up to nine months to receive welfare. A provision prohibited court appeals of denials of welfare benefits. Still another provision denied welfare recipients representation by legal service attorneys. Another section attempted to resurrect the unconstitutional state residency requirements. These measures and others attacked what Wiley and Sparer considered the heart of welfare "rights."
† Fred Harris and Eugene McCarthy did not run for re-election; Albert Gore was defeated by William Brock.

cil of Churches, and a thirty-six-hundred-dollar plan. Not only did NWRO lobby in its own right, but Wiley inspired creation of other lobbying groups, including one predominantly church group called Campaign for Adequate Income Now.

Wiley's style varied depending upon whom he was lobbying. Friends like Senator McCarthy and Congressman Ronald Dellums of California perceived him as the thoughtful intellectual. With them he would agonize over his own doubts about the legislation and how to improve the society. With George McGovern and members of the Senate Select Committee on Nutrition, he was a stern conscience. "He came in with a very simple statement of right and wrong," recalls committee staff-member Nancy Amidei, "and at every step of the way he was there. 'You cannot do this to poor people,' he would argue, and it would be painful, but he would not go away. With George, it was a matter of what was right and just, and you would wind up taking a very unpopular position because he made you live up to your beliefs."

In a debate before the governing board of the National Council of Churches, Wiley berated an opponent who advocated a modest pragmatic compromise, and appealed to the church people on moral principles, warning them that if they forsook those principles, "you might as well drop the 'of Christ' from the name of your organization." As David Ackerman, the Council of Churches lobbyist, later reflected, the church group really was compelled by Wiley on moral grounds to support the NWRO position throughout the debate, despite strong pulls within the organization to take a less ambitious position. The church groups were Wiley's strongest legislative lobbying allies, as well as NWRO's largest single source of funds.

With others he was more heavy-handed. "It was almost like he was dictating what should be done," recalled former Senator Harris' legislative assistant, Fred Gipson. "It was a very abrasive and forceful style." Congressman Dellums: "Washington is a world unto itself, and there are rules that are played in a very elaborate game that has no relation to the human misery out there in the real world. George Wiley understood this, and that is why he was a thorn in the side of Washington, D.C."

In the spring of 1971, Wiley concentrated his lobbying on the Congressional Black Caucus, the sixteen black members of the House of Representatives. He argued that if caucus members stuck together they could be a force, influencing at least sixty-five white congressmen with a significant percentage of blacks in their congressional districts. (He contended that Mills' H.R. 1 bill was "racist"—in that it called for twenty-four hundred dollars in annual benefits to an aged couple, 80 percent of whom were white. The same twenty-four hundred dollars would go to an AFDC family of four, 50 percent of whom were black.)

Representative John Conyers of Michigan: "George was scary to some black congressmen. His views were essentially different from the more or

less moderate views held by a consensus within the caucus. And they resented his style—dumping on us about what we should be doing. Here was a
guy who knew more about the bill than most of us, who was obviously
bright, and clearly determined, and had to be dealt with. You could not ignore George. If you told him you couldn't get him on the agenda of a Black
Caucus meeting, he'd find out where the meeting was anyway, and demand
that you hear him out." Not only were the black members of Congress
forced to confront Wiley's intense intellectual argument and his dogged persistence, but they were faced with the militancy of the black welfare mothers
who would swarm into their offices and demand to be heard. "He literally
grabbed us by the scruff of the neck until we finally began to see that we had
to support the NWRO viewpoint," Conyers concluded.

All sixteen members of the Black Caucus endorsed the NWRO bill, as
did a dozen white congressmen; they introduced it to Congress in April,
1971. At the same time, Wiley, moving behind the scenes again, tried to
push his other bills, which would ensure that no one would lose benefits in
the name of "reform." "George kept the heat on the white liberals who were
going to save the world for some poor black folks," recalled Ron Dellums.
"George lobbied not from a middle-class, black point of view but from the
reality that most blacks were still very poor."

Despite Wiley's efforts, Mills again guided his and the Nixon administration's joint effort through the House of Representatives on June 22, 1971.
And again Senator Long and the conservative Senate Finance Committee
blocked any action on the legislation—this time for fifteen months. On
August 15, President Nixon deferred the effective date of his welfare reform
proposal by one year, as a budget-saving measure. Friend and foe alike
realized that the president's interest had cooled markedly. In December,
1971, Congress passed little-noticed amendments offered by Georgia Senator
Herman Talmadge that required all welfare mothers with children over six
years of age to register for working and training. In April, 1972, the Senate
Finance Committee rejected the House-passed Nixon-Mills bill and approved Long's "workfare" plan. It would have replaced welfare with required
work, and guaranteed jobs at less than the minimum wage, to all welfare
mothers whose youngest child had reached school age. HEW Secretary Elliot
Richardson, who had replaced Finch, criticized Long's plan, which had other
stringent provisions, as "punitive—a retreat to the dark ages."

As in the previous Congress, any chance for welfare reform depended
on some kind of effective compromise in the Senate between Democratic liberals and the Nixon administration. Connecticut Senator Abraham Ribicoff
proposed such a compromise.* As negotiations began, Ribicoff's legislative
assistant Geoffrey Peterson recalled, Wiley kept liberals from giving too

---

* Ribicoff proposed that benefits begin at twenty-six hundred dollars and rise over several years
to three thousand dollars, and that no one lose present benefits.

much ground: "He had a stiffening effect—in making sure that in our efforts to compromise, we didn't sell out something that was really important."

"We would love to support your bill if we knew that it was going to come out in law," Wiley told Peterson. "But that won't happen. That will be the starting point from which you go down. And we just can't go along with that." Wiley privately debated the legislation all during the 1969–72 period with Tom Joe, an analyst who had been an early advocate of welfare rights in California and had worked in HEW during the Nixon administration.

Tom Joe: "We argued constantly over strategy. Wiley argued that the bill might do more harm than good, and I said, that's the chance we'll have to take. And he said he didn't know that he wanted to take that chance. I viewed it as an opportunity. He viewed it as a possible danger. We argued about raising the floor of payments. I said, 'Fine, let's raise the floor.' He said, 'Let's escalate the issue.' I said, 'Fine, escalate the issue as far as you can, but at what point are you going to support some legislation?' And he never would say, until the end, when he said he couldn't talk the welfare mothers into accepting anything less than their own plan. I think the failure to pass legislation was a step backwards for the welfare rights movement. It was a strategy argument, and maybe we were both wrong. He got carried away with the idea that welfare reform should be major revolutionary change. I never had that expectation." A mutual friend tried one last time in 1972 to arrange a "peace meeting" at which Joe and Wiley could reach some agreement, but it ended with Wiley saying: "You play your game and I'll play mine. I have an organization and you are working with the establishment."

Wiley did have an organization, and that was a reality he never could forget throughout the lobbying fight in Congress. For his own governing board, "$5,500 or Fight" meant just that. Wiley would have had difficulty participating in a compromise, even if he had so chosen. But he can be faulted for not impressing on his members how much even the Nixon plan might have helped the poorest people in the Deep South. Wiley refused to support the Ribicoff compromise, but so did President Nixon, who had virtually abandoned his own issue. Welfare had entered the presidential race. Candidates from Wallace to Nixon, even Hubert Humphrey, used welfare recipients as scapegoats for campaign venom.

Democratic presidential contender George McGovern took a beating from his own party—especially from longtime liberal Humphrey—when McGovern proposed a four-thousand-dollar guaranteed annual income plan. When McGovern then hedged on the plan (at first he couldn't even give the projected costs), Republicans never let him forget it. Nixon no longer wanted a welfare "reform" that would add benefits or recipients to the welfare rolls. In that atmosphere, the full Senate approved Russell Long's "workfare" plan in September, 1972, after first defeating the Ribicoff compromise. A month later, a joint Senate-House conference committee killed AFDC welfare reform completely (although Congress did approve federalization and an increase in benefits for other categories of welfare recipients: the aged, the disabled, and the blind.)

Daniel Patrick Moynihan reflected that the 1969–70 session of Congress was the one chance in a generation to make the breakthrough toward a guaranteed annual income. In response, Wiley stated: "The proposals under discussion were not the rosy and radical reform that we were led to believe, but represented at the best a small step toward change in the welfare system. At worst they were a serious repression against the people who are most vulnerable—the women and children who subsist on AFDC, whose rights were abridged, and 90 percent of whom could lose benefits. So far as the 'foot in the door' theory of reform, it would have taken years to improve benefits."

The benefit of several years' hindsight has led some of the key architects of compromise in the legislative battle between the Nixon administration's bill and a more generous one to revise their thinking about Wiley's political astuteness at the time. "In a sense," said Ribicoff aide Peterson, "Wiley probably looked further down the political road than we did in seeing what was going to be the ultimate result. He was probably politically correct." Mitchell Ginsberg,* who attempted to be the broker between the administration and liberal groups, reflected: "Wiley was a constructive influence on the liberals in saying that whatever they did was not enough. And in the end, I think he was right about the Senate not being the place where you could improve the bill. Nixon killed the bill."

Others thought that Wiley had little impact on the final outcome. "If Wiley had been in favor of the Family Assistance Plan, his support would have cost it votes," flatly stated John Veneman, who was under-secretary of HEW at the time. Vernon Jordan, who succeeded the late Whitney Young** as director of the Urban League, saw it another way: "George did the best organizing job of anybody after the sixties had reached their peak. When it came to welfare legislation, I was very impressed with his detailed knowledge. He wasn't just a podium type who could raise the rights of people and exhort. He could quote from page four of the bill and he knew what section A meant, and that was very important. He commanded support." And still others contend that Wiley played a negative role. "I count him [George Wiley] as one of the arch-villains of the welfare reform story," said Alice Rivlin, then a Brookings Institution scholar.

Another view is that Wiley added a unique dimension to the national

---

* Dean of the Columbia University School of Social Work and a former welfare commissioner in New York City.
** Young died of a heart attack while swimming off the coast of Africa on March 11, 1971.

debate, providing an ingredient which seldom has been present in Washington power struggles. As Senator Edward Kennedy said of himself and a number of other liberal senators: "Our interest in Wiley probably represented a turning point in the lobbying effort on social reform. For previously, legislators relied on professionals for positions to follow on legislation affecting the poor. This probably was the first time that many of us consciously looked at a representative of the poor for guidance on legislation that would affect their lives so extensively."

The legislation for welfare reform, abandoned by President Nixon, died in Congress in 1972 and was not revived for the next four years. But the broad issues of welfare reform, of a guaranteed annual income, of adequate jobs for all willing to work, of redistribution of American wealth and income remain very much with us. The issues will not go away, however long they remain unresolved, because they involve fundamental philosophical and political disagreements about the nature of American society. The history of the welfare reform fight from 1969 through 1972 probably will influence how those issues are dealt with in the future. But left unanswered by that debate is a crucial question: Is there a way of achieving welfare reform that would satisfy a majority of the American public, pass both houses of Congress, and be reasonably generous and equitable to the poor? Part of the difficulty in resolving the issue is the conflict between two principles: paying a decent income support, and maintaining the incentive of the work ethic.

Wiley believed in the power and utility of the work ethic and the need to maintain work incentives, as did the Nixon administration. The NWRO fifty-five-hundred-dollar-a-year plan contained a work-ethic provision, so that those who worked would always remain financially ahead of those who did not work. But by starting the payment level for the welfare poor at the Bureau of Labor Standard's "minimum standard" of fifty-five hundred dollars and maintaining a strong work incentive, Wiley's plan would have covered, with some benefits, all families with less than ten thousand dollars in annual income. At that time, his politically impractical plan would have affected 130 million people and cost somewhere between forty and sixty billion bollars. In contrast, the Nixon plan, by starting benefits at sixteen hundred dollars (or twenty-four hundred dollars in its second version) and cutting them off at thirty-nine hundred dollars in income (forty-three hundred dollars in the second version), held the cost to several billion dollars and the coverage to about twenty million people. The cost and range of coverage were kept down only by starting the benefits at a very low level, and even then, conservatives protested that too many people would be covered by welfare.

Therein lies the political dilemma. If one agreed that it would be unrealistic to forget about the work incentive, for example, how could one pay a guaranteed annual income of $4,000 a year to a family in which no one

worked, while a family that earned $4,001 would get no benefits? Given this dilemma, and knowing the political futility of NWRO's ideal plan, Wiley was asked in 1973 what future action he recommended. He replied: "The political problems are really serious, but I think no analysis of the political problem would lead you to want to accept a program that is worse than the present welfare system. I believe it is possible to devise some versions of welfare reform which protect the rights of recipients, which perhaps do not go for a terribly high benefit level in the first instance, but which set up a program which is in the right direction of reform. Our base-line demands were to protect the present benefit levels, look toward an adequate income, and protect the rights of recipients."

One reality is unescapable. Any welfare reform plan which provides minimum decency for the poor and also contains a work incentive feature will be costly and to some extent will provide an income guarantee to millions of Americans beyond those now on welfare. Facing that reality, said Wiley, is the starting-point on the road to reform.

31

The Juggler

NWRO was a precarious organization whose very existence often hung on George Wiley's ability to hold together a bewildering assortment of people who had nothing in common except a loyalty to him and to the cause of welfare rights. Somehow he managed to run the national office by a contagious personal magic harnessed to the force of his own stubborn will. As the membership expanded, so did the paperwork, and with it the numbers of volunteers, hangers-on, and paid staff. In 1969, NWRO took over the fourth floor of a run-down office building at Fourteenth and H Streets in downtown Washington, a few blocks from the burned-out ghetto and a stone's throw from the White House. The dusty second-hand desks overflowed with paper; every staff member was overworked and harassed; the atmosphere was seldom less than chaotic. Wiley set a punishing pace, and more than once, the staff was on the edge of revolt.

George's frenzied activities might wear down his colleagues, but his schedule always seemed orderly to him, even serene. His exhausted aides watched with fascination as he dealt with a hundred details at once. He assumed others would match his total dedication. Some employees simply burned out. But while they stayed at NWRO, Wiley managed to extract from them work that went beyond the call of duty or their meager salaries. He coerced, he charmed, he cajoled, he made outrageous demands.

Not only were NWRO salaries abysmally low, at times the payroll was not met at all. Wiley would pay the telephone bill rather than the staff—even though the employees complained that they couldn't pay their rent. NWRO would be out of business if the telephones were cut off, he felt. He expected people to "live off the land," pool their resources, cadge free meals and lodgings, or wangle their way onto the payroll of some other organization that would still allow them to work for NWRO. After all, he had done it. And he used a light touch. In organization of poorly paid workers and volunteers, stern commands would not get very far. Often Wiley made assignments by saying, "It would be nice if someone would prepare testimony for the House welfare hearings." That kind of request usually worked.

In the same way Wiley could extract extraordinary help from outsiders, the people NWRO workers called "Wiley's seven staffs." Alongside the regular staff were the volunteer academics who researched issues and wrote legislation, the unpaid fund-raisers, the lawyers who filed NWRO's lawsuits, the accountants and lawyers who kept NWRO out of legal trouble with the government, the staff lent to Wiley from other foundation-backed programs, and the dozens of organizers who worked for NWRO while on someone else's payroll. They greatly augmented the regular staff, which ranged from a few people to nearly a hundred, depending on NWRO's financial fortunes.

George had serious shortcomings as an administrator. His unique sense of order did not mesh with the needs of many of his people, who were simply confused. He often failed to delegate authority, or gave the same job to two people. He avoided confrontations within NWRO. He failed to resolve disputes, and he often failed to share with others his plans and goals. He often was not a shrewd judge of ability in picking employees, and he found it difficult to fire anyone. His aides believed that his toleration of incompetents and opportunists weakened the organization. Once, when board member Catherine Jermany pointed out how a member had used him and NWRO for selfish gain, he replied: "Everybody we help is not going to turn around and do something for the world, but if that person gets to the point where she can do something for herself, then you have accomplished a lot. The only real freedom from dependency is that which you obtain for yourself." And when administrative assistant Audrey Colom complained of the incompetence of a staff member, he replied, "There's a place for everyone; you just have to find out where they belong." Wiley's gentleness, or weakness, in such situations infuriated his more efficient staff; yet, in the context of the slapdash NWRO operation, his attitude about people's imperfections made sense. Wiley needed anyone who was willing to help his ragtag group. The whole thing was a juggling act and he often had to make do with second-hand equipment and second-rate people.

Wiley's most sensitive job was his relationship with the elected NWRO officers. In theory, the women were his bosses and he carried out policy made by the elected executive board. In practice, said chairman Johnnie

Tillmon, "we were partners; we worked together." At the beginning, things worked smoothly. The women saw Wiley as their helpful teacher and guide. They treated him like a son, protecting him, buying him clothes and sending him home to his family when they thought he was neglecting that responsibility. They were eager to be taught. "Just learn the facts, and go out there and tell them like you're telling me now," he would say to them. To his delight, the recipient leaders became articulate and impassioned speakers for the movement in roles he actively promoted, often giving them his choice speaking invitations. But as the women extended their own influence and activities, George lost some of his control. The women thrived on confrontation and sometimes caused more to happen than Wiley had planned.

There was, for instance, the scene at the May, 1969, National Conference on Social Welfare in the grand ballroom of the New York Hilton. The conferees were going to let spokesmen for other groups have their say. Wiley, Johnnie Tillmon, Beulah Sanders, and nearly forty members from NWRO's National Coordinating Committee stood waiting for their turn. There were other groups waiting, too—a radical social workers' group, a women's group, a hunger group, and various other radical and ethnic caucuses. NWRO planned to use the forum to demand that the conference contribute money to the NWRO cause. The plan was for Wiley to make a thoughtful appeal for support, based on the issues. Many of the social workers already were allies, and he would insist that others should be too. Tim Sampson tried to get the NWRO group coordinated and told Sanders and Tillmon they would have to be patient. They "should not get uptight," he warned. But they did.

"The ladies just got madder and madder as each successive group went up to the microphone to lay out their grievances," recalls Sampson. "They thought the others were stealing their thunder. So finally, when their turn came, Beulah Sanders shouted, 'Block the doors.' " The audience of thirty-five hundred was stunned. "We demand thirty-five thousand dollars or you're not going to leave this room," Johnnie Tillmon announced, as other NWRO members and supporters quickly blocked the exists. The police were called and the convention hall's temporary walls were eventually dismantled to let the delegates escape. While the commotion raged on, Wiley calmly and coolly negotiated with chairman Arthur S. Flemming, a former secretary of HEW. Despite intense resentment at NWRO's heavy-handed tactics, the conference eventually gave NWRO the thirty-five thousand dollars to support summer interns from schools of social work. The conference takeover added to NWRO's growing notoriety, outraging editorialists throughout the country. Wiley took the beating philosophically ("We got more press than we've ever had before") and he was philosophical, too, about the headstrong actions of his leaders.

At the beginning, the women viewed Wiley as their partner, but eventually they felt he was a rival for power. The leaders often came to meetings angry not only at the society but enraged at Wiley and the staff. They would curse him, scream at him, rake him over the coals. "They used him like a scapegoat, venting all their frustrations," said Wiley's personal secretary, Joanne Williams. "And when they had finished, he would come back into the conversation, and usually it would go his way. But if they did things wrong, he did not try to overrule them; he just went on to something else."

"Patience was the key," said Catherine Jermany, the board's West Coast representative. "Patience and end-of-the-road perspective. George had the patience to get beat on for two or three days, and then it would all come together and we would do what we were supposed to do." Accomplishing NWRO's business became more difficult as the organization's internal conflicts intensified. The women wanted more authority and services for themselves and for the existing chapters. The organizers wanted more action in the field and felt that Wiley's national political activities were ineffective and a waste of resources. The recipients felt that the staff acted condescendingly toward them and usurped power. The professional staff felt that the recipient leaders lacked competence and disrupted effective operations.

Sometimes the differences were merely of style and perception. The women had come from all over the country in 1969 to testify before Congress on proposed welfare legislation. Each had dug into her own pocket to buy new clothes for the occasion. They arrived looking like churchwomen at a convention: new dresses, shoes, hats, and gloves. When they assembled at the NWRO office for a final briefing before heading for Capitol Hill, an office staffer in charge of the testimony shouted: "You can't go up there looking like this—you're supposed to look poor." The women were hurt and infuriated. It was, as some later recalled, the biggest day in their lives. They wanted to look their best and had sacrificed to do so. Wiley chastized the staffer, a white Ph.D. who often dressed in overalls. He understood the women's pride in and desire for respectability, just as he understood the style of the white staff, as they donned uniforms of rebellion against their middle-class origins. He defended their freedom to wear long hair, beards, and scruffy jeans when board members complained that "those dirty hippies should be made to shave, bathe, and dress like respectable people." Salaries were always a sore point. Wiley was constantly called on to justify paying an organizer six thousand dollars a year, which seemed like a lot of money to a welfare recipient trying to support three children on an average welfare stipend of two thousand dollars a year.

The worst internal crisis to hit NWRO was a crisis in black and white, a grim reminder for Wiley of a similar struggle in CORE five years earlier. No issue more bitterly split civil rights and social activist groups in the late 1960s than matters of race, and NWRO was not exempt, despite Wiley's efforts to turn the focus of the movement away from traditional civil rights concerns towards a coalition of multiracial economic interests. Blacks were increasingly sensitive to white domination of American institutions, or even the appearance of such control. Some black NWRO staffers staged a revolt on this issue in the summer of 1969, nearly destroying the organization in the process.

John Lewis,* the NWRO director of publications, led the protest, charging that Wiley had surrounded himself with white aides in key jobs and that the white-dominated staff had usurped the policy-making role of the mostly black elected leadership. Moreover, he charged, black employees were mainly confined to menial jobs, such as those under his direction in the printing "back shop." On the surface, there was validity to the complaints. Certainly, Wiley and his staff engaged in policymaking. It was also true that several of Wiley's key aides were white. The leadership demanded that recipients be given jobs in the national office, and Wiley made some effort to comply, bringing in Joyce Burson and Jackie Pope from Brooklyn. But their talents were underutilized. Wiley, the instructor, had become too busy with other things to place any effective priority on staff development.

Wiley was perfectly comfortable to have white aides, but the appearance of whites in key jobs, he insisted, was principally a matter of economics. Fewer blacks could afford to work at subsistence pay or as volunteers. Furthermore, some black activists did not want to work for an avowedly multiracial organization, and many black men avoiding working for an organization dominated by black women.

The racial clash came to a head the first week in August, when blacks organized protest at a two-day staff conference held at Trinity College in Washington. Wiley was home in bed with flu and a high temperature when Hulbert James came to tell him that the confrontation had reached the stage where most of the staff, both black and white, were about to quit. Wiley wrapped himself in a blanket, and made a dramatic late-night appearance at the conference.

"NWRO was organized by and for welfare recipients and the very existence of a staff is only for the purpose of helping them," he said. "And it is the basic policy of this organization that it exists for the benefit of all poor people, black, white, Chicano, Puerto Rican, Indian, and that racial prejudices should have no place here as they should have no place in other elements of our country's life. At the same time, we must recognize that there is going on in this country a black revolution in which many of us are deeply involved, have deep commitments, and have a very basic visceral concern."

But the primary concern, Wiley said, was the future of NWRO, which was imperiled by attacks from all sides. Wiley said it was important to hire blacks, but he added: "John Lewis, you are more black-conscious than I am. You put that first and I put that second, I place the highest priority on people whom I know can get the work done. Some of those white staff people we are talking about are people who are there until one and two o'clock

* Not the John Lewis who headed SNCC and later the Voter Education Project.

every damned night of the week because they are doing their work."
Wiley's anger, his eloquent statement of NWRO's ideals and goals soothed
and inspired many of those present. He also took "affirmative action" by
making Hulbert James, a black man, his top aide. When the black dissidents, who were fired by James, protested again at the NWRO convention,
the elected leaders strongly backed Wiley. Johnnie Tillmon even cautioned
the black members of the NCC not to wear their splendid African-style evening dresses on the platform, "because we don't want to give the impression
this is an all-black organization."

The immediate black revolt was over, but Wiley had to continue to deal
with the accusation that, as he put it, he was at heart "a white man in a
daishiki."

His style did not bother Johnnie Tillmon. As far as she was concerned,
"George was rapping the need for people to survive, not just black people,
but a whole lot of folks."

Said his aide Joanne Williams, "George didn't ooze black culture, but he
oozed success and he came to help, and that's what counted with the
women." Hulbert James: "George did not identify with the vague concepts
of black power or black nationalism or black identity. For George I think
those were meaningless phrases, just rhetoric. I would try to get him to go to
some of those black-type meetings and he would say: 'What for? They never
do anything.' " Yet James said Wiley was fascinated with black nationalist
theoretician and poet Imamu Baraka because "Baraka was serious about grass
roots organizing in Newark, New Jersey." Anyone who could organize poor
people to win power and benefits was interesting, regardless of his ideological notions.

Black attorney Barbara Williams observed Wiley with other black
leaders: "He didn't fit. He was from New England. He was a chemist. He
was a Ph.D. who had taken on this ragged poverty struggle. He looked awful
to people in the way he dressed. He didn't rap easily. But what was really
important was that George raised uncomfortable images for other black
leaders. Many were more conservative than whites on the welfare issue.
They weren't ready to go as far as he was ready to go. And they knew that
George would use any opportunity, any meeting to press the points of his
agenda, and they didn't like that. He was aware when they were copping out
on an issue, and he never made it easy. You couldn't shuffle."

NWRO often waged a lonely struggle behind a lonely leader. Militant
black groups avoided NWRO because of its interracial character, while moderate black organizations, such as the NAACP, were put off by NWRO's militant tactics and radical goals. And, as Audrey Colom observed, "The black
community identified George with whites, and the white community identified him with blacks."

32

Decline and Fall

By 1970, the weaknesses inherent in a poor people's organization were all too apparent. Even at the peak of its strength, NWRO led a hazardous existence. Its very successes in expanding membership and encouraging enormous numbers of people to claim their rights and benefits were provoking a conservative reaction. It became clear that government would not react favorably to too many poor people claiming too many legal rights. Public resentment of government aid to blacks and poor people was out in the open.* An early but ominous response came in 1968 when two liberal states, New York and Massachusetts, eliminated special grants for furniture and clothing, after NWRO had pressed highly successful drives for these benefits. Still NWRO expanded in 1969 and 1970 into other parts of the country where the welfare system had never been forced to operate according to the law, despite a growing national antagonism for welfare recipients.

The public hostility once directed towards the civil rights movement and antipoverty programs was by 1970 clearly focused on welfare. The question became one of how long could NWRO sustain growth and vitality

---

* As early as 1969, the public opinion polls revealed that white Americans, by a margin of more than two to one, felt that blacks were asking for more than they were ready for. By a six-to-one margin whites opposed protest demonstrations by blacks or the poor. In sharp contrast, two-thirds of blacks thought progress was too slow in eliminating racism and poverty, and only one black in four still thought the government was trying to help his cause.

against this kind of opposition. The changing public and official mood was symbolized at the White House in a choice of songs. In 1972, President Nixon asked Johnny Cash to sing "Welfare Cadillac," a derisory song about welfare recipients. Just seven years earlier, President Johnson had dramatically embraced the title of another song, "We Shall Overcome." Stimulated by hostile public opinion and the burden of soaring welfare costs, nineteen states cut welfare benefits in 1971, and virtually every other state considered such action. For the first time in many years, the Supreme Court retreated on welfare rights. On the deciding votes of two Nixon appointees, the court limited welfare recipients' rights of privacy.

Wiley and NWRO were forced on the defensive, trying to protect old benefits rather than fighting for improvements. When the state of Alabama cut thirty-three thousand welfare recipients from the rolls in the summer of 1971, Wiley agonized but did not counterattack. He decided limited resources were needed to fight an even larger cutback in New York. Underfinanced and understaffed, NWRO could take on only one big fight at a time.

As Wiley told his staff: "We are now in a critical period because the honeymoon for NWRO is over. For any new organization, there is a period of glamor, when the organization can make it based on the fact that it is new, dynamic and exciting and can attract to it the attention and energies of a lot of different kinds of people. But as the organization matures, the glamor begins to wear off. The financial support falls away, and the foundations that tossed in seed money for a few years refuse to do it again. It becomes more difficult because the divisions and factions and splits begin to develop and these problems become more difficult to manage as time goes on. Everybody expects more and more help from the organization. As a result, the national organization becomes more and more extended. It becomes taken for granted and less appreciated by the people it serves. We are in a situation which is a crisis and a kind of crossroads." Wiley liked to say that social movements have a life of their own, not one of unlimited duration. The trick was to extend the life long enough to achieve significant results. From 1969 onwards, Wiley knew he was in a race against time.

The crisis grew steadily from 1969 to 1972, yet NWRO responded with some success by pursuing imaginative new strategies and employing old ones in yet untested areas of the country. When authorities would curtail one welfare benefit, Wiley would design organizing campaigns to push for another one. In September, 1969, for example, NWRO launched a campaign to win poor children their legal entitlement to free school lunches, and scored victories on the issue in Detroit, New York, Philadelphia, and many smaller cities such as Pueblo, Colorado, and Pontiac, Michigan. A 1970 campaign focused on the high cost of utilities brought victories for welfare recipients in Waterbury, Connecticut; Roanoke, Virginia; and Detroit. A 1971 campaign focused on making local school authorities comply with federal law by using Title I money from the Elementary and Secondary Education Act for the benefit of poor children. This action succeeded in a dozen major cities and throughout Indiana.

As it became more difficult to win at the state and local level, Wiley increasingly turned his attention to the federal government. NWRO won increased welfare benefits in 1971 in California, Connecticut, Arizona, and Indiana by pressing HEW to enforce a law requiring all states to update their welfare cost standards. A similar 1972 campaign forced HEW to require states to provide medical checkups for poor children. The Medicaid program had required such preventive medicine since 1969, but virtually every state ignored the law until NWRO successfully pressed a series of lawsuits.

Organizing became more difficult in the 1970s, yet NWRO established chapters for the first time in a dozen new states, including significant ones in Minnesota and Texas. Even rural Alabama finally yielded in 1971 as a woman in Marengo County won for the first time the right to a welfare hearing. Also in 1971, NWRO organized Indians in North Dakota, Nebraska, Montana, and Utah. In each case, state authorities were stopped from paying lower welfare benefits to Indians on reservations.

Every well-publicized NWRO victory after 1969 also had a negative effect, heightening opposition to the welfare rights movement. Wiley always expected NWRO's politics of protest to polarize friend and foe. But the polarized opposition now grew larger, and welfare recipients became an increasingly isolated minority. Therefore, Wiley decided that NWRO's survival depended on its internal expansion to include other poor people besides welfare recipients, and on joining in coalitions with other groups.

He reached out for allies with whom NWRO could trade support: helping to form the National Tenants' Organization; exchanging support with Cesar Chavez; involving NWRO in an experimental project to organize the working poor in New Bedford, Massachusetts; joining in an alliance with the Reverend Ralph Abernathy and SCLC; assisting the National Committee on Household Employment; and helping to sponsor the National Women's Political Caucus. He also became one of the few prominent black or poor people's leaders to join wholeheartedly in the leadership of the antiwar movement. He brought a large contingent to the November, 1969, New Mobilization march on Washington; helped lead the April, 1970, demonstration of the New Mobe and National Moratorium Committee; and was a key leader of the 1971 People's Coalition for Peace and Justice. In return, he got some modest reciprocal support for NWRO. "Wiley gave far more than he ever got in return," was the assessment of David Ifshin, who, as president of the National Student Association, assisted both NWRO and the antiwar effort.

Wiley's most ambitious scheme to broaden the membership of NWRO was a 1971 effort aimed at unemployed men and the working poor of New York. The plan was to organize these men by getting them to claim state benefits in a little-known and rarely used program for unemployed and poor working men. This organizing drive, with a battle cry of "Give us work or welfare," would serve as a counterattack against Governor Nelson Rockefeller, who had just cut all welfare benefits and proposed a bizarre experimental plan in which some recipients' benefits would be cut 50 percent. Women could win back part of the reduction by registering for and accepting any job offered, and by scoring points on a "self-improvement evaluation" for such activities as registering their sons in the Boy Scouts.

But Wiley's ideas for expansion were clearly unpopular with and received little support from NWRO's elected leaders. They felt that the inclusion of other groups would lessen the attention paid to their unique problems and endanger their own positions of leadership. Only after threatening to resign did Wiley get his board's reluctant approval for the New York campaign to organize men. Wiley succeeded in thwarting what he called Rockefeller's "Brownie Point Plan," but the effort to organize men was a dismal failure. The campaign was hastily planned, received little support from NWRO leaders in New York, and failed to stir interest among the unemployed men.

Even the traditional organizing of women had become much more difficult. The original recipient leaders, after six years in the streets, were tired and discouraged. On a bitterly cold winter day in 1971 outside the welfare department headquarters in New York, Wiley found out how tough it was to rally the women. He had hoped to rebuild NWRO in New York City by demonstrating against the welfare department's practice of coping with a housing shortage by stockpiling poor welfare recipients in unsafe, verminous hotels. But only a few dozen demonstrators arrived at the rally, in contrast to the hundreds who had marched in New York a few years earlier. As he watched the rally dissolve, Wiley pleaded with Beulah Sanders to lead one more demonstration later in the day, but the New York leader tearfully refused, explaining that she must take her daughter to a doctor's appointment, already thrice postponed. After years on the barricades, the urgent needs of her own family came first.

Listening to the conversation between Wiley and Sanders, another NWRO member angrily said: "He just doesn't understand our problems." But Wiley did fully understand that the movement could not function unless thousands of women were still willing to transcend their problems in order to make real sacrifices for the cause.

Wiley was convinced that in coalition politics lay the salvation of the movement, and he was determined to push the cause over the reservations of the elected leadership. NWRO's 1971 convention in Providence, R.I., was going to be a dramatic example. As the convention opened in the auditorium of Brown University, Wiley had crowded onto the stage representatives of the wide number of groups with whom he hoped to make common cause. There together were representatives of the rights of women, tenants, consumers, the working poor, white ethnics, black nationalists, household workers, unorganized workers, the elderly, the disabled, and many others, along with Senator George McGovern and Representatives Ronald Dellums and Bella Abzug. Speaker after speaker called for coalition and for a new populism, but this message was not uppermost in the minds of many NWRO delegates or staff. The organizers staged a rump caucus to protest that Wiley was neglecting grass-roots organizing. Welfare-recipient delegates complained that they felt like strangers at their own convention. "Who are all these outsiders?" they asked.

In the spring of 1972, Wiley, seeking to cash in his chips with the other groups, planned a massive one-day Washington demonstration called "The Children's March for Survival." He hoped to impress Congress and the country with the breadth of support for NWRO's position on welfare reform. All of his coalition allies participated, and nearly fifty thousand people marched, but the news media generally ignored the event except to criticize Wiley's use of Washington schoolchildren. Ironically, Wiley now had to defend the same one-shot demonstration tactics for which he had criticized King and others eight years earlier.

Wiley's pursuit of coalition allies yielded a few results in 1972. His new friends, led by feminist Gloria Steinem, persuaded the Democratic Party's Policy Council, headed by Senator Hubert Humphrey, to support a solid welfare reform resolution. Wiley then tried to expand on this policy victory at the Democratic National Convention. Considering the political weakness of his forces, Wiley put on an inventive performance at the Miami convention, where he led a coalition of NWRO, SCLC, and the National Tenants' Organization. Arriving at Miami with two unpaid aides and without official status, he seized opportunities as they developed, won a series of skirmishes in convention committees, achieved official recognition for welfare recipients, commandeered national television, and won convention approval for much of NWRO's "Poor People's Plan." Even NWRO's sixty-five-hundred-dollar-a-year guaranteed adequate income plan received one thousand delegate votes in a convention roll call.

But these victories seemed hollow in 1972. At the chaotic Democratic convention, the politics of protest had become almost a caricature. Competing for attention were advocates of legalizing marijuana, gay liberation, women's rights, amnesty for draft evaders, civil rights, welfare rights, and a dozen other causes. All of the causes may have been serious, but, given the political climate of the times, they blended together in the public mind as an unwanted chorus of protest and disorder. The country still favored welfare reform, but only as that term was understood to mean reducing the welfare rolls.

It was no longer possible to hide NWRO's weaknesses. Membership was off sharply. Financial support plummeted in 1972, and most of the staff were laid off or working without pay. Wiley's desperate pleas for financial help now often went unheeded. As a final blow, the organization, long battered from without, now splintered from within as long-standing disagreements between Wiley and the recipient leadership reached a climax.

It started out as just another executive board meeting, with the members badgering Wiley with questions and criticisms, but the argument soon became an indictment: Wiley had usurped for himself the policy-making role of the board. Old disputes were rehashed, including criticisms of Wiley for funding without board approval an Arkansas organizing project which sought the participation of working-class people. The disputes played into a prearranged plan of a board faction which believed that the time had come for a woman and a former welfare recipient to lead NWRO.

A motion was made to fire the executive director. The vote was five to five, with Beulah Sanders refusing to break the tie. After years of tightly self-disciplined behavior with the board, Wiley spoke out angrily. When he charged that the board "doesn't have the guts to fire me" one woman grabbed him around the neck and began choking him. Others pulled her away and peace was temporarily restored, but the unique partnership which had begun six years earlier and given birth to a new movement was fatally ruptured.

The board never actually fired Wiley, but he knew that they had reached an impasse and that NWRO would never become his vehicle for a larger, expanded movement. He resigned, effective January 1, 1973. Johnnie Tillmon took Wiley's place as executive director and Faith Evans became her assistant. The national organization continued for the next two years, with a skeleton staff working from a basement suite in Washington. But in the spring of 1975, NWRO could no longer pay its telephone bill or rent, and the office was closed. For the time being, at least, NWRO was dead as a national organization. A number of NWRO chapters still functioned effectively in 1976, but the movement had ended.

Most political scientists still contend that organizations of the poor are doomed to failure and that NWRO's existence was only an aberration of the 1960s. There is no question that NWRO was aided by the movements of the 1960s for the rights of minorities and poor people, and that the reaction to those movements helped kill NWRO. But those are little more than generalizations, telling little about NWRO in particular.

Wiley himself later tried to analyze the situation in an interview with his former aide Wilbur Colom: "I guess three things went wrong. First, it got much tougher to organize around welfare, because the welfare departments toughened up and clamped down. Second, we developed a national leadership cadre that was merely interested in being leadership and maintaining their own position. It got entrenched. At times those national representatives saw other groups as political enemies and really obstructed people's affiliation with NWRO. They erected barriers that kept a lot of people from joining. Third, as the effort became more difficult the glamor wore off, and it was harder to recruit and keep good organizers. New organizers just didn't hang in. A lot of them got discouraged and went into other things. The poverty program people copped out as welfare rights became less voguish. The organization was not able to respond to those changes. It responded some and developed some new techniques, relying more on the women members themselves, but not enough." To Wiley's three points NWRO members and critics would add another: his own failings as an administrator and leader.

It was a bitter irony for Wiley that NWRO suffered at the end from the same kind of "national superstructure, unresponsive to local issues and local needs" which he had deplored at CORE and sought to avoid at NWRO. Colom and others thought that the elected officers had misused the organization, becoming more concerned with the small perquisites of their office, such as free trips and expense accounts. For Colom the decay of NWRO was symbolized by a scene at the 1972 Democratic National Convention. The leadership, meeting with Senator McGovern, spent the time arguing that he pay their travel expenses rather than pressing for his support of the NWRO plank on welfare. And as board member Catherine Jermany observed, "The executive board cluttered up George's world with a bunch of irrelevant demands for personal service." Wiley was much more understanding of the fact that poor women, like anyone else, would take advantage of their few very small tastes of power and minor perks of office—which did not raise any of them from poverty. Far more significant in his view was that the women who perpetuated themselves in office no longer represented a substantial grass-roots following. Without that following, NWRO could not exercise power for the poor.

Wiley also speculated, accurately, that NWRO had been sabotaged, at least to some extent, by the Internal Revenue Service and the FBI. The IRS did succeed in disrupting NWRO's principal flow of funds from the Inter-Religious Foundation for Community Organization (IFCO), which had been set up by the National Council of Churches. Only much later, in the fallout from Watergate, was it revealed that IRS conducted a harassing audit of the IFCO-NWRO relationship, as well as of many other activist groups, on direct orders of the White House. Wiley believed but could not prove that an FBI-inspired provocateur deliberately created dissension within NWRO.

Only later did it become known that the FBI actually had a program for disrupting radical activist groups such as NWRO.*

Speaking of his own failings and what must be done differently in a renewed welfare organizing effort, Wiley said: "There would have to be a much more substantial leadership development program, having more and more people coming and learning in much more depth about the politics of the organization and of the country, learning what kind of things you have to do to make basic changes, learning where the power lies. I wasn't good at getting recipients to do a lot of jobs in the organization." Wiley gave lip service but little time or resources to systematic leadership development. Joyce Burson observed: "They moved so fast they didn't give people a chance to learn, and so very often people didn't know why they were doing things or what they were doing." In a similar vein, Tillmon complained that "there was too much mobilizing and not enough organizing," the same complaint Wiley had earlier made of most civil rights leaders.

Wiley was undoubtedly right in his pragmatic stress on short-term incentives and goals, but in the process he underestimated the need to emphasize long-range goals and ideals. This criticism was made by academics and also by recipient leader Jennette Washington: "We told people to come out and we'd get them furniture and clothing. So they joined us to get those benefits, and then left when there weren't any more material benefits. We didn't feed their souls. We didn't educate them as to why they should stay in the struggle." Wiley had defined an ideology, but he did not stress it or a long-range program that might have sustained NWRO's spirit.

Hindsight is valuable, but events moved quickly in the atmosphere of the 1960s. Civil rights bills became law because King managed to create the proper dynamics in Birmingham and Selma at opportune times. Wiley moved on the welfare organizing issues at precisely the moment when the system was most vulnerable and troops could be assembled to attack it. So his sense of urgency, of traveling fast and light, was in keeping with the times. In the process, either because he was in a hurry or out of vanity, he did not share leadership effectively. "He carried so much on himself that he inevitably undermined each piece," said administrative assistant Nancy Barnes. And, as Catherine Jermany observed, "George could unite everybody so long as he was there, but he couldn't stay with everybody twenty-four hours a day, three hundred and sixty-five days of the year, so there was not one-hundred-percent unity, and our organization sort of self-destructed."

Wiley may also have misjudged the times. He continued militant protests long past the time when others found such tactics counterproductive. He said that poor people had no other alternative. In the process, however,

---

* FBI files on Wiley, made available in part in May, 1977, under the Freedom of Information Act, show that the FBI, through its agents and informers, maintained surveillance of Wiley's civil rights and welfare rights activities from 1961 until his death.

he did learn that the nature of your opposition makes a crucial difference. The tactics of the civil rights movement and the early welfare rights movement were pushed nationally against liberal Democratic administrations and a neutral or apathetic electorate. In that case, government sometimes yielded to militant pressure, but a conservative government and electorate yielded very little.*

It appeared at last that George Wiley had been accepted as a black leader. It was African Liberation Day, in April, 1972, and Wiley was a featured speaker in ceremonies at the Sylvan Theatre at the foot of the Washington Monument. "George was surrounded by African Liberation flags and slogans, and he was really into it," recalled Audrey Colom. "For the first time I saw his 'soul side.' He was in an all-black setting and he was very comfortable." But as Wiley began speaking, a group of black women marched to the front of the platform and began chanting: "Where's your white wife? Where's your white wife?"

Visibly upset, Wiley changed his speech to focus on the fight he was involved in for black womanhood and to call on black men to support black women. But the chanting continued: "Talking black and sleeping white."

This attack, at this particular moment, was devastating for Wiley. He and Wretha were separated. The marriage had somehow survived the birth of the movement, the growing pains, the twenty-hour days; Wretha had managed the house, the children, and her own job, and had stayed away from the inner workings of NWRO. George was consumed by his work. It was a classic example of how a dedicated man lets his family come last. Sometimes Danny and Maya called the office, imploring him to come home. But there was no time for home. A separation of interest naturally followed. Wretha had become a highly skilled job consultant, but Wiley hardly knew what she did. She, on the other hand, was bored with the intense shop talk of NWRO social gatherings and soon stopped attending them.

The comfortable three-story house on Nineteenth Street, filled with Wretha's books, modern paintings, and sculpture, became merely a rest stop for George. He spent rare evenings at home watching Westerns on television. There still had been idyllic family moments together camping on the island in Canada or relaxing for a week at the mountaintop cabin in West Virginia. Then the old ties seemed to be renewed. "But that was unreal," says Wretha. "It was not of the real world in which we had to operate. Immediately on returning, the spell would be broken. The hectic pace, the twenty-hour days began all over again."

---

*Wiley concentrated a 1970 demonstration against HEW Secretary Robert Finch in part because he considered Finch the administration official most amenable to NWRO demands. Finch tolerated an all-day NWRO occupation of his office, but the only result was that Finch lost his job.

Finally, there were other women. At forty, Wiley seemed to be living through the adolescence, the teenage dreams that he had been denied. And then he fell in love with feminist writer Gloria Steinem, who physically, intellectually, and ideologically was so like Wretha. But Steinem's feelings toward him were of deep friendship, and he settled for the kind of close friendship he had established with men and women throughout his life. There were other relationships, and, after much thought on the matter, Wiley asked Wretha to indulge in an "open marriage." The idea seemed rational to him, but it stunned Wretha. She was enraged by his request that she share with other women what little time and emotion he had outside his work. At Christmastime, 1971, Wretha's parents came to Washington. Her father, who had not accepted the marriage (although her mother had), saw his grandchildren for the first time. Two days before he arrived, George and Wretha were separated.

Later, for the first time in his life, George developed a sustained, intimate relationship with a black woman. Barbara Williams, the talented attorney with whom he shared a house, learned the meaning of his lifelong phrase "God hates a coward" as she watched him risk his life on a boating vacation. A motor part dropped into the water, and although there were sharks swimming within view, Wiley dived for three hours until he found it.

She, too, was bothered by his obsession with work. He told Barbara that he had eight good years left in which he would be an organizer at the most energetic level. After that, at age fifty, he could write and do other things.

When Wiley broke with the women of NWRO, Barbara Williams said he was angry and very depressed, wondering what had gone wrong. But he revealed his inner anguish to few. With most close friends, he would say lightly, with a laugh: "Guess what? They fired me." Even when he felt lowest, however, Barbara Williams said, he was determined to continue his work. It was almost as if he were saying, she related, "that no person or disappointment will drive me away from my commitment to poor people." He awoke one morning in December, 1972, with his depression gone and his doubts lessened. He spent the day on the telephone, calling old friends and associates together for a meeting. He had a new plan.

33

The Movement
for Economic Justice

"He would tell us that everything has two sides and that
the easiest way to meet challenges is to just look at the easy
side."   —MAYA WILEY
"He would look at dangerous things as something funny.
He would always make things not as dangerous as they really
were."   —DANNY WILEY

George Wiley's ideas continued to evolve, and by 1973 he believed that the
poor and the black of America could not win further significant improvements in their status unless they became part of a new "majority movement"
to change the society. Its purpose would be to achieve a redistribution of
wealth and political power, helping both the poor and the average citizen at
the expense of the rich. In pursuit of this vision, Wiley created a new organization which he named the "Movement for Economic Justice." This organization was founded with the same spirit with which he had opened the
Poverty/Rights Action Center seven years earlier. And he returned in part to
his original concept, that welfare would be but one of many issues around
which the poor would be organized. His new insight was the need to
broaden greatly the base of the movement.

Reflecting on his new ideas, Wiley said: "While welfare rights is a good
example of what can be done by organizing a grass-roots movement for
change, it was a minority strategy. Only five percent of the population are
welfare recipients, and minority movements can succeed only if the majority
is either sympathetic or passive. In recent years hostility toward welfare re-

cipients and other minorities has increased. Even a coalition of minorities is
no longer politically sufficient. If you organized all the blacks, all the Chi-
canos, all the poor in this country into one organization, you would still have
only twenty-five percent of the population.

"Only a broad-based movement aimed at the economic interests of a
majority of Americans will ever succeed in bringing about the changes we
desire. In a majority strategy you try to convince or involve directly a majority around issues in which they have a self-interest. We're not saying to people that they have to deal with those issues because they're good for blacks
or welfare recipients, but because they are good for themselves. The issues
of income redistribution, of more adequate jobs, of tax reform, of decent
housing, of national health insurance are beneficial to a majority of Americans."

As Wiley met weekly in early 1973 with a dozen former associates from
NWRO, they assessed how their own efforts in NWRO had been used for
other purposes. "Minorities get isolated and manipulated one against another," said Wiley. "It is my belief that the success of those with wealth and
power has come from manipulating all of us to fight among ourselves, to act
against our own economic self-interest, which has allowed the maldistribu-
tion of wealth and power to continue. Nixon had divided us by saying that
the enemies of white workers are blacks, welfare recipients, kids. The Nixon
strategy has been successful. It focuses attention on victims instead of on
problems, like the need for income redistribution. We need a majority strategy to protect minorities and to develop enough political muscle to redirect
the country."

Wiley was just one of a number of people calling for some version of a
"new populism." But he differed from most who thought such ideas could
come about through the normal political process. In Wiley's view, real
change in the system required far deeper citizen involvement in the process
than merely voting. Without education and organized commitment, voters
might change the political officeholders but not the tax laws. Wiley understood the difficulty of implementing his strategy: "People talk about populist
movements as if all you have to do is articulate a set of issues and people will
rally around. I don't think that is going to work. What might work is people
actually organizing around some specific issues, and then developing a common political-economic agenda by bringing together the leaders and people
organized on different issues."

As Wiley planned the new movement, his attention ranged from the
tactics of how to build local grass-roots organizations to the strategy of how all
these groups might some day be pulled together around national issues. Bert
DeLeeuw, Wiley's chief aide: "George was constantly building models on the
blackboard. He talked about various means for building local organizations.
Finally, he built a five-foot-high board on which he laid out the steps for an
action campaign. August would be devoted to a national fund-raising effort

and October to an eight-state organizing campaign." In the weekly strategy sessions, DeLeeuw said, the conversation turned repeatedly to a single topic, "the dilemma of how to get the poor and the nonpoor together. The forays into different issues were attempts to make the bridge."

Wiley saw MEJ's potential constituency as coming from the 75 percent of Americans who lived on family incomes of less than fifteen thousand dollars. He began with two ideas about how to build workable alliances between the poor and the working and middle classes within this broad group. The first step was to concentrate on issues of common concern. At the national level, he thought that these issues were tax reform and national health insurance. The second ingredient for success was to permit maximum diversity between groups at the local level.

George Wiley: "I don't think it's going to be necessary for everyone to be members of the same organization. People have different styles, different sensibilities. I think that if we have learned anything over the last few years, the question of integration—of blacks and whites doing everything together—may not be the way to go. What we are looking for is not necessarily an integrated movement but a multiracial one. I think that plurality is the key. We think different groups will organize around different immediate interests with different styles. Perhaps senior citizens will organize one way, working-class blue-collar another, poor blacks yet another. We look for linking those different organizations together around issues. And that is the coalition aspect of people coming together not because they love each other, necessarily, but because they have a common interest in basic economic change."

During the first seven months of 1973, Wiley alternated between the roles of student and activist. He learned the intricacies of the tax system and spent a month as a Kennedy Institute Fellow at Harvard, picking the brains of professors he brought together from all over the Boston area. And he traveled widely, visiting new experimental efforts at community organizing. At the same time, Wiley kept in the public spotlight, pressing his own views as fast as he developed them, seeking to give a semblance of activism to his still tiny organization. Testifying before the House Ways and Means Committee on tax reform, Wiley was his old combative self: "I always found your welfare policies morally reprehensible but politically understandable, since welfare families represent at most about five percent of the population, about 55 percent of whom are black or Spanish-speaking. We have now begun examining your tax policies and find them just as outrageous. And the group which you are discriminating against here is over 70 percent of the voting population and over 80 percent white." As an example of unjust taxation, he cited the cumulative effect of tax exemptions and so-called loopholes. The 70 percent of taxpayers with incomes under fifteen thousand dollars received only sixteen billion dollars in exemptions, an average of $330 each, while richer taxpayers received forty billion dollars, an average of $1,915.

Wiley now made conciliatory moves to the leaders of liberal and labor organizations whom he had antagonized in the welfare reform fight. When lobbyists for liberal groups formed the Coalition for Human Needs and Budget Priorities to fight President Nixon's repeated 1972–73 vetoes of social legislation, Wiley joined the group's board, saying: "FAP was a fight of the past and this is a fight of the present. We are together on this one." Wiley reached out for opportunities to exert leadership and test new organizing ideas. When a demonstration was mounted in Washington against cuts in the poverty program, he told the protestors to "go home and fight for your share of revenue-sharing funds. We will help you." MEJ was flooded with requests for help and responded with a "how-to" kit showing local groups how to seek revenue-sharing for social needs.

His main focus was on federal tax reform and developing organizing tactics that would involve people at the local level in this complex issue. He hit on the idea of holding free tax clinics in which poor and moderate-income persons would be helped with their tax returns. MEJ sponsored more than a hundred tax clinics in 1973 as Wiley experimented to see whether providing this service could become a vehicle for educating and organizing people around the tax reform issue. Speaking before the National Council of Churches, he said: "The average taxpayer is a victim of the tax system because he has no tax lobbyist and must depend on an ineffective member of Congress. The complicated nature of the tax code keeps it as a province of a few Washington lobbyists and members of Congress who understand it. We need a taxpayers' revolt; not isolated taxpayers marching in the streets."

He did some of that marching himself, joining former Senator Fred Harris in a Wall Street tax protest rally. Even there he tried to educate: "The income gap between the rich and the poor is still widening. In 1947, the average income of the richest 20 percent of all families was $10,565 higher than that of the poorest 20 percent. In 1969, that gap was $19,071. The wealth gap is even greater. The richest 20 percent own over 75 percent of personal wealth. The top 1 percent alone own between 20 to 30 percent of personal wealth. Less than 2 percent of the population owns more than 80 percent of the individually held corporate stock, 90 percent of the corporate bonds, and 100 percent of municipal bonds."

He sought to distinguish between $6 billion in welfare programs for the poor and $68 billion in federal subsidies for the rich; between $23 million in housing subsidies for the poor and $750 million in tax breaks for owners of rental properties. He proposed beginning a tax reform and income redistribution plan: The $750 tax exemption for dependents would be turned into a $200 tax credit, since the present exemption was worth $525 to a taxpayer earning $200,000 a year, only $187 to a taxpayer with $15,000 earnings, and nothing to a taxpayer with less than $2,800 income. In Wiley's proposal, all taxpayers with less than $15,000 income would end up paying lower taxes, and the poor would be given the $200 as a tax credit. Wiley knew that other tax reformers had been advocating similar ideas and citing similar statistics for years, with little effect either on the public or in Congress. Yet he believed that a massive organizing and education campaign could make a difference.

At a series of Harvard seminars, Wiley was challenged on this optimistic, rationalist approach to politics—his belief that Americans could be adequately motivated by an appeal directed at their sense of fairness and direct self-interest. Contrary to this view, Professor Arthur Naperstak of the University of Massachusetts pointed out, many people believe the tax system should not be changed because it provides tremendous incentive to people who work hard. Even those who have worked hard and have not gained from their labors, he said, tend to regard lack of success as their own failure rather than that of the system.

Samuel Popkin, a Harvard professor of government and a polling expert, told Wiley that studies of public attitudes about inheritance tax laws again revealed no direct connection with personal self-interest. Instead of protest against the unfairness of the rich passing on their wealth from generation to generation, he said, the working man tends to ask: "Why would you want to make a million dollars if you couldn't leave it to your kids?" The political beliefs of many are based on hopes and dreams for their children rather than their own reality. "I realize that people don't necessarily move politically along lines of their economic self-interest," Wiley replied, "but I regard that as a problem to be solved rather than a condition to be lived with. I'm not saying we understand a lot. I'm saying we are trying to learn."

Wiley's theory called for a redistribution of income coming from the rich and benefiting both the poor and the middle-class, but he did not advocate socialism. As a pragmatic activist, Wiley rejected socialism as a cause most Americans would not adopt. But the George Wiley who had gotten ahead by his own efforts still believed in a system with high rewards for excellence and hard work. He still believed in the American dream. He thought that there needed to be a far more equitable sharing of both power and material wealth but that this could be accomplished by changing tax laws and providing a decent guaranteed annual income and enough jobs. Yet he resisted information from economists that not enough money could be gained by closing loopholes to accomplish a significant redistribution of income. Since the vast majority of American families are in the middle income range, any major redivision of income would require a leveling in which income was also taken in taxes from some in the middle class and given to the poor and lower-middle class. Faced with these statistics, he replied, "I don't believe it."

When editors of *Newsweek* magazine expressed skepticism about the feasibility of organizing a majority at the grass-roots level, Wiley explained: "You have to organize about 2 percent of the people in a group to get anything. Two percent of the welfare recipients means you have the welfare recipients. You need 2 percent of the various constituencies. An organizational nucleus really has a tremendous ripple effect on the people around it. We aren't trying to become the AFL-CIO. MEJ isn't going to have 130 million members. It's really a question of trying to get a nuclei of people in those constituencies organized so that it develops a political consciousness among those kinds of groups that there is really something happening."

A tired colleague from the movement wondered who would take on even this monumental organizing job. "Those who will do it, will do it," Wiley replied stubbornly. Again seeking to avoid creating a national super-structure without strong roots, Wiley said that this problem might be avoided by not forming a national organization too soon, by not having a per-manent chairman, and by letting the best organized groups variously take the lead on different issues. In keeping with this thinking, Wiley gave him-self the title of "coordinator" rather than director or chairman.

Wiley's greatest interest was focused on finding or creating the local or-ganizations, which would be the essential building-blocks of the reform ef-fort. Mark Splain, a young former NWRO organizer, agreed to provide an experimental model for MEJ with an organizing effort in Chelsea, a working-class area of Boston. Wiley and Splain sought the ultimate national goals of tax reform and national health insurance, but their immediate local concerns centered on questions such as: Where are the handles? How do you orga-nize? How do you produce victories for people? Within a two-year period, Splain's efforts had become "Massachusetts Fair Share," with more than thirty communities participating, working individually on local issues and together on state issues such as taxes and utility rates.

Wiley also was attracted to the Citizens' Action Program in Chicago because it brought under its broad umbrella both blacks and some of the same working-class whites who had rioted against Martin Luther King's ef-forts there six years earlier. The issues were local: preserving inner-city housing, fighting red-lining* of neighborhoods by mortgage bankers, win-ning property tax rebates, fighting a crosstown expressway, stopping pollution by the electric utility. Thirty neighborhood organizations and fifty senior cit-izens' clubs were working individually and collectively on their problems.

Another Wiley interest was a unique and growing organizing effort in Arkansas which he had helped initiate three years earlier. He had sent Wade Rathke to Little Rock first to organize welfare recipients but then to experi-ment with a broader constituency of working-class and middle-class groups. The result was ACORN (Arkansas Community Organizations for Reform Now), which had organized farmers to protest crop-destroying pollution from a power plant, Vietnam veterans to get state benefits, unemployed workers to fight unscrupulous employment agencies, property owners to fight against a freeway. ACORN soon encompassed forty local groups in all areas of the state, and spread new efforts to Texas and North Dakota.

* A system by which bankers designate an area in which they won't make loans.

When Wiley went to Little Rock to learn from his former student, Rathke was struck by the ease with which he established rapport with working-class southern whites. Bill Whipple, a white ACORN member, launched into a diatribe against welfare recipients as soon as they met. "Wiley smiled, praised the virtues of hard work, and soon they were deep in friendly conversation as George asked the man about the chemistry of the cleaning fluids he used in his carpet-cleaning business," Rathke recalls. "Regardless of the potential for power, George believed in the potential of people. In the cynicism which mass organizing tends to develop in people, this made George very rare indeed."

In 1973, Wiley was still at a crossroads in his personal as well as his professional life. He and Barbara Williams separated in the spring. He dated another woman, but much of his time was spent either with his children, in seeking out new friendships, or by himself. "During June and July, George was often lonely," recalled Bert DeLeeuw.

Seeing him that summer, friends from long ago might have thought they had encountered the old George. The daishiki was gone and a battered Austin Healey sports car was back. Dressed in a turtleneck shirt and sport coat, he drove around Washington with his children as his companions. He took them to the office, where they played; to hear all his "sweaty speeches"; and to his friends' homes. He was openly affectionate with them, wrestling with Danny and pulling Maya onto his lap. Out of their hearing, he worried about making up for all the time he had not been around as a caring father. As part of that process, he told friends, he was talking with the children about a great adventure they would have together. They would buy an old boat and explore the nearby Chesapeake Bay. But he could not keep his mind distracted for long from the demands of his ambitious new undertaking.

Bert DeLeeuw: "We changed many times the formula of what we were doing. It was painful for George, because we had said we were going to devote nine months to planning and then initiate major action. We had now spent eight months planning. We were about to begin. He was very excited about taking a vacation with the kids in early August. They were going to spend three or four days on the boat on their first trip. He was going to come back from the vacation with a resolution of the dilemmas facing us in MEJ." The dilemma was how to move from merely planning a populist-type new movement to actually bringing such a movement to life with concrete action. At age forty-two, he had given himself the challenge of starting anew. His past experience was an invaluable guide, but also a constant reminder of the incredible energy and effort he would have to invest in the myriad jobs from fund-raising to organizing.

The week before leaving on the boating vacation he was off on another trip, this time to learn about the community organizing being done by John Hunter in the mountain hollows of Appalachia. Wiley originally had met Hunter in Milwaukee and persuaded him to return to his native West Virginia mountains to organize white welfare recipients. Now he was organizing mostly whites in a community union. Wiley spoke with the members about the need for whites and blacks to work together. "He talked to me on that trip about wanting to move to his West Virginia farm, of wanting to get back to the world of real people," recalled Hunter, "and he talked about buying an old boat and going boating with his kids. He described how as a kid he used to go down to the water; he said he spent hours fishing, and seeing all the rich white kids out fishing and sailing in boats. He had spent hours dreaming about how great it would be to have a boat."

Wiley then drove over to spend the night at the West Virginia summer retreat of Leslie Dunbar, the director of the Field Foundation. Wiley had asked Field for a $150,000 grant for MEJ, and Dunbar was inclined to give it to him. "We sat out there on the patio facing the mountains and we had a couple of drinks," recalled Dunbar. "And we talked all night. He talked about his children and wanting to spend more time with them. The most important thing about the evening was that it was just commonplace talk."

Returning to Washington, Wiley met last-minute obligations before his boating vacation. On Sunday, August 5, he sat for a long interview with his former aide Wilbur Colom, who was writing a story. The interview ended with a question:

"Are you burned out, George?"

"We will have to wait and see," Wiley replied.

On Monday, August 6, George and his children drove down to the Chesapeake Bay, forty miles from Washington, to begin their adventure. The eighteen-foot wooden cabin cruiser was old and rickety, but for George it had character, just like his old cars. He had paid fifteen hundred dollars for it a few days earlier, after first getting a bank loan to cover the purchase. They spent the day painting, checking out the engine, and loading supplies. The next day they began exploring the bay and small communities along the Maryland shore. They docked for the night. The next day, Wednesday, August 8, was cloudy and windy. As George gassed the boat at a marina, the operator cautioned him against going out into the bay, warning that a storm was brewing.

Wiley disregarded the warning and steered the boat out into the bay. His action was characteristic of the man. "God hates a coward," he had always said, strong-willed, stubborn, and so confident of his own abilities that it didn't occur to him that he was taking chances. He and the children had only a few days, and he wanted them to enjoy the boat to the maximum.

Within several hours it started to rain, softly at first and then with some force. The waves were growing choppier and larger. The boat's windshield wiper did not work, and Wiley had difficulty seeing through the window. He left ten-year-old Danny at the wheel and worked his way around the walkway outside the boat to repair the faulty wiper. As the boat rolled from a wave, he slipped against the frail wooden railing. The railing snapped and he pitched backward into the water, his lifejacket being torn away as it snagged on the boat.

It was a moment of terror. Wiley was treading water and shouting instructions to the children. Danny and his nine-year-old sister were alone in the boat. Danny and Maya tried to steer the boat in the rough water and throw a line to their father. It did not reach. Wiley was a strong swimmer, but the Chesapeake Bay in foul weather is deceptive, with high waves and strong underwater currents. Two small children, inexperienced with boats, tried to manage one in a heavy sea. Wiley struggled, but finally, his strength sapped, he slipped beneath the water. He was gone. Danny eventually managed to bring the boat ashore. He ran inland searching for help. Despite the children's best efforts, it was too late. Wiley's body was recovered four days later. He had drowned in the Chesapeake Bay at age forty-two, only a few miles from where his great-grandparents had been born in slavery.

Just as the poor could not afford to march on Cleveland in 1966, but instead held demonstrations in their own cities to begin the welfare rights movement, the poor could not afford to come to Washington to pay homage to their leader. Instead, they held memorial services in more than twenty communities, from New York City to John Hunter's farm in West Virginia. More than 150 people gathered at the farm, where they planted a black walnut tree—to symbolize George Wiley's color and his strength. The principal memorial service was held August 12, 1973, in the New York Avenue Presbyterian Church in Washington, with more than a thousand people attending.*

"It was very much as if the different layers of George Wiley's complicated life had come in for a final counting," wrote *Washington Post* reporter Austin Scott. "One seldom saw them all together. There were welfare mothers, foundation executives, lawyers, liberal congressmen, energetic young white staff volunteers and black and white organizers—people who were often uncomfortable around each other, whose temperaments clashed, but through some magic of personality stayed bound together in a chaotic, high-pressure orbit around Wiley, working to support his ideas on developing power for poor people." One after another rose to speak.

There was Beulah Sanders, speaking in a soft sobbing voice about her lost brother. And former Senator Eugene McCarthy, who had led the fight against the war in Vietnam but who needed George to discover his own hu-

* Wiley was awarded a posthumous honorary degree from the University of Rhode Island in 1974.

manity with poor black people. Robert Ostrow, the legal and accounting expert, who stood with head bowed and said only, "He called me Bobby, and I loved him and he loved me." And there was Bruce Thomas, who told how George had changed his life back in the streets of Syracuse and now vowed to carry on. There were the old faces of the civil rights movement, like Jim Farmer, and the new ones, Andrew Young, Vernon Jordan, and Ronald Dellums. And then Dick Gregory, thin from many lonely fasts, whispered his ghetto poem:

> "Brother George who helped the
>   needy
> Defend themselves against the
>   greedy."

And finally Ed Day, the young white sidekick who said: "George was the master of the barely possible. George was a spiritual descendant of the Wright brothers. He patched together old bicycle parts and canvas and bailing wire, and while others looked on or idly dreamed or schemed, he made things fly. Where others saw the undoable, he saw the doable. George did things with resources that others would consider woefully inadequate. And that was, in fact, his delight in living. That was his vision, that was the spark that commanded in us a spirit, a dedication, a determination to do what must be done. George said that somehow we could do it. We believed him and therefore we did it, and were always a bit amazed that we had."

The Movement for Economic Justice was little more than a grand vision when Wiley died.* Its office closed in 1976, but the idea lives on.

"There are hundreds of grass-roots activist-type organizations around the country," said Bert DeLeeuw. "George's concepts have become the definition of what people in these groups say they are doing. They are doing the things locally that George Wiley talked about and dreamed about, building majority coalitions, trying to build bridges between the poor and the non-poor. Perhaps someday there will be an organization and a leader who can bring them all together to be a national force for economic justice."

Organizer Mark Splain: "There is activity all over the country, but there is no one with George's ability talking about and working toward making this into a national movement. He had the self-confidence, the considerable skills, and the political appetite to make it happen. He was the one in a million in being able to pull all the pieces together, being able to have the vision yet work with the practical details."

Wiley is also missed in Washington among those who care deeply about

---

* Bert DeLeeuw carried on the Movement for Economic Justice, aiding, encouraging, and incorporating grass-roots groups around the country, organizing around such issues as taxes and utility rates.

issues of race and poverty. In the three years since his death, the phrase "If only George Wiley were here" has been stated repeatedly, whenever callous attacks against the poor have gone unanswered. It is then that people recall the function he served in shaming the heartless and forcing the timid to confront hard issues and their own consciences.

George Wiley is also missed as a human being who communicated an enormous sense of vitality and life force. He left a strong, indelible imprint on hundreds of people who knew him in different stages of his life. A boyhood friend recalls a humorous incident with George and laughs as if the event happened only yesterday. A Syracuse University professor breaks into tears, recalling how Wiley moved him to a first act of social protest years ago. Gloria Steinem, in updating her address book, found herself transferring George's name and telephone numbers from her old book to a new one.

Any assessment of Wiley's accomplishments or significance as a public leader must focus on his work with welfare rights. He may not have changed the broad national perception of welfare recipients, but he brought the welfare poor out of the shadows and into the public arena. He could not remove the feelings of unworthiness experienced by many on welfare, but for thousands he offered inspiration, information, and a program by which they could re-examine their status in society, find and assert their own dignity, and act in their own behalf. He may not have proved that poor people can be organized into a permanent force, but he increased the likelihood of that possibility. He may not have totally reformed the welfare system, but he helped establish a whole series of legal welfare rights that cannot so easily be swept away. He may have hindered the passage of welfare reform legislation in 1969–72, but he asserted that the poor should have a voice in their own destiny and that reform should not be purchased at the cost of lost rights and benefits for poor people.

Wiley did not consider the welfare rights movement a failure. Its most concrete success, in his mind, was helping to ignite and fuel the explosion in the welfare rolls, with six million more people getting benefits and benefits rising by four billion dollars in the seven years following the birth of NWRO. Many point to these statistics as showing the failure of the Great Society programs and further deterioration at the bottom of American society, especially among the black poor. The popular view is that the welfare explosion is a national disaster, but at least a few students of the subject agree with Wiley.

Dr. Robert Lampman, a University of Wisconsin professor of economics and an authority on guaranteed annual income concepts, believed that the poor in the 1960s often served as pawns in contests to reform all government policies. He said the poor should not be blamed or punished because society has not figured out solutions to unemployment and all the perplexing other problems that have created an impoverished dependent group at the bottom of American society. Suggesting a "new test for national policy," namely,

"What does it do for the poor?" he concluded that the poor are better off, in at least getting welfare.

Gilbert Steiner, director of the governmental studies program at the Brookings Institution and the author of two definitive studies on American welfare, made a similar point: "Admitting more of the needy poor to the relief rolls, no matter how reluctantly, rather than keeping them off, no matter how ingeniously, is the quintessence of welfare reform. While the planners are frustrated, the welfare poor are better off."

Steiner had written in 1965 that the time was ripe for a welfare rights movement when the proper person came forward to lead it. In 1973, he reflected: "If Wiley had not done it, I don't think that group of poor people would have been organized. I don't see any other figure who would have undertaken that job."

There is a sense of mysticism about the death at early ages of black heroes at crucial turning-points in their lives, at times when they offered promise of a new beginning or fulfillment of centuries old dreams. One hears it from Vernon Jordan at the Urban League, from John Conyers in his congressional office, and from a welfare mother in her slum apartment. They speak of Malcolm X, murdered just as he sought to apply new insights of possible racial harmony; Martin Luther King, Jr., murdered as he tried to redirect the civil rights movement to issues of poverty; Whitney Young, struck down by a heart attack as he sought to broaden the purpose of the Urban League. And then George Wiley, who was reaching out for alliance with the very people who had attacked the poor.

In the eyes of some, all of these leaders were spared the disillusionment of seeing the failure of their new visions. For others, their lives are a dramatic testament to the human potential for growth and renewal; their deaths are a reminder of the unfinished work that remains.

At the end, Wiley no longer expected easy victories or quick ones. His views of life's possibilities had changed since his early days as a social activist. As with many of his generation, optimism about achieving social and economic justice in America was transformed into a more somber vision as real changes began to appear more elusive.

In a 1973 conversation with Barbara Williams, he spoke of his engagement in the struggle.

"When does it end?" she wondered. "When do you win, George?"

"When there are not any more poor people," he replied.

"Okay, there isn't going to be any end," said Williams, "because that's what the Bible says."

"Then you just keep struggling," he answered.

APPENDIX

NWRO—A CHRONICLE

Compiled from the official NWRO publications, *NOW!* and
The Welfare Fighter, 1966–1972.

1966

April Washington, D.C.—Poverty Rights Action Center (P/RAC) founded by George A. Wiley.

May 19–21 Chicago—University of Chicago's Guaranteed Annual Income Conference; Wiley meets with potential welfare rights leaders

June 30 First nationwide welfare rights demonstrations coordinated by P/RAC—6,000 participate in 40 cities

August 6–7 Chicago—P/RAC's first national meeting attended by 75 welfare recipient organizations. National Coordinating Committee of Welfare Groups (NCC) elected with member from each participating state

September–November Massachusetts—10 welfare rights organizations (WROs) ask state commissioner of welfare for special grants

Chicago—WRO organizers of sit-in in welfare office jailed. WRO now demands right to recruit and organize in welfare offices

Contra Costa County, Calif.—WRO campaigns against county welfare work program; 150 ask for vocational counseling

Los Angeles County, Calif.—WRO protests baby's death due to inadequate processing of mother's medical ID card. County makes improvements

California—California chapters of National Association of Social Workers develop Welfare Rights Support Project

December 3 Del Rey, Calif.—California WRO established at convention of 32 welfare groups

December 17 Pittsburgh—first meeting of NCC enlarges NCC to 25 members.

1967

January Philadelphia—15 WROs campaign for better housing

St. Louis—250 meet with state director of welfare to present welfare reform agenda

February 4–6 Washington, D.C.—P/RAC workshops on organizing techniques attended by 350 welfare recipients from 50 states

March P/RAC prepares organizing and welfare information packets to be distributed to P/RAC members

>   Mount Vernon, N.Y.—8 welfare recipients sit in at welfare department when unable to get checks during social workers' strike. After 1½ days they get their checks.

>   New York, N.Y.—1,500 attend welfare teach-in co-sponsored by P/RAC

>   Greensboro, N.C.—2,500 sign a petition calling for additional welfare appropriations, larger day-care program, right to have telephone and insurance, free medicine, public ambulance service, and emergency medical service

>   Raleigh, N.C.—40 people from Greensboro WRO meet with state legislators

>   New York, N.Y.—Welfare department rules recipients can have another person with them when they talk with welfare department people

April National Spring Campaign: (1) WRO membership drive begins; (2) local action on key local welfare issues and planning of nationwide demonstration; (3) 200 summer student volunteers recruited to work as organizers with local welfare rights groups

April 8–10 Washington, D.C.—NCC meeting votes for summer national campaign to raise welfare grant levels, national membership plan, and national convention in July

>   NCC meets with officials from HEW and Agriculture Department

April Other WRO actions in Philadelphia and New York, N.Y.

May Washington, D.C.—Wiley, Etta Horn, and Carl Rachlin (general counsel) testify before House Agriculture Committee on food stamp program

>   New York, N.Y.—300 recipients demonstrate against proposal to replace commodity food program with food stamps

>   St. Louis, Mo.—WRO campaign for AFDC for unemployed parents, higher grants, and Medicaid benefits; lobbying and testimony before state legislature

>   Ohio—WRO circulating petition in favor of legislation to raise grant levels

>   California—WRO initiates weekly lobbying effort

>   California—State Supreme Court rules that "midnight raids" violate recipients' constitutional rights

>   Other WRO actions in Oakland, Calif.; San Francisco, Calif.; Tulsa, Okla.; Baltimore, Md.; Columbus, Ohio; Contra Costa County, Calif.; Rochester, N.Y.

June Nationwide basic-needs campaign—recruitment of recipients to fill out basic needs form; June 30 demonstrations to present demands; July 15 fair-hearing requests filed for each person whose needs were not met

June 30 5,000 demonstrate for welfare rights in coordinated actions in: Philadelphia, Pa.; Washington, D.C.; New York, N.Y.; Jackson, Miss.; Durham, N.C.; Columbus, Ohio; St. Louis, Mo.; Cincinnati, Ohio; Mount Vernon, N.Y.; Wichita, Kan.; Detroit, Mich.; Miami, Fla.; Cleveland, Ohio; Los Angeles, Calif.; Toledo, Ohio; Gainesville, Fla.; Boston, Mass.; Patterson, N.J.; Providence, R.I.; Rochester, N.Y.; San Jose, Calif.; San Bernadino, Calif.; Louisville, Ky.; Lexington, Ky.; Newark, N.J.; Fresno, Calif.; Pittsfield, Mass.; Tulsa, Okla.; Springfield, Mass.; Phoenix, Ariz.; Wilmington, Del.; Milwaukee, Wis.; Sacramento, Calif.; New Orleans, La.; and other cities

July 14   Columbus, Ohio—9 WROs meet to file fair-hearing requests and stage sit-in at state house

July 15   Jackson, Miss.—statewide welfare rights workshop

July   Washington, D.C.—WRO demands meeting with welfare director after welfare department ignored 300 basic needs requests

Miami, Fla.—WRO obtains emergency county checks for members when state checks delayed

Chicago, Ill.—welfare department offers to give special grants for basic needs items, but money would be deducted from monthly grants; WRO rejects offer

Cleveland, Ohio—welfare department to meet basic needs requests for beds, mattresses, blankets, tables and chairs, stoves, refrigerators, and washing machines

Other WRO actions in New York, N.Y.; Philadelphia, Pa.; Utica, N.Y.; Waterloo and Muscatine, Iowa; Pittsfield, Mass.; Louisville, Ky.; and Lancaster, Pa.

August 3   "Welfare freeze" (H.R. 12080) adopted by House Ways and Means Committee

August 17   Kansas City, Mo.—Wiley speaks on "The Equal Rights of the Poor" at National Catholic Conference for Interracial Justice

August 25–28   Washington, D.C.—founding convention of NWRO attended by 300 delegates from 26 states and representing 15,000 recipients. Delegates march to Capitol Hill and HEW to lobby against welfare freeze

September 19   Washington, D.C.—NWRO officials and Wiley testify before Senate Finance Committee on welfare legislation; when Committee recesses, 50 recipients stage a wait-in

September 18–October 3   New York, N.Y.—2,000 fair-hearing requests filed in basic-needs campaign, bringing recipients $300,000

September 25   Pittsburgh, Pa.—100 attend rally to confront Office of Public Assistance with demands for changes in welfare

September   Ohio—200 fair hearing requests filed

Jackson, Miss.—WRO calls for HEW investigation of state welfare department after department schedules only 10 fair hearings out of 175 requests

October 14   Columbus, Ohio—statewide WRO basic needs and fair hearings workshop

October 20   Long Beach, Calif.—Carmelitos WRO pickets housing management on "the cockroach issue"

October 23   NET-TV film about NWRO aired

October   NWRO mobilizes behind Robert F. Kennedy's amendments to H.R. 12080

New York—NWRO demands representation in state social welfare conference

Los Angeles, Calif.—WROs join Committee for the Rights of the Disabled to fight Governor Reagan's Medicaid cutbacks

Philadelphia, Pa.—WRO forces welfare department to cut welfare application review time and to increase number of people eligible

WRO actions against "anti-welfare" bill in Boston, Mass.; Los Angeles, Calif.; Rochester, N.Y.; and Chicago, Ill.

November 3   Dover, Del.—150 recipients demonstrate at state capitol

November 8   Philadelphia, Pa.—"blood for shoes" publicity campaign takes unexpected turn; 25 of 27 recipients cannot qualify as blood donors, most because of iron deficiency

Des Moines, Iowa—60 poor people interrupt Iowa Welfare Association convention to seek support for welfare changes

November 10 Arizona—first annual forum on public welfare

November 18 Mount Beulah, Miss.—statewide welfare rights meeting

November 21 Waterloo, Iowa—50 meet with country social welfare director to protest H.R. 12080

Nationwide WRO "scapegoats for poverty" demonstrations in: Brooklyn, N.Y.; Modesto, Calif.; Hartford, Conn.; Gainesville, Fla.; Chicago, Ill.; Des Moines, Iowa; Washington, D.C.; Kansas City, Kans.; New Orleans, La.; Detroit, Mich.; Lansing, Mich.; Hattiesburg, Miss.; Kansas City, Mo.; St. Louis, Mo.; Newark, N.J.; and Columbus, Ohio

November 30 Harrisburg, Pa.—250 WRO members in meeting with public assistance officials ask why welfare recipients must live in poverty

November Detroit, Mich.—West Side mothers stage sit-in at Detroit Housing Committee to protest lack of housing for large families

Columbus, Ohio—Day-long WRO demonstration to dramatize proclamation for Welfare Rights Week (November 5–11)

Hinds County Welfare Rights Movement (Jackson, Miss.) and Ohio Steering Committee for Adequate Welfare charge HEW fails to require states obey federal fair-hearing regulations

New York, N.Y.—10,000 minimum standards lists distributed by CityWide Coordinating Committee of Welfare Rights Groups

Other welfare rights actions in Brockton, Mass.; Denver, Colo.; Troy, N.Y.; Rosedale, Miss.; Arlington, Va.; Gary, Ind.; Bluefield, W. Va.; and Binghamton, N.Y.

December 9 Detroit, Mich.—100 members of Westside Mothers protest to Wayne County officials about inadequate payments

December 15 Washington, D.C.—U.S. Senate passes Mills-Long welfare bill

December 18 Brooklyn, N.Y.—175 recipients picket, march, and sing outside Brooklyn welfare centers until 15 receive special Christmas grants

December Other welfare rights actions in Ohio; Washington, D.C.; and Chicago, Ill.

1968

January 24 Springfield, Ill.—Illinois Budgetary Commission votes to investigate welfare costs

January NWRO wins lawsuits challenging legality of one-year state residency requirement for welfare eligibility in Connecticut, Delaware, Washington, D.C., Maryland, Pennsylvania, Wisconsin, and Illinois. Challenges still pending in Florida, Michigan, Mississippi, Missouri, New Jersey, Texas, South Carolina, Oregon, Washington, and Arizona

Other WRO actions in Brooklyn, N.Y.; Philadelphia, Pa.; Columbus, Ohio; and Washington, D.C.

February 5 Chicago, Ill.—NWRO leaders meet with Martin Luther King, Jr., and join Poor People's Campaign

Chicago, Ill.—NWRO training workshops on welfare law, fair hearings, and organization attended by representatives from Illinois, Michigan, Ohio, Indiana, Kansas, Iowa, Virginia, Louisiana, and Kentucky

Other WRO actions in St. Louis, Mo.; Springfield, Ill.; Des Moines, Iowa; Richmond, Va.; Wilmington, Del.

NWRO claims 5,000 dues-paying members, representing 20,000 welfare recipients

February 29 NWRO participates in HEW compliance hearings on Georgia's implementation of welfare freeze

February 686,000 added to welfare rolls in 1967, twice the 1966 increase and three times the annual average in last five years

Other WRO actions in St. Louis, Mo.; Springfield, Ill.; Des Moines, Iowa; Richmond, Va.; Wilmington, Del.; Louisville, Ky.; Mount Vernon, N.Y.; Ohio; Brooklyn, N.Y.; Calexico, Calif.; Baton Rouge, La.; Chicago, Ill.; New York, N.Y.; New Haven, Conn.; Harrisburg, Pa.; and Barnwell, S.C.

March 6 Dover, Del.—50 meet with governor, who promises appointment of recipient to state board of welfare and examination of payment ceiling

April 15–22 Washington, D.C.—NCC training conference; speakers include Acting HEW Secretary Wilbur Cohen and Stokely Carmichael

April 21 Washington, D.C.—31 NWRO officers arrested during midnight prayer vigil for Martin Luther King, Jr., at U.S. Capitol

April 26 Denver, Colo.—25 persons meet with Colorado state welfare director to demand recipient participation on the State Welfare Board

May 12 Washington, D.C.—7,000 attend NWRO/PPC Mother's Day March and Rally; speech by Coretta Scott King.

Other Mother's Day Marches in Benton Harbor, Mich.; San Bernadino, Calif.; Atlanta, Ga.; Passaic, N.J.; Hazlehurst, Miss.; Toledo, Ohio; Barnwall, S.C.; Hattiesburg, Miss.; Long Beach, Calif.; Ann Arbor, Mich.; McKeesport, Pa.; Buffalo, N.Y.; McComb, Miss.; Cleveland, Ohio; New Orleans, La.; and Dayton, Ohio

May 21 Milwaukee, Wis.—150 post demands on the welfare center doors and attend rally for "dignity and more money for mothers on welfare"

Philadelphia, Pa.—sued by WRO, Philadelphia Housing Authority agrees to drop unwritten policy excluding families with illegitimate children

May 23 Washington, D.C.—Wiley leads 250 to congressional office building to demand welfare reform; 18 arrested

May 24 Washington, D.C.—Wiley leads 100 in demonstrations at USDA and home of Rep. Wilbur Mills to protest welfare freeze

May Other WRO actions in Tucson, Ariz., and Louisville, Ky.

June 17 Washington, D.C.—welfare-recipient "Board of Inquiry" convenes on Capitol Hill and questions witnesses from Congress and HEW, including HEW Secretary Wilbur Cohen

Washington, D.C.—U.S. Supreme Court strikes down "man-in-the-house" rule, affecting 19 states and D.C.

June 18 Washington, D.C.—500 march on Rep. Wilbur Mills' home distributing "wanted" posters for Mills' "crimes against poor people"

June 29 Chicago, Ill.—300 protest threatened cuts in welfare grants

June 30 & July 1 Marches celebrating NWRO's second birthday in Detroit, Mich.;

Los Angeles, Calif.; St. Louis, Mo.; Benton Harbor, Mich.; Newark, N.J.; Englewood, N.J.; San Francisco, Calif.; Ann Arbor, Mich.; Toledo, Akron, Columbus, Cleveland, Cincinnati, Steubenville, Ohio; and other cities

June 28–30 New York, N.Y.—12 WRO leaders stage sit-in in social services commissioner's office in campaign to force payment meeting minimum standards

June 30 New York, N.Y.—250 march outside the UN to draw attention to New York's proposed Guaranteed Annual Income (GAI) plan

July 1 New York, N.Y.—80 recipients block entrances to New York City welfare headquarters; 38 arrested

July 2 New York, N.Y.—WRO denied attendance at State Board of Social Welfare meeting; 40 take over social welfare commissioner's office; commissioner agrees to meet with 11 WRO representatives

July 8 New York, N.Y.—WRO calls for 24-percent increase in basic budget and continuation of special grants

July 12 Topeka, Kans.—after 2½-hour sit-in, 40 senior citizens meet with governor about state's decision against funding a federal old-age assistance program

July 16 Columbus, Ohio—30 welfare demonstrators stage a sleep-in on the statehouse steps after state officials fail to meet demands for increased welfare benefits

August 5 Brooklyn, N.Y.—WRO begins voter-registration action

Washington, D.C.—HEW adopts regulations to enforce Supreme Court's ban on "man-in-the-house" regulation

August 21 Chicago, Ill.—Wiley, Beulah Sanders, and Etta Horn testify before the platform committee at the Democratic National Convention

August 22–25 Chicago, Ill.—NWRO Action Conference (161 groups from 70 cities and 37 states represented)

August 28 New York, N.Y.—18 arrested in third day of massive resistance to New York City program substituting flat grants for special grants

September 2 Ann Arbor, Mich.—30 stage sit-in at County Building after Board of Supervisors refuses to hear demands for emergency allowance for school clothes

September 7 Ann Arbor, Mich.—after a week of demonstrations with college student participation and 242 arrests, county officials and recipients agree to an allowance of up to $70 per child

September 14 Newark, N.J.—60 women and 25 children picket and sit in for increased welfare allotments for children

September Other WRO actions in Detroit and Benton Harbor, Mich.; Rochester, N.Y.; Kansas City, Kans.; Waterbury, Conn.; Newark, N.J.; Washington, D.C.; and Boston, Mass. for school clothing allowances

November 14 Philadelphia, Pa.—over 1,000 women and children sit-in in office of regional director of Department of Public Assistance demanding special Christmas grants

Thanksgiving Day Toledo, Ohio—12 WRO members arrested in a welfare center during demonstration for basic needs and winter clothing grants

November 18 New Orleans, La.—22 mothers and 60 children arrested during protest against 10-percent cut in welfare payments

November 19 New Orleans, La.—250 protest November 18 arrests; 10 more arrested

Toledo, Ohio—28 people arrested in further demonstrations for basic needs and winter clothing grants

November 20 Baton Rouge, La.—600 protest state cut in welfare; representatives meet with the governor, who promised increase if there was a tax increase

November 21 Brooklyn, N.Y.—campaign begins for credit to welfare recipients at E. J. Korvette stores

New York, N.Y.—Winter Action Campaign launched with demonstration at Macy's Parade

November 27 Bakersfield, Calif.—70 WRO members from Wasco, Delano, and Bakersfield picket welfare department for winter clothing and Christmas allowances

November 30 Kansas City—WRO wins campaign to gain credit privileges at Montgomery Ward

December 3 Washington, D.C.—6 WRO members arrested picketing Cafritz Hospital for its failure to join Medicaid

December 5 Beaufort, S.C—100 demonstrate at county welfare department for 16 demands, including money for winter clothing, Christmas grants, and welfare rights representation on County Welfare Board; 7 people arrested

New York, N.Y.—sit-in demonstrations begin for winter clothing: 500 recipients occupy 18 welfare centers, with clients in Bronx and Harlem gaining payments ranging from $50 to $127 per family

December 6–9 Providence, R.I.—Central Falls Fair Welfare group holds sit-ins at local welfare department demanding clothing and furniture grants

December 9, 16 Baton Rouge, La.—200 demonstrate in continuing campaign against 10-percent cut in welfare

December 12 Detroit, Mich.—three-day sit-in by 50 mothers at Wayne County Department of Social Services demanding Christmas grants

December 13 Youngstown, Ohio—60 sit-in at county welfare office to ask for $100 winter clothing grants for ADC children

December 16 Springfield, Ill.—175 Chicago WRO members promised that legislative Committee on Public Assistance will hold public welfare hearings in Chicago

Worchester, Mass.—25 recipients demonstrate in welfare office for Christmas grants

December 20 Jersey City, N.J.—welfare mothers demonstrate for fair hearings and Christmas grants

December NWRO signs $435,000 contract with U.S. Department of Labor "to assist with job training of poor."

Other WRO actions in Memphis, Tenn.; Oklahoma City, Okla.; Kansas City and St. Louis, Mo.; Boston, Mass.; Toledo, Ohio; Tucson and Tempe, Ariz.

1969

January 1 Beaufort, S.C.—800 sign petitions in behalf of demands by Beaufort County WRO

January 2 Rochester, N.Y.—85 file fair-hearing forms after not receiving winter clothing grants

January 3 Rochester, N.Y.—75 file winter clothing forms and demand money promised after December demonstrations; sit-in when welfare director will not see them; 20 arrested

January 16 San Antonio, Tex.—WRO wins rent reductions for welfare recipients

January 17 Flagstaff, Ariz.—Demonstration to demand WRO representation on welfare administration advisory board

January 23 Ann Arbor, Mich.—40 sign statements making WRO their bargaining agent before County Board of Social Services

January 29 Bay Village, Mass.—50 demonstrate at welfare office for furniture and winter clothing allotments, and improved communication between mothers and welfare department

January Washington, D.C.—NWRO Executive Committee meets with Daniel Patrick Moynihan about administration's welfare proposals

Los Angeles, Calif.—400 WROs demonstrate for fair hearings

Other NWRO actions in Albany, N.Y.; Providence, R.I.; Tuba City, Ariz.; Toledo, Ohio; Oklahoma City, Okla.; Evansville, Ind.; North Adams, Mass.; Flint, Mich.; Reno, Nev.; Sacramento, Calif.; and New York, N.Y.

January–February Philadelphia, Pa., WRO signs up 1,000 new members; Los Angeles, Calif., WRO signs up 500 new members; New Jersey WRO signs up 200 new members; Chicago, Ill., WRO signs up 300 new members

February 21–24 Jackson, Miss.—NCC meeting adopts proposal of $6,000 GAI for family of 4 and votes Easter boycott of Sears Roebuck if credit is not given welfare recipients

February 25 Washington, D.C.—HEW Secretary Finch agrees after meeting with NWRO leaders (1) to investigate 12 states for possible violations of HEW regulations; (2) to check state compliance with HEW requirement that state regulations be available to recipients; (3) to press Congress for federal financing of welfare standards

March 3 Pittsfield, Mass.—13 present demands for household necessities

March 4–5 Washington, D.C.—300 take over local welfare office in demand for furniture

March 6 Newport News, Va.—31 begin basic-needs campaign

Washington, D.C—50 Beaufort County, S.C., WRO members meet with agriculture secretary to demand changes in food-stamp and commodities program

March 27 NWRO begins nationwide boycott of Sears Roebuck stores to demand end to credit discrimination

Buffalo, N.Y.—30 begin a "shop-in" when requests for credit are denied

Washington, D.C.—WRO pickets Sears store and distributes leaflets

Providence, R.I.—125 picket local store when management refuses to negotiate credit

Pomona, Calif.—March 26: WRO successfully negotiates with local Sears management

Chicago, Ill.—60 sing, march, and distribute leaflets at downtown Chicago store

March NWRO files lawsuits to repeal welfare cuts in New York State, Wisconsin, Louisiana, and Texas

Washington, D.C.—NWRO members testify at U.S. Senate Special Committee on Hunger hearing

April 8   Detroit WRO begins two-day "live-in" at Wayne County Department of Social Services to demand clothing allowance

April 16   New York, N.Y.—massive NWRO march protesting welfare cuts broken up by mounted police; 2000 protesters attend Central Park rally

April 21   Madison, Wis.—800 participate in demonstration protesting state welfare cuts

U.S. Supreme Court strikes down welfare residency requirements as impinging upon recipients' right to travel

April 26–27   Washington, D.C.—NWRO welfare rights conference; one session on how to avoid WIN program's job training

April   Harbor, Long Beach, and Hawaiian Gardens, Calif.—6-week NWRO special-needs campaign nets $6,000 in household items

NWRO joins lawsuits in 26 states to demand compliance with federal food programs

Other NWRO actions in Pike County, Ohio; Essex County, N.J.; Boston, Mass.; and New Orleans, La.

May 1   Hardin County, Tex.—140 children demonstrate at welfare department to protest welfare cuts

Houston, Tex.—135 mothers and children begin protest against state welfare administration by picketing welfare offices in Houston

May 24   New York, N.Y.—NWRO takes over National Conference on Social Welfare; demands $35,000 to finance participation of poor people at 1970 conference

June   NWRO claims 30,000 members in 250 chapters in 100 cities

June 11   Washington, D.C.—NWRO announces its GAI plan: minimum of $5,500 for family of four

June 30   20,000 demonstrate at 19 state capitols for GAI and enforcement of federal regulation that states add cost-of-living increases to welfare payments

Richmond, Va.—200 march from Virginia welfare offices to governor's mansion and meet with Governor Mills Godwin

Boston, Mass.—5,000 march to Boston Common to a rally to hear GAW and Dr. Benjamin Spock; 600 disrupt Board of Supervisors budget meeting and successfully lobby for a resolution recommending an increase in grants

Atlanta, Ga.—150 picket the state capitol, 20 meet with one of the governor's aides, Governor Lester Maddox orders state troopers to get "these bums out of here—they smell"

Phoenix, Ariz.—30 present demands at state capitol and stage sit-in at State Department of Public Aid when director refuses to meet with them

Little Rock, Ark.—60 present 5 demands to Governor Winthrop Rockefeller and state commissioner of welfare

Denver, Colo.—70 picket state capitol, sending a delegation to meet with Governor John Love

Sacramento, Calif.—20 demonstrate in state senate chamber

Los Angeles, Calif.—Marchers disrupt Board of Supervisors budget hearings, than 300 march to mayor's office while others go to state office building and Department of Social Welfare

Washington, D.C.—100 meet with mayor and City Council

Des Moines, Iowa—50 people from across the state gather to meet with Governor Robert Ray

Turtle Mountain Reservation, N.D.—100 members of Ojabuwa tribe march to B.I.A. welfare office and demand that Indian payments equal those of other North Dakota citizens

Jacksonville, Fla.—40 picket the state welfare office

Indianapolis, Ind.—100 march to Indianapolis and meet with governor

Baton Rouge, La.—200 attend rally at the state capitol, later meet with governor and state welfare commissioner

Lansing, Mich.—Michigan WRO officers meet with state senators and then join 500 at rally on state capitol steps

Trenton, N.J.—400 meet with commissioner of state institutions and agencies

Albany, N.Y.—300 meet on state capitol steps and march to HEW regional office to meet with first deputy commissioner

Columbus, Ohio—600 march to state capitol for rally

Harrisburg, Pa.—300 march to state capitol to issue subpoenas to state welfare officials; when they refuse to meet with marchers, they are tried in absentia

Austin, Tex.—15 Edinburg, Tex., WRO members present list of demands to governor

July 1   Nationwide march on welfare departments to file claims for cost-of-living increase

July 2   NWRO demonstrations against inadequate food programs; congressional wives spearhead "Live on a Welfare Budget Week"

July 3   Nationwide shop-in at Sears stores

August 9   President Nixon announces Family Assistance Plan (FAP): $1,600 for family of four

August 18   New York, N.Y.—WRO wins invasion-of-privacy case against welfare workers entering homes without search warrant

August 21–25   Detroit, Mich.—NWRO convention: 700 delegates, speakers include Representative John Conyers, Dr. Spock, Wiley, Fannie Lou Hamer, Whitney Young, and Jerry Wurf

August 28   Brooklyn, N.Y.—1000 disrupt Board of Education meeting to protest cutbacks in clothing allowance

August 31   Santa Maria, Calif.—NWRO stages sit-ins and boycotts for school clothing allowance

September 2   Fall Campaign begins:

Pueblo, Colo.—2,700 children boycott schools to press for school clothing allotments

Springfield, Mass.—300 welfare recipients demonstrate for cash for household supplies

Chicago, Ill.—150 mothers meet with assistant director of public aid, 200 meet with state director of welfare

September 4   Richmond, Va.—Portsmouth, Va., WRO meets with board of welfare and institutions director

Cleveland, Ohio—400 women and children occupy welfare department office to protest absence of school clothing allowances; 92 people arrested

New York, N.Y.—64 women arrested, bringing total to 239 in campaign in

Manhattan and the Bronx to protest welfare cuts and demanding school clothing allowances

Detroit, Mich.—NWRO mothers barricade doors of welfare offices; on third consecutive day of demonstrations, police spend four hours cutting chains on welfare department doors and arrest more demonstrators, bringing total arrested to 64

September 8 Jersey City, N.J.—100 mothers and children demonstrate at the welfare department to protest welfare cuts

Boston, Mass.—40 women stage a sit-in in a welfare center

Detroit, Mich.—welfare department closes after one week of demonstrations by welfare recipients

Other NWRO actions in West Point, Miss.; San Antonio, Texas; Fayetteville, N.C.; and Warren, Ohio

September HEW, after meeting with NWRO, sets up rules for group hearings

New Bedford, Mass., and Brooklyn, N.Y.—NWRO organizes working poor

NWRO, with Columbia Center on Social Welfare Policy and Law, files lawsuits for free or reduced-price school lunches in Philadelphia, Pa.; Detroit, Mich.; Kansas City, Mo.; Milwaukee, Wis.; North Carolina; Texas; West Virginia; Cleveland; Little Rock, Ark.; Syracuse, N.Y.; Kentucky; New Mexico; Atlanta, Ga.; Rochester, N.Y.; New Jersey; Maine; and Oklahoma

September 29 Madison, Wis.—after week-long march from Milwaukee to Madison, NWRO mothers, joined by supporters from NAACP, Brown Berets, and Father James Groppi, march to state capitol on first day of special legislative session called in response to protests about welfare cuts. At the capitol, 2000 demonstrators storm the empty chambers. In early evening, everyone is ordered to clear the building and at midnight remaining demonstrators are forceably evicted.

October 8 NWRO joins Cesar Chavez' Farm Workers' Union and National Tenants' Organization in joint program.

October 14 NWRO files suit against HEW Secretary to raise higher needs standards in 30 states

NWRO wins priority hiring of children of recipients for temporary post office jobs

NWRO wins school lunch suits in Colorado; Michigan; and San Antonio, Tex.

October 14-22 Washington, D.C.—as as part of NWRO contract with Public Health Service, first session is held to train 30 NWRO leaders on health issues

October 15 Boston, Mass.—Wiley leads 150 welfare mothers in a march on South Boston Army Base demanding end of Vietnam War so that money can be spent on poor

Springfield, Mass.—400 mothers stage sit-in at welfare center to get winter coats for mothers; 1,000 supporters, who came from Vietnam moratorium demonstration, picket outside

October 23 Nationwide Sears Action Day

October 27 Washington, D.C.—Beulah Sanders, Wiley, and Carl Rachlin testify before the House Ways and Means Committee about the welfare crisis and Nixon's proposal

October 29-30 Washington, D.C.—NWRO Executive Board votes major campaign to expose budget cuts in state welfare departments and force states to increase welfare grants

November 6 Des Moines, Iowa—15 welfare recipients forceably evicted from the annual Iowa Welfare Association's evening banquet

November 7 Newport, R.I.—35 people picket the Newport Housing Authority to protest its admission policies

November 7–14 Aquidneck Island, R.I.—20 volunteer families live on a welfare food budget

November Richmond, Va.—150 NWRO protesters driven from Richmond City Hall

Other welfare actions in Puerto Rico; San Francisco, Calif.; and Roanoke, Va.

December 1–4 Washington, D.C.—White House Conference on Hunger, after NWRO takeover, supports NWRO's $5,500 minimum-income plan

December 1–7 National NWRO "Fast Between Feasts" to test Nixon welfare plan, directed by Friends of NWRO, joined by National Council of Churches, Churches Crusade Against Hunger, United Methodist Church, Urban League, National Association of Social Workers, Women's International League for Peace and Freedom, American Freedom Hunger Foundation

December NWRO successfully negotiates pilot credit program with Montgomery Ward

HEW to hold hearings on Connecticut, Nevada, and Pennsylvania conformity to federal regulations after NWRO charges of illegal practices

Massachusetts, Virginia, and New York WROs assist striking United Electrical Workers Union workers to get welfare benefits

Denver, Colo.—WRO challenges right of public service company to raise rates

Pueblo, Colo.—WRO organizes campaign to protest harassment of welfare families by utilities departments

Other successful NWRO utilities actions in Vermont; Pontiac, Mich.; and Waterbury, Conn.

1970

January Lansing, Oakland County, and Pontiac, Mich.—WROs achieve demands in school clothing, school lunches, and waiver of utility deposits

January 12 Austin, Tex.—15 welfare mothers lobby at school board meeting for school lunch program

January Los Angeles, Calif.—"squat-in" succeeds in obtaining housing for large families; 900 Los Angeles County NWROs insist on receiving monthly checks on time

Actions protesting utility rate increases result in success in Milwaukee, Wis., and 7,200 WRO members march on welfare center in Washington, D.C.; Pueblo, Colo.; Madison, Wisc.; Waterbury, Conn.; Denver, Colo.; Roanoke, Va.; Detroit, Mich.; Kansas City, Kan.; and Massachusetts.

January 22 Milwaukee, Wis.—800 WRO members march to county welfare center to demand winter clothing money for children

February 5 Catano, Puerto Rico—200 members of the Association of Welfare Recipients picket department of social services protesting poor quality of food distributed in surplus food program

February Baton Rouge, La.—NWRO National Coordinating Committee selects NWRO priorities: to sign up more people for welfare and to build WROs in the South; to work on black referendum on war in Vietnam, enlisting mutual support of peace movement.

HEW, because of NWRO pressure, schedules two hearings to decide whether Nevada and Connecticut are breaking welfare law; NWRO stages sit-in in Washington and wins right to participate in hearings

February 16 Wyandotte County, Kans.—WRO begins legislative campaign against bill pending in Kansas legislature which would centralize the administration of welfare

February Colorado NWRO wins additional payment for utilities

NWRO school lunch actions in Houston, Tex.; Chelsea and Haverhill, Mass.; Cleveland, Ohio; Pottstown, Pa.; and Birmingham, Ala.

Washington, D.C.—NWRO rent strike

St. Paul, Minn.—furniture special needs campaign

Rhode Island—successful action against Landlord Eviction Company

March 18 Wyandotte County, Kans.—50 WRO members meet with Kansas Gas Service Company officials; after 7 hours of negotiations the company agrees that welfare recipients will no longer pay more than their welfare allowance

March 20 Richmond, Va.—60 parents and children attempt to purchase Easter clothing at a department store on the welfare department's account at the store; when this fails, they march to the welfare department

March Albany, N.Y.—5,000 NWRO members march on state capitol to demand GAI of $5,500

Pittsburgh, Pa.—NWRO wins special clothing grant

Massachusetts—WRO claims 5,000 members in 60 groups; wins campaign for clothing

NWRO actions in Schenectady, N.Y.; Illinois; California; Detroit, Mich.; Wisconsin; Denver, Colo.; South Dakota; Luzerne Co., Pa.; and Pima County, Arizona

April 6 NWRO Executive Board lobbies Senate against Nixon welfare bill and for GAI of $5,500

April Turtle Mountain and Fort Totten Reservations, N.D.—organizing activity among Ojabuwa and Sioux Indians

April 15 NWRO joins peace groups in 50 cities to demonstrate against the war and for adequate income

Oklahoma City, Okla.—400 march on state welfare department building; director of public welfare refuses to meet with them

Washington, D.C.—125 attend anti-FAP rally organized by NWRO and DCWRO in park in front of White House

Milwaukee, Wis.—600 march to county welfare department and then to court house plaza for rally for America's new priorities

Richmond, Va.—100 attend rally and march to welfare department and Medical College of Virginia for teach-in about welfare and Vietnam

Roanoke, Va.—100 participate in New Priorities Day activities to protest both war and welfare policies

New York, N.Y.—400 WRO members attend rally in Washington Square Park and join 40,000 to march on IRS building

San Francisco, Calif.—200 picket welfare office and conduct guided tours through building, later marching to Civic Center for rally

Chicago, Ill.—500 march to downtown Civic Center rally

Baltimore, Md.—Welfare Rights members join supporters from New Mobe, women's liberation groups, Black High School Student Union and Black Panthers in rally for $5,500 GAI

Boston, Mass.—50,000 peace demonstrators at Boston Commons rally hear Mamie Wilson of Massachusetts WRO, speak for peace and justice in U.S.

April 21 U.S. Supreme Court (*King* v. *Smith*) strikes down "man-in-the-house" rule

April Rapid City, S.D.—actions on school lunch program

Austin, Tex.—250 WRO members in Poor Peoples Campaign demonstration

Other WRO actions in Michigan; Colorado; Vermont; Arkansas; San Diego, Calif.; Richmond, Va.; Pierre, S.D.; Lansing, Mich.; and Minneapolis, Minn.

May 2 Strong, Ark.—300 participate in a march against fear and hunger

May 9 Cotton Plant, Ark.—Cotton Plant WRO and COMBAT, Arkansas CORE organization, march against inadequate welfare and for more jobs; 52 arrested

May 13 Washington, D.C.—Wiley and large group of mothers occupy HEW Secretary Robert Finch's office for 7½ hours to press for $5,500 GAI

May 14 Washington, D.C.—NWRO members take over HEW's main auditorium to hold hearings on NWRO's adequate-income proposal

May Other NWRO actions in Rhode Island; Muskegon, Mich.; Memphis, Tenn.; Wichita, Kans.; Canton, Ohio; Brooklyn, N.Y.; and Pittsburgh, Pa.

May 31–June 5 Chicago, Ill.—97th National Conference of Social Workers; Johnnie Tillmon speaks at opening-night meeting

NCC votes to stress southern organizing in Louisiana and Arkansas and to emphasize health rights

May U.S. Congress strengthens existing laws providing free or reduced-price lunches to poor

June Rhode Island—85 take over state food stamp director's office to present 143 complaints

June 21 Chicago, Ill.—NWRO disrupts AMA convention and presents indictment against medical profession for discrimination against poor

June 23 Washington, D.C.—6,000 march on welfare department, 44 persons arrested

June 25 Baltimore, Md.—WRO demonstrates to restore special diet fund

June 30 WRO demonstrations to support $5,500 GAI in Ohio, Rhode Island, Virginia, Georgia, and Wisconsin

July 8 HEW begins hearings in Arizona, California, Indiana, and Nebraska to determine compliance with federal law regarding ADC, as a result of NWRO lawsuit against HEW

July 16 Washington, D.C.—WRO, after 1,000 emergency requests for furniture and two weeks of protest, achieves meeting with mayor

July 22–26 Pittsburgh, Pa.—1970 National Welfare Rights Conference: 1,000 delegates, speakers include Representative Shirley Chisholm and Senator Eugene McCarthy

NWRO concentrates its resources on fighting FAP and supporting Adequate-Income Bill

August   NWRO actions succeed in getting money for school clothing from boards of educations under Title I of the Education Act in: Providence, R.I. (600 WRO members stage rally, win $96,000 in grants); Washington, D.C. (WRO wins $5000 for four schools); Richmond, Indiana ($19,000 in grants); Indianapolis, Ind. ($20,000 in grants); Evansville, Ill. ($102,000 for school clothing, books, and breakfasts)

Other NWRO actions in Harford, Md., on hunger; in Holly Springs, Greenwood, and Kilmichael, Miss., on Medicaid; and in Marengo County, Ala., on conditions in surplus commodities

Detroit, Mich.—WRO obtains food stamps for striking General Motors workers

Washington, D.C.—HEW, after meeting with pressure from NWRO, issues directive that eligibility for ADC means automatic eligibility for Medicaid benefits

September 17   Brooklyn, N.Y.—Several thousand mothers march on Board of Education headquarters demanding that school clothing allowances be made available with Title I funds

September   Washington, D.C.—D.C. WRO organizers arrested at Bureau of Indian Affairs after demanding audit of school board books and share in Title I funds

Washington Co., Wis.—WRO opens co-op self-help furniture store

Hennepin Co., Minn.—five welfare mothers arrested during demonstration over winter clothing allowances

Detroit, Mich.—WRO launches drive to secure $5 million in aid from 8 foreign countries for winter clothes for U.S. welfare children

October 9–11   Kansas City, Mo.—150 attend regional NWRO conference and workshop

October 16–18   Atlanta, Ga.—NCC decides on fall priorities: lobbying against FAP, concentrate on health programs, Indian affairs, and southern organizing

October 30   Baton Rouge, La.—every welfare mother is sent an application to enroll her children in a new free lunch program (WROs in and around Baton Rouge worked for institution of the program)

October 31   Winooski, Vt.—50 Chittendon County WRO members go to welfare office and successfully demand winter clothing vouchers

November 4   Milwaukee, Wis.—WRO members follow up on October 27 appearance before school board to demand that winter clothing allowances be made available under Title I; the board votes to release $50,000 for that purpose

November 13–15   Little Rock, Ark.—NWRO Southern Regional Conference

November 18–19   Washington, D.C.—McCarthy hearings on FAP after NWRO is not allowed to testify during formally scheduled hearings of Senate Finance Committee; 300 WRO members attend, 23 testify

November   NWRO school lunch actions in Detroit and Saginaw, Mich.; Kansas City, Mo.; Little Rock, Ark.; Haverhill, Mass.; Pittsburgh, Pa.; Pueblo and Trinidad, Colo.

Atlanta, Ga.—WRO "sleep-in" for better housing

Las Vegas, Nev.—NWRO charges that county welfare department discourages education for poor children

St. Paul, Minn.—200 WRO members apply to school board for winter clothing funds

Long Island, N.Y.—WRO conducts voter registration drive

Muskogee, Okla.—WRO members stage Thanksgiving sit-in at welfare department

Philadelphia, Pa.—WRO members prepare Thanksgiving dinners for senior citizens

NWRO actions on housing in Portsmouth, Stafford, and Norfolk, Va.

Other NWRO actions in Greenville, Miss., and Kansas City, Mo.

December   Connecticut WRO charges state with failure to comply with federal welfare regulations

New York City mayor and governors of California, New Jersey, and Washington announce plans to cut welfare programs

NWRO forms coalition with National Committee on Household Employment, National Legal Services Clients Council, and National Tenant Organization

1971

January 6–7   Arizona—Welfare Department announces that more than 7,000 recipients will no longer receive welfare

January 18–25   Indiana—WROs march to state office building to demand that state pay recipients 100 percent of basic needs and that unemployed fathers be allowed to collect welfare

January 19   Marengo County, Ala.—first fair hearing won in Alabama

January   New York, N.Y.—WRO joins demonstrations protesting "emergency" welfare hotels where six children have died

February 5–6   Las Vegas, Nev.—NCC-NWRO raises adequate-income goal to $6,500, continues lobby against FAP (H.R. 1); Right-to-Welfare campaign set for 1971

Tacoma, Washington—500 demonstrate against "flat grants" and welfare cuts

February 10   Minnesota—WRO members testify against proposed "flat grants" legislation

Massachusetts—WRO wins partial victory (deposits waived) in fights against utilities

February 15   Washington, D.C.—WRO members testify at Citizens' Board of Inquiry into Hunger and Malnutrition

February 23   Washington, D.C.—25 WRO members take over USDA National Outlook Conference

Olympia, Wash.—500 storm legislature to protest welfare cuts

February 24   Washington, D.C.—NWRO and SCLC form People's Lobby Against Poverty, War, and Repression

Williamsburg, Va.—WRO members interrupt follow-up conference to White House Conference on Hunger and Malnutrition

February 25   Annapolis, Md.—WROs converge on state capitol to ask 100 percent increase in welfare payment levels

February   Las Vegas, Nev.—Welfare leaders from 40 states attend NWRO meetings and work in Operation Nevada

March 1   New Mexico—welfare recipients are sent cards announcing welfare grant cuts; NWRO files suit to challenge procedure

March 6   Philadelphia, Pa.—new coalition of Philadelphia WRO is formed with

Women's Strike for Peace, women's liberation groups, United Farm Workers, Women's International League for Peace and Freedom, and Resistance

March 13 New Haven, Conn.—NWRO joins demonstrations at trial of Black Panthers

March 22 Richmond, Va.—25 protest termination and reduction of welfare grants at city hall; when city manager refuses to meet with all 25, they begin sit-in (one person arrested and charged with carrying a bomb—which turns out to be a sack of flour)

March 23 Seattle, Wash.—sit-in at welfare department to protest department's refusal to replace two stolen welfare checks; participants arrested

March Nebraska—legislature appropriates 10-percent increase in state standard of need

Tennessee—legislation proposed to prohibit welfare to any unwed recipient (with more than one child) who refuses to be sterilized

Atlanta, Ga.—WRO members collect money from Georgia Conference on Social Work; then 150 march on state capitol to protest budget cut

April 1 Seattle and Tacoma, Wash.—day-long demonstrations at welfare departments to protest welfare cuts

April 2–4 People's Lobby demonstrations in Chicago, Ill.; New York, N.Y.; Atlanta, Ga.; Philadelphia, Pa.; Memphis, Tenn.; Milwaukee, Wis.; St. Louis, Mo.; San Francisco, Calif.; Cincinnati, Ohio; Detroit, Mich.; Washington, D.C.; Austin and Forth Worth, Tex.

April 5 New York, N.Y.—5,000 attend People's Lobby rally on Wall Street

Baltimore, Md.—governor invited to, but fails to attend, welfare breakfast of dry toast and coffee

April 6 Washington, D.C.—21 congressmen, including Black Caucus, announce welfare-reform bill guaranteeing $6,500 a year income to family of 4

April 15 Washington, D.C.—People's Lobby meets with HEW officials

April 26 Washington, D.C.—WROs from New York, Philadelphia, Rhode Island, Washington, Virginia, Maryland, Connecticut, Florida and California lobby against FAP after two days of workshops on that legislation

April California—WRO files suit against Governor Reagan, President Nixon, Vice President Agnew, and HEW Secretary Richardson alleging conspiracy to obstruct justice and deprive welfare recipients of their rights

Superior court judge directs Governor Reagan to increase welfare grants to needy children by 21.4 percent

Connecticut—federal hearing examiner finds state out of conformity with federal law in 13 issues raised by NWRO

Virginia—WRO hunger campaign over issue of food stamps, with actions in Arlington, Alexandria, Cumberland, Norfolk, and Roanoke

Governors of New York and California apply to HEW for waivers of Social Security Act provisions; NWRO files suit to prevent this

St. Louis, Mo.—NWRO participates in Allied Health Manpower conference

Rhode Island—after pressure from Rhode Island Fair Welfare, state senate investigates welfare system; federal judge restores cuts in welfare

Milwaukee, Wis.—WRO opens day-care center with 8 WRO mothers as certified teachers

Other actions in Missoula, Mont.; Memphis, Tenn.; Birmingham, Ala.; Frederick, Md.; Wichita, Kans.; and Washington, D.C.

May 1 Albany, N.Y.—legislature votes 10-percent decrease in AFDC payments

May 4 Washington, D.C.—National Women's Political Caucus adopts resolution favoring $6,500 GAI

May Indiana—250 march on state capitol and give testimony before legislative committees; grants are raised $15 for mother and first child, $5 for each additional child

Spring, Vt.—WRO action wins Medicaid coverage for dental services and eyeglasses

Colorado—Denver, Boulder, and Colorado Springs WROs fight legislative cuts in aid to needy and disabled, win raised ceiling on rent allowance

Charleston, V. Va.—WRO testifies against proposed welfare budget cuts

Topeka, Kans.—WROs fight budget cuts, governor vetoes $5.2-million cut

Houston, Texas—WRO files complaint against misuse of Title I funds and poor service in food stamp program

June 1 Chicago, Ill.—NWRO and Chicago pediatrician file suit with FDA charging mislabeling and misuse of behavior control drug

June 6 Wiley accepts Doctorate of Humane Letters at Wesleyan; supports striking workers at Yale.

June NWRO and National Consumer Health Council form National Consumer Health Rights Coalition to present Adequate Health Care Act to Congress

HEW reports that only .07 percent of welfare recipients are involved in errors

July Alabama—WRO files 25 fair-hearing appeals each day for two months, files lawsuit against state welfare department, holds hearings, and pickets state capitol to protest cutbacks in grants

Minneapolis, Minn.—100 WRO members hold hearings to protest proposed 10-percent cut in welfare; senate votes against cut

California—WRO presents $6,500 adequate-income plan to state legislature in answer to Reagan welfare bill

Washington, D.C.—Senator George McGovern introduces NWRO adequate-income bill

July 28–August 1 Providence, R.I.—NWRO convention with 1,000 delegates; workshops on health, housing, women's rights, senior citizen's rights; speakers: Representative Ron Dellums, Representative Bella Abzug, Wiley, Ralph Abernathy, Pete Seeger, David Dellinger, Imamu Baraka, Gloria Steinem

August South Carolina—Greater Midlands WRO presents list of grievances to welfare director, campaigns for Title I school clothing money and against higher utility rates

Greeley, Colo.—500 WRO members demonstrate against county welfare cut; state supreme court orders county to pay

22 state governments attempt to terminate and/or reduce welfare grants

NWRO forms coalition with Federation of University Employees, National Conference of Household Workers, Trade Union Action and Democracy, National Women's Political Caucus, People's Coalition for Peace and Justice

Other NWRO actions in Monmouth County, N.J.; Sioux Falls, S.D.; Sikeston and Charleston, Mo.; Jacksonville, Fla.; St. Paul, Minn.; Kansas City, Mo.; Madison, Wis.; Louisville, Ky.; Little Rock, Ark.; and Topeka, Kans.

September 8 Phoenix, Ariz.—200 WRO members march on state capitol to urge statewide participation in food stamp program

September 9 Augusta, Me.—50 attend rally on capitol building steps to protest H.R. 1

September 23 Phoenix, Ariz.—federal court rejects Arizona's appeal against cut-off of food stamp funds

September 24 Providence, R.I.—80 from Rhode Island Fair Welfare picket, demand to address special session of legislature after speech by Representative Wilbur Mills

September 27 Washington, D.C.—social workers demonstrate at capitol against FAP

September 28 Seattle, Wash.—People's hearing on H.R. 1

September 29–30 Clark County, Nev.—People's hearing on H.R. 1

September Blair Co., Pa.—WRO fighting against state "welfare scrip" bill

Pasco Co., Fla.—20 WRO members confront Welfare Commission regarding service at commodity center

Illinois—WRO wins lawsuit against State Department of Public Aid; state grants retroactive payments to 1,400 who pay more than "maximum rent"

Springfield, Ill.—demonstrators march to state office building protesting FAP

Kansas City, Mo.—450 social workers and WRO members oppose HEW officials speaking for FAP

NWRO Title I (school clothing) actions in Milwaukee, Wis.; Evansville, Ill.; Richmond, Va.; South Bend and Indianapolis, Ind.; West Collingswood, N.J.; Springfield, Ohio; Santa Cruz, Calif.

Welfare cuts in Alabama, Arizona, Georgia, Kansas, Minnesota, Nebraska, New Jersey, New Mexico, New York, South Dakota; proposed cuts in California, Connecticut, Delaware, Georgia, Idaho, Illinois, Louisiana, Minnesota, New Hampshire, Nevada, Oregon, Pennsylvania, Rhode Island, Texas, Vermont

Grants raised in D.C., Maryland, Mississippi, Nevada, Ohio, Oklahoma, Wisconsin

October 1 California—WRO files suit against state in behalf of 800,000 recipients affected by October 1 welfare cuts

October 8 West Virginia—NWRO demonstrates against FAP during President Nixon's visit

October 15 Connecticut—600 WRO members stage 15-day protest on capitol grounds against flat grant system

October 21 Nevada—WROs demand funding for county food program

Rhode Island—300 WRO members march on governor's house to protest flat grant system; federal court delays implementation

October 28 Delaware—State Division of Social Service makes cuts of 12 percent and 29 percent affecting almost 40,000 welfare recipients

Washington, D.C.—25 serve "eviction notice" on head of D.C. welfare system and stage guerilla theater production at her door; six arrested

October 18 NWRO files lawsuit against HEW for failing to provide poor children with medical services required by law

October 29 NWRO files lawsuit against HEW regarding demonstration projects in New York

October Springfield, Ill.—5,000 demonstrators organized by NWRO and Chicago's Operation Breadbasket march on state capitol to protest welfare cuts

  Wiley proposes joint effort of NWRO, National Tenant Organization, United Farm Workers, and Household Federation Association for voter registration campaign

November 6–10 Washington, D.C.—260 WRO members from mountains of West Virginia, Kentucky, Tennessee, North Carolina, Virginia, Ohio go to Washington on Appalachian March for Survival to oppose strip mining, demand adequate health care, and lobby against FAP

November 9 California—CWRO serves 14¢-per-person Salute to the Poor dinners while there are $500-per-person Salute to the President dinners in Los Angeles, San Francisco, Sacramento, Fresno, San Diego, and Redding

November NWRO begins Operation New York to develop jobs for those who can work

  Washington, D.C.—Fair hearing granted against caseworker for sexual abuse of welfare recipients

  California—CWRO organizes statewide rent strike to fight flat-grant welfare system

December 1 Georgia—welfare cutbacks instituted

December 6–8 Washington, D.C.—150 testify during 3 days of public hearings on FAP sponsored by D.C. Family Rights Organization

December 6 Washington, D.C.—U.S. district court judge rules that if area suffers from severe economic conditions, USDA must implement both commodity distribution program and food stamp program

December 7 Washington, D.C.—U.S. Supreme Court voids California law supported by Reagan, requiring mothers to sign criminal complaints against absent fathers of their children

December 8 Indianapolis, Ind.—50 recipients demonstrate at state employment office for adequate jobs or adequate welfare

December 9 New York—1,000 WRO members and caseworkers demonstrate at office of state commissioner of social services against "incentives for independence" program

December 14 Minneapolis, Minn.—30 WRO members block Hennepin County board room to protest county cut in welfare budget

December Michigan—200 WRO members take over governor's office to lobby for increased welfare allowance; state legislature passes bill next day

  Jamaica (Queens) N.Y.—WRO works with South East Queens Committee for Children, sponsors Christmas party for 500 poor children, works with Queens Hospital to insure admittance of minority nursing students

  Kentucky—30 WROs meet with state commissioner of economic security presenting demands on various welfare issues

  Other actions in Pittsburgh, Pa.; Collingswood, N.J.; St. Louis, Mo.; Indianapolis, Ind.; Pima Co., Ariz.; Baltimore, Md.; Madison, Ala., Watertown, N.Y.; and Rhode Island.

1972

January 11   South Carolina—400 WRO members stage day-long protest against state mandatory work law

January 26   Jefferson City, Mo.—Kansas City WROs go to state capitol to protest welfare cuts

January 29   Baltimore, Md.—federal court strikes down regulations denying aid to unemployed fathers

January   NCC's election-year program: local WROs demand representation for poor on national political delegation and plan political organizing in 44 states

Brooklyn, N.Y.—WROs form Bay Ridge Coalition: 1,000 demonstrate for decent jobs with adequate salaries, free day-care facilities, upgrading of schools, and wholesale tax reform

February 1   Milwaukee, Wis.—50 WRO members "live in" for better housing

February 3   Annapolis, Md.—Maryland WROs hold legislative workshop and meet with lieutenant governor

February 10   Huntington, W. Va.—18 WRO members demonstrate at state welfare office against treatment by officials

February 12   Charleston, W. Va.—50 WRO members march on governor's mansion to protest failure of state official to participate in scheduled hearing

February 16   Sacramento, Calif.—Sacramento Superior Court rules against implementation of "emergency residency requirement"

February 23   Washington, D.C.—35 welfare recipients and their children attempt unsuccessfully to address welfare hearing at national governors' conference

February 23   Rochester, N.Y.—40 WRO members demonstrate against FAP

February 26   New York, N.Y.—NWRO Regional Conference plans Children's March for Survival in D.C., strategy for poor people's platform in general elections

February   Evansville, Ind.—Indiana WROs lobby at state house and help defeat four bills affecting recipients

Other NWRO actions in Chicago, Ill.; Baton Route, La.; and Atlanta, Ga.

March 24   New York, N.Y.—WRO holds Children's Fair to promote Children's March for Survival

March 25   Washington, D.C.—NWRO's Children's March for Survival: 50,000 march to protest FAP, cuts in child care, health, and food programs; 1,500 children given medical screening examinations; speakers include Jesse Jackson, Ralph Abernathy, Bella Abzug, Ron Dellums, Yolanda King, Beulah Sanders, Gloria Steinem, Peter Yarrow, Edwin Berson, Kim Weston, Eugene McCarthy, Coretta King, cast of *Jesus Christ Superstar*, Shirley MacLaine, and Richard Roundtree

March 24–28   Nationwide Children's Marches in Montgomery, Ala., with 300 participants; Las Vegas, Nev., with 600; Little Rock, Ark. 200; Indianapolis, Ind., 500; Evansville, Ind., 200; Madison, Wis., 200; Phoenix, Ariz., 300; San Francisco, Calif., 500; Chicago, Ill., 800; Columbia, S.C. 200; Kansas City, Mo., 100; Salt Lake City, Utah, 100; Lincoln, Neb., 250; and Seattle, Wash., 500

March   Washington, D.C.—NWRO organizes Children's Hearing at U.S. Senate, with sponsors Senators Philip Hart, John Tunney, Caliborne Pell, Edward Kennedy, George McGovern, Edmund Muskie, Mike Gravel, and Harold Hughes

Las Vegas, Nev.—300 WRO members participate in "eat-in" to protest lack of food stamp program in Las Vegas

Montclair, N.J.—WRO protest discrimination against food stamp users by supermarket chain

Marshalltown, Iowa—200 attend WRO conference

Other NWRO actions in Seattle, Wash.; Norfolk, Va.; Broward, Fla.; Genessee County, N.Y.; and Warren County, Ohio

April 13–17 Washington, D.C.—NWRO Executive Committee meeting sets goals: defeat of H.R. 1, programmatic child advocacy, and promotion of $6,500 adequate-income concept

April 28 Lexington, Ky.—25 WROs request participation in naming state Department of Economic Security commissioner

May 21 Washington, D.C.—NWRO Chairman Beulah Sanders, in speech at antiwar rally, pledges major demonstration at Democratic National Convention

May Houston, Tex.—after year-long struggle, WRO wins $325,000 from Board of Education in Title I school clothing funds

NWROs participate in regional platform hearings of Democratic Party in Indianapolis, Ind., and Omaha, Neb.

Other NWRO actions in Grand Junction, Colo.; St. Louis, Mo.; Hartford, Conn.; and Mud Creek, Ky.

June 30 Providence, R.I.—150 WRO members demonstrate at Department of Economic Security against July 1 implementation of Talmadge amendment

June 25 Miami, Fla.—Wiley addresses Democratic platform committee

June 8–10 Miami, Fla.—NWRO, NTO and SCLC present Poor People's Platform at Democratic National Convention

July 10 Miami, Fla.—NWRO leads march of 3,000 to protest lack of poor people's representation

Miami, Fla.—NWRO annual conference, 1,000 attend; workshops on child care, housing, health, nutrition and welfare reform, drugs and prison

Other WRO actions in Kentucky; New York; Las Vegas, Nev.; Baton Rouge, La.; Albany, N.Y.; Washington, D.C.; and Salt Lake City, Utah

August 1 Philadelphia, Pa.—300 WRO members protest in Work Incentive Program Office, where 12,000 welfare mothers were to register

October 12 Washington, D.C.—300 demonstrate at Democrats for Nixon headquarters; Wiley and 20 WRO members arrested

October 16 Congress votes against FAP

December 31 Wiley resigns as NWRO executive director

1973

April Wiley honored by NWRO at testimonial dinner

NOTES

The primary source of George A. Wiley records, speeches, and documents is the Social Action Collection, State Historical Society of Wisconsin (WSHS), Madison, Wisconsin, repository for George Wiley's papers, as well as for CORE documents. Materials used in this book, currently in possession of the authors, will be added to that collection. Abbreviations in the source notes follow those in the text. *NYT* refers to the *New York Times*, P/RAC to the Poverty/Rights Action Center.

1. Master of the Barely Possible

Flight to Las Vegas: Wiley datebook March, 1971—United Airlines flight #271, Dulles to Chicago; flight #723 to Las Vegas. Log of his long-distance calls at airport.

Wiley organized 100,000: NWRO claimed 30,000 paid members, representing 100,000 welfare recipients—*Welfare Newsletter NOW*, June, 1969, Vol. 3, No. 3.

Wiley on welfare reform: March 29, 1973, speech at John F. Kennedy School of Government, Harvard University.

Wiley's thoughts about quitting: from two letters written on the plane "to be opened in case of my death," one to his wife, Wretha, one to Gloria Steinem.

Wiley on Nevada rights: quoted in *Welfare Rights Newsletter*, April–May, 1971, Vol. 2, No. 6.

Johnnie Tillmon, "We're going to help you": ibid.

Court decision: ibid. ("Operation Nevada" coverage in *Las Vegas Sun*, January 9, 1971, through March 22, 1971, also in Ruby Duncan interview.)

2. "Remember, You Are a Wiley."

Blacks in Rhode Island: U.S. Department of Commerce, U.S. Bureau of the Census, *15th Census of the U.S.: 1930 Population,* Vol. III, Part 2 (Washington, D.C. Government Printing Office, 1932), p. 755.

Andrew Billingsley on black families: Black Families in White America (Englewood Cliffs, N.J.: Prentice-Hall, 1968), p. 98.

Providence's history of racial tolerance: Irving H. Bartlett, *From Slavery to Citizen: The Story of the Negro in Rhode Island* (Providence, R.I.: Urban League of Greater Providence, 1954), pp. 21, 27.

Frederick Douglass and discrimination on Rhode Island trains: Frederick Douglass, *The Life and Times of Frederick Douglass* (Boston: DeWolfe, Fiske, 1892), pp. 275–276.

Early twentieth-century race riots: Report of the National Commission on Civil Disorders (New York: Bantam Books, 1968), p. 215.

Membership in the Metropolitan Church: U.S. Bureau of the Census, Department of Commerce, *Census of Religious Bodies—1926—Metropolitan Church Association* (Washington, D.C.: Government Printing Office, 1928), p. 5.

Tenets of the Metropolitan Church: The Discipline of the Metropolitan Church Association, adopted November 15, 1930, © 1931, Metropolitan Church Association, Lake Geneva, Wisconsin (Library of Congress).

3. The White Negro

Wiley on growing up: George Wiley/Edward Daner interview, June, 1964.

William Wiley and the Providence Urban League: Richard F. Irving, "Toward Equal Opportunity: The Story of the Providence Urban League in the 1940s," Ph.D. thesis, Brown University, American Civilization Department, May, 1974, pp. 25, 41.

W. E. B. DuBois on black American's "twoness": W. E. B. DuBois, *The Souls of Black Folk,* introductions by Dr. Nathan Hare and Alvin F. Poussaint, M.D. (New York: New American Library, Signet Classic, 1969), pp. 45–46.

Wiley on swimming pool incident: Daner interview.

History of the Pond Street Baptist Church: founded 1840, Bartlett, pp. 37–45.

Wiley on teenage dating: Daner interview.

4. Joe College, BMOC

Controversy in fraternity's national office: Norris Culf interview; correspondence with national fraternity, 1974.

Wiley on Student Union activity: Wiley speech at University of Rhode Island, February, 1965.

James Rhea's Providence Journal *articles: Providence Journal,* 1953; twenty articles, including March 24 (p. 1), April 1 (p. 7), April 5 (p. 16), April 7 (p. 6), and April 9 (p. 24).

News stories saved by Wiley: Wiley personal papers, WSHS.

Wiley on dating in college: Daner interview.
Wiley on black tennis circuit: Daner interview.
Wiley on employment at DuPont: Daner interview.

5. Deeper Waters

Cornell University: Office of Registrar.
Wiley's letter of application to Cornell University Graduate School: Wiley papers, WSHS.
Wiley on Cornell's politics: Wiley letter to Professor Clifton J. Orlebeke, April 3, 1954.
Applications and rejections: Wiley papers, WSHS.
"I believe in the dignity of man . . .": draft of Telluride application, Wiley papers.
Wiley on university community: Wiley letter to Carol Stout Condie, March 17, 1957.
Wiley's seminar prospectus: "Seminar Prospectus: Chemistry," Wiley papers, WSHS.
Ralph Helverson sermon and Wiley's response: "Who Are the Unitarians?" sermon by Reverend Ralph Norman Helverson, Ithaca Unitarian Church, June 14, 1953, p. 2, mimeographed, Wiley papers.
"Oh, that rascal . . .": Malcolm Bell interview.
Wiley on winning a fellowship: Wiley letter to David and Gertrude Thompson, September 9, 1955.
". . . Toad on a Hot Griddle": Wiley letter to David and Gertrude Thompson, October 29, 1955.
Wiley on marriage: Daner interview.
Wiley rejects Fellowship of Reconciliation membership: Wiley letter to Fellowship of Reconciliation, Wiley papers, WSHS.
P. 56, footnote: from "The Talented Tenth," in *The Negro Problem: A Series of Articles by Representative Negroes of Today,* New York: James Pott, 1903, pp. 33–75; quoted in Broderick and Meier, *Negro Protest Thought in the 20th Century* (Indianapolis: Bobbs-Merrill, 1965), pp. 41–48.
Lerone Bennett on "myth of black progress": Confrontation: *Black and White,* Chicago: Johnson Publishing, 1965, p. 215.

6. Confronting the System

Wiley on eagerness for civil rights participation: Daner interview.
Make-up of Quartermaster School: ibid.
Petersburg, Va.: Wyatt Tee Walker interview.
Wiley on living in Petersburg: Daner interview.
Virginia's anti-NAACP legislation: Andrew Buni, *The Negro in Virginia Politics, 1902–1965* (Charlottesville: University of Virginia Press, 1967), pp. 186–187.
Wiley on joining NAACP: Daner interview.
Eisenhower and Little Rock: NYT, September 25, 1957, p. 1.
Wiley on reaction to Petersburg blacks: Daner interview.
J. Lindsay Almond campaigns against school integration: Benjamin Muse, *Ten Years of Prelude: The Story of Integration Since the Supreme Court's 1954 Decision* (New York: Viking Press, 1964), p. 150.

Wiley on Ph.D. in social education: speech to the Urban League, July 31, 1972, St. Louis; speech to NWRO National Coordinating Committee meeting, November 8, 1968; Daner interview.

Wiley on "officer rating" incident and aftermath: Daner interview.

7. A Man for All Seasons

Carbons of Wiley letters: WSHS.

On February 23: GAW datebook, 1958.

Los Angeles Herald *Dispatch on Martin Luther King, Jr.:* David Lewis, *King: A Critical Biography* (New York: Praeger, 1969), p. 107.

Wiley on Los Angeles stay: Daner interview.

Baha'i': Atomic Mandate, by Marzieh Gail (New Delhi: Baha'i' Publishing Trust, p. 4).

"A jeweled city": Wiley, letter to Lucille W. Davis.

Wiley as "Bachelor of the Year": "Leap Year's Eligible Men," *Ebony,* January, 1960, p. 66.

Wiley's advice to Black youth: San Francisco *Independent,* August 27, 1959, p. 7.

"And ordered coffee": Claude Sitton, "Negro Sitdowns Stir Fear of Wider Unrest in South," *NYT,* February 15, 1960, p. 1.

CORE "too radical": Daner interview.

Wiley on picketing Woolworth's: mimeographed flyer, Wiley papers.

Wiley on student political group: Daner interview.

Southern students arrested: "The Sit-In Movement, 1960–61," *New South,* Vol. 18, No. 10 (October–November 1963), p. 4.

Wiley on student confrontation with dean of students: Daner interview.

Wiley on his first demonstration: Daner interview.

Wiley on direct action: Daner interview.

Minsky: Letter to authors, June 27, 1975.

Wiley on challenge of interracial marriage: draft of letter to Mrs. Goldsmith, undated, Wiley papers.

Wiley's letter to Mrs. Goldsmith, ibid.

P. 73, footnote: from interviews with Professors James Cason, Andrew Streitwieser, and Kenneth Pitzer.

8. Wretha

Freedom Riders: James Peck, *Freedom Ride* (New York: Simon and Schuster, 1962), p. 149.

9. The Scientist

Wiley's research "innovative, daring, and successful": Dr. Henry Wirth, letter to authors, January 5, 1975.

Wiley's chemistry grants: applications for Renewal Research Grant, U.S. Department of HEW, Public Health Service, Grant #GM 08956-04, November 11, 1963, Wiley papers.

Sam C. Smith's letter to Chancellor William P. Tolley: carbon copy, April 21, 1961,
    Wiley papers.
P. 84, footnote: Chemical & Engineering News, Vol. 41, No. 37 (September 16,
    1963); *Journal of the American Chemical Society, Vol. 86,* No. 964 (1964); *Tetra-
    hedron Letters, Vol. 64,* No. 2509 (1964).

10. Joining the Movement

Wiley's letter on discrimination in sororities and fraternities: Syracuse Daily Orange,
    Wretha Wiley interview.
Freedom Rides: August Meier and Elliot Rudwick, *CORE: A Study in the Civil Rights
    Movement 1942–1968.* (New York: Oxford University Press, 1973), p. 139.
Wiley on tennis game: Philip Booth interview.
Wiley and Eduardo Mondlane: William Wasserstrom interview.
Everett Makinen on CORE members: Daner interview.
Wiley on CORE members: Wiley speech at University of Rhode Island, February,
    1965, Wiley papers.
Wiley on attitude at Syracuse University: keynote speech to Joint Student Legisla-
    ture, Syracuse University, September, 1964, Wiley papers.
Wiley on southern leadershp: ibid.
NYT on moral leadership: Harold Taylor, "The New Young Are Now Heard," *NYT
    Magazine,* January 29, 1961, p. 5.

11. A Direct-Action Victory

Jaquith quote: Ray White, "School Boundaries Retained by Board," *Syracuse Herald-
    Journal,* June 19, 1962.
*1960 Syracuse population: The Negro in Syracuse, His Education, Employment, In-
    come,* Alan K. Campbell, chairman, preface by Stephen K. Bailey, Papers on
    Adult Education, No. 30 (Syracuse: University College of Syracuse University,
    1964), p. 4.
1960 black population: ibid., p. 5.
Syracuse black unemployment: ibid., p. 17.
Syracuse black employment: ibid., p. 12.
Syracuse blacks' rent levels: ibid., p. 12.
Syracuse blacks free slave: John Hope Franklin, *From Slavery to Freedom: A History
    of Black Americans* (New York: Vintage Books), p. 266; Bennett, *Confrontation,*
    p. 27.
National Equal Rights League: Bennett, *Confrontation,* p. 72.
"*. . . we're not prejudiced . . .*": Alexander F. Jones, executive editor, "The Heyday
    of the Crackpot," *Syracuse Herald-American,* September 15, 1963.
Wiley on northern discrimination: keynote speech to Joint Student Legislature, Sep-
    tember, 1964, Syracuse University.
Syracuse educational segregation: "Racial Integration in the Public Schools of Syra-
    cuse, N.Y." prepared by Public Affairs Committee, May Memorial Unitarian
    Church, Memo No. 1, May, 1964, mimeographed.

National educational segregation: Racial Isolation in the Schools, a report of the U.S. Civil Rights Commission.

Wiley speech during school boycott: September 4, 1962, Wiley papers, WSHS.

"Action discipline" manual: Meier and Rudwick, p. 9.

James Farmer on converting segregation: ibid., p. 10.

12. The Fifteenth Ward

1962 boundaries of the Syracuse ghetto: The Next Steps Toward Equality of Opportunity in the Syracuse Metropolitan Area: Report of the Syracuse Conference on Human Rights and Housing, Dr. Michael O. Sawyer, chairman, July 2–3, 1962, p. 17.

80 percent of Syracuse blacks wanted to live elsewhere: The Negro in Syracuse, p. 14.

March 1963, national urban renewal displacement: Martin Anderson, *The Federal Bulldozer: A Critical Analysis of Urban Renewal 1949–1962* (Cambridge, Mass.: MIT Press, 1964), pp. 7–8.

Syracuse urban renewal displacement: "The Facts on Urban Renewal and the Proposed Civil Rights Commission: Joint Statement by CORE, NAACP, the Civil Rights Commission," Syracuse *Herald-Journal,* September 25, 1963, p. 33.

Syracuse employment for blacks: "Employment, Occupational and Income Characteristics of the Nonwhite Population, Syracuse 1960" (Syracuse: Friends of National Urban League, November 12, 1963, mimeographed.

$3,000 annual income for black families: report of Dr. Andrew Brimmer's speech at Tuskegee's Founders' Day convocation, *NYT,* May 22, 1970, p. 55.

James Farmer on CORE in North: Meier and Rudwick, p. 182.

Alice Tait on North's dilemma: report submitted to J. McCain (director of organization of National CORE), no date.

13. Baptism

James Farmer on the March on Washington: Robert Root and Shirley W. Hall, *Struggle of Decency: Religion and Race in Modern America* (New York: Friendship Press, 1965), p. 47.

John Kennedy on racial tensions: cover story, "The Long March," *Time,* Vol. 81, No. 25 (June 21, 1963), p. 16.

Birmingham violence felt by all blacks: William Brink and Louis Harris, *The Negro Revolution in America* (New York: Simon and Schuster, 1964), p. 45.

P. 112, footnote: Revolution in Civil Rights, 3rd ed. (Washington, D.C., Congressional Quarterly Service, 1967), pp. 75–78.

Wiley on Birmingham: speech at June 'Teenth Celebration, Syracuse, June 17, 1964.

Nine-point action program: Wiley papers, WSHS.

Urban renewal: "How Far from Birmingham: Syracuse, the Deep North," Wiley papers.

Wiley speech at Grace Episcopal Church: compilation of Wiley taped and written recollections, and interviews with Wretha Wiley, Ed Day, Ronald Corwin, Bruce Thomas, and Charles Goldsmith.

Reaction to Wiley's jail experience: Bruce Thomas interview, April 4, 1974.

Wiley on CORE's "lawlessness": speech, "The Philosophy and Direction of the Welfare Rights Organization," Raleigh, N.C., 1967.

Achievements of CORE: Faith Seidenberg interview.

Fern Freel on Syracuse CORE's success: Seidenberg interview.

Wiley on Syracuse CORE's inability to sustain pressure on political system: statement at Washington Journalism Center Press Institute seminar, Washington, D.C., December, 1972.

Wiley on Syracuse's return to old ways: speech, "The Protest Movement North: The Syracuse Story," typewritten draft prepared for publication, Syracuse, 1964. Wiley papers.

Wiley on North's racial problems: ibid.

14. Backlash

Syracuse CORE's November 23, 1963, statement: "CORE Cancels Demonstration," mimeographed press release, November 23, 1963.

Wiley letter on CORE boycott: Syracuse *Daily Orange*, November 22, 1963.

Bailey article: Stephen K. Bailey, "Lesson in Lawlessness," Syracuse *Daily Orange*, December 12, 1963, pp. 2, 6 (from text of Bailey's December 10, 1963, lecture to citizenship classes).

Wiley letter to Stephen Bailey: December 11, 1963, Wiley papers.

Charles Sparks on wanting job: transcript of meeting of CORE and Syracuse city officials to review CORE's Project 101.

Police actions: interview and files of Attorney Faith Seidenberg, Syracuse, N.Y.

P. 122, footnote: Benjamin Muse, *The American Negro Revolution: From Nonviolence to Black Power 1963–1967* (Bloomington: Indiana University Press, 1968), p. 224.

Police actions: Wiley "Syracuse CORE Report on Police Procedures," mimeographed.

Official response to St. Louis CORE demonstration: Meier and Rudwick, p. 237.

Casualties during Freedom Summer: Pat Watters, "Encounter with the Future, *New South,* Spring, 1965, p. 3.

David Dennis' eulogy for James Chaney: Meier and Rudwick, pp. 277–278.

Harlem riot: NYT, July 28, 1964, p. 14; also *Report of the National Advisory Commission on Civil Disorders*, p. 36.

Rochester, N.Y., riot: New York Times, ibid.

Wiley on restraining Syracuse police during Rochester riot: transcript of Wiley tape to Clint Byers.

Wiley confrontation with Sheriff Corbett: Arnold Abrams, "Time Bomb Ticks In Back Streets of Urban North," *Newsday,* August 1, 1964, p. 14W.

Wiley on mood of Syracuse's blacks: transcript of Wiley tape to Clint Byers.

Wiley's ambivalence about black riots: ibid.

Robert Gore's memo on Syracuse CORE: Undated memo from Bob Gore to Marvin Rich, Richard Haley, and James McCain, CORE papers

Wiley's analysis of Brooklyn CORE's stall-in: Wiley, handwritten notes for NAC Steering Committee meeting on April 11, 1964, CORE papers.

Wiley's analysis of U.S. racial struggle: transcript of Wiley tape to Clint Byers.

Wiley's list of options for U.S.: Wiley, "Syracuse: How Far from Rochester?" *Event,*
Vol. 5, No. 1 (Fall, 1964), p. 27.

Rudy Lombard on Wiley's waning optimism: Daner interview.

Wiley's statement to Senator-Elect Robert F. Kennedy: typewritten transcript of Robert F. Kennedy's speech and presentations of four men from Syracuse, Wiley
papers, WSHS.

Wiley's goals for civil rights movement: handwritten rough draft, Wiley papers,
WSHS.

15. Crisis of Victory

James Farmer on changing civil rights movement: Francis X. Clines, "CORE Plans
Role in Everyday Life," November 24, 1964, Eve Reinert, "Political Muscle for
Negroes: CORE Announces 'New Phase,'" *New York Herald Tribune,* No-
vember 24, 1964.

James Farmer's introduction of Wiley, NYT, November 24, 1964.

"Summit on Race": transcript of Meeting, January 1965, Wiley papers, WSHS.

Roy Wilkins and Andrew Young at "Summit on Race": NYT, January 19, 1965, p. 21;
also Wiley, handwritten notes of January 30–31, 1965, Conference of Negro
Leaders, National Council of Churches, New York City.

Kenneth Clark at "Summit on Race": ibid.

Bayard Rustin at "Summit on Race": minutes of January 15, 1965, special Steering
Committee meeting, National CORE office, p. 3, mimeographed, CORE papers.

James Forman at "Summit on Race": NYT, January 19, 1965, p. 21.

CORE's growing, budget and staff: Meier and Rudwick, p. 335.

CORE's declining income: NYT, January 19, 1965, p. 21.

Wiley's assessment of CORE's financial condition: Meier and Rudwick, p. 334.

Office reorganization: Edwin Day interview.

FBI/CORE: Wretha Wiley, James Farmer interviews.

August Meier and Elliot Rudwick on Wiley's administrative role: Meier and Rudwick,
p. 334.

CORE plans for South: Wiley, testimony before special Equal Rights Committee of
Democratic National Committee, Wiley papers

16. Lessons from the Deep South

P. 141, footnote: Muse, *The American Negro Revolution:* p. 141.

New Orleans meeting: transcript, Wiley papers, WSHS.

Ronnie Moore on community organizing: Meier and Rudwick, pp. 338–339.

Wiley on National CORE vs. local CORE activities: Dave Dennis interview.

Wiley's account of imprisonment in Mississippi: copy of witnessed statement made by
Wiley on July 12, 1965 in New York City for two FBI agents; typed essay by
Wiley, "The South on the Heels of the North," no date, Wiley papers.

Annie Devine's thank you to CORE: minutes of Twenty-third Annual Convention of
CORE, July 1–5, 1965, Durham, North Carolina, July 2, p. 10 mimeographed,
CORE papers.

James Farmer on jail "baptism": Martin Mayer, "CORE: The Shock Troops of the Negro Revolt," *Saturday Evening Post,* November 21, 1964, p. 82.

First mass protest against Vietnam War: Chester L. Cooper, *The Lost Crusade: America in Vietnam,* foreword by W. Averell Harriman (New York: Dodd, Mead, 1970), p. 284.

17. Failure in the North: Division in CORE

Syracuse CORE's Niagara Mohawk Power Company Campaign: "Comprehensive Report: Niagara Mohawk, Happenings to April, 1965," Syracuse CORE, mimeographed, Wiley papers.

Syracuse mayor's response to "Freedom Ride North": "Mayor to Welcome Selma Residents," Syracuse *Herald-Journal,* May 4, 1965.

Syracuse Herald-American *Response to "Freedom Ride North":* "The Dying Gasp of CORE," Alexander F. Jones, Syracuse *Herald-American,* May 2, 1965.

Stall-in: Edwin Day interview.

Wiley on CORE's failures at northern organizing: Hobart Burch, "A Conversation with George Wiley," *The Journal,* December, 1970, p. 10.

Wiley at 1965 CORE national convention: minutes of Twenty-third Annual Convention of CORE, July 1, 1965, mimeographed, CORE papers, WSHS.

James Farmer on failure of "new directions": Meier and Rudwick, p. 378.

Black Muslim's message: Meier and Rudwick, p. 402 (James X of New Jersey, Louis X of Boston, and Lonnie Shabazz of Washington, D.C., attended).

King spoke out against war: report of speech in Petersburg, Va., *NYT,* July 2, 1965, p. 6.

CORE's resolution against Vietnam War: minutes of twenty-third Annual CORE Convention, July 5, 1965; also James Farmer interview.

Wiley on nonviolence: minutes of National Action Council meeting, June 30–July 2, 1964, Hotel Muehlebach, Kansas City, Mo., mimeographed, CORE papers.

Watts: Report of the National Advisory Commission on Civil Disorders, p. 38.

Wiley statement to Time: handwritten draft by Wiley, Wiley papers.

Martin Luther King, Jr./Bayard Rustin in Watts: Lewis, p. 306.

LBJ warning on negative impact of riots: Congressional Quarterly, "Revolution in Civil Rights," p. 13.

18. Total Immersion

One-week period in summer, 1965: Wiley datebook, Wiley papers plus CORE papers, WSHS.

Wiley on need for flexibility in civil rights movement: Wiley, handwritten rough draft, "Civil Rights Coalitions," Wiley papers.

19. Seeking New Ideas

Johnson announcement: included in major civil rights speech at Howard University, June, 1965, reported in *Washington Post,* June 5, 1965, p. 4.

Daniel Patrick Moynihan on the Negro family: The Negro Family: The Case for National Action (Washington, D.C.: U.S. Department of Labor, Office of Policy Planning and Research, 1965), p. 5.

National efforts should be directed to the Negro family: ibid., p. 47.

Wiley's reactions to the Moynihan report: handwritten draft by Wiley, undated; Wiley tape analyzing Moynihan and his report; Wiley papers, WSHS.

Wiley's speech at White House Civil Rights Conference planning session: "A CORE Charge to the White House Conference, November 17–18, 1965, mimeographed, Wiley papers, WSHS.

CORE's agenda for change: document prepared for White House Conference, December, 1965, CORE papers, WSHS.

CORE reports: CORE papers, 1965, WSHS.

White House drafted new regulations: Wretha Wiley interview.

Growing military operation in Vietnam: Cooper, p. 491.

Wiley in South Carolina: James T. McCain interview; Wiley, typed memo, November 1, 1965 re "Conference with Mr. Waters" (U.S. Department of Agriculture field representative for rural housing loans); Wiley, typed memo, November 30, 1965, to Carl Rachlin, general counsel, re "South Carolina Legal Situation"; Wiley, handwritten notes of his meeting with County Clerk Smith, CORE papers.

Civil rights leaders' meeting with Attorney General Katzenbach: Drew Pearson, "The Washington Merry-Go-Round," *Washington Post*, December 7, 1964, p. B-11.

20. Defeat: Remembrance of Things Past

Wiley on reaction to James Farmer's resignation: typed introduction and outline of Wiley's presentation before NAC during December 31, 1965–January 2, 1966, meeting in New York City, Wiley papers, WSHS.

Wiley's plan of action for CORE: minutes of NAC meeting, December 31, 1965–January 2, 1966, National CORE office and Belmont Plaza Hotel, mimeographed, Wiley papers.

Separatist faction in NAC: James Farmer interview.

CORE's criteria for choosing new national director: minutes of NAC Meeting.

Wiley and Floyd McKissick before CORE's NAC: ibid.

Ruth Turner on supporting Floyd McKissick: ibid.

James Farmer's position in NAC leadership debate: ibid.

Marlene Wilson's letter in support of Wiley: undated carbon copy of letter to Floyd McKissick, CORE papers, WSHS.

Votes for CORE directorship: minutes of NAC meeting, December 31, 1965–January 2, 1966, CORE papers, WSHS.

"CORE is dead": Ed Day Interview, October 8, 1974; Marlene Wilson, undated letter to Wiley, Wiley papers.

Wiley letter to McKissick: carbon copy of letter, January 19, 1966, to staff, chapters, and friends of CORE, Wiley papers.

Wiley to press: Sue Reinert, "New CORE Director—And Three Resign," *New York Herald Tribune*, January 4, 1966.

Wiley on CORE defeat: George Wiley/Wilbur Colom interview, August 5, 1973.

21. Finding a New Strategy

Syracuse loss of federal funds: Ed Day interview.

Wiley on Cloward encounter: Wiley speech at Maxwell School of Citizenship and Public Affairs, Syracuse University, August 13, 1969, typed, Wiley papers.

Wiley resigns from Syracuse University faculty: handwritten draft of letter to Chancellor Tolley, undated, Wiley papers.

Wiley on "Action Center's" functions: "Proposal for the Establishment of an Anti-Poverty Action Center," April 7, 1966, mimeographed, Wiley papers.

Wiley on wanting to be activist for the poor: memo to Richard W. Boone (executive director, Citizens' Crusade Against Poverty), April 4, 1966, Wiley papers.

R. Sargent Shriver at Citizens' Crusade meeting: Eve Edstrom, "Boos Drive Shriver Out of Meeting," *Washington Post,* April 15, 1966, p. 1.

Johnnie Tillmon on Poverty Program: Nan Robertson, "Shriver Booed at 'Poor People's Convention' in Capital," *NYT,* April 15, 1966, p. 21.

Wiley's list on developing P/RAC: handwritten list, no date, Wiley papers.

Wiley's notes on phone conversation with Richard Cloward: typed copy, March 27, 1966, Wiley papers.

22. Birth of a Movement

Ed Day's data: Edwin A. Day, research report, "Public Assistance Cash Grant Programs in Baltimore, Md., Chicago, Los Angeles," April 5, 1966, Wiley papers, WSHS.

Program: The Guaranteed Income: A Leadership Conference, May 26, 1966, Law School Auditorium, University of Chicago, Wiley papers, WSHS.

Wiley's statement on eve of June 30, 1966, events: Wiley statement to the press, "The Birth of a Movement," June 28, 1966, Poverty Rights Action Center, Wiley papers.

Ohio Welfare policies: mimeographed flyer for Ohio Walk for Decent Welfare, Ohio Steering Committee for Adequate Welfare; William Howard Whitaker, "The Determinants of Social Movement Success: A Study of the National Welfare Rights Organization," Ph.D. dissertation, Brandeis University, 1970, p. 148.

Taunts during Ohio march: "Singing Welfare Walkers Begin Columbus March," *Cleveland Press,* June 20, 1966; Ladd Neuman, "Welfare Marchers Absorb Jeers, Keep on Walking," *Daily News,* June 29, 1966.

Cross burned during Ohio march: "Welfare Walkers Crossing Wayne County," Wooster, Ohio, *Daily Record,* June 23, 1966.

Welfare mothers' song: "Welfare Marchers Sing of Woes as They Near City," Mansfield, Ohio, *News Journal,* June 25, 1966.

Wiley in Columbus, Ohio: Columbus Citizen Journal, July 1, 1966.

Dick Gregory in Columbus, Ohio: "Ohio Welfare March Ends in Rally of 2000," *National Guardian,* July 9, 1966.

June 30 New York City demonstrations: Homer Bigart, "Welfare Protest March at City Hall," *NYT,* July 1, 1966, p. 44.

June 30 Boston rally: Jo Anne Levine, "Welfare Protest Planned," *Christian Science Monitor,* June 29, 1966.

June 30 Philadelphia "sleep-in": James H. Dolsen, "Fight for Adequate Relief in Phil-adelphia," Philadelphia *Worker,* July 10, 1966.

June 30 Louisville demonstration: "Protesters Push Food Stamps," Louisville, Ken-tucky, *Courier Journal,* July 1, 1966.

Stokely Carmichael begins "Black Power": NYT, June 17, 1966, p. 33.

Meredith march: Muse, *The American Negro Revolution,* p. 236.

King denounced "Black Power" slogan: Lewis, pp. 325–326.

Wiley's reasons for organizing around Welfare reform: Wiley, lectures, Harvard Uni-versity, John F. Kennedy School of Government, Black Students Seminar, March 23, 1973.

Wiley on P/RAC as interracial organization P/RAC, untitled statement on philosophy, history, and operation, September 8, 1966, mimeographed, Wiley papers.

Lilia Calloway on P/RAC: Seymour Hersh, article in *National Catholic Reporter,* May, 1966.

23. Impossible Mission

Description of Lumpenproletariat paraphrased from Marx and Engels, "The Class Struggles in France, 1848–1880," in *Basic Writings on Politics and Philosophy,* ed. Lewis Feuer (Garden City, N.Y.: Doubleday, 1959), p. 298.

Edward Banfield on organizing the poor: The Unheavenly City, the Nature and the Future of Our Urban Crisis (Boston: Little, Brown, 1968, p. 130.

George T. Martin, Jr., on the lives of the poor: "The Emergence and Development of a Social Movement Organization Among the Underclass: A Case Study of the National Welfare Rights Organization," Ph.D. dissertation, University of Chi-cago, 1972, p. 13.

Social protest movements of the 1920s and 1930s: Richard Cloward and Frances Fox Piven, *Regulating the Poor: The Functions of Public Welfare* (New York: Pan-theon Books, 1971), pp. 100–110.

1966 welfare statistics: P/RAC, "Public Assistance Fact Sheet," June 28, 1966, mim-eographed, Wiley papers.

Typical ADC recipient: William Howard Whitaker, "The Determinants of Social Movement Success: A Study of the National Welfare Rights Organization, Ph.D. dissertation, Brandeis University, 1970, p. 106.

Growing welfare rolls: Martin, p. 34; HEW, *Social Security Bulletin,* XXXIV (August, 1971), pp. 54–55.

Southern ADC statistics: Cloward and Piven, *Regulating the Poor,* pp. 116–117.

HEW declared children excluded from benefits: Martin, p. 57.

Thirty-nine out of fifty states out of compliance: Whitaker, p. 119.

Studies showed migrants did not come north for welfare: Larry R. Jackson and Wil-liam P. Johnson, *Protest by the Poor: The Welfare Rights Movement in New York City* (New York: New York City Rand Institute, 1973), p. 77.

Wiley on welfare rights as handle for social reform: "Strategy of Crisis: A Dialogue The American Child, Vol. 48, No. 3 (Summer 1966) (Wiley, Richard A. Cloward, Frances Fox Piven, Edgar Cahn, Robert Schrank, and Eli Cohen).

Wiley issues invitations to National Welfare Rights meeting: P/RAC, press release, August 4, 1966, Washington, D.C.

Attendance at meeting: P/RAC, minutes of National Welfare Rights meeting, Chicago, Ill., August 6–7, 1966; Wiley statement, August 8, mimeographed.

Variations in welfare payments: P/RAC, "Public Assistance Fact Sheet."

"Welfare Bill of Rights" (adopted at Chicago meeting, August, 1966): "Goals for a National Welfare Rights Movement," report of Workshop 2, National Welfare Rights meeting, August 6–7, 1966, mimeographed.

24. Putting the Pieces Together

Poor People's March on Washington: P/RAC, "Summer Report: Poor People's March on Washington," undated report, mimeographed, Wiley papers.

Meaning of WRO's emblem: Tim Sampson interview.

NCC's first meeting, Pittsburgh: "A Report of the First Meeting of the National Coordinating Committee of Welfare Rights Groups," December 17, 1966, Pittsburgh, Pa.

Wiley group's officers to be recipients: Etta Horn interview, November 20, 1974.

WRO activity in Chicago: Welfare Leaders' Newsletter, Vol. I, No. 2, November 14, 1966.

WRO activity in Paterson, New Jersey: ibid.

WRO activity in Cleveland, Ohio: ibid.

WRO activity in Providence: Welfare Leaders' Newsletter Vol. I, No. 3 December 21, 1966.

WRO activity in California: ibid.

WRO activity in St. Louis: Welfare Leaders' Newletter, Vol. I, No. 4, January 9, 1967.

WRO success in New York City: Welfare Leaders' Newsletter, Vol. I, No. 2.

NCC's second meeting in Washington, D.C.: Welfare Leaders' Newsletter, Vol. I, No. 7, February 20, 1967.

"Basic Needs Campaign": NOW! December 8, 1967.

Washington Conference: tapes and transcripts, Wiley papers, WSHS.

NCC Conference Conclusion: minutes of NCC Conference, August 8, 1966, Wiley papers.

HEW meeting with Meyers: Wiley, memo, February, 1967, Wiley papers; *Congressional Record,* 90th Congress, First Session, Vol. 113, No. 19, Wednesday, February 8, 1967.

Wiley itinerary: Wiley datebook, "Contact Sheets," Wiley papers, WSHS.

Wiley testimony before House Agriculture Committee: March 15, 1967, mimeographed copy, Wiley papers, WSHS.

25. Convention: The Founding Mothers

Founding convention: Tapes and transcripts of general sessions, NWRO Founding Convention, Wiley papers.

"Disrupting and praying": Whitaker, p. 3.

"National membership plan": NOW! membership and dues plan, undated, Wiley papers.

Resolution adopted at founding convention: official resolution of the National Organization for Welfare Rights, mimeographed, Wiley papers.

26. The Ladies

1965 USDA study on welfare food budgets: Eating Habits of Americans, (Washington, D.C., Economic Research Service, U.S. Dept. of Agriculture), 1965.
1966 AFDC payments: P/RAC, "Public Assistance Fact Sheet."
Shirley Dalton on life on welfare: Kathy Kahn, *Hillbilly Women* (New York: Avon Books, 1973), p. 34.
Bertha Hernandez and welfare: Nick Kotz, "The Welfare Tide: A Human Crisis," *Washington Post*, p. 21.
Wiley on mothers: speech at Southern University, New Orleans, June 15, 1972.
Number on welfare rolls in 1966: P/RAC, "Public Assistance Fact Sheet."
Findings of Leonard Goodwin study: Do the Poor Want to Work? A Social-Psychological Study of Work Orientations, foreword by Kermit Gordon (Washington, D.C.: Brookings Institution), 1972.

27. Organizing

Rathke experience: Wade Rathke interview.
Growth in welfare rolls between December, 1960, and October, 1970: Cloward and Piven, p. 183.
Wiley on organizing poor people: Wiley, tape of Mount Vernon, N.Y., meeting, 1968, Wiley papers.
Saul Alinsky on qualities of an organizer: Lawrence Neil Bailis, *Bread or Justice: Grassroots Organizing in the Welfare Rights Movement* (Lexington, Mass.: Lexington Books, 1974), p. 68., p. 77; Marion K. Sanders, ed., *The Professional Radical: Conversations with Saul Alinsky* (New York: Harper & Row, 1970), p. 68.
Moynihan on Wiley: "George A. Wiley: A Memoir," *The Crisis*, Vol. 82, No. 4, April, 1975, pp. 142–143.
Wiley on organizing around specific benefits: Martin, p. 15.
Wiley as militant speaker: Whitaker, p. 191.
Special-grant drives in New York City: Jackson and Johnson, p. 202.
New York City welfare membership: ibid., p. 207.
NYT on New York City welfare movement: NYT, August 1, 1968, p. 23.
New York City membership: Jackson and Johnson, p. 207.
NYT quote: NYT, August 1, 1968, p. 23.
AFDC benefits in Ohio: Whitaker, p. 113.
AFDC benefits in Detroit and Cleveland: ibid.
NWRO Bulletin: ibid., p. 114.
Philadelphia WRO's campaign for credit at Lit Brothers stores: Roxanne Jones interview, November 4, 1974.
Wiley tries the businessman look: Wretha Wiley interview.

28. Shaking the Money Tree

Growth of NWRO budgets: detailed Wiley financial files, Wiley papers, WSHS.
Hess family's NWRO contributions: NWRO files.

Marion Ascoli's reservations about contributing to NWRO: letter to Wiley, August 27, 1969, Wiley correspondence, WSHS.

Norman Foundation's NWRO contributions: Wiley financial files, Wiley papers, WSHS.

Stern family's NWRO contributions: Wiley financial files, Wiley papers, WSHS.

Philip Stern's contribution for D.C.: ibid.

Field Foundation's NWRO contribution: ibid.

Rockefeller Brothers Fund contribution: ibid.

IFCO contributions: ibid.

Social workers: see p. 281.

Work training program grant: Stephen Wechsler interview.

Wiley at staff training session on fund-raising: Wiley, handwritten notes for NWRO training conference in New Brunswick, N.J., October 3, 1968.

Sheer chaos: interviews with foundation directors Harold Fleming and Betty Troubh Vorenburg.

29. "Don't Mourn for Me. Organize!"

Martin Luther King, Jr., meets with NWRO leaders: Tim Sampson interview, December 8, 1974; Etta Horn interview, January 23, 1975.

Welfare bill: H.R. 12080, amendments to Social Security Bill, voted by House Ways and Means Committee, August 3, 1967.

Riots of 1967: NYT, July 25, 1967, p. 1.

McKissick—nonviolent action over: McKissick interview.

J. Edgar Hoover—Black Power means rioting to black Americans: NYT, January 6, 1968, p. 59.

Robert F. Kennedy on Mills' welfare legislation: Kennedy press release, October 25, 1967.

Senator Long on protesting welfare mothers: NOW!, National Welfare Leaders' Newsletter, Vol. 1, No. 9 (September 22, 1967) *Washington Post,* (September 21, 1967, p. 2).

Robert F. Kennedy amendments: U.S. Senate Amendment 425 to H.R. 12080, passed by Senate, November 20, 21, 22, killed by Conference Committee, December 8, 1967.

Martin Luther King's parting words to NWRO leaders: NOW! Vol. 2, No. 2 (February 23, 1968); Johnnie Tillmon interview.

Wiley on young blacks' discomfort with welfare issue: speech at Southern University, June 15, 1972.

NAACP convention: NYT, July 2, 1968, p. 12.

Whitney Young: NYT, May 1, 1968, p. 20.

Chicago meeting: NYT, March 24, 1968; Wiley datebook.

Martin Luther King, Jr., on economic issue: NYT, April 1, 1968, p. 20.

National Advisory Commission on Civil Disorders—on welfare: From *Report,* p. 457, Mitchell Ginsberg's testimony.

Wilbur Cohen's objection to Commission's emphasis: Eve Edstrom, "Riot Panel's Report Criticized," *Washington Post,* March 26, 1968, p. 1.

Wiley's letter to Ethel Kennedy: carbon copy, Wiley papers, WSHS.

Wiley at Kent State University: tape of a Kent State University conference, April 5, 1968.
Wiley at Martin Luther King, Jr.'s, funeral: John Marqusee interview, *NOW!* April 9, 1968.
Wiley's eulogy for Martin Luther King, Jr.: NOW! Vol. 2, No. 6 (April 15, 1968).
Michigan WRO Action: "Mothers Vow Boycott," *Ann Arbor News,* August 2, 1968, "ADC Mothers Receive Funds Asked for Children's Clothing," *Ann Arbor News,* September 9, 1968; *NOW!* Vol. 2, No. 3 (October, 1968).
Denver WRO Action: "Recipients Seek Welfare Board Seat," *Rocky Mountain News,* April 26, 1968; *NOW!* Vol. 2, No. 8 (June 6, 1968).
Kentucky WRO Action: Courier-Journal & Times; NOW! Vol. 2, No. 8 (June 6, 1968).
Wiley confronts Cohen on HEW guidelines: NOW! Vol. 2, No. 11 (July 22, 1968).
NWRO political cartoon: "NOW!" National Welfare Leaders Newsletter, Oct. 1968, Vol. 2, No. 13.
Agnew on ghettos: NYT, October 19, 1968, p. 1.
Harris and Gallup polls: NYT, August 4, 1968, p. 45.
Moynihan Invitation: Wretha Wiley interview.
Wiley on NWRO's influence in Nixon administration: NOW! Vol. 3, No. 1 (February, 1969).

30. A Thorn in the Side of Washington, D.C.

Moynihan announces Nixon's welfare plan: covered by Nick Kotz, then Washington correspondent for the *Des Moines Register.*
John Kramer on the Arithmetic of Poverty: NYT, August 12, 1969, p. 1.
Commissions on civil disorders—"Two Societies": Report of the National Advisory Commission on Civil Disorders, p. 1.
Wiley accuses Moynihan of failing to consult with poor people: Hulbert James interview.
Wiley/Tillmon letter to Nixon: letter to President Richard M. Nixon signed by Johnnie Tillmon and George A. Wiley, dated August 6, 1969, carbon, Wiley papers.
BLS data basis of NWRO guaranteed annual income: "NWRO Proposals for a Guaranteed Adequate Income," June 11, 1969, mimeographed, Wiley papers.
Wiley's feelings about Nixon plan: speeches, 1969–1973, WSHS.
Range of state welfare payments: Committee on Ways and Means, U.S. House of Representatives, *The President's Proposals for Welfare Reform and Social Security Amendments, 1969,* 91st Congress, 1st Session (Washington, D.C.: Government Printing Office, 1969), p. 43.
Moynihan on breakthrough: Hulbert James interview.
Mills on welfare bill: Wilbur Mills interview with Nick Kotz, 1969.
Steiner on welfare: Political Insecurity: The Politics of Welfare (Chicago: Rand McNally, 1966).
P. 265 footnote: Washington Post, August 3, 1971.
Wiley Testimony on FAP: Mimeo copy of statement to House Ways and Means Committee, October 27, 1969, "Welfare Crisis 1969 and the Nixon Proposals."
Hunger Conference: covered by Nick Kotz for *Des Moines Register,* December, 1969.
Cost of Apollo moon shots: NYT, July 21, 1969.

"... *money to send a man to the moon* ...": *Washington Post*, June 6, 1972, p. A18.

Photo of HEW sit-in: Washington Post, May 14, 1970, p. 1.

NWRO's minimum requirements for welfare bill: NWRO, press release, November 10, 1970.

NWRO cardinal precept: Wiley, notes on Lowell Beck/Wiley telephone conversation.

Common Cause cancels meeting: Carl Holman interview.

Editorial on welfare reform: Washington Post, August 26, 1971.

Testimony before Eugene McCarthy: hearings on Family Assistance Plan, H.R. 16311, Thursday, November 19, 1970.

Book recounting the fight: Daniel Patrick Moynihan, *The Politics of a Guaranteed Income: The Nixon Administration and the Family Assistance Plan* (New York: Random House, 1973).

Nixon on welfare: State of the Union Message to Congress, January 22, 1971.

"We've Turned Back the Anti-Welfare Tide": Welfare Fighter, April–May, 1971.

Nixon on emptying bedpans: Washington Post, May 15, 1971.

Single day of the debate: Washington Post, April 7, 1971.

Wiley berates National Council of Churches: transcript of National Council of Churches meeting, late 1969 or early 1970.

Wiley—Mills bill "racist": NWRO, "FAP and Welfare: Racist Institutions," press release, May 11, 1971.

FAP chronology: Wiley papers, mimeographed, WSHS.

Richardson critical of Long's welfare bill: NYT, April 29, 1972, p. 1.

Wiley on Ribicoff's bill: Jeff Peterson interview.

Wiley/Tom Joe exchange: Tom Joe interview.

Wiley answers Moynihan's criticism: Lecture, Harvard University, John F. Kennedy School of Government, April, 1973; GAW, handwritten draft of book outline, on same subject, Wiley papers.

Veneman on Wiley's impact: James Welch, "Welfare Reform: Born August 8, 1969; Died October 4, 1972: A Sad Case of the American Political Process," *NYT Magazine*, January 7, 1973, p. 16.

Alice Rivlin on Wiley's role: ibid.

Wiley on future welfare reform: transcript, Harvard University, John F. Kennedy School of Government, Wiley/Black Students Seminar, March 23, 1973.

31. The Juggler

Interviews with Audrey Colom, Faith Evans, Joanne Williams, Rhoda Linton, Andrea Kydd, Nancy Steadman, Mary Lou Oates Palmer, Tim Sampson, Joyce Burson, Peggy Winkler, and other NWRO staff assistants.

Takeover of NCSW conference: NYT, May 29, 1969.

Differences between staff and board: Evans interview.

John Lewis protest: John Lewis, "Black Noises," *Washington Afro-American*, August 19, 1969, p. 3.

Their talents were underutilized: Faith Evans interview.

Wiley on racial dissent: tape of his speech to staff, Trinity College, Washington, D.C., August 4, 1969, Wiley papers.

32. Decline and Fall

P. 285, footnote: 1969 Gallup polls.

Wiley to staff: Tape of speech, August 4, 1969, Wiley papers, WSHS.

NWRO campaigns: NWRO Newsletter, 1969–1972, Wiley papers, WSHS (see Appendix).

Coalitions: ibid.

Rockefeller's welfare plan: Nick Kotz in *Washington Post.*

Wiley/Beulah Sanders: Austin Scott interview.

Providence convention: August 30, 1971, covered by Nick Kotz.

Children's March for Survival: Woody West, "Children March by Thousands," *Washington Star,* March 26, 1972, p. A-1.

Democratic Party Policy Council: Gloria Steinem interview.

Wiley at 1972 Democratic Convention: interviews with Wilbur Colom and David Ifshin; Norman Mailer, *Some Honorable Men: Political Conventions, 1960–1972* (Boston: Little Brown, 1976).

NWRO board to fire Wiley: interviews with Audrey Colom, Faith Evans, Catherine Jermany, Beulah Sanders, and others.

Wiley interview: with Wilbur Colom, August 5, 1973.

IRS audit: account of the Reverend Lucius Walker.

Wiley comments on improved organizing of the poor: Colom interview, August 5, 1973.

Underestimated need to emphasize long-range goals and ideals: Martin dissertation.

33. The Movement for Economic Justice

Wiley's new ideas: "Progress Report on the Planning Phase of the Movement for Economic Justice. Press release, June 20, 1973. Wiley papers.

Difficulty of implementing his strategy: seminar, April 8, 1973, Harvard University John F. Kennedy School of Government.

Wiley on diverse styles in MEJ: December 28, 1972, meeting with editors of *Newsweek,* New York City, taped account in Wiley papers, WSHS.

Wiley testimony before House Ways and Means Committee: MEJ press release, March 9, 1973, GAW papers.

Coalition for Human Needs and Budget Priorities: press release, June 14, 1973, Wiley papers.

Wiley to protestors against cuts in Poverty Program: Bert DeLeeuw interview.

Speech before National Council of Churches: Wiley notes, March 5, 1973, Wiley papers.

Wall Street tax protest rally: MEJ press release, Wiley papers.

Seminar, "The Politics of the Working Class": Harvard University, John F. Kennedy School of Government, Institute of Politics, March 27, 1973, taped transcript, Wiley papers.

Newsweek editors—Wiley explanation of organizing a majority: December 28, 1972, meeting.

Monumental organizing job: Bert DeLeeuw interview.

Citizens' Action Program in Chicago: DeLeeuw interview.

Wiley concern about his children: conversation with the authors, July 14, 1973.

Boat accident: accounts of marina operator and of Danny and Maya Wiley.

Memorial service: Austin Scott in *Washington Post*, August 16, 1973; videotape, August 12, 1973, transcript, Wiley papers, WSHS.

Lampman and Steiner Views: The Great Society: Lessons for the Future (New York: Basic Books, 1974), pp. 47–83.

BIBLIOGRAPHY

Welfare: Books

Aaron, Henry J. *Why Is Welfare So Hard to Reform?* Studies in Social Economics. Washington, D.C.: Brookings Institution, 1973.

Bailis, Lawrence Neil. *Bread or Justice: Grassroots Organizing in the Welfare Rights Movement.* Lexington, Mass.: Lexington Books, 1974.

Bell, Winifred; Lekachman, Robert; and Schorr, Alvin C. *Public Policy and Income Districution.* New York: Center for Studies in Income Maintenance Policy, 1974.

Bowler, M. Kenneth. *The Nixon Guaranteed Income Proposal: Substance and Process in Policy Change.* Cambridge, Mass.: Ballinger Publishing, 1974.

Budd, Edward C., ed. *Inequality and Poverty: An Introduction to a Current Issue of Public Policy.* Problems of the Modern Economy Series. New York: W. W. Norton, 1967.

Burke, Vincent J., and Vee. *Nixon's Good Deed: Welfare Reform.* New York: Columbia University Press, 1974.

Cloward, Richard A., and Piven, Frances Fox. *Regulating the Poor: The Functions of Public Welfare.* New York: Pantheon Books, 1971.

————. *The Politics of Turmoil: Poverty, Race, and the Urban Crisis.* New York: Vintage Books, 1974.

Goodwin, Leonard. *Can Social Science Help Resolve National Problems? Welfare: A Case in Point.* New York: Free Press, 1975.

————. *Do the Poor Want to Work? A Social-Psychological Study of Work Orientations.* Washington, D.C.: Brookings Institution, 1972.

Graham, James J. *The Enemies of the Poor.* New York: Random House, 1970.

Handler, Joel F., and Hollingsworth, Ellen Jane. *The "Deserving Poor": A Study of Welfare Administration.* Institute for Research on Poverty Monograph Series. Chicago: Markham Publishing, 1971.

Harrington, Michael. *The Other America: Poverty in the United States.* Baltimore: Penguin Books, 1962.

Hutchinson, Shauneen; Humphreys, Joseph; and Yavis, Jean. "Welfare Reform: Issues and Legislative Development." Congressional Research Service, Education and Public Welfare Division, November 22, 1971. (Unbound report for the Library of Congress.)

Jackson, Larry R., and Johnson, William A. *Protest by the Poor: The Welfare Rights Movement in New York City.* New York: New York City Rand Institute, 1973.

Lampman, Robert J. *Ends and Means of Reducing Income Poverty.* Institute for Research on Poverty Monograph Series. Chicago: Markham Publishing, 1971.

Levitan, Sar A. *Programs in Aid of the Poor for the 1970s.* Policy Studies in Employment and Welfare, No. 1. Baltimore: Johns Hopkins Press, 1969.

————; Rein, Martin; and Marwick, David, eds. *Work and Welfare Go Together.* Policy Studies in Employment and Welfare, No. 13. Baltimore: Johns Hopkins Press, 1972.

Martin, George T., Jr. "The Emergence and Development of a Social Movement Organization Among the Underclass: A Case Study of the National Welfare Rights Organization." Ph.D. dissertation, University of Chicago, 1972.

May, Edgar. *The Wasted Americans: The Cost of Our Welfare Dilemma.* New York: Signet Books, 1964.

Moynihan, Daniel Patrick. *The Politics of a Guaranteed Income: The Nixon Administration and the Family Assistance Plan.* New York: Random House, 1973.

Milwaukee County Welfare Rights Organization. *Welfare Mothers Speak Out: We Ain't Gonna Shuffle Anymore.* New York: W. W. Norton, 1972.

Poverty Amid Plenty: The American Paradox. Report of the President's Commission on Income Maintenance Programs. Washington, D.C.: Government Printing Office, 1969.

Sampson, Timothy J. *Welfare: A Handbook for Friend and Foe.* Foreword by Hobart A. Burch. Philadelphia: United Church Press, 1972.

Steiner, Gilbert Y. *Political Insecurity: The Politics of Welfare.* Chicago: Rand McNally, 1966.

————. *The State of Welfare.* Washington, D.C.: Brookings Institution, 1971.

Streshinsky, Naomi Gottlieb. "Welfare Rights Organizations and the Public Welfare System: An Interaction Study." D.S.W. dissertation, University of California at Berkeley, 1970. (Microfilm—Xerography by Xerox University Microfilms, Ann Arbor.)

Theobald, Robert, ed. *The Guaranteed Income: Next Step in Economic Evolution?* Garden City, N.Y.: Doubleday, 1966.

Whitaker, William Howard. "The Determinants of Social Movement Success: A Study of the National Welfare Rights Organization." Ph.D. dissertation, Brandeis University, Florence Heller Graduate School for Advanced Studies in Social Welfare, 1970. (Microfilm-Xerography by Xerox University Microfilms, Ann Arbor.)

Wilson, Joseph C. *Report from the Steering Committee of the Arden House Conference on Public Welfare.* Albany, N.Y., 1967.

Welfare: Magazines

Banfield, Edward C. "Welfare: A Crisis Without Solutions." *Public Interest*, No. 16, Summer, 1969, pp. 89–101.

"Battleline of Welfare: The Hungry Can't Wait." *Nation*, May 22, 1976, pp. 649–652.

"Behind Rising Alarm Over Welfare Costs." *U.S. News & World Report*, November 30, 1970, pp. 32–35.

"Demonstration in Boston." *U.S. News*, June 19, 1967, p. 16.

"Down and Out: Report on Public Welfare Practices in Southern States." *New Republic*, January 6, 1968, pp. 10–11.

Eppley, David B. "The AFDC Family in the 1960s." *Welfare in Review*, VIII, No. 12 (September–October 1970), pp. 8–16.

"First Congress of the Poor; Total Participation of the Poor; Aim of Syracuse Convention." *Nation*, February 7, 1966, pp. 148–151.

Handler, Joel, and Hollingsworth, Ellen Jane. "Work, Welfare, and the Nixon Reforms Proposals." *Stanford Law Review*, Vol. 22, No. 5 (May, 1970), pp. 907–942.

Jacobs, Paul. "How It Is—Getting on Welfare." *Harper's*, October, 1967, pp. 74–75.

Nathan, Richard P. "Family Assistance Plan: Workfare/Welfare." *New Republic*, February 24, 1973, pp. 19–21.

"Poor Power." *Nation*, February 20, 1967, p. 228.

"Revolt of Nonpersons." *Time*, July 21, 1967 p. 46.

Ribicoff, Abraham. "He Left at Half Time." *New Republic*, February 17, 1973, pp. 22–26.

Salamon, Lester M. "Family Assistance: The Stakes in the Rural South." *New Republic*, February 20, 1971, pp. 17–18.

Sirkis, Nancy, and Berman, Susan K. "Two American Welfare Mothers." *Ms.*, June, 1973, pp. 74–81.

Tobin, James; Pechman, Joseph A.; and Mieszkowski, Peter M. "Is a Negative Income Tax Practical?" *Yale Law Journal*, Vol. 77, No. 1 (November 1967). Washington, D.C.: Brookings Institution, 1967.

Welsh, James. "Welfare Reform: Born August 8, 1969; Died October 4, 1972: A Sad Case of the American Political Process." *New York Times Magazine*, January 7, 1973, pp. 14–17.

"Welfare: Trying to End the Nightmare." *Time*, February 8, 1971, pp. 14–23.

Black History: Books

Aptheker, Herbert, ed. *A Documentary History of the Negro People in the United States*. Vol. III, 1933–1945. Preface by William L. Patterson. Secaucus, N.J.: Citadel Press, 1974.

Baldwin, James. *Nobody Knows My Name: More Notes of a Native Son*. New York: Delta Books, 1961.

Banfield, Edward C. *City Politics*. Cambridge, Mass.: Harvard University Press and MIT Press, 1963.

Bartlett, Irving H. *From Slave to Citizen: The Story of the Negro in Rhode Island*. Providence: Urban League of Greater Providence, 1954.

Bennett, Lerone, Jr. *Confrontation: Black and White*. Foreword by A. Philip Randolph. Chicago: Johnson Publishing, 1965.

Billingsley, Andrew. *Black Families in White America*. Englewood Cliffs, N.J.: Prentice-Hall, 1968.

Blaustein, Albert, and Zangrando, Robert. *Civil Rights and the American Negro: A Documentary History.* New York: Washington Square Press, 1968.

Blaustein, Arthur I., and Faux, Geoffrey. *The Star-Spangled Hustle.* Foreword by Ronald V. Dellums. Garden City, N.Y.: Doubleday, 1972.

Breitman, George, ed. *Malcolm X Speaks: Selected Speeches and Statements.* New York: Merit Publishers, 1965.

Brink, William, and Harris, Louis. *The Negro Revolution in America.* New York: Simon and Schuster, 1964.

Broderick, Francis L., and Meier, August, eds. *Negro Protest Thought in the Twentieth Century.* Foreword by Leonard W. Levy and Alfred Young. American Heritage Series. Indianapolis: Howard W. Sams, 1965.

Brotz, Howard, ed. *Negro Social and Political Thought 1850–1920: Representative Texts.* New York: Basic Books, 1966.

Buni, Andrew. *The Negro in Virginia Politics 1902–1965.* Charlottesville: University Press of Virginia, 1967.

Butterfield, Stephen. *Black Autobiography in America.* Amherst: University of Massachusetts Press, 1974.

Carmichael, Stokely, and Hamilton, Charles V. *Black Power: The Politics of Liberation in America.* New York: Vintage Books, 1967.

Chace, William, and Collier, Peter, eds. *Justice Denied: The Black Man in White America.* New York: Harcourt, Brace and World, 1970.

Clark, Kenneth B. *Dark Ghetto: Dilemmas of Social Power.* Foreword by Gunnar Myrdal. New York: Harper Torchbooks, 1965.

Cleaver, Eldridge. *Soul on Ice.* New York: Delta Books, 1968.

Revolution in Civil Rights. 3rd ed. Washington, D.C.: Congressional Quarterly Service, 1967.

Conot, Robert. *Rivers of Blood, Years of Darkness.* New York: Bantam Books, 1967.

Corwin, Ronald. "School Desegregation in Syracuse: A Study in Community Decision-Making."Ph.D. dissertation, Syracuse University, December, 1967.

David, Jay, ed. *Growing Up Black.* New York: Simon and Schuster, 1968.

Davis, John P., ed. *The American Negro Reference Book.* Englewood Cliffs, N.J.: Prentice-Hall, 1966.

Douglass, Frederick. *The Life and Times of Frederick Douglass.* Boston: DeWolfe, Fiske, 1892.

Draper, Theodore. *The Rediscovery of Black Nationalism.* New York: Viking Press, 1970.

Drotning, Phillip T., and Smith, Wesley W. *Up from the Ghetto.* New York: Pocket Books, 1970.

DuBois, W. E. B. *The Souls of Black Folk.* Introductions by Dr. Nathan Hare and Alvin F. Poussaint, M.D. New York: Signet Classic, 1969.

Fanon, Frantz. *The Wretched of the Earth.* Translated by Constance Farrington. Preface by Jean-Paul Sartre. New York: Grove Press, 1963.

Forman, James. *The Making of Black Revolutionaries.* New York: Macmillan, 1972.

Franklin, John Hope. *From Slavery to Freedom: A History of Negro Americans.* 3rd ed. New York: Vintage Books, 1967.

Goldman, Peter. *Report from Black America.* New York: Simon and Schuster, 1970.

Herbers, John. *The Lost Priority: What Happened to the Civil Rights Movement in America.* New York: John Day, 1970.

Hill, Robert B. *The Strengths of Black Families.* New York: Emerson Hall Publishers, 1972.

Irving, Richard F. "Toward Equal Opportunity: The Story of the Providence Urban League in the 1940's." Ph.D. dissertation, Brown University, 1974.

Jacques-Garvey, Amy, ed. *Philosophy and Opinions of Marcus Garvey.* Vols. I and II. Preface by Hollis R. Lynch. New York: Atheneum, 1971.

Johnson, Charles S. *Growing Up in the Black Belt: Negro Youth in the Rural South.* New York: Schocken Books, 1967.

Johnson, James Weldon. *Negro Americans: What Now?* New York: Viking Press, 1934.

King, Martin Luther, Jr. *Where Do We Go from Here? Chaos or Community.* New York: Harper & Row, 1967.

————. *Why We Can't Wait.* New York: Mentor Books, 1964.

Lewis, David. *King: A Critical Biography.* New York: Praeger Publishers, 1970.

Lomax, Louis E. *The Negro Revolt.* New York: Signet Books, 1963.

Malcolm X, with Alex Haley. *The Autobiography of Malcolm X.* New York: Grove Press, 1965.

Meier, August, and Rudwick, Elliot. *CORE: A Study in the Civil Rights Movement 1942–1968.* New York: Oxford University Press, 1973.

Moynihan, Daniel P. *The Negro Family: The Case for National Action.* Washington, D.C.: U.S. Department of Labor, Office of Policy Planning and Research, 1965.

Muse, Benjamin. *Ten Years of Prelude: The Story of Integration Since the Supreme Court's 1954 Decision.* New York: Viking Press, 1964.

————. *The American Negro Revolution: From Nonviolence to Black Power 1963–1967.* Bloomington: Indiana University Press, 1968.

Myrdal, Gunnar. *An American Dilemma: The Negro Problem and Modern Democracy.* New York: Pantheon Books, 1972.

Parris, Guichard, and Brooks, Lester. *Blacks in the City: A History of the National Urban League.* Boston: Little, Brown, 1971.

Peck, James. *Freedom Ride.* New York: Simon and Schuster, 1962.

Redding, Saunders. *They Came in Chains: Americans from Africa.* Philadelphia: J. B. Lippincott, 1973.

Political Participation. Report of United States Commission on Civil Rights. Washington, D.C.: U.S. Government Printing Office, May, 1968.

Root, Robert, and Hall, Shirley W. *Struggle of Decency: Religion and Rage in Modern America.* New York: Friendship Press, 1965.

Ryan, William. *Blaming the Victim.* New York: Vintage Books, 1971.

Sellers, Cleveland, with Robert Terrell. *The River of No Return: The Autobiography of a Black Militant and the Life and Death of SNCC.* New York: William Morrow, 1973.

Silberman, Charles E. *Crisis in Black and White.* New York: Vintage Books, 1964.

Stone, I. F. *In a Time of Torment.* New York: Vintage Books, 1967.

Thurow, Lester C. *Poverty and Discrimination.* Washington, D.C.: Brookings Institution, 1969.

U.S. Bureau of the Census. *The Social and Economic Status of the Black Population in the United States, 1971.* Washington, D.C.: U.S. Government Printing Office, 1972.

Watters, Pat, and Cleghorn, Reese. *Climbing Jacob's Ladder: The Arrival of Neg-roes in Southern Politics.* New York: Harcourt, Brace & World, 1967.

Woodward, C. Vann. *The Strange Career of Jim Crow.* London: Oxford University Press, 1966.

Wright, Richard. *Black Boy: A Record of Childhood and Youth.* New York: Harper and Brothers, 1945.

Black History: Magazines

"After the Riots: A Survey—How the Flare-Ups Affected U.S. Racial Attitudes." *Newsweek,* August 21, 1967, pp. 18–19.

Alilunas, Leo. "Legal Restrictions on the Negro in Politics." *Journal of Negro History,* April, 1940, pp. 152–202.

Anderson, J. "Profiles: A. Philip Randolph." *New Yorker,* December 2, 9, 16, 1972.

Aptheker, Herbert. "The Negro College Student in the 1920s—Years of Preparation and Protest: An Introduction." *Science & Society,* Spring, 1969, pp. 150–167.

Baron, Harold M. "Black Powerlessness in Chicago." *Transaction,* November, 1968, pp. 27–33.

"Black Power: Two Views." *Commentary,* Vol. 42, No. 3 (1966), pp. 35–46.

"Blacks, Democrats, and the '72 Convention." *New Republic,* October 16, 1971, pp. 11–15.

Bloach, Herman D. "Craft Unions and the Negro in Historical Perspective." *Journal of Negro History,* January, 1958, pp. 10–33.

Brewer, James H. "The War Against Jim Crow in the Land of Goshen." *Negro History Bulletin,* November, 1960, pp. 53–57.

Brittain, Joseph M. "The Return of the Negro to Alabama Politics 1930–45." *Negro History Bulletin,* May, 1959, pp. 196–199.

Brown, Earl. "American Negroes and the War." *Harper's,* April, 1942, pp. 545–552.

Browne, V. J. "Racial Desegregation in the Public Service with Particular Reference to the U.S. Government." *Journal of Negro Education,* Summer, 1954, p. 242.

Campbell, Alan K. *The Negro in Syracuse: His Education, Employment, Income.* Preface by Stephen K. Bailey. Papers on Adult Education, No. 30. Syracuse, New York: University College of Syracuse University, 1964.

Clark, Kenneth. "The Civil Rights Movements: Momentum and Organization." *Daedalus,* Winter, 1966, pp. 239–266.

———. "Fifteen Years of Deliberate Speed." *Saturday Review,* December 20, 1969, pp. 59–61.

———. "The Present Dilemma of the Negro." *Journal of Negro History,* Vol. 53, No. 1 (1968), pp. 1–11.

"Color Line Cracks a Little." *New Republic,* September 22, 1941, pp. 365–366.

Erskine, Hazel. "The Polls: Negro Employment." *Public Opinion Quarterly,* Spring, 1968, p. 132.

Frazier, E. Franklin. "The Negro Middle Class and Desegregation." *Social Problems,* April 4, 1957, pp. 291–301.

Gill, Robert L. "The Negro in the Supreme Court: 1940." *Negro History Bulletin,* 1965 (Special Summer Issue), pp. 194–197.

Good, Paul. "Bossism, Racism and Dr. King." *Nation*, September 19, 1966, pp. 237–242.

———. "A Tale of Two Cities." *Nation*, November 21, 1966, pp. 534–538.

Gosnell, H. F. "Chicago Black Belt as a Political Battleground." *American Journal of Sociology*, November, 1933, pp. 329–341.

Greenbaum, Fred. "The Anti-Lynching Bill of 1935: The Irony of 'Equal Justice Under Law.'" *Journal of Human Relations*, Vol. 15, No. 3 (1967), pp. 72–85.

Granger, L. B. "Barriers to Negro War Employment." *Annals of the American Academy of Political and Social Science*, September, 1942, pp. 72–80.

"Happy Anniversary: Convention, Durham, N.C." *Newsweek*, July 12, 1965, p. 21.

Hill, Herbert. "Employment, Manpower Training and the Black Worker." *Journal of Negro Education*, Summer, 1969, pp. 204–217.

———. "Patterns of Employment Discrimination." *Crisis*, March, 1962, pp. 137–47.

Hunter, Charlayne. "On the Case in Resurrection City." *Transaction*, Vol. 15, No. 10 (1968), pp. 47–55.

Jencks, Christopher. "Accommodating Whites: A New Look at Mississippi." *New Republic*, April 16, 1966, pp. 19–22.

Johnson, C. S. "Negro 1930–1940." *American Journal of Sociology*, May, 1942, pp. 854–864.

Johnson, Guy. "Negro Racial Movements and Leadership in the U.S." *American Journal of Sociology*, July, 1937, pp. 57–71.

Kahn, Tom. "Problems of the Negro Movement: A Special Report." *Dissent*, Winter, 1964, pp. 108–138.

King, Martin Luther, Jr. "Next Stop the North." *Saturday Review*, November 13, 1965, pp. 33.

Kushnick, Louis. "Race, Class and Power: The New York Decentralization Controversy." *Journal of American Studies* (Great Britain), December, 1969, pp. 201–219.

"Labor-Negro Division Widens." *Business Week*, July 9, 1960, p. 79.

Lee, Frank F. "The Race Relations Patterns by Areas of Behavior in a Small New England Town." *American Sociological Review*, April, 1954, pp. 138.

Lekachman, Robert. "Death of a Slogan: The Great Society 1967." *Commentary*, January, 1967, pp. 56–61.

"The Long March." *Time*, June 21, 1963, pp. 13–17.

"Lynching in Georgia." *Time*, July 28, 1941, p. 37.

Mayer, Martin. "CORE: The Shock Troops of the Negro Revolt." *Saturday Evening Post*, November 21, 1964, pp. 79–83.

McCoy, Donald R., and Ruetten, Richard. "The Civil Rights Movement (1940–54)." *Midwest Quarterly*, October 1969, p. 11.

Meier, August, and Rudwick, Elliot. "The Boycott Movement Against Jim Crow Streetcars in the South 1900–1906." *Journal of American History*, March, 1969, pp. 756–775.

———. "Early Boycott of Segregated Schools: The Case of Springfield, Ohio, 1922–1923." *American Quarterly*, Winter, 1968, pp. 744–758.

"Negro's War: 1/10 of U.S. Population Still—" *Fortune*, June, 1942, pp. 76–80.

"Negro America: What Must Be Done." *Newsweek*, November 20, 1967, pp. 33–65.

"A New White Backlash?" *Saturday Evening Post*, September 10, 1966, p. 88.

"Nixon on Racial Accommodation." *Time*, May 3, 1968, p. 21.

"Occupational Distribution of Negroes." *Monthly Labor Review*, April, 1936, pp. 975–976.

"One War at a Time: CORE's Annual Convention in Durham, N.C." *Newsweek*, July 19, 1965, p. 22.

Pfautz, Harold W. "The Power Structure of the Negro Sub-Community: A Case Study and a Comparative View." *Phylon*, Second Quarter, 1962, pp. 156–166.

Randolph, A. Philip. "The Unfinished Revolution." *Progressive*, December, 1962, pp. 20–24.

———. "Why Should We March?" *Survey Graphic*, November, 1942, pp. 488–489.

Rogin, Michael. "Politics, Emotion, and the Wallace Vote." *British Journal of Sociology*, March, 1969, pp. 27–49.

Rustin, Bayard. "From Protest to Politics: The Future of the Civil Rights Movement." *Commentary*, February, 1965, pp. 25–31.

Sager, Lawrence Gene. "Tight Little Island . . ." *Stanford Law Review*, April, 1969, pp. 767–800.

"Something Borrowed; Pres. Message on Civil Rights." *Newsweek*, February 27, 1967, pp. 27–28.

Sancton, Thomas. "The Race Riots." *New Republic*, July 5, 1943, pp. 9–13.

"The Sit-In Movement, 1960–61." *New South*, October–November, 1963, pp. 3–6.

Sullivan, L. "Negro Vote," *Atlantic*, October, 1940, pp. 477–484.

"There Must Be a Better Way." *Newsweek*, February 8, 1971, pp. 22–30.

"To the Sound of a Different Drum." *Newsweek*, April 27, 1964, pp. 25–26.

Von Eschen, Donald; Kirk, Jerome; and Pinard, Maurice. "The Disintegration of the Negro Non-Violent Movement." *Journal of Peace Research*, No. 3, 1969, pp. 215–234.

"Washington Conference on the Economic Status of the Negro." *Monthly Labor Review*, July, 1933, pp. 42–44.

Watters, Pat. "Encounter with the Future." *New South*, May, 1965, pp. 1–34.

Weaver, Robert C. "Defense Industries and the Negro." *Annals of the American Academy of Political and Social Science*, September, 1942, pp. 60–66.

Wiley, George A. "Syracuse: How Far From Rochester?" *Event*, Fall, 1964, pp. 25–28.

Zabel, William D. "Interracial Marriage and the Law." *Atlantic*, October, 1965, pp. 75–79.

Zangrando, Robert L. "From Civil Rights to Black Liberation: The Unsettled 1960's." *Current History*, November, 1969, pp. 281–286.

———. "The NAACP and a Federal Anti-Lynching Bill 1934–40." *Journal of Negro History*, January, 1965, pp. 106–117.

General: Books

Alinsky, Saul D. *Reveille for Radicals*. New York: Vintage Books, 1969.

———. *Rules for Radicals: A Pragmatic Primer for Realistic Radicals*. New York: Vintage Books, 1971.

Editors of *Fortune. America in the Sixties: The Economy and the Society.* New York: Harper Torchbooks, 1960.

Anderson, Martin. *The Federal Bulldozer: A Critical Analysis of Urban Renewal 1949–62.* Cambridge: M.I.T. Press, 1964.

Banfield, Edward C. *The Unheavenly City: The Nature and the Future of Our Urban Crisis.* Boston: Little, Brown, 1968.

Benson, Robert S., and Wolman, Harold, eds., *Counterbudget: A Blueprint for Changing National Priorities.* Foreword by Sol M. Linowitz. New York: Praeger, 1971.

Clark, Kenneth B., and Hopkins, Jeannette. *A Relevant War Against Poverty: A Study of Community Action Programs and Observable Social Change.* New York: Harper & Row, 1969.

Cooper, Chester L. *The Lost Crusade: America in Vietnam.* Foreword by W. Averell Harriman. New York: Dodd, Mead, 1970.

The Discipline of the Metropolitan Church. Lake Geneva, Wis.: Metropolitan Church Association, 1931.

Feuer, Lewis S., ed. Karl Marx and Friedrich Engels, *Basic Writings on Politics and Philosophy.* Garden City, N.Y.: Doubleday, 1959.

Gail, Marzieh. *Baha'i: Atomic Mandate.* New Delhi: Baha'i Publishing,

Ginzberg, Eli, and Solow, Robert M., eds. *The Great Society: Lessons for the Future.* New York: Basic Books, 1974.

Handler, Joel F. "Social Reform Groups and the Legal System: Enforcement Problems." Paper prepared for the Workshop on the Sociology of Judicial Process, Center for Interdisciplinary Research, University of Bielefeld, Bielefeld, West Germany, September 24–28, 1973.

Jencks, Christopher; Smith, Marshall; Acland, Henry; Bane, Mary Jo; Cohen, David; Gintts, Herbert; Heyns, Barbara; and Michelson, Stephan. *Inequality: A Reassessment of the Effect of Family and Schooling in America.* New York: Basic Books, 1972.

Kahn, Kathy. *Hillbilly Women.* New York: Avon, 1973.

Kershaw, Joseph A., with Paul N. Courant. *Government Against Poverty: Studies in Social Economics.* Washington, D.C.: Brookings Institution, 1970.

Kester, Howard. *Revolt Among the Sharecroppers.* New York: Covici, Friede, 1936; reprinted New York: Arno Press, 1969.

Lampman, Robert J. and Steiner, Gilbert Y., eds. *The Great Society: Lessons for the Future.* New York: Basic Books, 1974.

Levy, Jacques E. *Cesar Chavez: Autobiography of La Causa.* New York: W. W. Norton, 1975.

Mailer, Norman. *Some Honorable Men: Political Conventions, 1960–1972.* Boston: Little, Brown, 1976.

Manchester, William. *The Glory and the Dream: A Narrative History of America 1932–1972.* Boston: Little, Brown, 1974.

Nielsen, Waldemar A. *The Big Foundations.* Foreword by M. J. Rossant. A Twentieth Century Fund Study. New York: Columbia University Press, 1972.

Pechman, Joseph A., and Okner, Benjamin A. *Who Bears the Tax Burden?* Studies of Government Finance. Washington, D.C.: Brookings Institution, 1974.

Report of the National Advisory Commission on Civil Disorders. Introduction by Tom Wicker. New York: Bantam Books, 1968.

Rose, Thomas, ed. *Violence in America: A Historical and Contemporary Reader*. New York: Vintage Books, 1969.

Sanders, Marion K., ed. *The Professional Radical: Conversations with Saul Alinsky*. New York: Harper & Row, 1970.

Sowell, Thomas. *Race and Economics*. New York: David McKay, 1975.

Taylor, William L. *Hanging Together: Equality in an Urban Nation*. New York: Simon and Schuster, 1971.

Theobald, Robert. *Economizing Abundance: A Non-Inflationary Future*. Chicago: Swallow Press, 1970.

Theobald, Robert, ed. *Social Policies for America in the Seventies: Nine Divergent Views*. Garden City, N.Y.: Doubleday, 1968.

U.S. Department of Commerce, U.S. Bureau of the Census. *U.S. Census Population: 1930*. Vol. II. *General Report Statistics by Subjects*. Washington, D.C.: Government Printing Office, 1933.

————. *U.S. Census Population: 1930*. Vol. I. *Population*. Washington, D.C.: Government Printing Office, 1931.

————. *U.S. Census Population: 1940*. Vol. II, Part I. *Characteristics of the Population*. Washington, D.C.: Government Printing Office, 1943.

————. *U.S. Census Population: 1950*. Vol. II. *Characteristics of the Population*. Part 46. *Virginia*. Washington, D.C.: Government Printing Office, 1952.

————. *U.S. Census Population: 1960*. Vol. II. *Characteristics of the Population*. Part 34. *New York*. Washington, D.C.: Government Printing Office, 1963.

————. *Fifteenth Census of the United States: 1930 Population*. Vol. III, Part 2. Washington, D.C.: Government Printing Office, 1932.

————. Bureau of the Census, *Census of Religious Bodies, 1926*. Washington, D.C.: Government Printing Office, 1928.

U.S. House of Representatives, Committee on Ways and Means. *The President's Proposals for Welfare Reform and Social Security Amendments, 1969* Ninety-first Congress, First Session. Washington, D.C.: Government Printing Office, 1969.

U.S. Department of Agriculture. Economic Research Service. *Eating Habits of Americans*. Washington, D.C.: Government Printing Office, 1965.

General: Magazines

Burch, Hobart A. "A Conversation with George Wiley." *Journal*, November–December, 1970, pp. 10–20.

"Campus Rebels Find a Cause." *Nation*, November 28, 1959, pp. 395–397.

Carmody, John. "A 'Middle Class' George Wiley Puts in 20-Hour Days on Behalf of His Powerful Group of Welfare Ladies. *Potomac*, May 3, 1970, p. 27.

Cloward, Richard A., and Piven, Frances Fox. "The Weight of the Poor . . . A Strategy to End Poverty." *Nation*, May 2, 1966, pp. 510–517.

Congressional Record, Ninetieth Congress, First Session, Vol. 113, No. 19.

DuBose, Carolyn P. "Champion of Welfare Rights." *Ebony*, April, 1970, pp. 31–34.

Gass, Oscar. "The Political Economics of the Great Society." *Commentary*, October, 1965, 40(4), pp. 31–36.

Glick, Brian. "The Thirties: Organizing the Unemployed." *Liberation*, September–October, 1967, pp. 12–16.

Kazin, Michael. "Some Notes on S.D.S." *American Scholar,* Autumn, 1969, pp. 644–655.

"Leap Year's Eligible Men." *Ebony,* June, 1960, pp. 62–64.

Moynihan, Daniel Patrick. "George Wiley: A Memoir." *Crisis,* April, 1975, pp. 142–143.

"No One Has Starved." *Fortune,* September, 1932, pp. 19–25.

Rothenburg, Jerome. "An Economic Evaluation of Urban Renewal." *Nation,* June 4, 1967, p. 65.

Stephens, Oren. "Revolt on the Delta." *Harper's,* November 1941, p. 656–664.

"Strategy of Crisis: A Dialogue." *The American Child,* Vol. 48, No. 3 (Summer, 1966), pp. 20–32.

"Unemployed Survey, Rhode Island, January, 1936." *Monthly Labor Review,* November, 1937, pp. 1116–1119.

U.S. Bureau of the Census. *Statistical Abstract of the United States: 1969.* Washington, D.C.: Government Printing Office, 1969.

U.S. Congress. Joint Economic Committee. "The Effectiveness of Manpower Training Programs: A Review of Research on the Impact on the Poor." Study Paper No. 3. Washington, D.C.: Government Printing Office, 1972.

"What Is the Bahai World Faith?" *Negro History Bulletin,* October, 1959, pp. 13–14.

Wiley, George A. "Health Care in the Inner City—Like It Is: The Point of View of a Consumer." *Report of the 1969 National Health Forum,* March, 1969, pp. 10–12.

———. "Masking Repression as Reform." *Social Policy,* May–June, 1972, pp. 16–18.

———. "The Nixon Family Assistance Plan: Reform or Repression?" *Black Law Journal,* Spring, 1971, pp. 70–76.

———. "Why Workfare Won't Work." *New Generation,* Winter, 1970, pp. 22–25.

INDEX